SOUTH AFRICA
Limits to Change
The Political Economy of Transition

SOUTH AFRICA
Limits to Change
The Political Economy of Transition

HEIN MARAIS

Zed Books Ltd
LONDON & NEW YORK

University of Cape Town Press
CAPE TOWN

South Africa: Limits to Change: The Political Economy of Transformation was first published by UCT Press (Pty) Ltd, Private Bag, Rondebosch 7701, South Africa and Zed Books Ltd, 7 Cynthia Street, London N1 9JF, UK and 175 Fifth Avenue, New York, NY 10010, USA.

The rights of Hein Marais to be identified as the author of this work have been asserted in accordance with The Copyright, Designs and Patents Act, 1988.

© Hein Marais 1998

Reprinted 1999

ISBN 1-919713-13-1 UCT Press, limp
ISBN 1 85649 544 2 Zed Books, limp
ISBN 1 85649 543 4 Zed Books, cased

Cataloging-in-Publication Data is available from the British Library

US CIP has been applied for from the Library of Congress

Cover design: The Nimble Mouse, Kalk Bay 7975, South Africa
Typesetting and reproduction: RHT desktop publishing cc, Durbanville 7550, South Africa
Printing and binding: Clyson Printers, Maitland 7405, South Africa

Contents

Acknowledgements

This book began as a research project commissioned by Samir Amin and Bernard Founou, as part of a pan-African investigation (launched by the Dakar-based Third World Forum) into the experiences of democratic transitions and structural adjustment on the continent. It was their encouragement and support that saw it progress into this form.

I also owe deep gratitude to Vishnu Padayachee, Bill Freund, Dot Keet and Mike Morris whose discussions and notes were of inestimable value. Readers familiar with Morris's writings, in particular, will recognize their imprints in some of the sections that follow, although he himself might not concur with the directions in which they are developed here.

Debts are owed also to John Sender (for his valuable comments), Sandile Dikeni, Monty Narsoo and Pierre Beaudet (for their enduring intellectual camaraderie and courage), Alexander Cockburn, Colin Bundy and Eduardo Galeano (for being inspiring examples), Barney Mthomboti (for granting me time off work to complete the manuscript), Robert Molteno and Glenda Younge (for their perseverance), Stephen Wright, Joan-Anne Nolan, Steve Friedman, Dennis Lewycky, Jeremy Cronin and Langa Zita.

Needless to say, the flaws and omissions are entirely mine.

This book is dedicated to Susan.

Foreword

Commissioned by the Third World Forum, this book marks an important shift in analyses of the South African democratic breakthrough and the subsequent efforts to transform South Africa along progressive lines, as it locates the transformation critically in broader historical, political-economic and global contexts.

In the book, Marais demonstrates that the struggle for a just and equal society proceeds, but on terms and under conditions that by no means guarantee a happy outcome. In fact, South Africa has launched itself on a long and difficult trek to achieve a truly democratic, non-racist, progressive society. Not least among the dilemmas confronting it is its ambivalent place in the world system.

South Africa has always been hard to classify, in part because it represents a microcosm of the world capitalist system. There exists on its territory zones that correspond to all four constituent 'worlds' that make up the world system. There is the overwhelmingly white section of the population whose popular culture and standard of living seem to belong to the 'first' (advanced capitalist) world. A humorist would note, however, that the 'statist' policies of the former white rulers put the country in a category that used to include the so-called socialist countries of the 'second' world. Much of the urban black population belongs to the modern, industrializing 'third' world, while rural Africans do not differ much from their counterparts in 'fourth' world Africa.

Construction of this curious and exceptional situation began in the 17th century when Dutch settlers looked upon indigenous Africans much as the English settlers in North America regarded Amerindians or the Israelis the Palestinians. British Industrial imperialism, intent on exploiting the fabulous mineral riches discovered in the late 19th century, understood that black labour, if mobilized for that purpose, would present an effective solution to the problem of extraction. It was the British, therefore, and not the Afrikaners who invented apartheid.

They established the antecedents of the miserable homeland system – some within the boundaries of the Union, two as British 'protectorates' (Lesotho and Swaziland), all designed to supply cheap migrant labour for the mines.

In the aftermath of World War Two, the National Party took over responsibility for the overall running of the system under the aegis of an explicitly racist legitimating ideology.

The decades since then were characterized by industrialization in the peripheries of the global system. By nature uneven and unequal in its development, this industrialization split the old 'third' world into a new, industrializing 'third' world and a severely marginalized 'fourth' world, which has remained a producer and export of agricultural and mineral products.

South African capitalists developed within this framework a project aimed at moving up in the global system by means of an industrialization process that would be firmly protected and supported by the state. The apartheid system was perfectly rational in that context. Cheap productive labour does not necessarily create a problem of realizing surplus value when that demand can be stimulated by raising the incomes of the ruling minority and by expanding some exports. The claim that there existed a fundamental conflict between apartheid and capitalism misunderstood what was at stake.

The standard measure of success for a country of the periphery that has industrialized since World War Two is (in accordance with the globalization of capitalism) its ability to be 'competitive' on the world market. From this vantage point, countries can be classified into four groups:

■ those which have industrialized and achieved 'competitiveness', or could do so with relatively minor adjustments (the countries of east Asia, with communist and capitalist political regimes, as well as most major Latin American countries);

■ those which have industrialized but are clearly not competitive and require drastic restructuring to become so (South Africa and the industrialized Arab countries like Algeria and Egypt);

■ those which have remained preindustrial but have succeeded in promoting 'traditional' agricultural, mineral or oil exports and, for that reason, may appear comparatively prosperous (the Gulf states, Gabon, Ivory Coast belong here); and

■ those which have failed to promote 'traditional' exports (the majority of African countries).

Only the first group of countries constitutes the periphery of the global system. Their successes are routinely portrayed as evidence that they are progressing towards 'full development' and are 'catching up' with the Western capitalist states. The image is false. In the past, polarization was based on a clear distinction between the industrialized and non-industrialized countries, the latter constituting the periphery.

The polarization of the future will no longer be based on that distinction. The new centres will be those countries that control the global industrial system through their command of financial power and communications systems, their dominance in decision-making over the use of resources at the global level, and their monopolies of technology and weapons of mass destruction.

By these criteria, countries in the first of the four groups cannot belong to the 'first' world merely because they have successfully industrialized. They will constitute the 'third world' of the future while the other groups constitute the 'fourth' world.

Again, South Africa presents a peculiar case. Side-by-side within its national boundaries are zones whose characteristics assign them to the last three groups. Its industries have failed to achieve international 'competitiveness', while its industrial exports are negligible compared to those of South Korea, Mexico and Brazil, for example, and are absorbed mainly by captive markets in southern Africa. Moreover, South Africa's location in the world system is, in the main, that of an exporter of primary products. At the same time, its rural hinterlands remain among the poorest areas of the 'fourth' world and struggle to maintain even minimal levels of survival.

Now that formal apartheid has ended, the institutions of formal democracy have been introduced and the country is governed by a party of the majority, what are the chances that South Africa can break free of the patterns inscribed by its history? Contrary to the reality, the black majority is said to have inherited a magnificent country which, with the 'correct' adjustments, can ascend into the ranks of the world's industrialized success stories. Demanded of its workers and its poor are the standard sacrifices necessary for attaining 'competitiveness'. Were the irony not so vicious it would be laughable – for the working classes are now saddled with the task of achieving what capital, with the active support of the Western powers over several decades, failed to do. And, indeed, as Marais shows, that failure counted among the main factors that led to South Africa's political settlement.

The possibility of genuine democracy and progressive social change exists – if a start is made now. Even then it will be a long and painful process of change, one that will last several decades still. Some of the conditions for such progress are in place: a democratic political system, a progressive Constitution and a unitary state is needed for the redistribution of income socially and regionally as well as a geographical redistribution of investment. Other conditions still have to be struggled for. An immense effort is needed to develop the backward rural areas and achieve agrarian reform that can benefit the rural African population and create a bedrock for industrial development (as the east Asian countries showed). Also, a redistribution of income and social infrastructure (education, health, etc.) is required and will, inevitably, require a diminishing of the status of affluent whites (for it is a simple fact that the overall development of the country cannot support the 'first' world consumption levels of its most privileged layers). Finally, a gradual restructuring of industrial policy is essential and should be geared both at servicing needs and stimulating demand. This means more goods for popular consumption, improved productive capacity in the rural areas, more housing to meet the needs of people and less wasteful production to satisfy the desires of the white minority. In my opinion, these are some of the requirements for real democratization.

Marais' incisive analysis of the visions and strategies, and the political and social forces at work in South African society presents compelling perspectives on the questions raised here.

This book must be read – not only in South Africa but in Africa and beyond – by all who desire a fuller understanding of this country.

Samir Amin
Dakar, June 1997

Introduction

There is nothing unanimous about social transformation; its measure
depends on the meaning it is assigned by the various actors involved.[1]

South Africa's democratic breakthrough has earned its place among the
'miracles' of the twentieth century. In an epoch highlighted by the horrors
erupting in the Balkans, the Rwandan genocide and the prolonged violence
of the Israeli–Palestinian struggle, a seemingly intractable conflict at the tip
of Africa ended in a political settlement that appeared to refute the rhythms
of history. Not only was it achieved without the apocalyptic conflagration
many had feared, but it seemed to spur a newfound sense of unity, conciliation and common purpose in a society that had become synonymous with
terminal discord and division. It yielded a constitution bristling with features that justifiably earned the envy of people around the world. It produced spectacles of reconciliation that baffled even its own citizens. It set in
motion not economic collapse but tentative recovery. It brought closer the
prospect of change in the lives of millions.

Little wonder then that the bemused admiration of the world was
matched by a sense of triumphant pride and hope among the majority of
South Africans and the liberation organization, the African National
Congress (ANC), they voted into power in 1994. A history marked by bru-
tally enforced inequalities appeared to have been ruptured, enabling the
black majority to pass through portals beyond which lay equality, dignity
and freedom.[2] The march of history could now proceed along an irrevoca-
bly benign and progressive route, propelled by the ANC's determination to
redress the devastation wrought under apartheid and mapped by visions of
change outlined in the Reconstruction and Development Programme
(RDP).

This book shares those hopes but questions not only the inevitability but
also the likelihood of their fulfilment under prevailing conditions. Its apprehension stems not from pessimism but from an analysis of the political

economy of the South African transition, an inquiry that excavates the many, stout historical trends and continuities which, far from having been erased by the 'miracle' of 1994, bedevil the prospects of progressive transformation. Some of them are plain to the eye, many others are rendered visible only by a more inquisitive gaze.

Most accounts of the transition have sought to dissect the post-1990 developments by focusing on the minutiae of political engagements and the personalities at their helm. These are valuable enquiries which, at their best, sketch a kind of sociology of the transition. In doing so, however, they risk over-personalizing history and they obscure the structural underpinnings of the transition.

Some readers might feel that in attempting to broaden this enquiry beyond the confines of political drama, it errs in the opposite direction – by laying undue stress on the economic. One hopes that such judgements would take into account the extent to which the South African struggle itself became defined by a political reductionism that collapsed the political economy of privilege and deprivation into the form of the apartheid state. Generated was an instrumentalist conception of state, one that regarded it as a site of concentrated power which, once captured, would become the central agent of transformation. Thus, the key objective of the liberation struggle became the seizure of state power in order to work its levers in the interests of the majority. Of course, this did not happen. Instead of seizing power, the democratic movement negotiated its partial transfer. Instead of taking over and transforming the state, the movement found itself assimilated into it. This alone, however, does not explain the apparently foreshortened horizons of change that now confound that movement. For in capitalist society the circuits through which power and privilege are reproduced course not only through the state but also through civil society, which is dominated by the formations of capital. This requires an expansive understanding of the transition and the developments that presaged it.

The analysis that follows seeks to fill some of those lacunae by locating the transition in a historical context. This requires probing South Africa's political-economic undercarriage, the developments that led to the political settlement, the terms upon which the transition proceeds, the ideological and structural shifts that accompany or drive it, and the relative strengths and weaknesses of the main forces contesting its outcome.

In doing so, the book argues that the transition should be understood less as a miraculous historical rupture than as the (as yet inconclusive) outcome of a concerted and far-reaching attempt to resolve an ensemble of political, ideological and economic contradictions that had accumulated steadily since the 1970s. It departs, therefore, from the conventional narratives that gauge the transition in predominantly political terms. In doing so, it does not propose that the tilt towards seeking a negotiated settlement or the ensuing developments were *inevitable* – other, equally risky options existed. But it does concur with Stuart Hall's contention that:

> ... material circumstances are the net of constraints, the 'conditions of existence', for practical thought and calculation about society ... [and that] what is 'scientific' about the Marxist theory of politics is that it seeks to understand the *limits of political action* given by the terrain on which it operates.[3]

The basis for the transition lay in a historic deadlock achieved between the ruling bloc and the democratic opposition in the late 1980s. The impasse rested on the apartheid state's inability to indefinitely suppress the challenges from the democratic opposition, which, in turn, had become powerful enough to prevent that bloc from devising and imposing a resolution that could unequivocally favour it. At the same time, the opposition was unable to force the capitulation of the old order.

The 1980s had been characterized by an increasingly aberrant mix of repression and reforms, the latter geared primarily at restructuring the social and economic basis for capital accumulation. They were responses to trends identified by Harry Oppenheimer, then chair of the Anglo American Corporation, as early as 1971:

> We are approaching the stage where the full potential of the economy, as it is at present organized, will have been realized, so that if structural changes are not made, we will have to content ourselves with a much lower rate of growth.[4]

Partly because these reforms only marginally and ineffectively addressed the demands of the opposition, they failed to halt the surge of resistance and, instead, fuelled successive waves of popular action which climaxed in the uprisings of 1985–6. Subsequent state repression dismantled the movement's capacity to capitalize on the 'insurrectionary climate' it claimed prevailed at the time. Animated by visions of change that focused on the overthrow of the apartheid state, the democratic movement found its path at least temporarily blocked by the end of the decade, while an ensemble of other local and international factors combined to consolidate the stand-off. Upon this precarious impasse an ambitious and far-reaching attempt to restructure the political sphere began.

A ruling bloc based on the political exclusion of the majority and revolving around a beleaguered minority political party had become a manifest liability. The rise of a well-organized and militant working class movement, politically allied with the excluded political opposition, and the spread of other popular organizations severely compounded the predicament. A negotiated political settlement would not resolve these difficulties, but it could serve as the gateway for an ongoing bid to modernize South African capitalism. For the democratic forces, a settlement could usher in a transition that heralded – but did not guarantee – far-reaching adjustments aimed at undoing the patterns for the allocation of power, privilege and opportunities.

One of the key propellants of the negotiations process, therefore, was the realization among sections of the ruling bloc that the capitalist system in South Africa had to be 'modernized' – in both economic and political terms. In short, South Africa had to become a 'normal' capitalist society. Despite its haphazard reform efforts of the 1980s, the National Party (NP) administration had proved manifestly unequal to the task.

From the vantage point of capital, two salient and risky adjustments were required. The abandonment of the exclusionary political framework of apartheid and its replacement with a democratic system meant that the NP would no longer function as the political axis of the ruling bloc. That role would befall the ANC, albeit on terms, business hoped, that inhibited its ability to advance the interests of the disadvantaged majority at the expense of the key prerogatives of capital. The fundamental importance of 1994, therefore, was not simply the end of apartheid but the dissolution of the dominant alliance of social, economic and political forces in South Africa – the old ruling bloc. The ANC's ascent to political power did not fill the resultant vacuum. Rather, it intensified a struggle over which set of forces would come to constitute a new ruling bloc. The ongoing contest over economic policies, the reshaping of the labour market and the social bias of development initiatives would form some of the key battlegrounds of that contest – which cuts to heart of the second area of adjustments.

The political restructuring of South African society served as a formative aspect of broader attempts to revise an economic growth strategy that had become steadily derailed since the 1970s – a dimension overlooked in overly politicized analyses of the transition. The political transformation has drastically modified the conditions under which the main social forces are now engaged in determining the content and extent of economic and socio-economic adjustment. The democratic movement demands changes that redistribute power, resources and opportunities in favour of the disadvantaged majority: broad-ranging transformation. South African capitalists hope that political democratization will serve as a grounding for structural adjustments that could inaugurate a new cycle of sustained accumulation, a process that would include efforts to cultivate and incorporate a black economic élite as junior partners within the white-run economy. This has left the ANC in a curious position. It is cast both in the role of agent and subject in a process aimed at enlisting it as the political axis of a modernizing alliance of social forces oriented around servicing, in the first instance, the interests and aspirations of the most privileged sectors of South African society. This might come to include organized, skilled workers who, through regressive changes to the labour market, could find themselves cloistered as a self-conscious 'labour élite', concentrating on defending a narrowed vista of interests. Such a process has been abetted by the increased stratification of the working classes and could lead to once powerful sections of them becoming appended, perforce, to a new ruling bloc as subordinate partners and beneficiaries of the new South Africa.

Far from having dissolved into a kind of fraternity of common purpose, tranquillized by the levelling language of nation-building, South Africa is in the midst of an intense, renewed struggle. The outcome will determine which interests, ideas and ideals determine the course of the new South Africa.

Already ossifying within the ANC are trends that ally it to an agenda which conflicts fundamentally with the hopes and rights of the majority of South Africans. The neo-liberal features of the ANC government's macroeconomic strategy, the élitist nature of many black economic empowerment ventures and the supine postures struck before the demands of corporate South Africa are, in such a reading, not anomalies. Spurring these developments is the tendency to judge the possibilities of national development on the basis of deeply conservative and empirically questionable interpretations of globalization. Indeed, post-1994 developments seem to amplify Ellen Meiksins Wood's lament that:

> ... it is not only that we do not know how to act against capitalism but that we are forgetting how to *think* against it.[5]

To what extent these inclinations are merely conjunctural or reflect the distillation of dominant interests in the ANC's social base remains unclear. But a survey of the ANC's history reveals telling legacies which, although submerged during the anti-apartheid struggle, have been pushed to the fore during the transition. Indeed, they raise the question whether a process of change centring on the deracialization of power and privilege (but without dismantling the structural foundations of inequality) might not be compatible with the organization's historical discourse.

Left unchecked, the defining trends of the transition seem destined to shape a revised division of society, with the current order stabilized around, at best, 30 per cent of the population. For the rest (overwhelmingly young, female and African) the best hope will be some trickle-down from a 'modernized' and 'normalized' new South Africa. This raises not only moral but political dilemmas, not the least of which is the danger that the incumbent élites come to view the excluded majority as a threat to newly acquired privilege and power, thereby introducing the spectre of a new bout of authoritarianism in response to social instability.

But South Africa also remains invested with a robust array of popular organizations, including the ANC, many of which played decisive roles in bringing about the stalemate of the late 1980s. Loosely grouped as a putative popular movement, these formations seem to represent a powerful antidote to the prescriptions advanced by capitalists inside South Africa and beyond its borders. Most, however, are prone to dramatic organizational upheavals and severe strategic disorientation, some of it unleashed by the transition itself, some of it the outcome of decisions and postures (both chosen and imposed) that can be traced back through their histories. Many of these features have converged in the form of towering challenges which, if not surmounted, will likely forestall the ideals that animate their millions of members and supporters.

There is nothing inevitable about the outcome of these ongoing struggles. That will be determined by the choices made and the creativity displayed, as well as the intellectual and practical courage mustered, by popular organizations, both existing and emerging. South Africa's history bears testimony to the prevalence of those strengths and the vagaries they are subjected to, a history that accounts for the fact that this book adopts a tone that is neither fatalistic or triumphant.

The pages that follow do not pretend to offer compact answers to the trends and challenges they identify. They are presented in the conviction that an intrepid interrogation of the past and the present is necessary if the transition is to spawn a society that does justice to its citizens. For history has bequeathed to South Africa a daunting array of limits to change, limits that have to be changed.

Notes

1 Mexican sociologist Carlos Vilas, cited by Blade Nzimande (1997).
2 South African realities unfortunately force us to resort to racial categories. Thus, 'African' refers to indigenous inhabitants whose ancestors' presence in the region pre-dated the arrival of European and other settlers; 'coloured' refers to people of mixed-race origins; 'Indian' refers to descendants from South Asia; 'white' refers to descendants of European settlers; 'black' refers inclusively, in the manner of the black consciousness tradition, to all South Africans who are not 'white'.
3 Stuart Hall, 'Marxism without Guarantees' in Morley and Chen (1996:44–5) (emphasis added).
4 Harry Oppenheimer in his chairman's address to the Anglo American Corporation, cited in Gelb (1991:20).
5 Wood (1995:11).

CHAPTER ONE

Origins of a divided society

A wealthy country by continental standards, South Africa is also one of the most unequal societies on earth. By the World Bank's calculations, the poorest 40 per cent of its citizens earn less than 4 per cent of the income circulating in the economy. The wealthiest 10 per cent pocket more than 51 per cent of income.

That apartheid entrenched these features with grotesque fastidiousness and anti-human severity is a matter of painful historical record. Yet, tracing the lineages of this inequality strictly to the apartheid system obscures the profound political-economic contours of inequity that define South African society. It also confounds the efforts to forge a society that not only extols but realizes the dignity, desires and rights of its citizens. In many respects South Africans' visions of the future rest on foreshortened perspectives of the past. This applies centrally to the millions who engineered, administrated and savoured the complex of exploitative practices that penetrated every aspect of lived reality – few of whom will today admit to their authorship of, or moral culpability for, the devastation they achieved. Nor are they under much pressure to do so; their indifference is indulged, even encouraged, in the quest for reconciliation.

But an abbreviated and elliptical sense of the past is evident also, though in very different respects, within the democratic movement. The history of successful liberation projects tends to be rendered in terms that portray an unequivocal and linear advance towards triumph. History is cleansed of failure, ambivalence and blemish. And yet, left celebrated and uninterrogated, the past ferments discreetly in the present.

It is not unlikely, though by no means certain, that the transition will extend the accumulated continuities of South African history in ways that reinforce the inequities visited on the majority. Sadly, the signs pointing to a happier outcome are irresolute and dwarfed by more encompassing dynamics that fortify the sanctity of privilege against human need. The pages that follow have one purpose only: to render these less opaque.

The roots are sunk

The definitive origins of South Africa's status as a 'Two Nation' society – marked by the systematic and violent segregation between privilege and deprivation – lie in the late nineteenth century, when the development of capitalism accelerated rapidly after the beginning of diamond mining in 1867 and gold mining in 1886.[1]

Pockets of commercial and agricultural capitalism had been established in the coastal regions colonized by Britain. But the hinterland remained essentially pre-capitalist, with Boer *trekkers* engaged in rentier exploitation, living off rents in labour and in kind extracted from indigenous peoples whose land they had seized. Racial prejudice was already rampant, though by some accounts it was often overshadowed by class division and religious bigotry as the basis for systematic social polarization.[2] In large parts of the country an economically independent African peasantry survived.[3] In many cases these societies remained organized within their own social and political systems; in some cases they were militarily powerful enough to inflict bloody defeats on British colonial armies.

The discovery of gold and diamonds, however, upped the ante – transforming the territory, at least in the eyes of British colonialism, from a geopolitical asset (hence the focus on controlling coastal strips) into a potentially huge capital asset.

These discoveries set in train processes that would definitively shape South African history for the next century. A huge influx of foreign, mainly British, capital put the mining industry on the world map and spearheaded the highly centralized character of an industry which would remain at the centre of the South African economy for the next century. There was a rush of European immigrant labour, which supplied the semi-skilled and skilled labour required by the industry and boosted the numbers of white settlers beyond the levels typical in other African colonies.[4] Also generated was the need for a steady supply of cheap, unskilled labour. The dismantled African peasantry would become the chief source, while a range of measures would be applied to guarantee and regulate the supply of labour. Administrative measures were introduced to establish and police a racial division of labour separating skilled white (mainly European) labour from gangs of unskilled African labour. Organized white labour would lobby strongly (and act militantly) to entrench those measures. This established the basis for a political alliance between the capitalist class and white labour, which was to survive until the 1970s.

For the next 50 years, the accumulation strategy centred on mining and, to a lesser extent, agriculture, with manufacturing industry at best an incipient feature of the economy.

With the huge gold fields yielding low grade ore, the mining concerns were faced with two central needs: a hefty flow of capital to establish and run mines, and a reliable, cheap labour supply to keep the profit margin attractive.

The first requirement saw the integration of the 'South African'[5] economy into the world economy as a source of primary commodities (the value of which was set in the European metropoles) and a destination for investment capital. The second sketched the pattern of labour and social relations that would become the definitive feature of this society. Capital accumulation would be based on the exploitation of a low-wage, highly controlled, expendable African workforce which was to be reproduced in a system of 'native reserves' at minimal cost to capital. Importantly, this workforce would be recruited from the entire subcontinent: until the 1970s, the mining industry employed more non-South African than South African workers.[6]

This accumulation path seemed to correspond to those in other African colonies, with the important distinction that a large settler population, itself segmented culturally and socio-economically, soon became ascendant in the political, administrative and, later, economic realms. The resemblance would lead the South African Communist Party (SACP) to develop its theory of 'Colonialism of a Special Type'.[7]

The economic independence of the African peasantry was gradually removed through a barrage of administrative and punitive measures which transformed this surplus-producing peasantry into a pool of labour for the mines and emergent capitalist agriculture. The African peasantry dwindled from 2,5 million in 1936 to 832 000 people in 1946. A trio of factors drove this process: increased mechanization of agriculture, the crushing effects of the Depression and, centrally, state expropriation of land. A legislative climax was the mammoth expropriation effected by the 1913 Land Act which barred Africans from acquiring land outside 'native reserves' (7,3 per cent of the South African land area). That process was augmented by the 1936 Natives Land and Trust Act which doubled the land area 'set aside' for 'native reserves' in a bid to reverse the 'incapacity of the Native Reserves to provide even the minimum subsistence requirements', as one government report later put it.[8]

Accompanying the establishment of capitalist mining at the centre of the South African economy – and its incorporation into the world economy on terms that would remain relatively consistent over the next half century – was the introduction of some of the definitive, systematic divisions in society:

■ There was a racial division of labour in urban centres between skilled white labour (both immigrant and domestic) and unskilled African labour (essentially 'economic refugees' fleeing the remnants of wrecked pre-capitalist zones). White workers imported the trade union tradition, organizing artisans and craftsmen, and vehemently defended their status against 'encroachment' by African workers when mining bosses, for instance, attempted to loosen the colour bar in a bid to lower wage costs by allowing black workers some upward mobility.[9]

- There was an increasingly fierce marginalization of African societies, who were not only converted into reserve armies of labour but were also burdened with the principal costs of reproducing that labour supply. Deprived of their means of production – land – they were physically barricaded into 'native reserves' outside the mining and industrial zones, where they were denied access to the types of health, education, welfare and recreational networks introduced in the urban centres. Measures like the pass law system regulated the flow of labour into the cities and deflected the cost of reproducing labour to the periphery – thus laying the basis for a highly profitable cycle of capital accumulation. In essence, the 'native reserves' (and later the homelands) would subsidize capitalist growth in South Africa.

- There was the proletarianization of large numbers of Africans, 'which distinguished the class structure of South Africa from the peasant economies of African colonies to the north' (Fine & Davis, 1990:14). By 1946, the number of urbanized African people had increased by 36 per cent over the previous decade. One third of them were women, suggesting long-term urbanization. But the urban/rural dichotomy was not rigid – hundreds of thousands of people *traversed* these zones. With the rise of an urban working class would come new forms of resistance: trade union organizing, strikes, boycotts and other mass protests.

- Within white society, increased divisions were also materializing. Marked by the consolidation of large farms and their mechanization (a process accelerated by the 1929–32 Great Depression), the advance of capitalist agriculture drove thousands of Afrikaner settlers off the land and into the cities, which they entered at a disadvantage to European immigrant workers. A category of newly proletarianized 'poor whites', mainly Afrikaners, arose. Until the 1930s what passed for 'Afrikaner capital' was restricted mainly to the agricultural sector, which represented a tiny fraction of gross domestic product (GDP). This material marginalization combined with a history of enmity towards British imperialism (expressed explosively in the two Boer wars) and a hermetic cultural framework derived from apocalyptic readings of the Old Testament of the Bible – all of which aided the exposition of a 'distinct' Afrikaner identity, a process which, by the 1920s, would begin evolving into a political project, Afrikaner nationalism.

- Significant tensions developed between mining capital, and agricultural and industrial capital. Internationalized in terms of markets and capital input, mining capital preferred 'free trade' policies. Agricultural and industrial capital was localized and required state intervention in the form of subsidies and protection, financed largely through taxes drawn from mining capital. The rudiments of different approaches to state–capital relations were taking form.

During this period a skewed, integrated regional economy was shaped, centred around migrant labour for the mines but extending also to trade, water supply, transport and capital investment patterns. As noted by Davies *et al.* (1993:14):

> ... the principal poles of accumulation came to be located in South Africa (and to a lesser extent in Zimbabwe) while the other territories were incorporated in subsidiary roles as labour reserves, markets for South African commodities, suppliers of certain services (such as transport) or providers of cheap and convenient resources (like water, electricity and some raw materials).

The rise of the working class

By the 1940s, manufacturing industry was growing in earnest, thanks to lavish state support in the form of protective measures and tariffs, subsidies and major infrastructure projects that facilitated its growth. The shift from artisinal to mechanized production was rapid, and the African proletariat swelled to number some 800 000 by 1939. Workers had become increasingly combative, with African and white workers (usually separately) staging strike actions.

In 1913 about 19 000 white miners and 10 000 African miners struck; a year later the state mobilized thousands of troops to crush a railway strike. In 1918 African miners won a wage increase after striking. Two years later 70 000 African miners struck for better pay, while in 1922 a white miners' strike was put down by 20 000 troops, killing 214 people. Five years later the black Industrial and Commercial Workers' Union (ICU) claimed a membership of 100 000.

The rise of an urban African working class raised the prospect of multiracial industrial action which could evolve into a more forthright challenge against the system. This precipitated a political realignment which brought to power, in 1924, the Pact government, which strove to give white workers a bigger stake in the system. Heightened (racial) wage differentials, job reservation for whites and expanded social benefits all deepened white racism, and encouraged white workers to throw in their lot with a system constructed around a racist class alliance.

Evident was the hardening of the 'Two Nation' society. The trappings of a social welfare state were extended gradually to a tiny, racially defined minority, while the majority was expelled to the physical and socio-economic margins of the system, subsidizing the privilege of the 'insiders'. By the mid-1930s several related developments were afoot that would leave deep imprints on the future of the country.

Resistance and defeats

Strong economic growth after 1933 boosted the industrialization process, though the manufacturing sector remained relatively small (until the 1940s when it grew considerably during mobilization of production for the war effort). This in turn increased demands for African labour, some of it skilled. At the same time, the reserves into which Africans had been driven were becoming increasingly unsustainable, with overcrowding and resultant poor environmental management of marginal land rendering huge parts of the periphery economically unviable. The result was an accelerated urbanization process. In the urban areas, meanwhile, at least one generation of African workers had sunk its roots. These trends, the intense poverty and the violent manner in which labour relations were controlled spurred a healthy rise in trade union organization – from which sprang the first sustained cycle of modern, militant resistance in South Africa's history.[10]

These trends should not be exaggerated, however. Despite the rise of an African proletariat, the vast majority of Africans still survived in rural areas. Although in decline, the peasantry remained a social and economic force in rural South Africa. In addition, the urban African proletariat retained strong links with rural communities, due to the migratory character of African labour. The greatest concentration of African labour was to be found on the mines where, separated from broader society, they were subjected to fierce disciplinary regimes – thus limiting their role as an organic element of a 'wave of resistance' which, some historians have claimed, generated a crisis in the ruling bloc by the mid-1940s. The upshot was that the social weight of the working class during the 1930s and 1940s – and the threat it posed to the ruling forces – was actually less formidable than claimed in many left-wing historical accounts:[11]

> We have to abandon the simplified image of the organisation and combativity of black workers ever escalating in the 1940s and of the defeats inflicted on labour struggles … serving only as a stimulus for yet more militancy from below (Fine & Davis, 1990:99).

The 1946 miners' strike is commonly portrayed as a landmark event, announcing a crisis in South African capitalism. In this view, worker militancy in support of higher wages and better working conditions challenged the basis of a system that pivoted on an abundant supply of very cheap, controlled labour. Common has been the view that:

> The violence of the state's response not only indicated the degree to which it felt threatened, but foreshadowed the extreme repression after 1948.[12]

The NP's victory at the polls became interpreted as a consequence of that trepidation and a mandate for the hardline solution to the crisis favoured by the NP.

The 1946 strike – with 70 000 miners and 6 000 iron and steel workers out on strike – surely was an impressive event, but honest appraisal has to take into account the ease with which it was smashed by state repression. Indeed, the strike was something of an anomaly: the number of black workers organized in trade unions as well as strike actions were in decline by 1946, suggesting rather that the 'miners' strike of 1946 represented the last gasp rather than the high point of the wartime strike wave'.[13] In 1947 only 2 000 workers would embark on strikes; by 1948 the number dropped to 1 500. Two years later, the African Mineworkers' Union (which had organized the 1946 miners' strike) had been reduced to barely a shadow of its former self and could claim only 700 members. According to government calculations, 66 trade unions became defunct between 1945 and 1951.[14]

More persuasive is a reading that links the rise of apartheid not to an alleged surge of sustained challenges from a militant working class, but rather (in part) to the telling defeats suffered by that class. Those defeats can be ascribed to several factors.

Firstly, the liberal wing within the ruling class (and with it the reform programme it was counselling) had been marginalized. Several of the reforms which would be introduced piecemeal fashion from the late 1970s onwards were already considered – and rejected – by the ruling bloc at this point. As Saul and Gelb reminded, several commissions had suggested nurturing a stable, semi-skilled labour force and accepting urban Africans as a given (1981:14). Secondly, state repression had a crushing effect on resistance. And thirdly, 'the lack of numbers, concentration and bargaining power of the black industrial proletariat' prevented the black working class from sustaining the threats it appeared to pose.[15]

A fourth, subjective, factor also needs to be considered. After the Nazi invasion of the USSR in 1941, the Communist Party of South Africa (CPSA)[16] abandoned its support for intensified class struggle and switched to a people's front policy which called for support for the Allied war effort and opposition to industrial action – putting CPSA and ANC policy on an accommodationist track.[17] This steered CPSA policy into (and deepened the ANC's commitment to) a 'liberal-democratic paradigm' which:

> ... presupposed that the rulers of South Africa were ready to reach an accommodation with the black working class and that the black working class had the social weight to force an accommodation on the rulers. On both counts the policy was mistaken. The state turned against consensual politics, directing its fire instead to extinguish the threat posed by black workers, while black workers themselves lacked the power to resist the attacks mounted on them (Fine & Davis, 1990:56).

The rise of African nationalism

After an impressive rise, black working class organizations had suffered a series of telling defeats, the effects of which were compounded by the sectarianism that plagued the Left. As a result, the late 1940s saw a drift away from class politics – preparing the stage for the dramatic rise of African nationalism which, although periodically challenged, would not only definitively shape the course of resistance strategies but eventually help establish the parameters of the accommodation reached with the ruling bloc in the 1990s. Portentous roots of the defeat of South African socialism are imbedded in these developments during the 1940s.

At the same time, the extreme hardships confronting the urban proletariat had spawned spontaneous community-based struggles which indicated a ferment of grassroots resistance that stood at an angle to the demonstrable failure of the policies followed by the ANC, and periodically shared by the CPSA. Still lodged on an accommodationist track, the ANC was unable to capitalize on those struggles and transform them from sporadic expressions of discontent into a challenge that threatened the ruling bloc.[18] State repression had confirmed the failure of the constitutionalist route trekked by the ANC since its inception in 1912.

Formed on 8 January 1912 as the South African Native National Congress, the ANC had functioned until the 1940s as a vehicle for the aspirations of the African middle classes. Initially built around a relatively privileged layer of independent African peasants, the organization followed a liberal trajectory, petitioning for the extension of voting and other rights to 'civilized' Africans. Its jaundiced view of so-called 'blanket' or 'uncivilized' Africans is unabashedly captured in leaders' statements and writing. As late as 1942, ANC president general Dr A. B. Xuma would write to General Jan Smuts, assuring him that:

> ... we are anxious not to embarrass the government ... We humbly and respectfully request the Prime Minister to receive a deputation from the ANC and CNETU [Council of Non-European Trade Unions] ... to assist you toward settlement of recent strikes and prevention of future strikes.[19]

By 1935, the CPSA's J. B. Marks would pronounce the ANC 'literally dead'. Its descent had been fuelled by its failure to register gains for its constituency and by the rapid erosion of its peasant social base, whose ranks had been seriously denuded during the Depression years. The ANC could not point to a single concession wrested from the state. Furthermore, the decline of the liberal wing of the ruling bloc removed any prospect of belated success for its policy. Less than ten years later, the CPSA would lament the fact that the 'African people have been frustrated by a Congress leadership which does not organize mass support nor carry on mass action

to improve their living standards'.[20] This assessment was hardly controversial, as ANC veteran Govan Mbeki has confirmed:

[The ANC] was not in a position to go to the people with any plan of action,
being top-heavy with very little support amongst the masses of people ... As
a result, not only were the masses not provided with an effective leadership,
but those who were at the head of the ANC felt helpless to do anything
(1992:37).

It was into this vacuum that a new generation of more militant urban
African intellectuals stepped in the mid-1940s, organized within the newly-
formed ANC Youth League (ANCYL). Reacting to the moribund state of
the ANC – labelled as 'an organization of gentlemen with clean hands' by
A. P. Mda, president of the ANCYL[21] – the ANCYL fashioned a fierce
brand of African nationalism which drew heavily on the 'Africa for
Africans' philosophy popularized by the followers of Marcus Garvey. These
militants – mostly doctors, lawyers, teachers and clerks – scorned in equal
measure liberal ideology and class politics. They idealized an imagined past
of unity and harmony among Africans, and posited a liberation struggle
that would be led by the 'African nation' and a new society that would be
ruled by it. This would be achieved by reviving mass struggle under the
aegis of a reconstituted national movement in which the politics of African
nationalism would eclipse class politics as the driving dynamic of struggle.

By 1949 the African nationalists had established their authority in the
ANC, which had adopted key parts of the ANCYL's manifesto in its
Programme of Action. The focus would be on organizing mass struggle in
urban areas – along the lines of the subsequent 1952 Defiance Campaign.
However, the African nationalist upsurge was already diverging into two
currents. Eventually dominant within the ANC was a more moderate
stream which viewed South Africa as comprising four nations (African,
Indian, coloured and white), of which three were oppressed. Meanwhile, an
ultra-nationalist stream insisted that South Africa belonged to Africans
only; in 1959 it would split from the ANC and form the Pan-Africanist
Congress (PAC).

The historical developments that made this possible deserve emphasis.
Blame for the dramatic decline of the working class movement cannot fairly
be laid at the feet of the ascendant African nationalists. Instead, that decline
and the defeat of a socialist project in the mid-1940s enabled the rise of
African nationalism as the hegemonic force within a broad, evolving resistance movement. Certainly, later efforts (particularly during the 1950s and
1980s) to revive class politics would draw fierce reaction from the nationalists, but this should not cloud an understanding of the dynamics which
precipitated the conversion of the South African struggle from a potentially
class-based one to a nationalist one. Nevertheless, it was this historic turn in

the South African resistance struggle that not only made possible but made likely the class compromise which in the 1990s would underpin the transition. The class contradictions which determine the society's 'Two Nation' structure would become submerged within a discourse – African nationalism – which in the 1990s would prove unequal to the task of transforming a restructuring project led by capital into a transformatory project that could break South Africa's insider/outsider mould. Read in this context, post-1994 developments appear less than surprising.

The system hardens

South Africa's 'Two Nation' character hardened radically after the surprise victory of the white supremacist National Party (NP) in the 1948 election under the banner of Afrikaner nationalism.[22] The NP's margin of victory was a slim, five-seat parliamentary majority won with a minority of votes cast. But it immediately set about implementing a meticulously codified racist project. Henceforth, race would become the definitive criterion for South Africans' access to privilege and opportunity, further restricting the social and economic mobility of black South Africans through a battery of legislative and administrative measures. Hardest hit was the African population. Deprived of political rights and full citizenship of the nation, Africans would eventually be decreed to belong to specific 'nations' assigned homelands on the 13 per cent of land reserved for Africans.

However, the NP's policies did not rupture the country's historical continuum. While they fiercely intensified the levels of oppression inflicted on the majority, they proceeded along routes staked out over the preceding half century. Although deepened along much more explicit racial lines, the patterns of inclusion and exclusion from the productive and consumptive centres of a growing economy rested on trends already present.

Mainstream historical accounts have consistently overlooked this continuity, preferring to view the NP's apartheid policies as a *sui generis* programme generated strictly in fulfilment of the perceived needs of Afrikanerdom. Such accounts have tended to seek an understanding of the 'apartheid era' via ethnographic studies of a purportedly undifferentiated group. As O'Meara has shown, the NP would become viewed through the prism of ideology and cod psycho-politics. Thus, the NP victory would be 'taken to represent the triumph of the frontier over the forces of economic rationality – of ideology over economics'.[23] Hardline policies would be ascribed to Afrikaner 'intransigence', the '*laager* mentality' or an enduring 'frontier mentality'. Softened approaches would be attributed simply to the rise of 'modernizing' currents within the party. In such analyses the NP is made to float above history and society, its decisions determined solely by the dictates of the ideology of Afrikaner nationalism. The effect was to obscure the capitalist character of the apartheid state, leading to a fixation on the secretive, highly ideological *Broederbond* as the hand engineering apartheid state policies strictly in accordance with the interests of the Afrikaner *volk*. While the *Broederbond*'s importance within the NP is well documented, its enduring centrality to NP government policies must be questioned. Any analytical enterprise that rooted NP policies in the dictates of a hermetic ethnic cabal tasked with ensuring the well-being of the *volk* ran aground during the late 1980s. How was it that the *Broederbond* then suddenly lost its role as the NP's puppeteer, and receded into insignificance?

A secretive organization formed in the 1930s, the *Broederbond* comprised largely Afrikaner intellectuals and *petit bourgeois* figures. As O'Meara has shown, an understanding of the rise of the NP and its subsequent policies in government could not rest on an abstraction of Afrikaner nationalist ideology from 'the material conditions, contradictions and struggles in the development of capitalism in South Africa' (1983:3). As elaborated and pursued from the 1930s onwards, Afrikaner nationalism had at its core the ambitions of a layer of aspirant bourgeois Afrikaners, who assiduously articulated and promoted Afrikaner nationalism, 'the ideology through which Afrikaner capital developed' via an 'extensive network of cross-cutting organisations'.[24] One might conclude that the demise of the *Broederbond* reflected, simply, its *fulfilment* of that historic role.

The NP rode to power on the back of a nationalist class alliance, the rudiments of which had been established 30 years earlier. It included agricultural capitalists, white workers (especially newly proletarianized Afrikaners), a growing layer of the Afrikaner *petit bourgeoisie*, and fledgling manufacturing capital. The party pledged to advance the interests of these sectors by restructuring the economy in their favour – consequently, its 1948 election rhetoric reflected the ambiguous and often contradictory demands of these constituencies.[25] Of prime concern is the material context in which this occurred, primarily the emerging contradictions within the capitalist system of production (differentially affecting the branches of capital) and the state's temporary inability to resolve them.

Key to the development of South African capitalism was the dependency of capital accumulation in mining, agriculture and industry on a guaranteed supply of cheap, African migratory labour. Labour costs were suppressed by the reserve system, which by the 1930s had proved economically unsustainable. This, combined with the intense exploitation of labour-tenants by white farmers and increased mechanization of agriculture, led to an increased flow of African workers into urban areas, producing a growing, semi-permanent African proletariat. One result was a new cycle of urban resistance in shanty-towns and a rise in black trade union organizations and strike actions. The challenges posed by these developments, however, should not be exaggerated. For example, O'Meara's claim that 'the problem of political control over Africans became acute' seems unwarranted

(1983:229). As indicated, trade union organizing and action was in decline by the end of 1946, the ANC as a political organization was ailing (with its revitalization at the hand of the ANCYL's young turks still a work-in-progress), while the boycotts and other protests launched in the shanty-towns were sporadic and localized, lacking a political centre of gravity.

More tenable is the view that 'it was through the defeat of [black] resistance that apartheid was able to resolve the crisis of segregationism in its own racist and dictatorial fashion' (Fine & Davis, 1990:7). The 'crisis' which led to the rise of the NP and the application of the apartheid system can be framed more accurately as a set of growing disjunctures within the capitalist system and the state – as the branches of capitalist production sought different solutions to their dilemmas. Indeed, the harsh repression unleashed by the NP government had been prefigured by its predecessor's sharp turn to repression after the end of the Second World War.

Manufacturing production had risen sharply during the Second World War (the sector's share of GDP had topped that of mining by 1943). Manufacturers favoured reforms that would ensure a large, permanent urban labour supply which could be regulated through recognized trade unions and bargaining structures. They preferred the relaxation of influx control, pass laws and the job colour bar (to enable cheaper African labour to do semi-skilled and skilled work), as well as the extension of still limited labour rights to urban African workers.

Mining capital, on the other hand, reasoned that the collapse of the reserve system undermined their cheap migratory labour supply. Rather than turn to a stabilized but more expensive urban workforce, it sought to shore up the rural reservoirs of migrant workers. And agricultural capital (especially in the then Transvaal, Orange Free State and Natal) wanted influx control and the pass laws tightened so as to stem the outflow of African labour towards the cities and towns. O'Meara has captured this fission well:

> As the 1940s progressed, the differing forms of state policy demanded by various capitals came into increasing contradiction with each other, opening deep divisions within the capitalist class ... The ruling UP was no longer able to organise together the increasingly contradictory demands of the various capitals and act as the political representative of the entire capitalist class ... [this] gave rise to a gradual realignment in the party political organisation of class forces (1983:232).

The state of affairs described by O'Meara was not extraordinary or peculiar. Capitalism is constantly marked by shifting tensions between the different branches of production and the resultant contradictory demands placed on the state, which has to attempt to reconcile or resolve them. Under the United Party (UP) government, the state was unable to fulfil that task which, after 1948, befell the NP. Some of its anti-capitalist rhetoric invited concern, but it was geared mainly at marshalling the class alliance that would bring it to power. Indeed, history would show that 'apartheid was designed to secure labour for all capitals, not to deprive any employer of it' (O'Meara, 1983:237).

This is not to say that there existed a precise 'fit' between the imperatives of capital and apartheid state policy, nor that the racist ideology of Afrikaner nationalism was a mere shadow play.[26] But it is to argue for caution against the Poulantzian insistence on the 'autonomy of politics', a line of analysis that over-dramatizes the fact that in capitalist society the state and the political system retains a compromised 'relative autonomy' from the system of production.[27] Apartheid would spawn laws which prohibited sexual union between whites and blacks, or excluded blacks from 'white' buses and park benches – so-called 'petty apartheid', implemented and policed at considerable cost to the system. But these were hardly central elements of the accumulation strategy pursued by South Africa capital. The sweep, the vehemence and many of the details of the apartheid system disclosed the powerful hand exerted by Afrikaner nationalist ideology. It was around this cultural, historical and political mythos that a differentiated group was organized into a political and economic force. After 1948, it was this ideology (and its translation into practice) that preserved the political base of the NP. But this does not alter the fact that the apartheid system for almost 40 years remained functional to the needs of the capitalist class; had it not, the state would have been plunged into a genuine crisis.[28] Indeed, some aspects of 'petty apartheid' were functional to the aspirations of the white *petit bourgeoisie*. The average white supported the expulsion of Indian and African traders from 'white' urban zones on the basis of racial exclusivity. But the core function of these exclusions lay elsewhere: they were expropriations aimed at guaranteeing the entrance of white merchants into the market or the removal of competition from that market.[29]

The NP won subsequent 'white' elections by broadening the class alliance that constituted its core political base (by effectively implementing measures that advanced Afrikaner material and cultural interests) within a broader programme which intensified the rate of exploitation and profit in South Africa and which ensured that the benefits were dispensed intensively within the white community. Within white South Africa, formidable hegemony was achieved. The NP regime offered something for everyone, even if a tiny minority of whites would recoil from some of its excesses.

In short, from capital's point of view, the contradictions of the 1940s were resolved by the apartheid state with comparative ease and little disruption. The costs were visited upon the black, particularly African, majority.

Restructuring under an iron fist

The NP regime quickly introduced two key sets of interventions. Influx control of African labour and the pass law system were expanded and tightened, intensifying efforts to reduce the African population to a labour army serving capitalist industries and agriculture.[30] Organizations representing the interests of the African majority (especially trade unions and the CPSA, which was banned in 1950) came under sustained attack. One result was that African wages were dramatically driven down and continued to fall in real terms until 1958/9. Adjunct to these interventions was a gallery of racist measures which segmented every aspect of social and economic life along racial lines.

Central, too, was the notion of an 'activist' state (common internationally in the post-war years) which actively and often forcibly would intervene in social and economic affairs. The state's ability to 'manage' aspects of the economy – specifically the allocation and control of labour – was enhanced. Webs of administrative structures were set up, including the notorious Bantu Administration Boards, which managed the influx control system. The resultant increase in profitability led to a surge of foreign investment, much of it channelled into the manufacturing sector. In spite of the NP's earlier threats, it did not introduce any anti-monopoly legislation. On the contrary, 'tariff protection policies … and fiscal and taxation policies favourable to efficient firms, all encouraged the trend towards monopoly capitalism'.[31]

The state also intervened with vigour to aid the survival of marginal capitalist enterprises (particularly in agriculture) and assist the birth of new, mostly Afrikaner-owned, ones. Through a concerted affirmative action programme it augmented the Afrikaner capitalist class and advanced Afrikaners in all spheres of life. Government bank accounts were moved to an Afrikaner-controlled bank, government contracts were handed to Afrikaner-owned firms, Afrikaners were appointed to serve in and head scores of state departments, top bureaucratic and military posts, official boards and commissions. Cultural production by Afrikaners was encouraged and widely disseminated through a range of cultural bodies, festivals and publishers. History books were rewritten in accordance with the ideology of Afrikaner nationalism, and school curricula were altered accordingly. The contracts for new textbooks went to Afrikaner-owned publishers. The state bureaucracy was expanded and made to absorb huge numbers of Afrikaner workers who thereby gained access to soft loans, housing bonds and other benefits[32] – 'a parasitic layer' living directly off the state, and from which evolved rapidly an Afrikaner middle-class. Afrikaners, hitherto confined largely to the 'Third World', were propelled into the 'First World'. In all these respects, the achievement by the NP of state power stood at the hub of the Afrikaners' elevated status and roles in South Africa society.

The post-war accumulation strategy

Dramatic changes were also wrought within the capitalist class. In two decades, Afrikaner capitalists were propelled into the upper reaches of the economy and integrated into the steadily evolving web of conglomerates that would dominate the economy by the 1970s. Significant were the joint ventures launched by English monopolies with Afrikaner corporations: in one instance the Anglo American Corporation practically handed over its General Mining and Finance Corporation to a subsidiary of the Afrikaner-owned insurance giant Sanlam. The graduation of Afrikaner capital as a junior partner in the (still English-dominated) economy was in full swing.

Even more far-reaching were the restructurings applied in pursuit of a new accumulation strategy, which rested on two central pillars: an industrialization strategy based on import-substitution and the ongoing dependency on cheap African labour.

The strategy of import-substitution industrialization was selected as the route into the company of 'First World' industrialized economies. Like Chile, Argentina and Brazil, South Africa focused on developing basic industries (an emphasis not dissimilar to Soviet forms of industrialization), with strong state intervention to protect a burgeoning manufacturing sector against foreign imports. The expansion of mass production of consumer commodities was linked to the rising consumptive power of whites, especially white workers who enjoyed a dramatic rise in wages. A key element of the accumulation strategy, therefore, was 'racially structured', leading economist Stephen Gelb to describe the post-war growth model as 'racial Fordism' while noting that the foundation of this model 'was the expansion of exports of gold and other precious metals, and their stable prices on world markets' (1991:2).

Rather than adopt a 'hands-on' role throughout the economy in terms of a comprehensive economic strategy, the apartheid state tried to establish optimal conditions for capitalist growth to occur. It did so by erecting high tariff and non-tariff protective walls around vulnerable industries, setting up massive parastatal corporations (like the steel manufacturer Iscor, electricity supplier Eskom and energy supplier Sasol), and expanding and upgrading transport and telecommunications infrastructure. From this path emerged deep social transformation, a modern working class and pockets of relatively modern industrial capitalism marked by increasingly concentrated ownership patterns.

The strategy did not match the later example of East Asian Newly Industrialized Countries (NICs) which restructured capitalist production by intervening in investment and production decisions, research and development, and more, to move from the import-substitution stage to a primary export-substitution stage. The *export-substitution* paths adopted by Taiwan and South Korea centred on strong state intervention in the economy, with a focus on the production of non-durable, labour-intensive goods and the development of markets for them. This path addressed the problem of an urban influx of workers from ailing agricultural areas, by structuring the economy in ways that would absorb the labour surplus.

In contrast, South Africa chose to persist with an exclusionary regime of accumulation, barricading the labour surplus on a periphery which took economic, social, political and geographic forms.[33] Furthermore, the growth model favoured capital-intensive industry, which meant limited absorption of labour surplus, and an (increasingly mechanized) agricultural sector marked by very low wages and dismal working conditions.

Dependency on the reproduction and exploitation of cheap African labour increased, chiefly in the mining and agricultural sectors, thus elaborating and intensifying a process which had been integral to the development of capitalism in South Africa. The homeland system saw the insider/outsider division expressed geographically, enabling the state to deflect the social and economic costs of reproducing African labour and absorbing unemployment onto a literal periphery. Massive forced removals saw the labour tenant system replaced by a contract labour system. Between 1960 and 1982, 3,5 million people were forcibly removed by the state; almost half were Africans who had lived on white-owned farms or on their own land in African districts. About 700 000 more people were removed from urban areas declared 'white' (Surplus People Project, 1983). Most were removed to homelands. Influx control measures were tightened, preventing Africans from being physically present in urban ('white') areas without state permission (in the form of the notorious 'pass books'). The prime function of the homeland system was, to paraphrase Alain Lipietz, the production of an immense reserve army of children available for wage-labour as and when required (1987:149). As late as 1980 an apartheid think-tank would still propose that 'the problem of race relations' be solved through 'a system of separate political sovereignties' joined in 'economic cooperation' with 'white' South Africa.[34] However, one should guard against an economic reductionist reading of the homeland policy. Political factors were also to the fore, as apartheid administrators sought to deflect the post-war continental surge of nationalist liberation politics into barricaded political entities.

The popular forces fight back

Popular resistance, though still fragmented, quickly revived in reaction to the apartheid measures – in the form of sporadic strikes and consumer boycotts in towns and cities, and more militant (occasionally violent) action in rural areas.[35]

Goaded on by its newly-formed youth wing, the ANC emerged from its slumber. Its 1949 Programme of Action had incorporated several elements of the ANCYL's manifesto and signalled a turn to 'mass struggle' under the ambit of African nationalism. Although the ANC's core base had shifted to the urban African working class, the organization was by no means under working class leadership: its top ranks – including the rising stars of the ANCYL like Nelson Mandela, Oliver Tambo, Walter Sisulu and Joe Matthews – were still drawn from the African middle class.

The predominance of African nationalism within the resistance move-ment was not yet assured, however. Following a leftward turn by the CPSA after 1948, the party generated a scathing critique of African nationalism and the ANC. Its 1950 Central Committee report warned that 'the class conscious proletariat cannot rally under the "national" flag of the bour-geoisie', and lambasted the black middle class for failing to provide effective leadership to the masses.[36] However, Fine has argued that the central thrust of the report was less towards shifting resistance onto the track of socialist struggle than at radicalizing the nationalist struggle (Fine & Davis, 1990:113). The CPSA would continue to fight for socialism, but the imme-diate task was the struggle for national liberation under the leadership of a revolutionary organization. In essence, the framework for an alliance between the CPSA and ANC had been proffered. Relations between the two organizations were not tranquil, as shown by the fierce reaction from ANC conservatives to the joint May Day stayaway called by the CPSA and Transvaal ANC in 1950.[37] A month later, the CPSA dissolved, in anticipa-tion of the promulgation of the Suppression of Communism Act by the NP government. Three years later it reconstituted itself as an underground organization, the South African Communist Party (SACP).

The first major resistance action organized by the ANC was the Defiance Campaign of 1952, in which African women – led by the example of figures like Dorothy Nyembe, Lilian Ngoyi and Annie Silinga – played a central role. The ANC Women's League, hitherto an ineffective group dominated by the wives of ANC leaders, was 'transformed into a fighting arm of the ANC' (Mbeki, 1992:73). The campaign also spawned joint actions with other political groups, a move that would lead to the formation of the mul-tiracial Congress Alliance in 1955,[38] and the drafting of the Freedom Charter. At the height of the campaign, ANC membership rocketed from 4 000 to 100 000 (Mbeki, 1992:64).

Given the disparate nature of resistance and the earlier quiescence of the ANC, the Defiance Campaign was a landmark attempt to mount a co-ordinated challenge against the apartheid state. Again, though, official his-tory tends to exaggerate the accomplishments. The campaign was aimed at forcing the NP government to repeal six sets of legislation introduced or reinforced since 1948[39] – which it failed to do. By early 1953, the flow of volunteers for civil disobedience actions had slowed to a trickle, and the government had responded with new repressive legislation outlawing political protest. By the end of the year, the ANC's membership surge had been reversed, dropping to 28 000. This prompted an anonymous ANC writer to complain that 'the building of the organisation did not correspond to the enthusiasm the campaign had aroused ... As a result we did not consolidate our gains'.[40]

Attempts to consolidate the fragmentary elements of popular resistance under the banner of African nationalism continued in earnest – including the creation of the Congress Alliance and its historic adoption of the Freedom Charter, and the launching of the ANC-aligned South African Congress of Trade Unions (SACTU). The Freedom Charter for the first time presented South Africans with the outline of a democratic alternative to apartheid. Its pronouncements were sweeping, but they pointed to a new order where liberal democratic rights could be combined with a welfarist socio-economic system. The Charter and its drafting process would, in decades following, become intensely mythologized: the Charter became the touchstone of ANC policy and assumed sacrosanct status as the product of the 'will of the people'. That status is perhaps controversial.[41] Nevertheless, the Charter acquired immense political utility – particularly as an instrument in the ANC's efforts to establish its hegemony amongst the anti-apartheid opposition. The state, meanwhile, used the Freedom Charter as the basis for laying charges of treason against 156 leaders of the Congress Alliance. All the accused were eventually acquitted, but the five-year Treason Trial effectively removed them from political activity.

Formed in 1955, the non-racial SACTU represented the trade union wing of the Congress. With 19 affiliate unions, its membership would more than double by 1961 and reach some 55 000. It was tasked with furthering 'political unionism', a conception that linked workers' struggles for better wages and working conditions to the broader struggle for national liberation. SACTU played a significant role in the rise of industrial militancy between 1955 and 1958. The number of strikes rose markedly between 1954 and 1958, and some historians have suggested that the reinvigorated militancy contributed to halting the steady decline in African wages by 1959.[42] The number of organized African workers was tiny, however, although some 300 000 Africans worked in factories, 150 000 in transport, 800 000 in services, and a million in agriculture by the end of the decade.[43]

By mid-1958, though, SACTU had experienced fully the suffocating weight of 'political unionism'. It had pushed for a national strike in support of demands for a minimum wage, shorter working hours and trade union recognition,[44] but ANC leaders were intent on launching a mass campaign to coincide with the whites-only election in April. In the end, a three-day stayaway was called, nominally including the union demands but, in reality, focusing on the election – as the slogan 'Defeat the Nats' made clear. It was called off after the first day, to the dismay of some union leaders,[45] while leftists blamed the ANC leadership for undermining the militancy of the masses. Great controversy still surrounds the election stayaway and the decisions taken around the earlier 1957 bus boycotts, when ANC leaders were also accused of restraining the apparent militancy of workers. Whatever the verdict, by the end of the decade, the working class movement was decidedly weak – in Fine's view, partly because of the 'internal fragmentation of the working class', its 'structural position' in production, and 'the lack of distinction of the working class as a party in its own right from other class forces' (Fine & Davis, 1990:153). More than ever before, its demands and aspirations were being refracted through the prisms of race and nation.

Meanwhile, tensions between the ANC mainstream and its Africanist elements had grown, producing the 1959 split when a breakaway group led by Robert Sobukwe formed the Pan-Africanist Congress (PAC) in April. It was the PAC that organized the anti-pass law campaign during which police shot dead 69 protestors in Sharpeville township and 17 in Langa outside Cape Town. Pretoria used the opportunity to declare a state of emergency, and banned both the ANC and PAC on 8 April 1960.

The swing to armed struggle

The banning of the ANC forced the organization underground and occasioned a dramatic shift away from its strategy of non-violent resistance. There remains some dispute about the manner in which the decision to launch an armed struggle was taken. Govan Mbeki has acknowledged that there was strong disagreement within Congress on the matter as late as June 1961 (1992:90), whilst other writers have asserted that the decision came about fitfully.[46] Nevertheless, an armed wing, Umkhonto we Sizwe (Spear of the Nation), or MK, was set up under a National High Command, comprising ANC and SACP leaders, and carried out its first bombings on 16 December. In its manifesto, MK declared:

> The time comes in the life of any nation when there remain only two choices: submit or fight. That time has now come to South Africa. We shall not submit and we have no choice but to hit back by all means within our power in defence of our people, our future and our freedom … Refusal to resort to force has been interpreted by the Government as an invitation to use armed force against the people without fear of reprisals. The methods of Umkhonto We Sizwe mark a break with that past.[47]

The focus was to be on rural areas, where recent peasant uprisings (in Pondoland, Witzieshoek and Zeerust) seemed to indicate an untapped potential for a guerrilla war – an improbable enterprise in a countryside dominated by white-owned farms and white-run towns and lacking impenetrable natural features usually associated with such warfare.[48] Even more surprising is the fact that this strategic turn was taken by an organization whose major organized support base indisputably lay in the urban working class. Consequently, as historian Colin Bundy reminds, not all ANC and SACP leaders were convinced and strategists like Walter Sisulu and Bram Fischer slammed the decision as the 'unrealistic brainchild of some youthful and adventurous imagination'.

Left analysts (notably Harold Wolpe[49]) have, in varying ways, adopted a periodicization model for resistance strategies, segmenting it into distinct phases during which largely objective conditions purportedly prescribed certain forms of struggle. Thus, 1948–1960 saw legal, non-violent forms of mass resistance, 1961–1973 was a period of illegality and armed struggle in the form of guerrilla war, and post-1973 allowed for a synthesis of the two forms. The central determinant in each phase was the posture of the apartheid state. For instance, the state's decision after 1961 'to rule by force alone', thereby shutting out 'all lawful modes of opposition'[50] is typically presented as the singular rationale for the resort to armed struggle. But, in the view of Fine and Davis, that line of analysis ignores:

> ... the conscious, rational side of social movements; their capacity to make programmatic and operational choices, to learn from the past and from theory, to combine their own experience with the experience of other movements abroad, to question themselves through debate and criticism and to rebuild afresh (1985:25).

Armed struggle might have been the most attractive option but it was not the only viable one, despite the severity of the state's crackdown. In the aftermath of the Sharpeville and Langa massacres, protests erupted in the country's industrial heartland and in Cape Town, along with widespread strike action. The state's repressive capacities were strained as police reinforcements were shuttled frantically from flashpoint to flashpoint – it had not yet established a blanketing, systematic and co-ordinated repressive presence. In addition, local and foreign capital had grown markedly nervous. A strong outflow of capital commenced even before the Sharpeville massacre, and accelerated afterwards. Gold and foreign reserves dropped by 55 per cent, while the stock market and gold price plummeted. This amplified tensions in the ruling bloc: neither in the state nor the capitalist class was there unanimity about the appropriate response – indeed, acting prime minister P. O. Sauer openly supported reforms in key areas (pass laws, some political rights for Africans, improved wage levels), while five major business associations petitioned the government for policy reforms.[51]

Without exaggerating these developments, in theory all other strategic options had not been sealed off. Although very difficult under prevailing conditions,[52] a 'war of position' approach was perhaps available – by marshalling the militancy of African workers, women and other sectors of the urban African population. The fundamental question was whether such an option was *feasible*. An answer required an assessment of the comparative strengths and weaknesses of the popular sector, and the extent of disorientation and strategic heterogeneity in the ruling bloc. Instead, the movement's historians and strategists have bequeathed a version of history which denies the existence of any other strategic path.

Into the doldrums

The turn to armed struggle marked not only a major strategic shift, but also a critical paradigmatic shift.[53] Henceforth, reforming the system was declared impossible. The ANC and SACP adopted:

> ... an assumption that revolutionary armed struggle was not merely the means by which ultimately to contend for state power but also the principal means by which to progress in each phase of escalation towards that goal.[54]

This characterization would become dominant within the liberation movement, yielding an all or nothing approach that launched resistance struggles on a path of outright conflict with the state, and which rubbished bids to wrench reforms from the ruling class. SACP leader Joe Slovo's formulation of the strategy at a December 1960 SACP conference captured this thinking well. It would entail:

> ... a long-term, multi-staged campaign of disciplined violence in which a hard core of trained militants, supported by mass-based political activity and crucial external aid, *confront state power with the ultimate goal of seizing it.*[55]

As analyst Mike Morris has noted, 'a tendency was born which threatened to equate armed struggle with revolution and legal struggle with reformism'. The paradigmatic shift was immense. Removed from the range of options was any:

> ... conception for political activity [that] centred on open internal struggle, on taking advantage of fissures within the state, of incremental change, of operating within the system, of using existing institutions for organisational activity or policy work.[56]

Whilst rhetorically deemed an element of the new strategy, mass struggle was moved onto the backburner and armed struggle (based on *guerrilla* warfare) occupied the strategic centre-stage, thereby also fortifying the vanguardist and militarist tendencies in the movement. The urban masses – though demonstrably still capable of mounting telling resistance initiatives – were reduced to passivity, their return to the stage of history having become predicated on the materialization of a *deus ex machina*, guerrilla war, which would founder for the next two decades. If anything, the next 10 to 15 years would validate philosopher Paul Virilio's warning:

The principle aim of any truly popular resistance is thus to oppose the establishment of a social situation based solely on the illegality of armed forces which reduces a population to the status of a movable slave, a commodity.[57]

These observations are hardly heterodox. Entrenched by the armed struggle was, by Slovo's own, later admission,

> ... an attitude both within the organisation and amongst the people that the fate of the struggle depended on the sophisticated actions of a professional elite. The importance of the masses was theoretically appreciated, but in practice mass political work was minimal.[58]

The ANC's 1969 Morogoro consultative conference endorsed the guerrilla warfare strategy but emphasized that it could not occur in a political vacuum. Political struggle had to be primary. Consequently, the decision was taken to build the ANC's underground structures inside South Africa. The advocates of guerrilla war held their ground until 1978, when a study tour to Vietnam persuaded many of the enthusiasts (Slovo included) that an armed struggle had to be based on and arise out of mass political support – 'therefore all military activities at all times had to be guided and determined by the need to generate political mobilisation, organisation and resistance' (Bundy, 1989:7).

This dominant paradigm of armed struggle would prefigure the strategic disorientation of the movement after the late 1980s. Henceforth, apartheid could 'not be reformed', it had to be destroyed – an 'all or nothing' approach would eventually yield the tenets of 'ungovernability' and 'non-collaboration', and generate the calls for 'insurrection' and a 'people's war'. Its legacies would haunt the movement long after the achievement of liberation.

In the medium-term it would usher the resistance movement into the 'dark decade' of the 1960s. 'By the end of 1962,' Govan Mbeki has recalled, 'most units could no longer operate since they did not have the materials to carry out their sabotage activities' (1992:94). During the early 1960s, most of the ANC leadership that had not been imprisoned, moved into exile and guerrilla training camps were set up in Tanzania. The ANC was cut off from its support base inside South Africa and turned its attention to mustering international support for its struggle. Conditions hardly favoured guerrilla warfare. South Africa was surrounded by a *cordon sanitaire* – the Portuguese colonies of Mozambique and Angola, white-ruled Rhodesia and South African-occupied South-West Africa. Internally, the country offered few of the geographic features associated with rural guerrilla warfare: large, secluded mountain ranges and forests. It was not until 1967 that a major effort would be made to launch a guerrilla war, when guerrillas tried to infiltrate into South Africa through the Wankie Game Reserve in Rhodesia –

apparently in response to growing disaffection among cadres in the training camps. The attempt failed when Rhodesian security forces intercepted the 80-man force, killing 30 guerrillas and capturing 20.[59] For the next decade, the armed struggle remained largely a strategy on the drawing board.

Meanwhile, the state was able to reorganize its repressive capacities, viciously crush any remnants of internal resistance, and resolve some of the main conjunctural sources of tension in the ruling bloc.[60]

Apartheid's harvest

The post-war accumulation strategy established for whites an affluent welfare state. White workers were guaranteed access to jobs, experienced rising wages and were cushioned by a wide-ranging social security system plus easy access to credit and loans. This increased their consumptive power, making them (and the ballooning middle class) the consumptive core of a growing economy. Vast resources were invested in education, health, cultural, recreational and sports infrastructure and services for whites. White trade unions won collective bargaining agreements for white workers and successively defended their privileges against some employers' attempts to cut wage costs by shifting the job colour bar upwards and elevating low-paid African labour into semi-skilled jobs. In sum, the class alliance that returned the NP to government in successive whites-only elections was shored up. As long as the claim by black South Africans to full political rights could be held in check, the political survival of the system could be ensured – or so it seemed.

In African communities, the effects were the reverse, with the great majority of Africans ruled out of these circuits of production, distribution and even consumption. Access to skilled jobs was heavily restricted, through discrimination in the workplace and an education system which, until the early 1970s, was explicitly designed to equip Africans only with the rudiments required for entry into the lower ranks of the labour market.

Class formation in African communities was curbed, flattening class differentiation in the townships. Some segmentation did occur within the African working class, as a semi-skilled urban layer emerged, but an African middle class remained a distant prospect. The state had closed off access to most accumulatory activities and continued to drive African businesspeople from the central business districts. Even the informal sector was closed down through a barrage of regulations, forcing African consumers to spend their money at white-owned businesses. Wages rose but, in the absence of a social security net and with destitution increasing in the homelands, they had to be distributed widely within extended family networks. The rate of savings was negligible, and disposable income remained too small to afford most items deemed 'essential' by whites.

At the same time, the weight of the apartheid system was distributed unevenly among blacks (i.e. Africans, coloureds and Indians), as state budget allocations to housing, education and health departments showed. Along with white workers, Indians and coloureds predominated in the expanding sectors of the economy and were accorded some mobility within and between jobs (Hindson, 1991:229). By the 1970s there had developed in both 'groups' a significant middle class, comprising mostly professionals and merchants. Although disenfranchised, these small minorities were deemed to be citizens of 'white' South Africa.[61]

The 'boom' years

The economy performed strongly, with GDP rising at an average rate of almost 6 per cent between 1960 and 1969.[62] This strong growth cycle continued until the early 1970s,[63] attracting large inflows of foreign capital, much of it routed into the manufacturing sector. By the mid-1960s, the manufacturing sector was growing at almost 12 per cent annually, but much of the growth was capital intensive and did little to stem the chronic rise in unemployment.

Although performing impressively at first glance, the economy stood on shallow, rickety foundations. The manufacturing sector did not became export-oriented. Even though manufacturing's contribution to GDP in 1960 was almost double that of the mining and agricultural sectors combined, it comprised a small part of foreign earnings, which depended overwhelmingly on the export of primary products (with gold the biggest earner). By 1975, agriculture and mining accounted for three-quarters of merchandise exports with manufacturing relying on an almost saturated domestic market (Davies et al., 1984:53); a decade later mining, whilst representing only 11 per cent of GDP, contributed 70 per cent of foreign exchange earnings. Also, the manufacturing sector did not possess a capital goods branch of any note. This meant that the capital intensive growth registered in manufacturing during the 1960s rested on a high rate of capital goods imports (destined both for the private manufacturing industry and the massive parastatal industries set up by the NP government) which strained foreign reserves.

The fortunes of the South Africa economy still hinged on two *external* factors: the gold price and access to foreign exchange. At this fundamental level, its location in the world system still resembled that of most 'Third World' countries.

The model falters

After the oil shock of 1973, the growth rate slowed demonstrably. Annual GDP growth dropped to 1,9 per cent until 1984 and to 1,5 per cent for the rest of that decade – signs that the post-war accumulation strategy had encountered serious difficulties. Orthodox economic analysis recoiled from diagnoses that detected the onset of a long-cycle crisis. Rather, the natural soundness of the economy was said to be distorted or undermined by

inappropriate government policies and/or disruptions in the global economy. At the macro level, such analyses stressed the increasing dysfunctional-
ity of the government's apartheid policies to the economy, policies which
were said to limit the natural workings of the free market and to invite
external distorting factors like sanctions. Thus, the economic difficulties
were regarded as downswings occasioned by, among other factors, the oil-
price increases following the oil shock of 1973, periods of capital flight and
sanctions (particularly in 1976 and 1985), and drops in the price of gold.[64]
But the problems that had congealed in the economy were too severe and
cumulative to represent a mere cyclical downturn. Against the background
of a global recession and post-1972 revival of working class organization
and action, several chronic handicaps had emerged. In summary:

- Capital intensive growth prevented the economy from absorbing surplus
  labour.
- The manufacturing sector's dependency on imports and its failure to
  become a major exporter deepened the economy's vulnerability to external factors (such as world market prices for precious metals and currency
  fluctuations) and caused chronic balance of payment difficulties.
- Manufacturing investment had become tardy, betraying a tendency
  towards over-accumulation.
- The market had become too small to sustain manufacturing centred on
  luxury import-substitution.
- Productivity growth had slowed, partly because of a shortage of skilled
  black labour and the deliberate depreciation of social capital under the
  apartheid system.

As in other industrializing economies on the periphery, growth in the manufacturing sector depended on capital goods imports, which during periods
of expansion grew at much quicker rates than export earnings. In addition,
the effects of the slowdown in the advanced world economies 'were trans-
mitted to the South African economy ... through a rise in the price level of
imported machinery' (Gelb, 1991:20). Aggravating matters was the failure
of the manufacturing sector to penetrate export markets (which would have
relieved the economy's dependency on mineral exports for foreign exchange
earnings), and the wild fluctuation of primary commodity export prices
(notably gold prices) after 1971. Chronic balance of payment problems set
in. South Africa's industrial development was being severely stunted and its
essential status as a primary commodity exporter confirmed.

The boom had been financed by large foreign capital inflows that were
contingent on sustained economic growth. But by mid-1976 – *before* the
Soweto uprising – South Africa was experiencing a net outflow of capital,
raising the spectre of a debt crisis. The economy lost a quarter of its foreign
exchange reserves in the first three months of 1976, forcing resort to an

emergency loan from the International Monetary Fund (IMF). Total investment dropped by 13 per cent between 1975 and 1977 (Saul & Gelb, 1981:
23). In industry, productivity remained low, with manufacturing outputs
dropping and production costs rising. The economy had entered a period of
stagflation. Rising rates of inflation fuelled a revival in worker resistance in
the early 1970s – signalling the breakdown of the disciplinary regime in the
workplace.

The rigid racial structuring of production and consumption patterns
made whites (and, to a much smaller extent, the coloured and Indian
minorities) the core market for the manufacturing sector.[65] That market was
now too small to sustain production growth. As the local chief executive of
General Motors would put it in 1980: 'We need people to sell to' (cited in
Saul & Gelb, 1981:27). This consumer shortage was deepened by the lack
of infrastructure in African areas: consumers without electricity, for
instance, were not going to buy electrical goods. Simply increasing wages
would not solve this problem: the soaring unemployment rate and rising
inflation meant that wage-earners' pay packets had to stretch further, since
more people within extended families depended on them as breadwinners.
Thus, even when wages increased (as they would in the 1980s), disposable
income did not expand at the same pace.

Destitution in the homelands, increased mechanization in agriculture,
and the expulsion of labour tenants from 'white' farms forced more of the
huge labour surplus to seek salvation in the urban centres. The state continued to apply influx control measures fiercely and introduced a variety of
grandiose schemes (including very costly efforts to redirect these economic
refugees into new 'economic growth zones' set up inside or on the borders
of homelands). The idea of blockading Africans in literal peripheries was in
crisis. The reality of an exponentially growing, permanent urbanized
African population had become irreversible.

Meanwhile, it was not salvation that awaited Africans in the urban areas.
Work was scarce, on the whole wages remained extremely low and the
oppressive realities of diffuse racist state apparatuses continually confronted
residents. The economy was experiencing a terminally high rate of black
unemployment, despite the high growth rates achieved through the 1960s.
In the lived experienced of Africans – and many coloureds and Indians – this
ubiquitous, all-encompassing nature of oppression led to the struggle to survive being couched more and more in political terms.

There remains enduring debate over whether the economic crisis was
centred on the demand side or the supply side.[66] Demand side analyses
have concentrated on the contradictions that arose between industry's
need for expanding consumptive capacities and the restrictions imposed
on black – particularly African – incomes. The state's attempts in the late
1970s to extend wage and other benefits to semi-skilled layers of the

urban black working class partly seemed to respond to a demand-side conception. More conventional Marxist analyses have characterized the crisis as one of overaccumulation of capital: '[A] situation in which goods cannot be brought to market profitably, leaving capital to pile up without being put back into new productive investment' (Bond, 1991:27). This view seeks corroboration in the dramatic rise in speculative activity, the increase in mergers and takeovers since the late 1970s and declining industrial output. Certainly, capital became increasingly centralized with hosts of companies absorbed into seven massive conglomerates through mergers and takeovers. By 1983 they controlled 80 per cent of the value of shares listed on the Johannesburg Stock Exchange (JSE) and straddled different sectors. Mining monopolies moved into the financial, industrial, property and agricultural sectors; insurance giants launched raids into the mining and industrial sectors.[67] In short, the overaccumulation thesis emphasized the terminal nature of the difficulties which, allegedly, could not be resolved within the capitalist system. What it did not explain was 'capitalism's mutability and continued survival through several crises' (Gelb, 1987:35).

Notes

1   For a terse account, see Colin Bundy's 'Development and inequality in historical perspective' in Schrire (1992:24–38).

2   According to Davies et al., in the British-held Cape Colony, for instance, class position 'rather than outright racial discrimination determined the patterns of economic and political power' (1985:6).

3   An independent African peasantry survived in significant numbers until the early 1930s, when its dissolution was intensified by the Depression. See Bundy (1979). Until then this peasantry served as the main social base of the ANC. Its decline coincided with the ANC's slump during the 1930s and early 1940s.

4   With the exception of Algeria, where a similar pattern of settler domination occurred.

5   South Africa, of course, would only emerge as a geopolitical entity in 1910, with the establishment of the Union of South Africa.

6   For more, see Legassick and De Clerq (1978).

7   See *The Road to South African Freedom: Programme of the South African Communist Party* (adopted in 1962). Central to that theory was the notion of 'two South Africas', which must be distinguished from the 'Two Nation' divide referred to in this book. The SACP's theory distinguishes between a 'White South Africa' with 'all the features of an advanced capitalist state in its final stage of imperialism' and a 'Non-White South Africa' with 'all the features of a colony'. Hence, the notion of 'internal colonialism'.

8   *Economic Planning Council Report No 9*, 1946, cited in Fine and Davis (1990:15). The intervention failed. Seven years later, the Lansdown Commission would conclude that 'reserve production [is] but a myth' (cited in O'Meara, 1983:230).

9   In one of many anomalies, white workers combined this racist chauvinism with militant action, under the banner of socialism, against capital. In 1922, a miners' strike mushroomed into the Rand Revolt – a bid to overthrow the state and replace it with a 'White Workers' Republic'.

10 The famous Bambata revolt of 1906 belonged to the pre-capitalist epoch. The 1922 white miners' strike ostensibly fitted the tradition of trade union militancy but was geared mainly at shoring up racial privileges. By 1945, however, about 40 per cent of African industrial workers were unionized, with some 119 trade unions fighting often fierce wage struggles (Davies *et al.*, 1985:12–16).

11 As argued, for instance, by Saul and Gelb (1981) and Davies *et al.* (1985).

12 Historian Dan O'Meara cited in Saul and Gelb (1981:14).

13 Fine and Davis (1990:12).

14 Botha Commission, cited in Fine and Davis (1990:11).

15 Fine and Davis, *op. cit.*, p. 18.

16 The CPSA was formed in 1921 out of the International Socialist League, which was founded in 1915 following a breakaway from the South African Labour Party.

17 Since 1935, CPSA policy had vacillated, largely in response to directives from Moscow. From 1936 to 1939, CPSA policy centred on mustering a popular front based on opposition to 'imperialism, fascism and war'. The 1939 Hitler–Stalin pact precipitated an abrupt shift (following the Soviet Communist Party's decision to portray the Second World War as an 'imperialist war') towards advocating heightened class struggle. The Nazi invasion of the USSR in 1941 triggered another sharp turn, towards building a people's front. For an exposition of these twists and turns see Fine and Davis (1990:36–57).

18 Also, the African peasantry continued to resist the restructuring of the countryside, although these actions were largely unconnected to the wellsprings of resistance politics lodged in the urban areas.

19 Cited in Fine and Davis (1990:47).

20 *Inkululeko*, 18 September 1943, cited in Fine and Davis (1990:95).

21 Cited in Fine and Davis (1990:74).

22 The best study of the Afrikaner nationalism's rise to power remains O'Meara, D., 1983, *Volkskapitalisme: Class, Capital and Ideology in the Development of Afrikaner Nationalism, 1934–1948*. O'Meara, D., 1996, *The Apartheid State and the Politics of the National Party (1948–1994)* is an unrivalled account of its subsequent exercise of power.

23 O'Meara (1983:5).

24 O'Meara, *op. cit.*, p. 149.

25 Its anti-capitalist, anti-monopoly and anti-imperialist postures, for instance, were designed to win over white farmers and workers, and were abandoned soon after the election victory. Surprisingly, serious efforts to organize Afrikaner workers did not occur until the Second World War when the *Arbeidsfront* (Labour Front) and *Blankewerkers se Beskermingsbond* (White Workers' Defence League) were formed, in 1942 and 1943, respectively.

26 ANC intellectual Harold Wolpe would later critique the notion of a tight fit between apartheid and capitalism; the relationship, he argued, was 'historically contingent' and 'Janus-faced, being simultaneously functional and contradictory' (1988:8).

27 The work of Marxist Nicos Poulantzas exerted a strong pull on the thinking of left intellectuals inside South Africa during the 1970s and 1980s, particularly his *State, Power, Socialism* (1978).

28 A drastic reconfiguration of (white) political society would have ensued. Instead, the NP rapidly established itself as an integral element of a reconstituted ruling bloc which would survive until the early 1980s. Recall that white South Africans lived in a (racially exclusive) parliamentary democracy. After its precarious victory in the 1948 election, the NP succeeded in expanding its base. It won subsequent elections by ever-widening margins, an unlikely feat had its exercise of state power proved dysfunctional to the overall needs of the capitalist class.

29 The economic logic of violent racism, even on this 'parochial' scale, was not unique. US historian Ivy Compton Burnett has shown that 68 per cent of lynchings in the American south targeted black businessmen who were competing with white counterparts (cited in IPS news report, 'Black scholar decries U.S. existential crisis', 13 July 1994).

30 The earliest influx control measures actually date back to 1760 and were applied against slaves in the Cape Colony (Davies *et al.*, 1984:171).

31 Davies *et al.* (1984:23). Contrary to its title, the 1955 Regulation of Monopolistic Conditions Act did not curb monopolies.

32 This also served as a stimulus for housing, vehicle and other durable goods markets.

33 This is not to imply that South Africa as easily could have aped South Korea, a country where social polarization was much less severe and which lay closer to expansive markets.

34 Bureau of Economic Research, Organisation and Development report cited by Saul and Gelb (1981:52).

35 The 1950 Witzieshoek rebellion, for instance, when at least 15 people were killed (including two policemen) and more than 100 injured.

36 See Fine and Davis (1990:111) where Fine also accused the CPSA of disingenuousness: '[T]he Central Committee failed to mention that it was the Communist Party itself which for most of the 1940s had allied itself with the old guard of the ANC on a patriotic programme of constitutional reform and the curtailment of illegal forms of direct action, so that one function of the report was to displace all responsibility for this strategy from the shoulders of the Communist Party onto those of African nationalism'.

37 Nineteen workers died in the action and twice as many were injured.

38 The Congress Alliance mirrored the racial categorizations introduced by the NP government and comprised the ANC, the South African Indian Congress, the Coloured People's Congress and the Congress of Democrats (a grouping of progressive whites).

39 The Group Areas Act, the Suppression of Communism Act, the pass laws, the Voters' Representation Act, the Bantu Authorities Act, and the Stock Limitation Policy.

40 See Lodge (1983:44). It was in response to the defeat of the campaign and growing state repression that Nelson Mandela devised his 'M-Plan', designed to enable the ANC to operate under conditions of illegality.

41 For instance, in academic Tom Lodge's assessment, 'popular demands were canvassed but the ultimate form of the document was decided by a small committee and there were no subsequent attempts to alter it in the light of wider discussion' (1983:72), while Fine has suggested that key elements of the Charter had been decided on beforehand (Fine & Davis 1990:138–45).

42 The overall number of participants was low, though – a mere 6 158 workers participated in the 113 strikes launched in 1957, for instance; see Fine and Davis (1990:159).

43 Part of the problem lay in the many divisions that traversed the working class – racial, ideological and administrative (with or without legal recognition).

44 See Fine and Davis (1990:168–75) for a critical overview.

45 The NP won the election handsomely, while the opposition UP was virtually wiped out at the polls.

46 Stephen Ellis and the pseudonymous Tsepo Sechaba contend that 'the ANC's National Executive Committee in June 1961 debated the issue but took no position on it' (Ellis & Sechaba, 1992:32).

47 For the entire text, see Karis and Gerhardt (1977:716).

48 Govan Mbeki recalls that 'the most important books on guerrilla warfare that were available at the time in South Africa were the writings of Mao Tse-Tung on the Chinese experience and of Che Guevara on the Latin American experience ... [which]

emphasised the importance of enlisting the support of the peasantry if a revolutionary war is to succeed' (1992:89).

49 See Wolpe (1980) and Wolpe (1984).

50 Nelson Mandela, 1978, *The Struggle is my Life* speech at the Rivonia Trial, IDAF, London, p. 156.

51 Fine and Davis (1985:41).

52 It is worth noting that the state's crackdown, while severe, was not instantaneous: the new security legislation only took effect in 1963, although detention without trial had been introduced in 1961.

53 For a lucid overview, see Barrel (1991).

54 Barrel, *op. cit.*, p. 69. A great deal of the theoretical impetus towards armed struggle stemmed from the SACP's Colonialism of a Special Type thesis, according to Bundy: 'An analysis which viewed class as subordinate to the national question looked to guerrilla action not only for its military gains but also for its contribution towards politicising and mobilising the masses' (1989:5).

55 J. Slovo in Davidson *et al.* (1977:186) (emphasis added).

56 Morris (1993b:6).

57 Virilio (1978:55).

58 Davidson *et al.* (1977:193).

59 Leading the force was Chris Hani, later secretary-general of the SACP. According to Ellis and Sechaba, 'the security forces noted with consternation that the guerrillas' performance and training was far superior to anything yet seen in Rhodesia' (1992:49).

60 SACTU was buckled by state repression and, after 1964, shifted its focus to international solidarity work. By 1969 only 13 black unions remained in existence, down from 63 in 1961.

61 In the Cape Province, coloureds lost their qualified vote only in the 1950s, a move that triggered heated disputes even within Afrikaner ranks where the linguistic and cultural bonds with coloureds were recognized and even celebrated. In South Africa's first democratic election in 1994, coloured voters would provide one-third of all votes cast for the NP.

62 Figures cited by Anthony Black, 'Manufacturing Development and the Economic Crisis' in Gelb (1991:157). Other, higher figures are also cited – Merle Holden, in Schrire (1992:315), has pegged average growth for the same period at 7,4 per cent.

63 This view is disputed. Economist Nicoli Nattrass has contended, for example, that profit rates actually declined throughout the post-war period. See her 'Wages, Profits and Apartheid' (unpublished D.Phil, Oxford, 1990); and Moll (1991). Radical economists have countered that Nattrass' critique 'is focused too much on one variable, the rate of profit' (Bond, 1992:25).

64 They would often point to the 1980–1 rise in the growth rate as proof that the economy was undergoing short-term cyclical swings. That brief upswing, however, was triggered by a gold price rise in response to the 1979 oil price shock following the Iranian revolution.

65 Hence Stephen Gelb's description 'racial Fordism'. In Western Europe, Fordism had rested on boosted mass consumption (through wage increases, larger social spending) and stabilized labour relations (through collective bargaining agreements). Similar measures were applied in South Africa, but only within the white society.

66 For an instructive summary of these debates, see Bond (1992).

67 Of these four had controlling interests in major mining, manufacturing and financial ventures: Anglo American Corporation, Rembrandt Group, Sanlam and Old Mutual; see Lewis (1991:33).

CHAPTER TWO

Managing the crisis

By the end of the 1970s there had arisen what some analysts have described as an *organic crisis*, linking the economic, social and political dimensions. Pressured by capital, the state would respond with a fitful series of adjustments in the social and economic spheres over the next 15 years, deferring formative reforms in the political dimension until the late 1980s.

The use here of the term 'crisis' requires explanation. The definition employed is not that of orthodox Marxism, of a terminal breakdown of the system which necessarily inaugurates profound social transformation. More appropriate is the definition developed within regulation theory, where a crisis denotes a 'turning point' arrived at because 'the capitalist economy cannot continue to develop in the same form and along the same path as before'. This crisis registers also in the social and political structures which underpin an accumulation strategy but which have become increasingly dysfunctional to it (Gelb, 1991:2). Required is profound restructuring which, crucially, can and often does occur within the capitalist system – with distressing regularity and often without altering the patterns of inequality in a society.

In South Africa's case, severe contradictions were engendered within an accumulation strategy that depended on cheap, expendable African labour, but also rested on an import-substitution (and capital-intensive) industrialization strategy which required an ever-expanding market for its products. Simultaneously, the expulsion of the vast majority of the population from the enclave of (even comparative) privilege generated a variety of social and political responses which ranged from low productivity to forms of resistance that threatened the legitimacy and authority of the capitalist state. The result was a burgeoning, multi-dimensional crisis. In itself this did not augur the collapse of the system, but it did produce intense fission within the ruling bloc, rendering it even less coherent and opening new possibilities for advance by resistance organizations. Indeed, Harry Oppenheimer, chair of the country's largest corporation, Anglo American, already had noticed in 1971 that:

… we are approaching the stage where the full potential of the economy, as it is at present organized, will have been realized, so that if structural changes are not made, we will have to content ourselves with a much lower rate of growth … Prospects for economic growth will not be attained so long as a large majority of the population is prevented by lack of education and technical training or by positive prohibition from playing the full part of which it is capable in the national development.[1]

Resurgence of resistance

In 1972 the first signs emerged that a crucial underpinning of the post-war accumulation strategy – the disciplinary regime in the workplace, which helped enforce a stable, low-wage labour force – was disintegrating. Despite the formidable battery of measures aimed at preventing African workers from organizing independently,[2] industrial workers explicitly challenged the labour relations system by staging the first strike wave in decades. It began with the October 1971 protests for higher wages by 4 000 dockworkers in Durban and Cape Town. Months later the strikes spread to textile factories and transport companies, followed by actions in East London and Johannesburg and on some mines.

The strikes were triggered by extremely low wages and the rising prices of basic consumer items[3] but gradually spurred demands for the legal right to organize. If anything, they announced the end of apartheid's 'golden age' – with class struggle, for the first time in almost 25 years, reaching an organized pitch that could unsettle the rhythms of capital accumulation. A clutch of new black unions was formed, including the Metal and Allied Workers' Union (MAWU), the National Union of Textile Workers (NUTW), the Chemical Workers' Industrial Union (CWIU) and the Transport and General Workers' Union (TGWU), many of them centred around Durban. Unions also mushroomed in the Western Cape and the Witwatersrand regions where training and other support structures were set up. Active in these organizing efforts were former SACTU and ANC activists who had been in hiatus for most of the 1960s, as well as a new generation of radical white students and intellectuals. Mindful of SACTU's experience of state repression, most of the new unions eschewed the 'political unionism' approach and concentrated on shopfloor issues.

Having reached their peak in 1973–4, the strikes continued until 1976.[4] Most, however, were crushed by police and management. On the whole, workers' demands were not met and membership of the new unions declined swiftly. A painstaking process commenced to build sturdy worker organizations capable of weathering the setbacks of strike defeats. But more than two decades after the defeats of the late 1940s and the subsequent rise of African nationalism, working class resistance had re-emerged in its own right. Meanwhile, the country would be rocked by the Soweto uprising, triggered by students protesting a decree that half the subjects in African schools be taught in the *Afrikaans* medium.

Unexpectedly, both capital and the apartheid state were tumbled into damage-control mode, albeit with the odds still stacked dramatically in their favour as they sought to suppress and defuse rising opposition.

The resurgence of popular resistance in the 1970s was propelled by four developments. The first related directly to the economic crisis. Unemployment levels had risen more sharply than in the 1960s and inflation climbed steeply, imposing severe hardship even on employed African workers, who reacted with the post-1972 strikes. The second development was the advance of national liberation struggles in southern Africa where both Mozambique and Angola won independence in 1975. These victories reverberated in South Africa, deepening a growing sense of siege among whites and immeasurably boosting courage and resolve among blacks. Logistically, the makeshift armed struggle benefited also as the infiltration of guerrillas and the exodus of new recruits into exile became easier, and communication channels could be revived with underground cells operating inside South Africa. For the first time since being banned, the ANC was able to narrow (to some extent) the distance between itself and the realities unfolding inside South Africa.

Thirdly, drawing on the writings of African radicals and US black nationalists, an ideological rejuvenation occurred in the form of Black Consciousness (BC). A new emphasis on self-reliance and non-violent militancy emerged from the Black Consciousness Movement's (BCM) propagation of 'psychologism' – the conviction that the key to black liberation lay in psychological liberation – which was expressed explosively in 1976, when the Soweto uprising erupted.[5] BC was perhaps the last independent ideological current to filter into the discourse of the liberation movement.[6] By the late 1970s, however, it had dissipated. State crackdowns had deprived BC of its leadership (through murder, as in the case of Steve Biko, or imprisonment). After the Soweto uprising, thousands of younger adherents fled the country, determined to return with guns in their hands. In exile, however, they discovered they could survive only by joining either the ANC or the PAC – and were thus absorbed into the mainstream liberation traditions.[7] BC turned out to be a godsend for the ANC, which drew into its ranks a new generation of committed and astute young leaders.

The fourth development was the growing tendency within the broad opposition to attribute all forms of deprivation, oppression and discrimination (in short, the multiple travails and contradictions experienced in lived reality) to the apartheid system, thereby enabling a heightened and more widespread politicization of the oppressed. A fresh resolve became evident in popular organizations which multiplied in numbers, drawing ever younger cohorts and cadres into resistance activities. The desolate 1960s were over. From here onwards, the state and capital would have to contend with a steady wave of resistance as they sought antidotes to dilemmas that were beginning to extend into all spheres of society.

The lights dim

In the economic sphere, the apartheid growth model had begun to decay, while in the political, ideological and social spheres, the 'conditions which had hitherto sustained a form of capital accumulation based predominantly on cheap, unskilled black (African) labour' began to function in contradiction to that form of accumulation (Davies *et al.*, 1984:37). Drawing on Antonio Gramsci's writings, Saul and Gelb, in an influential intervention,[8] declared the crisis to be 'organic':

> A crisis occurs, sometimes lasting for decades. This exceptional duration means that incurable structural contradictions have revealed themselves ... and that, despite this, the political forces which are struggling to conserve and defend the existing structure itself are making efforts to cure them within certain limits, and to overcome them. These incessant and persistent efforts ... form the terrain of the conjunctural and it is upon this terrain that the forces of opposition organize.[9]

The authors tried to avoid a shallow contradistinction between 'reform' and 'revolution', reminding that 'while "reform" is not genuine transformation ... it is not meaningless or irrelevant either, for it can affect the shape of the field of battle'.[10] Discourse within the resistance movement, however, had come to orbit around a facile schema that saw reform and revolution in mutually exclusive terms. Centred on the dictum that 'apartheid cannot be reformed', reforms were disparaged as mere attempts to undermine the revolutionary momentum and which, therefore, demanded outright rejection.

This conception was integrally linked to the paradigm shifts introduced by the turn to armed struggle, and was later reinforced by the victories of the MPLA and Frelimo in Angola and Mozambique, respectively. The crucial thrust of Gramsci's analysis – that a 'war of position' had to supplant the 'war of manoeuvre' – would hardly feature in the ANC and SACP's strategic debates, although it earned greater favour within the intellectual strata of the new trade union movements. The exiled organizations' strategies were geared to mobilizing resistance forces for an outright conflict aimed at a cataclysmic outcome: the overthrow of the apartheid state. Generalizing, Morris would later characterize this approach as follows:

> Radical participation in state structures to take advantage of spaces and gaps created by the regime, to create cracks and exacerbate crises, is mostly dismissed as collaborationist, granting legitimacy, confusing the masses, and reactionary. Often those advocating such courses are regarded as more

dangerous than the regime. The discourse of opposition becomes concerned with a fear of cooptation, preservation of the real principles of the struggle, and the correct strategies to create islands of alternative power to that of the regime. (1993a:99)

As well as imposing strategic limitations, this thinking would consolidate within the resistance movement a dominant culture based on a mix of coercion and loyalty, a matter explored in more detail below.

From the mid-1970s onwards, the ruling bloc's efforts to establish a new configuration of social, economic and political relations would open a myriad of spaces and gaps through processes of 'reform from above'. With the eventual (though partial) exception of the trade union movement, popular forces would not take an effective hand in shaping these reforms.

There was no conspiratorial game plan guiding the state reforms. The complex of difficulties arising in the 1970s amplified tensions within, as well as between, the state and capital. Simultaneously, popular organizations exerted fresh pressures, while changes in the regional and international contexts also influenced the search for solutions. Each set of reforms, then, was shaped as much by 'objective need' as it was by a shifting balance of forces within and between the state, capital and the popular forces. Yet, these reforms should not be read as the mere products of panic. Challenges were certainly mounting, but they would not (until the mid-1980s and then only temporarily) force the state and capital into a defensive mode.

Without pretending that the state or leading capitalist organizations viewed matters in such enveloping terms, resolving the accumulating difficulties required innovations on two fronts. A new basis for national consent had to be constructed which, ultimately, implied adjusting (and, eventually, overturning) the political and ideological bases of apartheid rule (Morris & Padayachee, 1989). Secondly, the post-war accumulation strategy had to be restructured, which necessitated adjustments not only in economic policies but also in the extra-economic underpinnings of that strategy – social relations, state structures, political formations and the webs of interaction between the state, capital and popular organizations.

From the mid-1970s onwards, the fitful array of reform initiatives introduced at both the macro and micro levels touched on some of those elements, sometimes stimulating and sometimes retreating before revived bouts of resistance. At their most basic level, they were aimed at shoring up the two fundamental foundations of state power in capitalist society – coercion and consent – and at reshaping the spheres of production, distribution and consumption in order to resuscitate faltering economic growth. As summarized by Stadler, this involved attempts 'to remodel political institutions, increase economic and educational opportunities for blacks, and institutionalize relations between capital and labour, in order to generate some legitimacy for the social order' (1987:160).

Hindsight allows us to compartmentalize these reforms into three phases (Morris & Padayachee, 1989), without suggesting they were conceived or pursued with such coherence. Nor should it hide the fact that they crystallized out of intense differences and debate within and between the state and capital about appropriate courses of action, and that their forms and implementation were often shaped by intensifying popular pressures, heightened class struggle and shifting social dynamics.

The first phase reforms: 1977–82

This phase was marked primarily by bids to restructure two important aspects of the social relations underpinning the accumulation strategy – the labour regime and urbanization policies. Some political adjustments did occur, but mainly inside the state itself. The overarching political crisis continued to be regarded as a security problem. A 'total strategy' was unveiled to defend the system against the 'total onslaught' mounted by the liberation forces and their allies. It called for the large-scale militarization of white society, closer co-operation between the state and capital, and new initiatives geared at taking 'into account the aspirations of our different population groups' in order to 'gain and keep their trust'.[11]

At the level of macro policies, several commissions were appointed to investigate possible adjustments – reflecting a marked shift towards technicist approaches and a greater emphasis on 'neutral', scientific solutions. To help achieve this, the state-funded Human Sciences Research Council (HSRC) was substantially reorganized and expanded; it would commission and conduct a wide range of surveys and policy research. In 1977, capital's disquiet over the lack of formative government reaction to the Soweto uprising prompted the Anglo American Corporation and the Rembrandt Group to set up a new research body, the Urban Foundation, which would focus on urbanization strategies and housing policies.[12]

Two commissions were specifically tasked with adapting the social relations underpinning the accumulation strategy – urbanization (Riekert) and industrial relations (Wiehahn) – in order to satisfy demands from monopoly capital for an enlarged, stable source of African semi-skilled and skilled labour. In the broadest sense, the key thrust of the resultant reforms was to 'ensure that as many people as possible share in prosperity and find their interests best served by an alliance with capitalism',[13] as part of a wider bid to preempt the overthrow of the system. Viewed more closely, their effect was to accelerate the process of class and intra-class differentiation within African communities.

Reshaping the divide

The 1979 Riekert Report sought 'to underpin, on a new basis, territorial segregation by legislatively strengthening the division between urban and rural Africans' (Morris & Padayachee, 1989:75). Thus, it proposed that Africans be divided into two categories: 'qualified' urban dwellers and the 'disqualified' rest, who would be banished to the homelands.

The aim of dividing South Africa between capitalist and pre-capitalist sectors persisted (Morris, 1991:45). The Two Nation model of society was to be hardened, with the terms of the division redrawn to admit a small layer of urban Africans into the enclave of 'insiders'. In Saul and Gelb's view the effect would be 'to tighten, not relax, the mechanisms of influx control' (1981:49). The new rights and concessions envisioned for the layers of 'officially urbanized' Africans would increasingly differentiate them from their 'insurgent' compatriots. After forcefully compressing classes within African townships, the apartheid state was now relaxing that pressure. This shift stemmed from industries' need for a more settled and sophisticated semi-skilled African labour force, and the political hope that a layer of comparatively privileged urban Africans would emerge to douse the ardour of the masses, as an article in the *Financial Mail* made clear:

> [T]he small group of privileged urban blacks whose quality of life will undoubtedly improve 'may well become less urgent in their demands for political power and serve as the lid on the kettle of revolution for some years to come'.[14]

This dream of a buffer of African moderates was reflected in the Commission's proposal that control and revenue generation in townships be decentralized with local township councils elected and tasked with duties hitherto performed by white apartheid officials. A kind of privatization within an authoritarian framework was attempted,[15] with the central state appearing to retreat from the day-to-day management of Africans' lived realities. In part this was aimed at defusing township discontent. But the attempts to 'depoliticize collective consumption in the townships produced its direct opposite – the massive politicization of struggles', as Morris observed (1991:46). Residents rebelled against huge increases in rent and service fees and targeted the new councils as 'puppets of apartheid'.

Among the other consequences of these adjustments was the intensification of competition for jobs and resources between the settled or permanent sections of the African urban working class and migrant workers. This would fuel animosities between these layers and lead to open, violent conflict in the years ahead,[16] as well as provide a bridgehead for the Zulu Inkatha movement in the industrial heartland around Johannesburg.

Reshaping the labour regime

The Wiehahn Commission on black trade unions was enlisted to restructure labour relations, with two broad aims. It had to revise the control of black workers in the workplace and design measures to increase the productivity and spending power of a well-trained, skilled African urban workforce. The Commission was explicit about its aims: 'The unions' potential strength meant that they must be controlled – their present weakness – meant that this should be done soon.'[17] It warned that reliance on outright repression 'would undoubtedly have the effect of driving black trade unionism underground and uniting black workers – against the system of free enterprise' (Saul and Gelb, 1981:72). Instead repression was to be replaced by a network of mechanisms which could lock black trade unions into the disciplinary and controlling workings of the labour relations system.

The 1981 Labour Relations Amendment Act accorded black trade unions the right to register and negotiate as well as participate in the Industrial Council system, a mediating apparatus designed to deflect worker issues from the shopfloor into a highly legalistic and bureaucratic process. Statutory job reservation for whites was also abolished. A select urban layer was to benefit from reforms – in keeping with the aim of refashioning and entrenching the insider/outsider dichotomy along less rigidly racist lines, as Morris and Padayachee recognized:

> The purpose of this new 'reform policy' was to ensure maximum division and differentiation of the popular classes: divide the black petty bourgeoisie from the working class by satisfying some of the former's socio-economic aspirations; pacify the working class by granting trade union reform; divide the general black population by driving a wedge between 'insiders' (with access to urban residential rights) and 'outsiders' (with no urban residential rights)' (1989:74).

The resultant legislation, however, departed from the Commission's recommendations in important respects. Most significant was the state's decision to forsake the proposal that unions seeking registration could only comprise African workers deemed permanent urban residents; migrant workers would not be allowed to join the unions. But protests from black unions pressured the state into removing those elements from the eventual enabling legislation.[18]

Unions were divided over whether to enter the new system. Some argued that registration subjected them to a debilitating set of controls while others believed that, despite the restrictions, registration offered new opportunities that could be exploited creatively. The Western Province Garment Workers' Union, for instance, rejected registration, while the Federation of SA Trade Unions (FOSATU) supported it on condition that non-racial unions would be able to register. FOSATU's approach was controversial in another respect. It opted not to engage with community and political issues that did not bear directly on labour, thus departing from the tradition of 'political unionism' spearheaded by SACTU during the 1950s. Importantly, it also developed a strong commitment to building shopfloor democracy.

Seizing spaces

The fate of the reforms needs to be couched within broader contexts, as well. Economic policy took a sharp turn to the right towards the end of the 1970s, leading to a host of 'free market' adjustments (exchange controls for non-residents were lifted, key surcharges were dropped and monetary policy was tightened). This occurred against the background of a deepening global recession. As a result, 'the liberalization of South Africa's economic links allowed for the easy transmission of the worsening international economic situation into [the] South African economy' (Morris & Padayachee, 1989:76). This led to rising inflation, increased job losses and the removal of state subsidies on basic consumer items. The black working class responded by using the new spaces accorded by the restructured labour relations system to rebuild its organizations and launch a fresh wave of strikes. In the process, the unions also became vehicles for political protest.

The Riekert strategy also backfired. The attempt to redraw and entrench the division between the capitalist and pre-capitalist sectors of African society failed to take into account some far-reaching structural changes. The division between homeland residents and 'settled' urban residents was not as watertight as Riekert and other apartheid planners imagined. Homeland residents were increasingly, though precariously, integrated into 'modern' South Africa – through the migrant labour system, their dependency on wages earned in industrial centres, transport systems and their geographic proximity to urban areas – although their access to its benefits was minimal. The urban/rural divide could no longer be formalized in spatial and geographic terms:[19]

> The classic patterns of labour supply and reproduction based on the migrant/settled rural/urban dichotomies were being superseded by the restructured urban regional economies around the industrial metropolitan areas (Morris & Padayachee, 1989:76).

Attempts by the central state to lessen its fiscal burden by offloading the provision of township services also failed. In order to fulfil their financing and regulatory role, the new township councils were forced to pass on the costs to residents (higher rents, rates and service charges) which generated a surge of opposition.

Instead of consolidating control over the urban proletariat, the reforms became the basis for renewed and reinvigorated protests as the beneficiaries pushed the reforms beyond the limits imposed by the state. By 1982, this set of reforms was frayed and bedraggled.

Several other developments had meanwhile conspired to stir up fresh tensions in the NP which undermined the quest for some strategic coherence in the ruling bloc. They included the revival of resistance activities (the Soweto uprising, the strikes of 1980–1, school and other boycotts during the same period), a large outflow of capital and the onset of a recession in the late 1970s. Intense power struggles within the NP and the government erupted publicly in the form of a government scandal (Muldergate) which was used by a rising band of reformist challengers (grouped around defence minister P. W. Botha) to unseat the incumbent leadership (gathered around prime minister B. J. Vorster). 'Modernizing' fractions of Afrikaner capital became dominant within the party (thanks also to wider support from other capitalist organizations outside the party), confirming a dramatic shift in the class alliance on which the NP had been built. The traditional core of the NP (white workers, Afrikaner *petite bourgeoisie* and small farmers) – the rightwing of the party – became marginalized[20] and the party came to pivot on the organizations of a maturing Afrikaner capital. Both the ideology and class basis of Afrikaner nationalism were being transformed – prerequisites for further, more far-reaching reformist adjustments.

The second phase of reforms: 1982–7

These reforms were bolder, having been preceded by a change of leadership within the ruling NP, a decisive shift in the class alliance that constituted the party's social base, the rapid spread in the scope and sophistication of black worker organizations, the revival of organized community and political protest, and heightened international hostility. State policies (and the *institutional form* of the state) increasingly became shaped by shifting relations between the contending classes – hence the dizzy and desultory character (and implementation) of many of the ensuing reforms.

The interplay of conflicting demands and initiatives would also generate other social dynamics. Class differentiation in African townships sharpened, though it could not be ascribed only to state reforms. Worker struggles had won increased social benefits, covert entrepreneurship (including organized crime) had increased, informal trading boomed and even the influx of homeland refugees in many cases became a source of accumulation for shacklords and home owners (who rented and sold living space and other services to newcomers). The state was caught in the slipstream of dynamic social developments to which it would respond with reforms aimed at directing a process of change that, in fact, had acquired considerable momentum of its own.

The reforms, therefore, were a mix of proactive and reactive measures – tactical adjustments – which tended not to attain strategic harmony. One reason was the increasing incoherence within the state, which had several causes. At one level, different government departments vied to shape and control reforms. The tensions were both ideological and practical: as resistance intensified, security departments demanded (and won) greater authority as they were relied on to contain the opposition. This meant that traditional bureaucratic procedures often were either truncated or circumvented. (This problem was partly overcome when a parallel system emerged in the form of the National Security Management System (NSMS), which vested massive administrative powers in the hands of the security forces.) The 'political distance' between the state and capital further undermined the achievement of a strategic programme of change, despite efforts in the 1970s to shape new policies via consultative committees that actively involved business organizations. Capital continued to engage the state not through corporatist channels but in fragmented fashion through discreet lobbying processes. Often different business organizations represented the same industries, adding to the confusion. Meanwhile, different branches of capital desired different forms of adjustment.[21] Crucially, the state's reforms ran up against the political enclosures erected by the apartheid paradigm. As long as the state tried to 'solve' the national question through attempts to retain the literal division of South Africa along racial and ethnic lines, its reforms would be hobbled by their built-in obsolescence, as the opposition capitalized on the failure to address the central political crisis and exploited the liberalizing openings.

Recasting the terrain

Despite the constraints, the reforms of the second phase went much further than the earlier adjustments and exhibited five, main features.

Most dramatic was the official end to influx control in 1986, when the abolishment of pass laws allowed Africans to enter and work in urban areas without official state permission. This announced a major shift in the apartheid accumulation strategy and was based on a new acceptance of the 'interdependent and interconnected nature of the South African political economy' (Morris, 1991:51). The urban African population was accepted as a given but would be regulated through other means (principally, access to housing). Labour would henceforth be reproduced 'wholly within the confines of capitalist society' through a revised process of regulated urbanization (Morris & Padayachee, 1989:80).

Dovetailing with the new urbanization strategy were a host of initiatives geared at redistributing resources and accelerating class differentiation among urban Africans (through measures like the 99-year leasehold of homes granted to a select layer of residents). These schemes were not plucked from thin air. Key was the Urban Foundation's attempts to devise new urbanization and housing strategies. Diligent, sophisticated and proactive, the Foundation exerted a definitive influence on government housing and urbanization policies,[22] although earlier statements had declared the overall motive with candour:

> [O]nly by having this most responsible section of the urban black population on our side can the whites of South Africa be assured of containing on a long term basis the irresponsible economic and political ambitions of those blacks

who are influenced against their own real interests from within and without our borders.[23]

The redistribution of resources was selective. Targeted for upgrading were those townships deemed to pose potential security problems, resulting in a process of so-called 'oil spot' development. The state pumped more resources into black education and supported improvements in township infrastructure (such as electrification schemes in Soweto). The intention was to undermine political mobilization by removing some of the most distressing material sources of discontent. Again, one of the consequences was to redefine and deepen the divisions between insiders and outsiders, divisions which exploded violently in the late 1980s – albeit in forms unanticipated by the anti-apartheid opposition.[24] In cases like the Crossroads settlement near Cape Town, ominous divisions were prised wide even *within* the most marginalized sections of the African working class.[25]

The state continued to scale back on its fiscal commitments, a move that corresponded to international trends but was also inspired by domestic realities. The economic recession had imposed budgetary constraints which made it necessary to cut back on state spending (where possible) and increase state revenue. At the same time, the integration of the African urban population into 'modern South Africa' threatened to impose a massive new spending burden on the state. In order to sidestep this, the state tried to decrease its social welfare functions. Housing provisions in townships now befell private developers. The state slashed its support to social welfare services and continued to withdraw subsidies on basic consumer items. The effect was to push the marginalized further into destitution while forcing the comparatively 'privileged' sections to rely on privatized social services. Some African business entrepreneurship was boosted through the deregulation of the transport system (giving rise to the taxi industry) and by allowing informal trading. Towards the end of the decade, in a bid to raise additional revenue, the state also privatized several state assets.

Aspects of social life were also deracialized. Non-racial trade unions were allowed to register, thus opening space for the emergence of the trade union federation COSATU (Congress of South African Trade Unions) in 1985. 'Petty apartheid' measures were dropped, although the class undertones of this relaxation were obvious since access to deracialized consumptive and recreational activities was determined by income. Laws prohibiting interracial sexual intercourse and marriage were also abolished. The most telling effect of these reforms lay in their ideological impact: the 'relaxation' of apartheid contradicted the stern dogmatism of the post-war hegemonic project, further alienating the former hardcore social base of the NP and opening the way for further pragmatic shifts in the future. The reforms were accompanied, however, by other attempts to re-racialize political life – for instance, the establishment of the tricameral parliament (with its racially exclusive white, coloured and Indian chambers) and racially segregated affairs government departments.

Often overlooked was the limited democratization that occurred at the beginning of this reform phase. One example was the limited extension of voting rights to coloureds and Indians, who could vote in racial elections for their 'own' representatives, despatching them to the new racially-segregated tricameral parliament. Still, the state proved unable even nominally to address the national question by, for instance, incorporating Africans into such a manoeuvre. Thus, the long-mooted 'fourth' (African) chamber in parliament never materialized. As a result, the limited liberalization became the basis for a new wave of protest and the first campaign of the United Democratic Front (UDF) would be to oppose the tricameral system.

The restricted democratization was intended to let the opposition 'blow off steam' in more regulated and less tumultuous fashion. Instead the openings were used to revive old popular organizations, build new ones and strike fresh alliances around an increasingly unequivocal opposition against the apartheid system. New organizations mushroomed, ranging from high-school students (mobilizing through students' councils) to township residents (who set up civic bodies and mobilized around advice offices), women (grouped in several women's organizations), professionals (who set up progressive lawyers and doctors' structures) and teachers. This inter-sectoral, cross-class mobilization in 1983 merged around the UDF and was directed at challenging the state's reform measures.

As resistance activities mounted, the reforms became more inchoate. The partial relaxations in the political and ideological spheres were reversed in 1986, after the imposition of a state of emergency. But this did not signal a sheer regression back to the 'old days'. The 'democratizing' reforms were withdrawn and a series of repressive measures were introduced to restore the stability required for the other, redistributive reforms to proceed. Indeed, 'the slogan of the early 1980s – "there can be no security without reform" – [was] turned on its head', according to Swilling and Phillips (1989b:147). Thus the state stayed its course in the other areas – particularly the restructured urbanization process and the selective redistribution of resources. In a sense, the state had crossed at least a tributary of the Rubicon.

From resistance to 'revolution'

The first two phases of reforms coincided with the emergence of widespread organizing and mobilizing by the popular forces, particularly among the black working class.

The reactivation of union organizing after the 1973–4 strikes was of a scale that exceeded all previous revivals – affirming a dramatic change in the potential strength of the black working class. The number of workers involved in strike action did decline between 1974 and 1980 but this was a poor indicator of the organizing momentum that had taken hold. Among the several factors fuelling the resurgence, three stood out: the manufacturing sector had become dominated by black workers (many of them occupying skilled and semi-skilled jobs), the effects of the economic recession were disproportionately deflected onto the black working class and the legalization of black trade unions had opened new organizing opportunities. Rather than embark on 'do-or-die' actions, most of the new unions focused on the painstaking process of building their organizations and seeking recognition from employers.

Working class organization and action proceeded by leaps and bounds after 1979. The legalization of black trade unions (recommended by the Wiehahn Report) boosted their total membership to 1,4 million by 1984,[26] while the number of strikes increased from 101 in 1979 to 342 in 1981. The importance of the union movement was not restricted to its own capacity for combative action (which also catalysed township resistance through complimentary tactics such as consumer boycotts). Civics and other popular bodies often drew their leadership from union ranks, a trend which introduced 'a greater degree of leadership accountability, democratic participation, and organizational structure'.[27] Moreover, for the first time since the 1940s, strong components of the resurgent black opposition were self-consciously animated by their working class identities.

Two distinct trends were discernible in the union revival. The twelve unions which joined to form FOSATU in 1979 were openly reluctant to become embroiled in wider political struggles. Their focus was on 'strong factory organization as the expression of a truly independent working-class consciousness' (Lodge & Nasson, 1991:28). Contesting that approach were a variety of 'community unions' which deemed 'it impossible to separate workers' factory demands from their township problems' and which openly identified with the liberation movement. In essence, this was a continuation of the 'political unionism' practised in the 1950s by the ANC's union wing, SACTU.[28] Inscribed into the revitalized workers' struggles of the 1980s, therefore, was the enduring tension between nationalist and class consciousness, which gave rise to fierce, even violent, conflict between so-called 'workerists' and 'populists'. The 'workerist' label, though, rested on a profound misrepresentation of class politics. 'Workerists' were accused of treating 'other issues beyond the point of production … as secondary matters' and of downplaying 'the very important struggle for state power'.[29] Consequently, 'attempts to revive socialism in the South African struggle', as Dave Lewis pointed out, were equated with 'a narrow workerism' despite the fact that 'the struggle to build socialism is the struggle to unite under the leadership of the working class the disparate groups and classes that are oppressed and exploited under capitalism'.[30]

Nevertheless, the tensions would persist within and beyond the ranks of COSATU, which was formed when FOSATU and the 'community unions' joined forces.[31] The Charterist tradition's emphasis on national oppression would win the day, although some COSATU affiliates continued to manifest a strong socialist bias.

The emergence of this formidable array of popular organizations occurred in a context shaped by two key factors: state reforms and the economic recession. A brief economic upswing in 1980–1 was followed by a steep drop in the gold price and a ballooning imports bill (caused by large-scale capital equipment purchases). The result was a balance of payments crisis. The government reacted by heeding IMF loan conditions which demanded swift measures to offset the difficulties. The burden of these adjustments was deflected onto the black working class. Subsidies on essential consumer items were withdrawn and sales tax was raised (hoisting the inflation rate to almost 17 per cent by 1985), while rents, rates and service payments were hiked in black townships.[32]

The recession also caused a sharp rise in unemployment. Job creation slowed to a crawl, while many industries applied large-scale retrenchments; in the metal industry alone, 84 000 jobs were shed between 1982 and 1984. In agriculture, rising production costs and a sustained drought led to massive retrenchments, triggering a concentrated influx of African workers into cities and towns.

The main spur to action lay with these intensifying material hardships, which led to the setting up of local township organizations. While their organizational forms differed, they all focused on so-called 'bread and butter issues' such as housing, services, transportation, rents and township infrastructure. Activists set up civics in Johannesburg (notably Soweto and Alexandra) and the Eastern Cape (where the Port Elizabeth Black Civic Organization led the way), while a network of 'advice offices' was established in townships in the Cape Peninsula (where they collaborated with feisty grassroots media projects). Their focus was on local community issues, which often included boycott and other activities in support of worker demands. Many of these organizations exhibited a strong class consciousness.[33] Along with the trade unions, student and youth organizations were at the forefront of resistance by the early 1980s.[34]

The national schools and campus boycotts organized by COSAS and AZASCO in 1980–1 also confirmed the generational tensions between youth and parents which had exploded into prominence during the Soweto uprising.[35] Although both organizations thereafter sought to close that gap through greater involvement in broader community issues, generational schisms persisted. As Lodge noted, the members of the youth congresses and other bodies that sprang up:

... were the children of the strongest and most sophisticated urban working class in Africa. Their instincts were shaped by a community that had undergone one of the most rapid industrial revolutions in recent history. A large proportion of them were considerably better educated than their elders. Of all generations, the 'children of Soweto' were the least inclined to accept the limits and restrictions of the apartheid system (Lodge & Nasson, 1991:38).

The ferment of organizing extended broadly. The women's movement was rekindled, with the revival in the Transvaal of the Federation of South African Women (FEDSAW), which had been dormant since the 1960s, and the formation of the United Women's Organization (UWO) in the Cape Province. Black professionals joined as lawyers, doctors and teachers in progressive groupings. Activist religious organizations were formed or revived, with some (like the Young Christian Students) providing formative leadership training for young activists.

It was this multiplicity of organizations that the UDF sought to unite. Launched in August 1983, it targeted the elections for new black local authorities and the new constitution, specifically its introduction of a tricameral parliament intended to draw coloured and Indians into the political system. Misnamed, the UDF was in fact a broad popular front whose affiliates grew from an initial 85 to 565 when it was officially launched. Its links with the workers' movement were weak, however, with trade unions comprising only 18 of the UDF's affiliates in 1984. Preponderant were youth, student and civic organizations – among whom the symbols, traditions and rhetoric of the ANC proved especially resonant. The UDF successfully projected itself as the standard bearer of the nationalist movement, but it did not become an organized national movement. Its influence was spread unevenly across the country and was formidable in the Eastern Cape and parts of the Transvaal but relatively weak in Natal and the Western Cape. Depending on the township, its affiliates were either a handful of activists or well-organized, 'representative' grassroots groups (Friedman, 1987).

The Front's leadership was structured at three levels: national (dominated by veteran ANC activists; only two officeholders had a labour background), regional and local. On the whole, the UDF's national and regional leaderships tended to be drawn from radical, middle-class intellectuals and professionals – although the Eastern Cape represented an important exception to that pattern.

Lodge and Nasson (1991) have divided the UDF's development into five phases, each emerging from a mix of proaction and reaction. The first, lasting until mid-1984, was marked by blustering, national campaigning akin to the ANC's populist campaigns of the 1950s 'in which large and excited gatherings, powerful oratory, and strong, attractive leaders substituted for systematically structured organizations, carefully elaborated ideologies and well-coordinated programs' (1991:62–3). A dramatic shift then occurred. The second phase (coinciding with the Vaal uprising of September 1984) saw the UDF lose the initiative to militant, local resistance activities dominated by township youth and schoolchildren. Partly in a bid to catch up with local dynamics, the UDF in early 1985 adopted a controversial line which held grave implications for the democratic movement: it endorsed the ANC's January 1985 call for South Africa to be 'rendered ungovernable' and was caught up in the insurrectionary reveries that swept through the movement.

The third phase followed the declaration of a state of emergency in July 1985, with the UDF reacting often creatively to the effects of increased state repression but having lost the strategic initiative. The withering impact of the June 1986 state of emergency marked a fourth phase, with the UDF pushed into retreat and resistance activities becoming much less coherent and disciplined, culminating in the UDF's banning in early 1988. From this period of decline emerged a fifth phase, in late 1988, when the popular forces regrouped as the Mass Democratic Movement (MDM) around the leadership of church and union organizations, and launched a campaign of mass disobedience.

The UDF resembled the kind of broad popular front outlined by the ANC's Politico-Military Strategy Commission in 1979, a front that 'should express the broadest possible working together of all organizations, groups and individuals genuinely opposed to racist autocracy'.[36] The Commission had been set up as part of the ANC's 1978–9 strategic review conference where unusually strong criticism of the ANC's performance was vented. Its report (summarized in a document known as the 'Green Book') accused the organization of having 'for too long acted as if the repressive conditions made mass legal and semi-legal work impossible' and warned that its 'efforts would reach a dead-end unless they had a broader political base'.[37] Some of the campaigns of the early 1980s took after recommendations by the Commission. The Freedom Charter was to be re-inserted into resistance discourse (utilizing its thirtieth anniversary). Significantly, the Commission urged campaigns against township authorities aimed at their 'permanent destruction' in order to thwart 'their effective functioning and [reduce] the capacity of the enemy to govern out people' (Barrel, 1991:88). The report reflected a revival and elaboration – not a revision – of ANC strategy. Long neglected, mass political mobilization inside South Africa had to be shored up. Political and military struggle became hitched together in a perspective which held that:

> Preparation for the people's armed struggle and its victorious conclusion is not solely a military question. This means that the armed struggle must be based on, and grow out of, mass political support and it must eventually involve our whole people. All military activities must, at every stage, be

guided and determined by the need to generate political mobilisation, organisation and resistance, with the aim of progressively weakening the grip on the reins of political, economic, social and military action.[38]

A tactical, not a strategic shift had occurred. The instrumentality of political mobilization and organization within an overall strategy that pivoted on an armed seizure of power remained clear, as Barrel noted:

> The perspective developed by the 1978–79 strategic review still turned on the popular armed struggle for the seizure of state power … The strategic vision remained one in which political organization was ultimately seen as subject to military imperatives (1991:89).

During the early 1980s, the ANC moved more to the fore and began occupying the symbolic centre of resistance and narrowing the distance between itself and the action. Covertly, it more effectively than before 'caught up' with the masses, setting up activist cells and underground networks. Its statements and propaganda, issued from Lusaka, reached local activists and came to function as increasingly authoritative reference points. ANC figures like Govan Mbeki have contended that the internal organizations 'were not random developments but the result of a deliberate strategy to form all kinds of mass-based organizations', claiming further that 'there is no doubt that a majority of them were led by people who belonged to the ANC underground or were sympathetic to the ANC' (1996:46). But political affinities did not necessarily produce situations where the ANC furnished the organizational impetus of those structures, nor does it warrant the claim that the organizations arose as sheer internal expressions of ANC strategy (Barrel, 1991:91). A much more complex process had occurred. The flowering of organizations inside South Africa and the radicalizing impact of the influx of Soweto uprising activists into the ANC confirmed to the organization's leadership not only the need but also revealed the conditions for reasserting its hegemony over internal resistance activities.

The formation of the UDF had occurred largely on the basis of internal dynamics that were organizationally independent of the ANC. Nor is it accurate to claim that the ANC was able to direct resistance tactics (even via the UDF, whose capacity to provide strategic leadership had weakened demonstrably by the mid-1980s). But its growing authority at the ideological and symbolic levels did enable it to strongly influence the overall terms in which resistance actions were couched – hence the formidable resonance of its calls for 'ungovernability' and a 'people's war'. By the late 1980s, the ANC was clearly the main political beneficiary of the UDF's campaigns. These were not unmitigated advances, however. In some cases, activists used the symbols and rhetoric of the ANC to discourage or prevent independent organizing initiatives and suppress ideological heterogeneity, prompting Friedman to observe that 'the symbolic strength of the exile movement has often weakened attempts to build grassroots power within the country' (1991:61).

The third phase of reforms: 1987–9

In 1987 the state suspended the 'democratization' aspects of its reforms in a bid to restore stability. But the broad trajectory of the reform process would be maintained albeit in a strikingly different manner. Redistribution would become co-ordinated and carried out within a security framework, the National Security Management System (NSMS).

The NSMS had been set up in 1979, as part of the 'total strategy', although, in the early 1980s, according to one former state functionary, NSMS officials 'were just keeping the seats warm'.[39] By 1987 it had been fully activated and became 'a parallel system of state power' which vested massive repressive and administrative powers in the hands of the military and police.[40] The NSMS spanned a national network of several hundred committees, each of which comprised local security officials, administrators and businesspeople – forming a 'shadow bureaucracy running alongside the official government bureaucracy'.[41] Its nerve centre lay in these committees which had the task of surveying, monitoring and recommending appropriate actions (by the state and its civil society allies) in 'trouble spots'. Each had to identify potential 'security problems' in its area (for example, a shortage of medical facilities or transport or schools) and design measures to defuse the risk. Implementation agencies would then be assigned to carry out the required upgrading in a speeded up process which, if necessary, would by-pass the sluggish procedures of the state bureaucracy.

The distribution of state power had already shifted somewhat by the early 1980s, after executive powers had been vested in the previously cere-monial office of the state president. But the power of the executive was still counter-balanced by the cabinet, parliament and the state bureaucracy. With the full-scale activation of the NSMS the balance of forces within the state shifted profoundly, with power increasing anchored with the state president, the security forces and the law and order ministry. In some circles these developments were likened to a 'palace coup' which allegedly trans-ferred state power to the security establishment. Lost in such a dramatic reading of the NSMS was the continuity of reformist restructuring that the network serviced. The NSMS did not substitute itself for the state; it func-tioned parallel to it. While the overt political dimension of reforms were put on the backburner from 1986 onwards, the short-term aim of the state was to restore stability and defuse the threats posed by the democratic opposi-tion. But the redistributive (and class restructuring) thrust of reforms con-tinued. Much of the selective redistribution was now applied not through the traditional channels of the government bureaucracy, but through the NSMS's shadow apparatus, with the commandist approach specifically designed to ensure speedy and efficient delivery. Thirty-four of the most volatile townships (the so-called 'oil-spots') were targeted for rapid upgrading, while a further 1 800 urban renewal projects were launched in 200 other townships (Swilling & Phillips, 1989a). The thinking behind these initiatives was that:

> ... [t]he lack of a classroom is not a security matter, but a lack of proper facilities or sufficient facilities can become a security problem ... Nobody can tell a [government] department they must build a new school. But from the security point of view you can tell them that if they don't there is going to be a problem. It is now your problem to build the school; if you don't it will become my problem and the [security] system's problem. And prevention is better than cure.[42]

The NSMS therefore made it possible to expedite the implementation of reform measures, as Swilling and Phillips noted: 'Some of these reforms were articulated by the political reformists before 1986, but they have since been appropriated and recast by the "counter-revolutionary warfare" strategists' (1989b:145). State tactics had not regressed into the sheer reactive repression commonly highlighted. If security measures could keep a lid on the revolt, the commandist delivery programme co-ordinated within the NSMS could, it was hoped, provide the kinds of social services that would stabilize the most rebellious townships. This foray represented the most sophisticated attempt yet by the ruling bloc to combine reforms and repression in ways that could alter the balance of forces. Still eluding the state, however, was a strategy to succeed the temporary containment of resistance.

The vagaries of insurrectionism

Two signal developments had impacted on the democratic movement, each reinforcing the other: the ANC's success at achieving hegemony (though not organizational control) within the movement, and its push for a 'people's war'. The all-or-nothing paradigm heralded by the turn to armed struggle became predominant in internal resistance discourse which, increasingly, looked to a headlong onslaught against the apartheid state.

Between 1981 and 1985 debates had raged in the SACP's *African Communist* journal between activists advocating the 'arming of the people'[43] and critics who argued against 'too narrow and military-technical a view of arming the people'.[44] The SACP and ANC leaderships, however, officially still opposed the insurrectionist strategies. Soon, this changed. At the ANC's Kabwe Consultative Conference in 1985, the national executive again spoke of preparing for a 'people's war'.[45] In July 1986, Joe Slovo came out supporting the insurrectionist line which, while not precluding 'a protracted conflict', meant that liberation movement's supporters 'had also to prepare and be ready to adjust to a much swifter transformation which would involve insurrectionary ingredients'.[46] By 1987, one of the chief theorists in the ANC and SACP – Mzala – was writing confidently that an insurrection was on the cards.[47] A year later, SACP analyst Harold Wolpe declared that 'the mass insurrectionary political movement is the principal agent of the struggle for national liberation'[48] – a considerable shift away from perspectives centred on a lengthy guerrilla war as the ideal form of armed struggle.

The insurrectionary approach presumed that a revolutionary situation was developing, a corrupt reading of the dynamics at play.[49] The ideological dominance of the ruling bloc was at its lowest ebb and was being challenged by crystallizing visions of an alternative order. But even in 1987, with state repression at its most intense, the continuance of socio-economic reforms (causing ideological and organizational disruption among the popular masses) prevented its complete collapse. Severe tensions had surfaced, as shown by the 1982 split in the NP, struggles between state departments (especially after the activation of the NSMS) and the defection of some ruling class intellectuals. But these were mitigated by other developments: the centralization of power in the NP and the government, the failure of capitalist organizations to produce coherent alternative strategies challenging those pursued by the state, and the government's success at marshalling support from the capitalist class for its repressive interventions. In Bundy's judgment, 'the cohesion and capacities of the state remained largely intact' (1989:16). By mid-1986, the prevarications of liberal sections of capital had grown faint and the state was entrusted with the restoration of 'order'.

The security apparatuses remained relatively cohesive, unthreatened at the military level and insulated at the ideological level against the swell of resistance. They were able to contain and invert militant energies within townships, by spatially isolating certain townships and concentrating repressive force on them and by introducing or supporting vigilante groups. This turned the 'revolutionary' violence inwards, catalysing a frenzy of internecine bloodletting that assisted state control. In addition, the core elements of these apparatuses were white and, despite the efforts of the End Conscription Campaign (ECC), stayed for the most part unmoved by calls on their consciences.[50] There was not the dimmest prospect of meeting a central precondition for revolution – the breakdown of the armed forces.[51] The state's security capacities were at no point stretched to the full, indicating that the state could still contain any feasible attempt to overthrow it by force.

Whether or not 'dual power' situations arose is moot. In some townships, certain state functions were arrogated. These instances, though, were sporadic and localized with little if any spillover effect on the broader functioning of state administration. Thus, the state could seal of these initiatives within particular communities, and attack them through a combination of repressive force and developmental interventions – often successfully.[52] In most cases, these organs were ephemeral and quickly escaped the bounds of disciplined co-ordination; only in exceptional, shortlived cases were they 'controlled by, and accountable to, the masses of people in each area'[53]. As Friedman noted at the time:

> … while some street committees appear to have enjoyed the support of residents, others seemed to have been imposed on them. While some 'people's courts' seemed to enjoy a high degree of legitimacy, others were allegedly used to impose the will of small groups of unelected activists (1987:62).

Even in the most militant townships the 'dual power' situations detected by insurrectionists could be more accurately described as 'ungovernability', reflecting not the usurping of power but its dispersal. They were marked by the absence of effective control by either the state or its challengers. As long as those zones were isolated by the police and army they posed no wider threat to the functioning of the state. At no point were 'liberated zones', in any meaningful sense of the term, established where popular forces could organize and defend elements of a 'proto-state'.[54]

If anything it was the explosion of political activism in a wide assortment of forms that emboldened the insurrectionists. Great potential was vested in these developments. Yet, closer scrutiny might have tempered expectations. Firstly, there was the mistaken notion that the country's townships were simultaneously attaining a critical pitch of militant resistance. In reality, the geographical focus shifted constantly as the state concentrated its repression on the 'hot spots'. As Steve Friedman noted, the 1986 state of emergency was remarkably successful at narrowing the options for mass mobilization:

> Short-term mobilization is likely to pose an enduring threat to white rule only if it creates a space in which long-term organization can emerge. Boycotts, stayaways and similar actions are often the products of organization, but many have been imposed by small groups of activists without thoroughly consulting their constituents (1987:61).

The spectacle of mass campaigns and the seemingly inexorable succession of militant actions hid from the casual gaze the UDF's failure to build and consolidate an organized national power base. Despite constant efforts the Front failed to overcome the poor communication with its grassroots components and, hence, a weak capacity to direct and discipline their activities. In Friedman's assessment:

> … its national leadership is often not in control of events on the ground. Despite gains over the past three years, it is a long way from becoming a disciplined and organized national movement which could pose a direct threat to white rule (1987:63).

Moreover, its 'reliance on mobilization and protest often conflict[ed] with organizational requirements, and resources which could [have been] devoted to organization [were] dissipated in attempts to mobilize dramatic local and regional campaigns'.[55] Throughout, the UDF launched attempts to overcome these shortcomings.[56] The formation of the South African Youth Congress (SAYCO) in April 1987, for instance, was intended to draw the youth back into line, but its fierce rhetoric instead seemed to spur activist youth along paths of action that had become unnervingly morbid. Many real or potential supporters were alienated by a situation where 'the children called the tune and our only role was to sit and listen, in angry silence'.[57] It was not surprising, in such a context, that more and more vigilante groups (usually composed of older African men) sprung into action, with the support of the security forces; or that the victims of so-called 'black-on-black violence' seemed to outnumber those killed directly by the security forces. The resort to violence in the townships had paradoxically strengthened the state's ability to hold at bay the challenge from the democratic movement.

State repression induced and compounded many of these weaknesses – by 'decapitating' popular organizations',[58] fomenting internecine violence, banning organizations, and (especially from late-1986 onwards) severely narrowing the political space opened earlier in the decade. At first, the state did not wield its repressive force with complete abandon; until late-1986 the 'liberalization' of political space had not been entirely reversed. Indeed, the security police chief, General Johan Coetzee, was said to believe that the threats posed by the UDF and other organizations 'could be countered most effectively through propaganda, highly selective restrictions, and the "defusing" of conflict by allowing outlets for political expression'.[59] Towards the end of 1986 that thinking was abandoned and political space became choked. By late 1987, most of the UDF leadership was either in prison (70 per cent of detainees were alleged members of UDF affiliates), in hiding or dead.

Ideologically the UDF functioned as an interlocutor for the ANC/SACP alliance but it failed to apply a coherent strategy to guide an escalation of resistance. By its own account, it was forced to react to the 'spontaneity of actions in the townships', and was 'trail[ing] behind the masses, thus making it more difficult for a disciplined mass action to take place'.[60] In Friedman's view, the UDF failed to become 'a disciplined and organized national movement' (1987:63). Meanwhile, the ANC by late 1986 had not yet extensively set up underground structures and built links between trained cadres and 'mass combat groups' – as it acknowledged in a NEC and Politico-Military Council document.[61] Its ideological predominance amongst the popular masses did not substitute for these shortcomings.

Viewed in this light, the insurrectionists seemed animated by a kind of chaos theory of revolution, whereby often uncoordinated and poorly strategized activities would, through an undefined alchemical process, achieve a critical mass and sweep away the apartheid state.

In the short term, the strategy of insurrectionism combined with the brutal weight of state repression to push the resistance campaigns of the 1980s off the rails. Coercive tactics and 'revolutionary violence' had by 1986 become acceptable methods of struggle among many of the youth who occupied the frontlines. While it is true that the UDF never openly endorsed these practices, its leaders were slow to denounce them. It was only after Winnie Mandela's infamous statement in April 1986 ('With necklaces and our little boxes of matches we shall liberate this country') that the UDF unequivocally condemned these methods. The UDF and its key affiliates did try to regain the initiative by mounting new, co-ordinated campaigns. but the driving impetus of resistance at the local level lay with youths whose millenarian determination placed them beyond the reach of coherent, strategized initiatives that could consolidate and extend gains. Such initiatives had to include tactical entry into the spaces opened by state reforms – a point confirmed by the labour movement's success at exploiting the restructuring of labour relations. Dominant among other popular organizations was a struggle ideology that mirrored the very exclusionism of the system that was being opposed: any engagement with the enemy other than outright confrontation was deemed to carry the risk of contamination and betrayal. Instead of separating 'those elements of reform, such as "democratization" and "deracialization", that were integral to their own struggles and required defending, all reforms were denounced as mere window-dressing'.[62] This tunnel vision was by no means unique to South Africa, as Morris has pointed out:

> Ideologically exclusionary regimes of a totalitarian nature, when viewed from the perspective of those who are excluded, create conditions which often make it extremely difficult for the excluded to comprehend the possibilities, and hence take advantage of, incremental reformist measures in order to stretch these to the maximum and create internal regime crises ... Principles and strategies are conflated and ... slogans such as boycottism, non-collaboration, non-participation predominate (1993a:98–9).

The success at resisting and scuttling reforms became confused with the ability to selectively reject some reforms and extend the parameters of others within an alternative strategic programme. Several ironies were at work here. The absolutism took hold during a period when, for the first time since 1948, the state's fitful restructuring efforts were creating highly favourable conditions for a 'war of position'. The democratic movement eschewed that route at a point when, for the first time since the 1950s, it was strong enough to exploit those openings. And rejectionism had by no means been an intrinsic feature of the Congress tradition, with which the democratic movement had clearly identified itself. Why then did it take hold? Firstly, the turn to armed struggle had marked an important shift in that tradition, by introducing a confrontationist/militarist paradigm. Secondly, the ANC had since the late-1970s taken on board the rejectionist approaches of the BCM (themselves inherited from the old Non-European Unity Movement) when large numbers of BC activists joined the organization. But it would also be wrong to allege that the insurrectionist line was merely imposed by the exiled ANC and SACP leadership or that is purchase among militant youth was an inevitable outgrowth of the militarism induced by the armed struggle paradigm. Important as those factors were, the prospect of a cataclysmic confrontation with the apartheid state resonated loudly with township youth. The ANC's call for ungovernability must, therefore, be seen in a wider context. While it fitted with the militarism of an armed struggle strategy, it was also an opportunistic attempt to slipstream behind the militancy erupting in townships. The alternative (to advise a more cautious and incremental strategy) would likely have diminished the ANC's stature among the leading militant currents inside the country. Having finally arrived on the brink of achieving hegemony over the internal resistance forces, the ANC would have been disinclined to urge a more circumspect and restrained approach.

The sum of these developments was an upsurge in resistance which came to rest on flimsy organizational and misconceived strategic buttresses.

Moments of truth

The insurrectionary challenge was defeated. The same could not be said of the democratic movement in general, however. Although the union movement had been bruised both by the ongoing effects of the recession (which reached its deepest ebb by 1988–9) and by some of the massive strikes and stayaways, it had confirmed its status as the most powerful component of the democratic movement. More than any other organized force, it retained the capacity to challenge the ruling bloc through tactical engagements that included but were not restricted to mass protests. With the UDF battered onto the sidelines, popular organizations regrouped around the union movement and progressive church bodies, which assumed the mantle of political leadership of the MDM. But the defiance campaigns that ensued in 1989 could not be slotted into a linear narrative of cumulative challenges pushing the ruling bloc into a corner. They represented the beginnings of an arduous process of rebuilding the democratic movement.

The imminent defeat of the system was not on the cards. But the interventions fashioned by technocrats and security strategists (and implemented under an exclusionary, repressive administration) merely bought time. They amounted to a set of tactics; the content of a more encompassing strategic response awaited the resolution of profound divisions that had emerged within the ruling bloc.

After 1987, capital had temporarily grouped around the state's turn to outright repression. But severe differences had surfaced within the ranks of capital, the state and the NP government over how to defend the capitalist system in the medium- to long-term. Internally the state was beset by continuing interdepartmental feuds and growing ideological rifts as conservatives reacted against the meandering adjustments advocated by the leadership. The economic crisis persisted and was being exacerbated by increased international isolation. It registered in increasingly grim terms: formal sector unemployment hovered around 30 per cent, services in most townships had collapsed, violent crime boomed, balance of payments problems worsened, the far-right (exploiting the economic and physical insecurities of rural and working class whites) was maturing into a potential political threat, and the anti-apartheid opposition was slowly regrouping around the MDM.

This was the signal achievement of the challenges mounted by the democratic movement during the 1980s: deepening and extending the complex of difficulties encountered by the ruling bloc and forcing it to try and fashion a response that would transcend the exclusionary political framework.

The wilting of civil society

The democratic movement came into its own during the 1980s. But the upsurge of resistance did not represent an irrepressible juggernaut as much as it did an aggregation of widespread but uneven organizing and mobilizing initiatives which, while occasionally pushing the state onto its heels, never threatened the overthrow of the system.

The decade represented perhaps the heyday of South African civil society. For a while, the variety and sweep of initiatives, broadly gathered under the canopy of the anti-apartheid struggle, offered hints of Gilles Deleuzes's concept of rhizomatic phenomena: a flowering of autonomous activities, linked laterally and not subjugated to hierarchical ideological and strategic conformity. Internal resistance had adopted innovative forms in a process suggestive of the 'deterritorialization' championed by Deleuze – the replacement of orthodoxy with flux and experimentation. Fine would describe this as the search for 'third way'. But by 1985, a process of 'reterritorialization' had occurred, as the codes of post-Bandung era liberation movements were reimposed, principally by the ANC and SACP.

The paths navigated by the popular forces became staked out by two key factors: state repression (which influenced their margin of manoeuvre) and the paradigmatic constraints imposed by the dogma that apartheid could not be reformed but could be overthrown. A few short years before negotiations would start, activists were widely invoking the examples of the Bolshevik and Iranian revolutions as 'suggestive alternative precedents for a South African insurrectionary change of regime' (Lodge, 1989:45). Morris has aptly summarized the thinking that propped up such misconceptions:

The mass of the population had recently embarked on the process of spontaneously gaining an angry consciousness of their potential power. The insurrectionist strategy mistook this for a period when a disorganized state and capitalist class, unable to rule, were confronted with a nationally consolidating real organs of alternative and countervailing popular power (1991:49).

There is no point casting the resistance upsurge in unambiguously romantic terms. The fortitude, determination and perseverance demonstrated by millions of South Africans carried traumatic costs. Thousands had died and countless more bore the physical and psychological scars of conflict. Thousands of protestors and activists were killed – in police attacks on protests and marches, by police death squads and a distressing number in internecine battles between political factions and organizations. Fighting escalated between rival factions (sometimes even within organizations) as resistance became increasingly violent, disorganized and alienated. The 'comtsotsi' phenomenon (lumpen township elements combining politics with crime), the use of young gangsters as political shock troops, the remorseless and sometimes violent intolerance shown towards dissent and heterodoxy within the popular movement combined with the brutal methods used by the security apparatus to exploit these dynamics and sap resistance of direction and discipline.

The suppression of dissent was manifest also in exile, where it led to tragic episodes in the ANC's Angolan camps.[63] Even a prominent intellectual like Pallo Jordan did not escape the Stalinist culture imposed in exile; he was detained by the ANC's security apparatus, Mbokodo, for criticizing the security system. According to the Motsuenyane Commission, later appointed by Nelson Mandela to investigate abuses committed in the camps, detention centres like the notorious Quadro 'developed a widespread reputation as a hell-hole where persons were sent to rot'.[64] In many cases, the distinctions between seditious activity, the expression of genuine grievances and sincere dissent, or sheer ill-discipline was made to disappear.[65]

A culture developed whereby any means were justified in the struggle against the apartheid state – bequeathing to the popular movement a variety of morbid tendencies which were more commonly associated with the apartheid regime and its allies. These tendencies existed alongside and sometimes eclipsed the publicly hallowed traditions of pluralism, debate and tolerance. They were displayed across the country, perhaps most horrifyingly in the 'Natal war', between supporters of the UDF and the conservative Zulu Inkatha movement led by homeland leader Mangosuthu Buthelezi.

Stalemate

The end of the decade became something of a respite. Battered popular forces were slowly regrouping around tactics reminiscent of the 1950s. The armed struggle had been eliminated from the ANC's arsenal by the USSR's decisions to push for a settlement and the shutting down of ANC bases in the region. On the security front, the state held the upper hand but was riven with internal conflict. In the background, a proto-negotiations process was gathering steam. A point had been reached where all sides could – indeed, had to – raise their heads above the parapets, scan the terrain and weigh their options.

More than a decade of chopping and changing the system had profoundly restructured the social and ideological undercarriage of the postwar accumulation strategy, and fitfully adjusted the economic realm. But because the reforms had steered a wide berth around fundamental political change, South Africa was not turned away from what appeared to be a slide towards chronic instability, tempered only by crisis management. No matter the alarmist rhetoric of the state, it was not so much the prospect of a revolution that had jolted the apartheid managers: it was the likelihood that the state and opposition would become entangled in a death embrace that could destroy South Africa's integrity as a nation-state and a viable zone for capital accumulation – and with it white privilege. Security measures and socio-economic reforms had not improved the outlook.

A stalemate had been reached. One option was to resort to an indefinite period of unmitigated totalitarian management of society – essentially a tactical response awaiting the emergence of an alternative strategy. Another was a further phase of political liberalization which was likely to accelerate the recovery of resistance organizations and generate another security crisis. The other option was to dramatically restructure the political basis of the system – a response which could proceed on the basis of the restructurings achieved since the 1970s in the social and economic spheres.

State analysts had viewed the political crisis in two, often complementary ways: as a security issue and, at a deeper level, as a symptom of socio-economic 'dysfunction'. The political was seen as contingent on more elemental material contradictions (mimicking Marxist accounts of societal crisis). Each of the three reform phases had circumvented the political aspects of the crisis, although the third phase (1987–9) had the hallmarks of a 'preparatory' intervention aimed at undermining the organizational capabilities and political appeal of the opposition, in order to tilt the balance of forces more in the state's favour. The influence of US counter-revolutionary theory (practised in countries like El Salvador during the same period) is discernible in the groundwork laid during the 1980s for a strategic shift towards a tightly managed transition of the type the SACP's Jeremy Cronin described as 'low-intensity democracy'.[66]

What the regime's strategists underestimated was the extent to which poverty, dispossession, landlessness and social disintegration had become politicized by the democratic movement. Every conceivable ill had been made attributable to apartheid.[67] The 1980s had confirmed that the state could not engage the popular forces within a reformist project based strictly on adjustments in the socio-economic realm. Early in the 1980s, former president P. W. Botha had warned that whites had to 'adapt or die'; by the late 1980s it was clear that adaptation within the paradigm of apartheid offered no escape. The political and social stability needed to restore and consolidate a new cycle of accumulation required a new political model which had to incorporate the basic demands of the political opposition: a non-racial democracy based on universal suffrage in a unified nation-state. As early as March 1986, NP ministers had already grasped this point; bedeviling them was how to proceed. This excerpt from notes of a special cabinet meeting on 1 March 1986 conveys the rudderless mood of the time:

> Internal violence and foreign pressure was on the increase, and (President PW Botha) wanted to know whether the NP should implement more dramatic things in the country, in place of the programme of gradual adaptations which apparently was not taken to heart by anybody. Mr Heunis [Minister of Constitutional Planning and Development] responded by saying (a) the NP did not know where it was going, and (b) the government was not in a position to deal with the circumstances in the country. Mr De Klerk was of the opinion that (a) negotiations with people who counted were on the rocks, (b) he was almost powerless because qualifications which accompanied change were often allowed to lapse, (c) there were fundamental differences between ministers over the question of where the NP and the country was heading, and (d) measures of the present did not meet the demands of the time.[68]

The need for a leap had been recognized. Yet, the strategic coherence required to make it seemed not to exist. The blame could not be laid solely at the door of the apartheid state. It stemmed also from the 'political incoherence' of capital (Morris & Padayachee, 1989) – a common feature of capitalist society, which tends to be overcome only during extraordinary periods. Capital traditionally engaged the South African state through discreet channels, mostly through engagements performed by business organizations grouped according to sector and even language. Its input into political and social policy tended, therefore, to be hide-bound and parochial. Concentrated pressure and coherent macro-reform proposals did not materialize (the notable exception being around urban planning, where the corporate-sponsored Urban Foundation made telling interventions). Instead capitalist organizations generally preferred to slipstream behind state policies, intervening when specific interests were at stake. The result was a political distance between state and capital, despite the state's attempts during the 1980s to rationalize the political input of capital by organizing consultative conferences and channels. This political incoherence had several origins:

- The economic crisis differentially affected different sectors of capital. Attempts to stabilize the balance of payments in the late 1970s benefited mining (the main export earner) at the expense of manufacturing, which was hit hard by rising wages and expensive working capital (caused by rising interest rates). The weakened currency favoured exporting sectors but made imports more expensive. As a result, bankruptcies in the manufacturing and commercial sectors grew, while the mining and finance sectors boomed. Finance capital went on merger and acquisition sprees as the casualties of the crisis were bought or bailed out, leading to even greater concentration of ownership in the economy. The crisis, therefore, registered distinctly within different sectors of capital.
- Cultural and linguistic schisms continued to divide South African capital, with so-called English and Afrikaner capital (despite increasing functional enmeshing since the 1970s) organized in separate business organizations. The ideological aspects of the system retained some (though diminishing) currency within Afrikaner business organizations like the *Afrikaner Handels Instituut*. These cultural tensions also hampered relations between English capital and the state. Common circuits for élite engagements had not evolved until the 1980s and were unenthusiastically utilized.

A consistent institutional intimacy did not exist between the state and capital. Even by the late 1980s, no common vision was evident amongst state and capital about routes out of the political crisis. Sections of capital had long sponsored a succession of gadfly opposition political parties opposed to the naked racism of the apartheid system. As late as 1983, with the crisis in full view, these sections loudly opposed the introduction of a tricameral parliament. In 1986, with the uprising in full swing, capital fell in line behind state repression – but without offering a congruous strategy as to what might follow once the uprising had been crushed. However, by the mid-1980s, sections had also begun actively entertaining the possibility of a negotiated settlement. These tendencies were not hegemonic within capital. It would be up to a cluster of 'visionary' fractions of capital and a band of reformist adventurers within the NP and the state (including top security officials) – alert to the fact that racial political domination was not inevitably and perennially functional to South African capitalism – to devise an exit.

Meanwhile, two developments had combined to establish a favourable balance of forces within the NP and the government. The weight of the white working class and *petite bourgeoisie* had been supplanted by the white middle classes and the capitalist class as the core social base of the NP, and power had been centralized within the NP and the government.

The crushing of the mid-1980s uprisings saw the reformists take heart: by 1990, a five-member committee headed by Coetzee and National Intelligence Service chief (NIS) Niel Barnard had met with Nelson Mandela 47 times.[69] The 'facilitation' provided by social-democratic institutes like Idasa – and funded by Western governments and development agencies – was instrumental in establishing the climate and forging the relations that would lead to formal political negotiations. In February 1990, the ANC, PAC and other anti-apartheid organizations were unbanned, and Nelson Mandela and other political leaders released from prison. A new pack of cards had been dealt, but the ruling bloc still held a strong hand.

A new conjuncture

The multitude of factors that combined to create this conjuncture have been discussed in detail elsewhere,[70] but they bear repetition. Many resonated simultaneously (but distinctly) in the ANC and the NP party and government camps, tilting the balance of forces within them towards the proponents of negotiations. Others helped to established an objective context that could be interpreted to favour that route. The precise internal dynamics within the two camps remain obscured by a lack of information. Official accounts and even personal memoirs that have emerged offer little insight into the debates and struggles that raged within the ANC, NP and government leadership circles. Nevertheless, those debates occurred on the basis of these (and possibly other) factors that conspired to produce this unique conjuncture. An ensemble of factors weighed on the minds of the NP and the government:

- Efforts to slow the slide of the economy were being hampered by international sanctions – although just how severely remains a point of debate. Certainly, the government's options in dealing with internal resistance were influenced by the chances of increased sanctions. At the same time, South African exports experienced an upturn from 1987 onwards, despite sanctions. The main value of sanctions appeared to lie in their negative effect on foreign investment flows and on the government's ability to secure financial assistance to offset balance of payments difficulties. Those pressures would not be relieved substantially until a political settlement was reached.
- The absurd duplication of state institutions (three chambers of parliament, multiple government departments performing the same tasks for racially defined sections of the population, expensive homeland administrations), as well as the cost of the Namibian occupation and the war in Angola, increased fiscal strains at a point when the economy was slumping into its worst recession since the 1930s.
- Maturing within ruling circles was an understanding that economic recovery was impossible without social and political stability. The failure of the

reforms introduced since the late 1970s to defuse political resistance confirmed that medium-term stability could not be achieved without addressing the political demands of the majority. Shifting to the outright totalitarian management of society appeared unattractive since it would postpone rather than resolve the political question, leading to ongoing instability. The economic costs would be destructive since capital inflows needed to avert balance of payments crises would not materialize, triggering a sequence of predictable effects. Sanctions would make it difficult and hugely expensive to secure foreign loans and other forms of finance; foreign debt repayment obligations would tighten, forcing the government to introduce economic austerity measures that would spur further waves of resistance, producing a constricting cycle of deepening economic decline and political instability. In other words, rescuing the economic made it essential to restructure the political framework of the accumulation strategy.

- The internal popular forces had regrouped within the MDM and were still capable of mounting resistance campaigns which, although they did not pose immediate threats to the state, could escalate into more formidable forms in the future, thereby further raising the costs of avoiding a political settlement.
- Negotiations required the existence of a coherent political force with sufficient legitimacy and authority among the popular masses to make a deal stick – the ANC had clearly emerged as that force. At the same time, the sweep of its authority and power could conceivably be limited by destabilization campaigns (of the sort launched with the Inkatha Freedom Party – IFP – in KwaZulu-Natal since the mid-1980s).
- A dramatic process of class restructuring had been unleashed within African communities – further undermining efforts to achieve unequivocal unity among the oppressed and yielding a small but distinct black élite, especially in the homelands where this stratum was also invested with political and administrative power. The rise of the IFP in particular – and with it organized, politicized ethnicity – raised hopes that the hegemony of the liberation organizations could be reduced during and after a negotiations process.
- The latter developments fuelled exaggerated expectations within the NP that a 'non-racial' centre-right political alliance could be mustered to challenge or hold in check the ANC.
- Militarist hardliners were pushed onto the defensive within the state by the military defeat suffered by the South African Defence Force (SADF) at Cuito Cuanavale in Angola, Namibia's almost anti-climactic achievement of independence, and progress in Angola towards a peaceful settlement.
- The NP had weaned itself from its old multi-class social base, enabling it to free its policies from the ideological straitjacket of apartheid, and

transform itself into a party championing the interests of the white middle classes and bourgeoisie.[71]

■ A power struggle within the ruling NP was resolved with the election of F. W. de Klerk as leader, with the party's 'young turks' grouping around him.

■ Pressure from Western governments, principally the US, and their touting of the reassuring examples of 'managed transitions' to democracy in the Philippines and Namibia diminished the reluctance to opt for negotiations.

The options appearing before the ANC, in particular, and the democratic movement, in general, were influenced by the following factors:

■ The dream of overthrowing the apartheid state had been dashed by withering state repression, as well as by organizational and strategic dysfunction within the democratic movement. A lengthy period of rebuilding the internal popular forces lay ahead. This weakened the power of ANC elements that favoured an unremitting confrontational engagement with the state.

■ The armed struggle never matured to the point where it posed a military threat to white rule. By the late 1980s its potency had faded to the point where the ANC would later admit that 'there was no visible intensification'.[72] The radical social transformation projects attempted in Mozambique and Angola had been destroyed, in large part through a massive destabilization campaign by the apartheid state, reinforcing South African hegemony throughout the subcontinent.[73]

■ After the Namibian settlement, the ANC lost its military bases in Angola and was forced to transplant them as far afield as East Africa. There was no foreseeable prospect of re-establishing them in the region.

■ The collapse of Eastern Europe and the USSR's shift towards demilitarizing its relations with the West (and dramatically lessening its support for revolutionary projects in the South) deprived the ANC of its main backers and effectively curtailed its armed struggle,[74] and accelerated an endemic retreat by radical forces world-wide.[75]

■ During the 1980s, the ANC had achieved substantial ideological hegemony among the popular masses and their main forces, bolstering its claim to be the government-in-waiting.

■ Overall, the balance of power within the ANC tilted towards a well-organized pro-negotiations faction which got the upperhand over hardliners embarrassed by the collapse of their insurrectionary strategy and alarmed by the disappearance of long-term support traditionally drawn from the Soviet bloc.

Internationally, the main Western imperialist powers had since the early 1980s successfully pushed for and facilitated a series of 'peaceful' transitions to democracy on terms that prevented or set back efforts by the popular forces to achieve deep social transformation in their respective countries.[76] Pressure was exerted on the South African government by its counterparts in Washington, London and Bonn to follow suit. They argued that their support (although at times ambivalent) had presented Pretoria with the strategic room to bring about a negotiated settlement, and probably warned it that shirking this historic opportunity would end their policies of 'constructive engagement'. At the same time, the ANC was almost certainly notified that it, too, had to seize the opportunity if an ANC government was to qualify for substantial 'rewards' from the West (in the form of development aid, new investment, favourable trading terms, and political support in international fora). The collapse of the Soviet bloc and the USSR's abandonment of its commitments to radical states of the South (even given the wavering and mercenary nature of that support) meant that post-apartheid South Africa would be knotted into a world economic system dominated by the Western powers, principally the US, Western Europe and Japan.

None of this should be taken to imply that South Africa had attained much more than peripheral importance for the West, whatever the inflated sense of importance harboured by South Africans of all political stripes. What significance it did have derived primarily from the activities of anti-apartheid solidarity movements and from the Cold War context into which South Africa, like other contested Third World countries, had been slotted. Once the Cold War ended, South Africa's 'strategic significance' – already putative and exaggerated – ebbed markedly. It is highly questionable whether a negotiated settlement was viewed by, for instance, Washington as a priority by the late 1980s – although a failure to settle the conflict probably carried sufficient 'nuisance value' to warrant words of encouragement from Washington. At the same time, the potential utility of a democratic South Africa to expanded spheres of US influence in southern, central and east Africa would not have passed unnoticed in the State Department.

While neither side could claim to have triumphed, the balance of forces still favoured the incumbents, who remained firmly in control of the economy, the state (and its repressive apparatus) and the media. The ruling bloc had won space to manoeuvre in. Although confronted by a crisis, it was not acting in panic-stricken mode.

The apartheid state had emerged from turbulent uncertainties with the support of most Western governments and South African capital intact, though provisional. The retreat of radical projects internationally before homespun failures, imperialist intervention and strategic and theoretical disorientation enabled the consolidation of centrist political alternatives (viz. the growing number of 'transitions to democracy' in the Third World). The claims of the liberation movement to represent the undifferentiated 'oppressed masses' were in doubt. Accelerated class differentiation and the growing prominence of other contradictions in African communities emboldened those who believed the NP could traverse and survive the gauntlet of negotiations.

The leap into the unknown

The launch of formal negotiations in 1990 confirmed the realization that an enduring resolution of the crisis first required addressing its political dimensions by fundamentally restructuring the political and ideological basis of the post-war accumulation strategy. But NP politicians embarked on this path without a strategic master plan. Clarity existed on the need to incorporate the democratic opposition into the political system and restructure the system in order to achieve this. Less clear were the terms on which incorporation could occur, short of the fact that these had to constrain the ANC's ability to wield political power in the service of a radical agenda of socio-economic transformation. As a result, the NP throughout the negotiations process would experiment with a bewildering assortment of proposals,[77] causing ANC negotiators to complain throughout that their NP counterparts were 'constantly cutting and changing their positions'.[78] Doubtless, there were nervous recollections of the insurrectionary course taken by popular forces when much narrower political openings had appeared during the early 1980s. It was not as if the floodgates of possibility had suddenly been opened, but the outcome of such forthright political restructuring was by no means certain.

Understandably, the ANC and its allies claimed a historic victory. Alongside the insurrectionary headiness of the mid-1980s were pronouncements by the ANC leadership that seemed to illuminate a path that might end in negotiations. In 1985, at the height of insurrectionary fervour, the Lusaka leadership had issued preconditions for negotiations – the same year in which its customary 8 January statement had called on supporters to prepare for a 'people's war'. Throughout the subsequent period, the organization issued starkly contradictory statements – some conciliatory, others patently martial. In part these were directed at specific audiences: moderate postures were designed to shore up the ANC's impressive knack at winning support on the international front, while the injunctions issued to its supporters glossed over any talk of compromise and negotiations with 'the enemy'. By the end of 1987 (after Mandela had commenced his talks with the government, and with the internal movement on the retreat), the organization appeared more inclined towards a negotiations route. It refined its preconditions, and two years later formalized them in the Harare Declaration which made it public knowledge that the door was open for negotiations.

Yet, the swiftness with which De Klerk moved through that portal and began meeting the preconditions caught by surprise the base of the ANC and the popular movement – and, indeed, even key ANC theorists, if

Mzala's observations shortly before Mandela's release in February 1990 (though published later) were earnest:

> There is no prospect of the apartheid regime under De Klerk agreeing to the most elementary demands of the ANC such as the establishment of a one-person, one-vote political system (1990:571).

That incredulity was anchored partly in the tenet that 'apartheid cannot be reformed' – change would be achieved by sweeping away the old order, not by enabling it to help decide its fate through negotiations. Linked was the cliché that the NP government could not meet the basic preconditions for negotiations set by the ANC, because doing so would be akin to signing its own death warrant.

By early 1990, the regime was meeting, steadily though stealthily, many of the preconditions set by the ANC for 'genuine negotiations'. What surprised the base of the ANC and its allies was that the government opted to approach the negotiations table in circumstances that were far from 'insurrectionary'. In contrast to the ruling bloc (which had sought to avoid far-reaching adjustments in the political sphere), the popular movement and the ANC in particular were guilty of over-privileging the political – reducing not only the oppression experienced by the majority but the entire system of exploitation to the political and ideological form of the apartheid state. In such reasoning, the ordering of economic and social relations pivoted on the state – once it changed, everything else would follow. Therefore, it was argued, the apartheid regime would – and could – not initiate the kinds of reforms demanded by the ANC, since they would amount to the regime wilfully engineering the collapse of the entire system of white privilege. Alas, such political reductionism did not prepare the movement for the ruling bloc's gamble that the defence of capitalism required abandoning the exclusionary political and ideological framework of the post-war growth path – and that a conjuncture had arrived when, perhaps for the last time, the balance of forces still favoured that bloc strongly enough to enable it to make the formative moves in that direction.

The confusion gripping the internal popular movement had important ramifications for the negotiations process and the settlement it produced. Still smarting from its setbacks in the late-1980s, the movement was only beginning to regroup when its organizational disarray was compounded by the profound strategic disorientation caused by the advent of negotiations. A mere five years earlier, the ANC had been labouring to catch up with dynamic internal developments; now the woozy state of the internal movement rendered it more prone to the organizational and strategic discipline of the ANC. The UDF was disbanded on 4 March 1991, with UDF leader Patrick Lekota justifying the decision with the claim that 'the purpose for which we were set up has been achieved' – apparently endorsing the mistaken view that the UDF (and, by implication, the bulk of the popular movement) was a mere stand-in for the ANC-in-exile. The move evoked widespread but impotent disgruntlement at rank-and-file level. Shortly afterwards, Lodge warned with prescience that:

> ... rendering the UDF's lively and heterodox following into neat bureaucratic units that can be incorporated into the organizational forms of a disciplined political party represents a task which will be not only difficult but also dangerous; the process of imposing bureaucratic uniformity on a popular movement may take away is spirit and vitality (Lodge & Nasson, 1991:204).

Within a short space of time SAYCO and several women's organizations opted to become conflated into their counterpart structures within the ANC. SACP deputy general secretary Jeremy Cronin has termed this the 'B-team mentality':

> People abandoned their organizations and joined the main political organization. The real experience and worth of the popular movements was not understood; they were seen as a kind of 'B-team', a substitute until the 'A-team' [the ANC] could enter the playing field.[79]

The ANC's ideological pre-eminence was now supplemented by organizational supremacy – with the partial exception of COSATU, which, despite its political allegiance to the ANC, retained an independent base and massed organizational strength. In slightly more than a decade, the ANC had returned from the wilderness and assumed the now incontestable mantle of a government-in-waiting.

A few secrets of success

As an assembly of different classes, traditions and cultures, the ANC's ideological character and strategic direction has been contested throughout most of its history. One of its several achievements has been its success at preventing this heterogeneity from generating the sorts of internal turmoil that have plagued many other liberation movements (including the ANC's offshoot, the PAC).[80] Whilst dominant strategic and tactical positions were intermittently fought for and established, they did not achieve invulnerability. The fierce discourse angled towards the overthrow of the apartheid state was shadowed by another, more moderate one which seemed inclined towards a negotiated settlement. The latter was more consistent with perspectives that predominated during the ANC's first five decades of existence and which endured among older exiles and Robben Island prisoners.[81] Both strategic visions incorporated other pressures that included economic sanctions and boycotts, international isolation of the apartheid state, mass action by the popular organizations (strikes, protests, marches, boycotts, armed action, etc.), and armed struggle. The relative importance of these ingredients was disputed – except in the case of armed struggle which had remained paramount.[82] Indeed, it was the patent failure of a strategy centred on an insurrectionary variant of armed struggle that probably tilted the ANC onto the negotiations path reconnoitred by Nelson Mandela since 1986.[83]

One might expect an organization which opts for negotiations during a period which, in its estimation, bristles with radical fervour to be inviting turbulent internal disputes and perhaps even open rebellion. Yet, there is little to suggest this happened inside the ANC. One reason is that the organization traditionally kept a tight reign on heterodoxy and dissent within its ranks. As important is the fact that the co-existence of radical and moderate postures in the leadership and historical discourse of the ANC equipped it with an ambiguity that could cushion sharp policy turns. Entering into negotiations therefore could not be portrayed as an about-turn or a betrayal of organizational principles. Likewise, the basically social-democratic constitutional principles issued by the ANC in mid-1989 could earnestly be presented as a distillation of its historical vision of change.

That vision, of course, resided in the Freedom Charter – which formed an ideological bedrock and key hegemonic instrument for the ANC. Idealistic and emotively phrased, it bore close resemblance to the French Declaration of the Rights of Man or the Declaration of Independence of the North American colonies.[84] It was not a policy document and its specific points steadily became detached from concrete moorings as time passed. From its adoption, the Charter had been hoisted above debate and dispute; it came to hover in a sacred zone of popular consciousness in the ANC. In order to marshal as broad and large a constituency as possible behind the banner of African nationalism, the ANC had pointedly refrained from elaborating and imposing a precise ideological 'line' derived from the Charter. In exile, the organization generally avoided substantive (and potentially divisive) elaborations. Discussion of alleged contradictions and ambiguities in the Charter was either actively suppressed or smoothed over with platitudes. Its formulation of post-apartheid policy was unexplicit, functioning not as road signs for transformation but as flagstones for mobilization and organization. Thus the promotion of the Freedom Charter ('The Year of the Freedom Charter' campaign in 1985), in a period when the country was deemed to be poised on the brink of liberation, was not used to refine and develop the document as a rough draft of some post-apartheid policies. Instead it was sanctified and deployed as a set of symbolic reference points geared at asserting the pre-eminence of the ANC in the liberation struggle.[85] The outcome was that the ANC retained considerable ideological manoeuvrability.

Indeed, the ANC's rise to pre-eminence stemmed less from its officially exulted 'successes' – mass mobilization and the armed struggle – than from its mastery in two other arenas: international diplomacy and symbolic struggle. Its achievements in those realms also reflected the absence of viable alternative political forces.[86] The only possible challenger, the PAC, was racked by interminable organizational dysfunction, internal rivalries and corruption scandals; it was not until the late 1980s that it recovered a semblance of international respect, thanks mainly to pressure from the governments of Nigeria and Zimbabwe.

In the diplomatic field the ANC achieved dazzling victories. By stressing the non-racial and moderate aspects of its programme it built a huge network of international representatives (far outnumbering the embassies of the apartheid state) and a powerful network of backstage and public solidarity groups and sympathizers. Internationally, the bulk of the publicity, mobilizing and campaigning work was carried out by the latter. The ANC's inclusive rhetoric – counterpoised by the increasing visual representations of apartheid violence in international media – drew waves of international solidarity that vexed other liberation organizations. In continental (the Organization of African Unity) and international fora (United Nations, sports and cultural bodies) the ANC established for itself the status of a 'government-in-waiting'. This enabled it to spearhead a formidable array of international boycotts and sanctions aimed against the apartheid system. Meanwhile, the SACP cultivated strong material, logistical and training links with socialist bloc countries. By the mid-1980s South Africa had become a domestic issue in most Western countries and the ANC was able to position itself centre-stage in these solidarity initiatives as the 'authentic voice' of the oppressed majority.

These accomplishments also enabled the ANC to capitalize on the exodus of youth into exile after 1976, at a point when the political stage belonged to the BCM. Awaiting them beyond South Africa's borders, thanks to the web of relations established internationally, were two choices: join the ANC or the PAC.[87] The former was much better organized and positioned for the intake, which infused the ANC with a new generations of radicalized recruits often with links to internal popular organizations.[88]

In important respects the ANC's success stemmed from its ability to dominate the symbolic aspects of struggle through a variety of adroit interventions, particularly in the 1980s.[89] At the (organizational and tactical) helm of the internal cycle of resistance of the 1980s were, first, unionists and student leaders and later township youth. However, the ANC made up lost ground through (among other methods) acting as international spokesperson for the uprising and by pushing key symbols to the fore. One such coup was the Free Nelson Mandela campaign (started in the early 1980s). The ANC in particular and the liberation struggle in general was personalized, condensed within the persona of Mandela: a link was thus established between Mandela, the legality of the ANC and the legitimacy of the struggle for national liberation. Likewise, the campaign celebrating the thirtieth anniversary of the Freedom Charter in 1985 served to place the uprising within the historical tradition of the ANC and provided it with a rough but embracing manifesto that resonated across ideological lines. The armed struggle, too, was more effective as a galvanizing, morale-boosting symbol of resistance than as a military strategy. Though armed attacks had multiplied in the 1980s,[90] they never posed a military threat to the state which developed a disarming success rate at pre-empting attacks. The import of attacks on the Sasol refinery or Air Force Headquarters lay in their symbolic demonstration that the system could be struck at its 'heart' and in the resulting cathartic, vicarious thrill this imparted. Later, armed action was also linked to community and union resistance. While this often had practical impact, again its prime effect was to stiffen the activists' resolve (as opposed to militarily threaten the apartheid state or effectively defend activists against repression) and confirm the pre-eminence of the ANC in the liberation struggle. In Lodge's view, 'Umkhonto's most significant contribution to the liberation struggle was helping the ANC exercise political leadership over constituencies it was unable to organize directly' (Lodge & Nasson, 1991:183).

For all these successes, the ANC's conceptions of a post-apartheid society remained rudimentary and impressionistic – a shortcoming that would become telling during negotiations and beyond. Roughly hewn, they had, until the mid-1980s, drawn heavily on the Soviet model and 'Third World' visions of the Bandung era. In most policy areas, the sweeping injunctions of the Freedom Charter ('There shall be houses, security and comfort! ... The people shall share in the country's wealth! ... The land shall be shared among those who work it!')[91] had been barely elaborated in the preceding 35 years.

Shortly before 1990, the ANC hurriedly set up embryonic policy structures to explore economic and land policies. The failure of the SACP – prominent in most other aspects of the organization – to take a profound role in policy debates was remarkable. ANC policies, according to Tito Mboweni (current labour minister and former deputy head of the ANC's economic planning department), would after 1990 emerge from an interplay of inputs from the ANC's:

> ... organizational structures; the policy departments; the positions of allies of the ANC (in particular Cosatu); the experiences of developing countries; the lobbying efforts of capital, the media, western governments, and independent commentators; and the policy research work of the IMF and World Bank (1994:69).

Less than five years had passed since a writer in the ANC's journal *Sechaba* had exhorted supporters with words that seemed to resonate loudly:

[T]he enemy has no role in the solution of our problems … There can be no going back to the practice of frittering away our energy in activities calculated to prise the case-hardened conscience of white oppressors to invite us to negotiations to bring about a dispensation acceptable to them and us.[92]

At roughly the same time, Nelson Mandela was initiating dialogue with the apartheid regime – at first without the explicit consent of the ANC leadership in Lusaka. A propensity for negotiating an end to the conflict had emerged also within a ruling bloc aware that the formidable array of political, social and economic barriers could no longer be surmounted within the apartheid framework. The need for dramatic political restructuring had become manifest and the courage to proceed had been mustered.[93] Implicit was the recognition that:

> … [w]hen the problem-solving capacities of the rulers begin to fail, the hegemony enters a crisis; control will keep these social and political forces in power for a certain period, but they are already doomed.[94]

The political basis of the South African system had to be revised – a project which had to include (and, most likely, pivot) on the ANC. The gamble taken by the state – and supported in rough outline by capital – was to suspend the desultory attempts to achieve stability via socio-economic reform packages and to try to resolve, instead, the political dimension of the multifold crises gripping South Africa. This could provide a relatively stable basis for restructurings in the economic and social spheres. The eventual settlement would constitute the most sophisticated and successful attempt yet to achieve this – essentially through 'élite-pacting', a political reformist path which, as summarized by Cronin, demands that 'élites, capable of "delivering" major constituencies, jointly manage the transition to a new constitutional dispensation'. In doing so, he continued, 'a new centrist (ruling) bloc is consolidated and right and left forces are marginalized'.[95] The survival of such a breakthrough, though, required that the consensus be extended across the political and social terrain.

The next four years would determine whether a sturdy enough envelope of restraint could be fashioned to ensure that the ANC and its popular allies did not transgress the boundaries of permissible change desired by the ruling bloc.

Notes

1 Cited in Gelb (1991:19–20).
2 These included outright repressive measures (banning unionists, violently crushing strikes) and a system of parallel unions whereby African workers' interests had to be presented to management and the state via white-controlled union bodies like the Trade Union Council of South Africa (TUCSA).
3 African workers in Durban were earning an average weekly wage of R13 at the time (Baskin, 1991:17).

4 In 1972, black workers staged 71 strikes. In the next years, the figures rocketed –
   370 strikes (1973), 384 (1974), 275 (1975), 245 (1976). Severe repression saw the
   figure drop to 90 strikes in 1977 (Davies *et al.*, 1984:34).
5 The precise organizational lineage of the uprising has proved difficult to discern. The
   South African Students' Movement (SASM) was a prominent force. Equally important was the fact that in the early 1970s a new generation of African students had
   begun teaching in township schools. Influenced by the BCM, they conveyed BC
   thinking to their students. The ANC's role in the uprising is unclear. There is little evidence of an active hand, although some researchers have claimed that the ANC managed to establish underground cells in Soweto via SASM; see Marks and Trapido
   (1991: 4–5).
6 For a valuable review of BC, see Pityana *et al.* (1991).
7 Politically, BC underwent traumatic detours, with the Azanian People's Organization
   (AZAPO) eventually emerging as the standard bearer of the tradition. It soon drifted
   to the far-left and entangled itself in rejectionist postures that saw it boycott even the
   April 1994 election.
8 Saul and Gelb (1981).
9 Gramsci, A., *Prison Notebooks*, p. 178, cited in Saul and Gelb (1981:3).
10 Saul and Gelb (1981).
11 Army Chief of Staff (later defence minister) General Magnus Malan, cited in
   O'Meara (1983:253).
12 For a summary of the Urban Foundation's origins and brief, see Davies *et al.*
   (1984:122–5).
13 The editorial view of the *Financial Mail*, the country's flagship business weekly, cited
   in Davies *et al.* (1984:39).
14 *Financial Mail*, 25 January 1980, quoting liberal critic Sheena Duncan; cited in Saul
   and Gelb (1981:49).
15 In the Riekert Commission's phrasing, 'black communities [should] bear to an
   increasing extent a greater part of the total burden in connection with the provision
   of services in their own community'.
16 These antagonisms were not new. In the 1950s, Soweto was rocked by violent riots
   when migrant hostel dwellers attacked 'permanent' township residents (Stadler,
   1987:175). By the early 1970s, however, these tensions appeared to have abated.
   Migrant workers strongly supported the new trade unions that emerged earlier in the
   decade. Indeed, researcher Ari Sitas found that, until the late 1970s, 'the distinction
   between urban and migrant workers was apparently dissolving as was the relationship between migrant trade unions and the community' (cited in Marks & Trapido,
   1991:14).
17 Paraphrased in Baskin (1991:26).
18 See Baskin (1991:26–8).
19 This is not to suggest, as ANC ideologues argued, that the romanticized 'unity of the
   oppressed' was taking shape – the contrary was in fact happening, as class and other
   forms of social differentiation became more pronounced in African communities.
20 In 1982 the NP split, and the far-right Conservative Party (CP) adopted these former
   core constituencies, equating their interests with the defence of 'classic' apartheid ideology. Violent racism and bigotry, and the promotion of hermetic and nostalgic versions of Afrikaner culture became the preserve of the far-right. This freed the NP, as a
   party, to spearhead further reforms that departed from 'classic' apartheid. But it also
   raised the spectre of a challenge to its authority within the white electorate emerging
   from the far-right.
21 Poulantzians has defined these fractions in terms of sectors – branches of production
   (mining, manufacturing), 'ethnicity' (English, *Afrikaans*), domicile (local, foreign)

and types of accumulation (financial, industrial, commercial). The conglomerizing tendency in the economy saw major corporations straddle many of the divides.

22 See, for instance, Cole's account of its role in squatter crises around Cape Town (1987).

23 Urban Foundation statement, cited in Davies *et al.* (1984:122).

24 These upgrading schemes, for instance, bypassed migrant worker hostels whose residents were becoming marginalized and alienated from wider society. It was on the basis of such material and social tensions that Inkatha later intervened politically, establishing footholds in hostels, while tensions between residents living in formal townships and those living precariously in squatter camps or hostels would later explode violently. See Cole (1987), Segal (1991), Everatt (1992), Marais (1992a), Hindson and Morris (1992).

25 Importantly, Cole reminded that 'reducing (these divisions) to state strategies alone merely mystifies the reality on the ground' (1987:163). Other contributing factors included economic recessions (forcing reliance on state and other forms of patronage), the disorientation caused by social systems transplanted into new settings, and communities' own differentiated histories.

26 *A Survey of Race Relations in South Africa*, South African Institute for Race Relations, 1985, Johannesburg.

27 Lodge and Nasson (1991:39). However, this 'democratic culture' within the ranks of the opposition would later become offset by coercive and authoritarian forms of mobilization and action.

28 Baskin (1991:28); Lodge and Nasson (1991:28). Borrowing another tactic of the 1950s, the unions buttressed their factory actions by enlisting community support for consumer boycotts against employers.

29 'Izizwe', 1987, 'Errors of Workerism' in *SA Labour Bulletin*, Vol. 12, No. 3, cited in Fine and Davis (1990:278).

30 Dave Lewis, 1986, 'Capital, the Trade Unions and the National Liberation Struggle', *Monthly Review*, No. 37, cited in Fine and Davis (1990:278).

31 In October 1985, COSATU federated the four largest trade union bodies, triggering a massive strike wave that coincided with the 1985–6 uprising; see Chapter 9 of this volume.

32 The new councillors exemplified the process of class differentiation in African townships: 'Councillors were often members of a growing commercial and entrepreneurial middle class ... [who] had benefited from the government reforms.' Their duties of fiscal administration in the townships 'greatly expanded the opportunities for venality ... and made them the target of widespread discontent generated by the economic recession' (Lodge and Nasson, 1991:31).

33 The Uitenhage Black Civics Organization, for instance, was formed by shopstewards from the Volkswagen factory in Port Elizabeth.

34 Lodge and Nasson (1991:51).

35 COSAS aligned itself with the 'charterist' tradition of the ANC while AZASCO at first adopted a BC outlook but soon embraced the non-racial approach of COSAS.

36 Barrel (1991:85–6).

37 Paraphrasing of the report by ANC officials interviewed by Barrel, *op. cit.*

38 'Green Book', ANC Files, p. 5, cited by Mbeki (1996:43).

39 Swilling and Phillips (1989a:76).

40 Morris and Padayachee (1989:87–95). For more a detailed overview of the NSMS, see Swilling and Phillips (1989a:75–89).

41 Morris and Padayachee (1989:88).

42 Senior NSMS official, quoted in *Weekly Mail*, 3 October 1986, cited in Morris and Padayachee (1989:89).

43 See, for instance, Mzala (1981) and (1985).
44 Trevor (1984).
45 The phrase was not new. It had featured in the Operation Mayibuye planning document, drawn up in 1963 by the high command of MK – but with starkly different meaning, functioning in the context of a rural-based guerrilla war.
46 Slovo, 1986, 'SACP: One of the Great Pillars of our Revolution', *African Communist*, No. 107 (Second Quarter); paraphrased by Bundy (1989:8). Supporters wrote enthusiastically of the factors required for a transfer of power: '[T]he South African state and its military power must be destroyed; the country must be conquered; the will of the enemy must be subdued'; see Cabesa (1986).
47 Mzala (1987).
48 Wolpe (1988), cited in Bundy (1989:9).
49 This section draws on Bundy (1989:14–18).
50 For a survey of attempts to undermine the military system from within, see Cawthra *et al.* (1994).
51 'No government has ever fallen before revolutionists until is has lost control over its armed forces or lost the ability to use them effectively' – C. Brinton, *The Anatomy of Revolution*, cited in Bundy (1989:1).
52 The mere existence of civics and youth groups did not, of themselves, constitute such organs of popular power – they were the potential basis for constructing such organs, a point often lost on celebrants of those initiatives.
53 As claimed, for instance, by Zwelakhe Sisulu in his keynote address to a National Education Crisis Committee (NECC) conference in Durban, 29 March 1986. Only in the small, compact towns of the Eastern Cape (especially the Karoo) did such claims contain even a measure of accuracy, and then only for short periods.
54 Along the lines of, for instance, El Salvador during the same period when the Popular Liberation Forces (FPL) and People's Revolutionary Army (ERP) respectively controlled large areas of Chalatenango, San Vicente and Morazan regions. In South Africa, earnest debates over 'dual power' would persist into 1990, when the popular forces were licking their wounds – see Niddrie (1990).
55 *Op. cit.*
56 Among them the 'Black Christmas' campaign of 1986; the 'People's Education' campaign of the NECC which, however made only marginal inroads against the 'No Education Until Liberation' rhetoric popular among many students; and worker stayaways.
57 Journalist Nomavenda Mathiane's account of a 1986 meeting called by students (cited in Lodge & Nasson, 1991:97). Her description applied also generally to adult township residents' reactions to the careening militancy of activist youth.
58 By mid-1986, 50 national and regional UDF leaders had been removed from active politics through arrests. Within another year, almost 30 000 activists (70 per cent of them members of UDF affiliates) had been arrested or detained, and more than 3 000 blacks had been killed (either by the police or in internecine violence).
59 As paraphrased by Lodge and Nasson (1991:89).
60 Report to UDF national congress, 5 April 1985.
61 See Bundy (1989:16).
62 Morris and Padayachee (1989:84). There were exceptions to this trend, notably in small Eastern Cape towns like Port Alfred. In 1985, through boycotts and other campaigns, telling divisions were fomented within the business community and local state structures. Rather than press ahead blindly, local activists exploited the disarray of their opponents by negotiating – and winning – specific local reforms.
63 See Marais (1992b:14–17).
64 *Motsuenyane Commission Report*, 1993, 'Executive Summary', Johannesburg, p. iii.

65 For an elliptical but instructive account of those trends, see *Appendices to the African National Congress Policy Statement to the Truth & Reconciliation Commission*, August 1996, Johannesburg; see also Marais (1992b).

66 See Cronin (1994a:3–6).

67 An eminently practical basis for mobilization, enabling activists to 'make visible' the underpinnings of oppression and suffering, and to focus protests more acutely. But it also fed the notion that the removal of apartheid would unlock a cornucopia of opportunity and power.

68 Excerpts from an expurgated political biography of former President P. W. Botha, *Sunday Times*, 28 August 1994.

69 See Sparks (1994).

70 See, for example, essays collected in Moss and Obery (1991); Saul (1993).

71 Shadowing this was a measure of uncertainty about the NP's political fate. In the September 1989 election, the party lost support to both the right (CP) and the 'left' (Democratic Party). Also, leading figures had abandoned the party. Reformists within the party were almost certainly alert to the fact that staying the course of political vacillation would have exacerbated these trends.

72 ANC National Executive Committee, 'Negotiations: A strategic perspective' (November 1992), discussion paper, Johannesburg.

73 For a survey of that campaign, see Hanlon (1986).

74 This development also removed the ruling bloc's fear of strong Soviet influence in the policies of an ANC-led post-apartheid government.

75 Particularly in Latin America, where radical forces had failed to seize state power (El Salvador), were besieged (Nicaragua) or were repositioning themselves to enter existing political systems on highly compromised terms (Brazil, Chile, Colombia).

76 The textbook example was the Philippines, though it would soon be joined by Namibia, El Salvador and South Africa.

77 The confusion was worsened by the fact that the NP's negotiating postures had two objectives: shaping the constitutional settlement and addressing the concerns of its constituency. Thus its insistence (as late as 1991) that a non-racial democracy in a unitary South Africa was not on the cards was not a bargaining principle but rather a sop to restive whites.

78 Author's interview with ANC negotiator Mohammed Valli Moosa, November 1992.

79 Presentation to the 'Prospects and Constraints for Transformation' workshop, December 1994, Johannesburg.

80 Although there were periodic, small-scale breakaways and departures by individuals.

81 The dynamics of this dramatic reversal from insurrectionist postures to negotiations overtures remain obscured in renditions of this period in ANC history. Most suggestive perhaps was Lodge's reference to the 'strong respect for tradition and continuity' in the ANC's 'historical consciousness' (1989:53).

82 Whether in the guise of a protracted guerrilla war (as it was originally conceived) or an urban insurrection (the strategy from 1985 onwards). Belatedly, thinkers within the ANC alliance are now acknowledging the negative effects of this fixation – for tentative criticism, see Cronin (1994a:15) and Barrel (1990); for stronger dissent, see Fine and Davis (1990:251-5).

83 The fact that Mandela opened a channel of communication with the regime – while his Lusaka colleagues were detecting the emergence of a 'pre-revolutionary' climate in South Africa – suggests an acute awareness on his part of the foolhardiness of that strategy.

84 This section draws on insights provided by Bill Freund.

85 As illustrated by Raymond Suttner and Jeremy Cronin (1986).

86   This, of course, is not a rare phenomenon in oppositional struggles. The socialist parties in Portugal and Spain, for instance, adroitly capitalized on the organizational deficiencies of the respective communist parties and popular forces – which were manifested in acute forms on the eve of these countries' transitions to democracy in the mid-1970s. For a detailed analysis, see Poulantzas (1976: 134–62)

87   Exiles could not remain in several African countries without the blessing of the ANC or PAC; the BC movement had no external presence to speak of.

88   Along with other factors (notably sectarianism) also accelerated the decline of the BC tradition, an independent current of resistance ideology which stood outside the charterist tradition.

89   The apartheid state inadvertently helped: its frantic efforts to demonize the ANC had the opposite effect – and added to the organization's stature.

90   Up from about 23 in 1977 to 228 in 1986 by Tom Lodge's count (Lodg & Nasson, 1991:178). See also Lodge (1987).

91   From the Freedom Charter, adopted by the Congress of the People on 26 June 1955.

92   Cassius Mandla, 1985, 'Let us move to all-out war', *Sechaba* (November), p. 25, cited by Lodge (1989:46).

93   According to journalist Allister Sparks, for De Klerk (and the NP élite) 'it was not a question of morality … but of practical politics – it was part of a gradual realization within the National Party that apartheid was unworkable and had to be changed' (1994:91).

94   Gruppi, L., 1969, *Democrazia e socialismo,* Edizioni del Calendario, Milan, cited by Pellicani (1980:32–3).

95   Cronin (1994a:7). It must be noted that Cronin does not necessarily share the view that this description applies neatly to the South African transition.

CHAPTER THREE

The shape of the transition

South Africa entered the twilight zone of the interregnum in February 1990 with the coherence presented until then by a repressive state replaced by the flux of process. A fitful, convoluted and often impenetrable process of 'talks about talks', 'protocol meetings' and, finally, negotiations was unleashed. This occurred against the background of the convulsive violence that raged across the country – signalling a 'centrifugal pull towards anarchy in South African society' (Saul, 1993:104). To a considerable extent, the violence was promoted through the action and inaction of the apartheid state, as subsequent revelations would confirm. The effect was to embolden attempts by the leadership of the democratic movement to reach a negotiated settlement:

> South Africa is on fire from end to end. The horrifying catalogue of assaults and killings must be brought to an end if we are not to sink into a state of self-perpetuating violence in which all our hopes of reform and social progress will be destroyed.[1]

The intrigues and manoeuvres of the public meetings, secret consultations, consultative seminars and talk-shops, the two main multiparty negotiating forums, breakdowns and worse are documented in reporting, analysis and punditry which, if stacked, would probably rise hundreds of metres into the sky.[2] Fascinating as some of those chronicles are, this chapter is concerned not with the minutiae of negotiations but the underlying agendas, trends and shifts which laid the basis for the settlement and established the parameters of the transition.

The stakes are stacked

Notwithstanding the ensemble of specific factors that inaugurated negotiations, in broad outline this phase was the outcome of the apartheid state's failure to resolve the political dimensions of a multifold crisis. By 1990, important sections of the state and capital were scanning the future through the prism of politics. As Mike Morris noted:

[Capital sees] a specific political role for redistributive policies: economic growth will not occur without a political settlement, and long-term peace and stability demands policies that can restore political and social conditions for economic growth (1993c:9).

South African capitalists would differ about the policies most likely to restore profit-making to the heights last relished in the early 1970s, producing desiderata that contained a mix of neo-liberal and crypto-Keynesian features. Nonetheless, the central concerns of capital were transparent and aggressively expressed: the need for a market economy, for social and political stability, for continuity in state institutions and for restraint from radical redistributive programmes. Unanimity was also absent among the democratic forces. Officially, the ANC supported a mixed economy. Its constitutional proposals, political analyst Tom Lodge noted, fell 'well short of a socialist reconstruction of South Africa'. Indeed:

> ... the political provisions of the guidelines suggest a more radical degree of restructuring than do the prescriptions for the economy (1989:49).

But within the ANC, and among its allies, debates raged on how robust a role should be reserved for the state. Even within the ANC, the Jacobin call for 'a dispensation that excludes the enemy as a factor in its making' retained some currency.[3] Though disoriented by the collapse of 'existing socialism' in the Soviet bloc, many SACP members harboured a residual commitment to a commandist state. Others rejected a commandist approach and, like former unionist Alec Erwin, argued for a 'planned socialist alternative' based on a 'democratically controlled economy which goes beyond simplistic notions of nationalisation'.[4] Overshadowing such specific differences, though, was the shared desire to fashion a development path that could redress the legacies of apartheid.

Required by South African capital was 'the reorganisation of hegemony through various kinds of passive revolution ... while providing for the continued development of the forces of production'.[5] Whilst eminently *political*, the required changes would not constitute an end in themselves. A resolution to the crisis had to rest on two key pillars.[6] It required, firstly, a political settlement which could enable the reconfiguration of the ruling bloc around a political axis capable of constructing and managing a new national consensus. Secondly, a new development path capable of guiding South Africa out of its economic and social crisis had to be devised and implemented. Both between and *within* the democratic forces and capitalist organizations there was considerable disagreement about the details of such a path.[7]

In Gramscian terms, the first element required that the hegemony of the ruling bloc be refurbished along dramatically new lines and become based on inclusive principles.[8] This implied a major risk: that the main political force in the democratic movement (the ANC) could be saddled with the task of salvaging South African capitalism by accepting and then managing a historic class compromise. As indicated, the ANC's history had not equipped it with an intrinsic aversion to such a role. As a liberation movement its struggle orbited around the ideals of democracy and civil rights. Its remarkable political unity had been cemented partially by consigning the class dimension to the margins of its analyses, which located the core fount of oppression and inequality in the apartheid state. The key to liberation, therefore, lay in a process of political transformation which centred on the winning of state power, which would serve as a *deus ex machina,* enabling it to gradually vanquish social and economic inequalities.

The negotiations process rested, therefore, on the fact that similar *methodological* predispositions had emerged in the ANC, and in the apartheid state and capital. In short, a convergence had occurred around the need to recast the *political* and *ideological* bases of state power. The major differences revolved around the extent to which the terms of this process would break and/or maintain continuities with the past. The ANC's historical privileging of the *political* over the economic[9] allowed for the possibility of a settlement based on significant restructuring of the political sphere, and broad continuity in the economic sphere. For obvious reasons, the restructuring could not be imposed unilaterally by the incumbent state but had to be negotiated with the political opposition – a perilous venture, nonetheless.

The NP maintained crucial advantages. It still controlled the state apparatus (not the least its repressive machinery which had been augmented by an assortment of covert and allied forces which became euphemized as the 'Third Force'), and retained the generalized support of the capitalist class. But negotiations launched the country into treacherous waters. The NP government could (be forced to) abandon the process and retreat into the defensive *laager* of the repressive state if the terms of the likely settlement seemed unacceptable. Likewise, the democratic movement could rekindle the insurrectionist fires of the mid-1980s and exploit the new space to try and topple the NP government and seize control of the state.[10] Active on the fringes, meanwhile, were increasingly militant white, ultra-right groupings, skittish homeland administrations, and, most ominously, an IFP institutionally ensconced in the KwaZulu homeland and militarily supported by security apparatuses.

The old and the new

'[T]his was a war without absolute winners ... the two major political forces in South Africa had fought to a draw,' the ANC's Govan Mbeki later wrote, 'And so it happened that the oppressor and the oppressed came together to chart the road to a democratic South Africa.'[11]

At hand was not the replacement of the old by the new, but their assimilation, according to terms that had yet to be established. In Morris' view:

> The negotiations process is not about a government negotiating its surrender because it was defeated by a superior force. It is not about an already cemented nation poised on the brink of decolonisation or the seizure of power. It is about a political struggle to forge a new nation and new alliances that can ensure the broadest basis of social consent. The opposition is not sweeping aside the old institutions of state power. It has to try and shape the terms on which it is incorporated into the state as a new ruling group (1993c:8).

An ensemble of factors seemed to indicate the boundaries of possible change – some of which were quite candidly itemized in a November 1992 paper by the ANC's National Executive Committee (NEC).[12] It noted that the government appeared highly divided but still commanded 'vast state and other military resources' and 'enjoyed the support of powerful economic forces'. The liberation movement, whilst having attained 'a very high level of mass mobilisation and mass defiance', was hamstrung by 'many organisational weaknesses' and a paucity of financial and military resources. These rendered it 'unable to militarily defeat the counter-revolutionary movement or adequately defend the people'. Meanwhile, the radically redrawn international context had increased pressures for a peaceful settlement that fell 'in line with the emerging international "culture" of multi-party democracy'.[13]

The NEC's conclusion was that this stalemate could best be surmounted through:

> ... a negotiations process combined with mass action and international pressure which takes into account the need to combat counter-revolutionary forces and at the same time uses phases in the transition to qualitatively change the balance of forces in order to secure a thorough-going democratic transition.[14]

It stressed that the balance of forces is 'not static'. But weighing heavily on the minds of the ANC leadership was the fear that South Africa could implode and fragment along the lines of the former Yugoslavia. Euphemizing this concern, the NEC declared that 'the new democratic government would need to adopt a wide range of measures in order to minimize the potential threat to the new democracy', some of which 'may have to be part and parcel of a negotiated settlement'.[15]

Evident here was the view that the ANC's moral and political weight would, during negotiations, be heavily mitigated by the perceived need to bring its main antagonists 'on board' through compromises which might rile many of its supporters. Yet, it had to reduce the risk of unleashing a

sequence of events that could lead to civil war. Shadowing the ANC's negotiating positions would be the need to preserve the South African nation-
state. According to SACP deputy general secretary (and ANC NEC
member) Jeremy Cronin, so alarmed was the ANC by the perceived
counter-revolutionary threat that:

> ... most of its energy went into trying to engage those forces ... We may have
> exaggerate the threat (our sources were often the government intelligence
> forces), but we shouldn't be complacent about the threat we were facing.[16]

For Cronin, the main political compromise eventually negotiated – the
Government of National Unity (GNU) – has to be understood 'as an
attempt to hold it all together and avoid a Bosnia'.

By late 1992, the ANC had geared itself to forging a political consensus
through 'certain retreats from previously held positions which would create
the possibility of a major positive breakthrough in the negotiating process
without permanently hampering real democratic advance'.[17] Prominent
among them was a 'sunset clause' providing for a period of compulsory
power-sharing in the form the GNU, an offer not to purge the security
forces and civil service of 'counter-revolutionary' elements, and the willingness to establish (during negotiations) a set of Constitutional Principles that
could not be violated by the final Constitution.

This caused considerable consternation throughout the democratic movement. NEC member Pallo Jordan accused his colleagues of elevating negotiations to the level of strategy and warned that they risked giving 'away what
we have won on [other] fronts' (1992a:15). SACP Central Committee
member Blade Nzimande accused Slovo of developing a scenario in which
'the masses are absent and, instead, the issue becomes primarily that of trade-
offs between negotiators, constrained by the logic of the negotiations process'
(1992:20). Troubling both were signs that negotiations would replace the
other traditional prongs of the ANC's struggle and produce a corporatist outcome cemented by an élite consensus. Many activists concurred. However, as
writer Anthony Marx observed, the ANC's arsenal had been depleted:

> The ANC's suspension of its armed struggle and reorganisation of under-
> ground structures into legal entities, together with international pressure to
> end sanctions, had by early 1991 weakened three of the congress's 'four pil-
> lars of struggle', leaving mass mobilisation as its only remaining form of
> pressure on the state (1992:264).

Traumatic levels of violence provided the backdrop to these strategic
debates. Fighting continued to rage in KwaZulu-Natal – ostensibly between
ANC and IFP supporters. Transformed from a moribund cultural organization in 1975, Inkatha (the IFP), with a politically adroit Mangosuthu
Buthelezi (a former ANC member) at the helm, achieved a 'political

mobilization of ethnicity to compete for power and privilege'.[18] By manipulating Zulu history and identity, Buthelezi positioned Inkatha as the vehicle for rescuing what he portrayed as a proud but denigrated people and culture.[19] Controlling access to resources in the KwaZulu homeland (via a system of patronage deployed through the homeland administration and networks of appointed chiefs), Inkatha expanded its support in rural areas and extended it into some urban pockets. The strategy was assisted by Inkatha's control of the KwaZulu police and by the often overt support of the apartheid security forces.[20] When the UDF tried to unseat Inkatha-supporting chiefs in rural areas, a *de facto* civil war erupted – pitting the pan-ethnic, nationalist traditions of the ANC against the Zulu chauvinism advanced by Inkatha. This conflict continues today, overlapping and blending with other conflicts – although the tendency within the democratic movement has been to collapse this web of conflict for political, social and economic advantage into the rubric of the *political*.[21]

By the end of 1990, the death toll in political violence had risen 163 per cent over the already high 1989 figures. This was attributable largely to the IFP's attempts to expand its base into townships around Johannesburg. Massacres (such as the attacks on funeral vigils in Sebokeng, Alexandra and Soweto) became commonplace, as did terror attacks on train commuters. Many of the incidents showed evidence or indications of state complicity in the violence – prompting international human rights organizations to accuse the security forces of going about 'business as usual'.[22] Subsequent evidence[23] suggests that the strategy of low-intensity conflict, employed in neighbouring countries to devastating effect, was applied also inside South Africa through covert units such as the cynically named Civil Cooperation Bureau (CCB) and structures of Military Intelligence. These units exploited and exacerbated the multifold lines of tensions coursing through many African townships. Inkatha shock troops were trained in SADF bases and provided with arms, intelligence and logistical support. Reports abounded of police allowing marauding Inkatha gangs access to township areas, not intervening in the attacks or arresting the attackers. Apparently motiveless attacks on train commuters and taxis, combined with the violence of vigilante groups and warlords to severely destabilize African townships, creating a pervasive sense of insecurity, demoralization and disorganization. Attempts by residents and the ANC structures to marshall community defence units turned many townships on the East Rand and in KwaZulu-Natal into virtual war zones. Overlapping were other dynamics – competition for scarce resources, feuding between warlords and criminal gangs, disputes over the control of taxi routes, tensions between settled residents, squatters and hostel dwellers, political conflicts, and more. As Canadian analyst Pierre Beaudet noted, the enduring social and economic crisis thrust some social segments (notably among the youth) 'towards violence and greater marginalisation', making them 'the social base for the emergence of urban gangsterism and political warlordism' (1994:217). For millions of South Africans the constant threat and reality of violence became commonplace.

The view that the NP government was following a 'twin-track strategy' – negotiating with the opposition while simultaneously attempting to destabilize it – became axiomatic within the ANC. The June 1992 Boipatong massacre, in which 48 residents were slaughtered, eventually prompted the ANC to walk out of the Codesa negotiations. It launched a campaign of 'rolling mass action' which unofficially culminated in early September when Ciskei homeland troops mowed down ANC protestors outside Bisho. A mood of panic was palpable in ruling circles. Not only was the patchwork of political allies the NP government had tried to assemble around the negotiating table disintegrating,[24] but there was deep concern whether the ANC could 'control' its supporters, and resume negotiations. On the latter score, their fears were unfounded. The mass action campaign was halted when the NP signed a Record of Understanding with the ANC in late September, 1992. This not only salvaged but reconfigured the negotiations process to orbit primarily around the NP and ANC.[25] Consensus-building became the name of the game, directly giving rise to the strategic debates outlined here, with Joe Slovo's 'strategic perspectives' view holding sway to define the contours of the negotiated settlement. Meanwhile, Mandela had made his views of rank-and-file anger known:

> We are sitting on a time-bomb. The youths in the townships have had over the decades a visible enemy, the government. Now that enemy is no longer visible, because of the transformation taking place. Their enemy now is you and me, people who drive a car and have a house. It's order, anything that relates to order, and it is a very grave situation.[26]

The upshot was a strategic perspective that saddled the ANC with the responsibility of establishing a new political and social consensus – a mission that would become elaborated into the ANC government's nation-building endeavours. At the micro-level, this produced specific political compromises which could later restrict the scope of changes desired by an ANC government.

Another consequence was more encompassing, however. A kind of short-term 'two-stage theory' emerged. Defining the ANC's negotiating strategy was the need to nurture compromises that could yield a settlement. This meant that the ANC – only temporarily, it believed – retreated from positions necessary to establish and safeguard an institutional bedrock for a socio-economic programme that could weaken the structural foundations of the 'two-nation' society. The political/ideological project of nation-building became paramount and supplanted – or at least overshadowed – the socio-economic features of the crisis. 'The tendencies propelling us towards a new 50 per cent solution,' Morris warned at the time, 'lie ... in the downplaying of the social and economic fault lines in our society' – a tendency he detected throughout much of the democratic opposition's history (1993c:8). Societal crisis tended to be cast in political and not economic terms, spawning the assumption that once the political and constitutional issues were resolved, 'the dozing South African "economic giant" would lumber to its feet and cart us off to the land of promise' (Morris, 1993c:9). Nzimande was among the few alliance figures to draw public attention to this legacy. Quoting Mexican sociologist Carlos Vilas, he reminded that:

> ... most important about 'transitions' [initiated by previously repressive regimes] is that 'they do not project into the economic sphere, nor do they provide a framework for any substantial changes in the level of access of subordinate groups to socio-economic resources – by income redistribution, creating employment, improving living conditions, etc.'.[27]

Outlines of the settlement

Interrupted periodically by deadlocks and brinkmanship, three years of formal negotiations ended in late 1993 with a political settlement that detoured significantly from the positions held by both the NP and ANC at the beginning of the process.

The political basis of post-apartheid South Africa would be a liberal-democratic system, as defined in an interim Constitution agreed to in late 1993. Completed and adopted in 1996, the final Constitution replicates much of the 1993 version – with the exception of refinements and nuanced changes introduced in some areas, notably on property rights, access to information, minority rights and the delegation of powers to provincial governments.

The new system is based on universal suffrage in a unitary South Africa; the separation of legislative, executive and judicial powers; multiparty elections every five years; gradual (and circumscribed) delegation of power from central to local levels of government; and the enshrinement of individual and collective rights in a Bill of Rights that ranks among the most progressive in the world.

A Constitutional Court adjudicates disputes arising from the constitution. Parliament comprises two houses: a National Assembly (400 members) and a National Council of Provinces (10 members from each of the nine new provinces). Several parastatal bodies would be created to monitor and advance implementation of the Constitution. These include a Public Protector's Office (to ensure democratic and ethical practices in the public service), a Human Rights Commission, a Commission on Gender Equality, an Electoral Commission (to help organize democratic elections), an

Independent Broadcasting Authority (to regulate the electronic media), an Auditor-General, and a Cultural Commission (to protect minority cultural rights).

The final Constitution had to comply with a set of 33 binding Constitutional Principles[28] which crystallized important compromises agreed to in the final stages of negotiations. Altering these principles requires a two-thirds majority in a constitutional assembly (Parliament). They demand, for instance, that:

- the 'diversity of language and culture' be protected;
- 'collective rights of self-determination in forming, joining and maintaining organs of civil society' be recognized and protected;
- 'the institution, status and role of traditional leadership' be recognized (possibly undermining the commitment to democratic representation at all levels of government);
- exclusive and concurrent powers and functions be delegated to provincial governments;
- national government be prevented from exercising its powers in ways that 'encroach upon the geographical, functional or institutional integrity of the provinces';
- minority parties be enabled to participate in the legislative process; and
- the 'independence and impartiality' of the Reserve Bank be protected.[29]

The Bill of Rights outlaws discrimination on the grounds of 'race, gender, sex, pregnancy, marital status, ethnic or social origin, colour, sexual orientation, age, disability, religion, conscience, belief, culture, language or birth'. It also allows for the declaration of states of emergency under certain circumstances.

Most dramatic was the postponement of majority rule to 1999. Until then, the country would be governed by the GNU, with executive power shared between political parties that won more than five per cent of the popular vote (the ANC, NP and IFP, as it turned out). Consensus-making was thus formalized within the executive in the hope of establishing political stability.

The system contains significant federal elements, reflecting the ANC's belated conversion to the belief that the country requires 'strong national government for national tasks, strong regional government for regional tasks, strong local government for local tasks', in the words of the ANC's Albie Sachs. At the insistence of the NP, IFP and Democratic Party (DP), key powers will be exercised exclusively or concurrently by provincial governments (for instance, provincial governments are forbidden to budget for a deficit but can decide on the allocation of monies within certain parameters). Critics felt this threatened the authority of the central government. But it represented a coup for the NP and IFP, providing each the chance to secure a solid institutional and administrative base in the 1994 election, when the NP triumphed in the Western Cape and the IFP in KwaZulu-Natal. Still, this did not meet the confederate demands of the IFP, which responded by boycotting the final Constitution drafting process.

The terms of the settlement also reflected the influence of forces outside the multiparty negotiations, specifically the IFP and the white far-right. In both cases the destabilizing pressures they exerted were welcomed (if not encouraged) and deflected by the NP onto the ANC. As a result, the ANC made some surprising concessions in the final stages of negotiations.

As part of its attempts to defuse right-wing reaction, it allowed a racist guarantee which reserved 30 per cent of the seats in some local government structures for minorities.[30] According to some interpretations it also afforded minority representatives in municipal councils a 'formal veto over redistributive budgets'.[31] The ANC agreed to support the investigation of the feasibility of an Afrikaner homeland ('volkstaat') by the far-right. Fearful of disloyalty in the security forces, the party also agreed to an amnesty which allows human rights violators to evade criminal and civil action court cases – on the condition that amnesty seekers fully disclose their crimes. Drawing on recent Latin American experiments, a Truth and Reconciliation Commission (TRC) was chosen as a potentially less destabilizing method to pursue human rights abuses (the TRC began functioning in April 1996). The powers of the Zulu monarchy and, less publicly, other traditional leaders through the country were protected, lending politicized ethnicity a menacing lease of life while also threatening to diminish and delay democratization in rural areas. The NP had demanded an 'education clause', allowing parents and students to choose the language of instruction in state or state-assisted schools; eventually, the ANC agreed to a compromise clause guaranteeing that right where it could 'reasonably be provided'. Finally, the ANC agreed to refrain from purging the civil service, thus leaving intact much of the institutional culture and personnel of the old order.[32]

Capital succeeded in fashioning, among others, a crucial detail of the settlement: the Bill of Rights sports a clause protecting property rights. Although diluted in the final Constitution, this limits the circumstances in which the state can expropriate privately-owned property, narrows the scope of a land reform programme[33] and reduces the redistributive options of an ANC government.

The settlement favours capital in another, less obvious respect. The justiciable Bill of Rights provides for constitutional litigation as a pathway towards sabotaging or holding up attempts to push ahead with socio-economic reforms that transcend the boundaries patrolled by capital.[34] Furthermore, the 'independence' of the Reserve Bank (historically intimately attuned and subservient to the needs of capital) now enjoys constitutional protection.[35]

Despite these limitations, the settlement represented a political milestone which, justifiably, earned the admiration and envy of citizens and governments internationally. A seemingly intractable and potentially catastrophic conflict had been resolved, yielding a constitution that ranked among the most liberal in the world. It included guarantees of the right to collective bargaining, to strike (although limited to collective bargaining issues and counterposed by employers' right to lock-out striking workers), to freedom of expression, speech and assembly, to privacy, equality before the law, access to information and to sexual orientation, opening new pathways towards freedom and equality. 'I think we've reached an effective instrument for governing the country, one that does not in any way constitute an obstacle to the process of completely transforming the country into a democratic state,' was ANC and SACP leader Joe Slovo's understandably blithe verdict in early 1994.[36]

The settlement paved the way for the historic 1994 elections which, despite far-right bombing campaigns during the run-up, were not marred by the anticipated bloodshed. The ANC won a landslide victory. Its 62,7 per cent of the vote earned it 252 of the 400 National Assembly seats, putting it well clear of the NP (20,4 per cent of the vote) and the IFP (10,5 per cent).[37] In some provinces, the ANC's share of ballots rose as high as 90 per cent.

Less joyous results awaited the ANC in KwaZulu-Natal and the Western Cape, however. The NP's appeal to coloured and white voters in the Western Cape handed it control of that provincial government in post-apartheid South Africa. The outcome in KwaZulu-Natal was more controversial. Weathering complaints of chaotic logistics and widespread fraud, the Independent Electoral Commission adjusted the results to reflect an allegedly projected outcome. The IFP won the province, its 50 per cent share of votes outstripping the ANC's 32 per cent. To prevent widespread violence in the province, the ANC's national leadership suppressed furious demands by its provincial colleagues that the result be challenged in court.

The results confirmed the ANC's status as by far the most popular and the only national party in South Africa. Even where vanquished, it won a third of the votes, a feat no other party could match. Political and symbolically the threshold of a new South Africa had been crossed.

Hidden contours of the transition

The task assumed by the ANC was to construct and administer a hegemonic project that would be based on a radical break with the exclusionary paradigms enforced under apartheid. The principles of conciliation and concession replaced conflict and triumph as the key catalysts for societal change. Abandoned were visions of change that centred on momentary historical ruptures, the seizure of power, the destruction of the old, and the construction, *ab initio*, of the new. The exclusionary basis of South African society would be replaced with an inclusionary one. The partitioning of South Africa into confederal units was abandoned, likewise the deprival of citizenship and the franchise to the African majority. A century-old ideological model was discarded. This notwithstanding the attempts of the IFP and right-wing Afrikaner organizations to establish federal units – respectively, KwaZulu-Natal and an unspecified 'Afrikaner homeland'.

One cannot underestimate the profundity of these conceptual sea-changes, as Mike Morris has noted:

> All the secure landmarks of the past, the defining features and political geography of the apartheid regime and its counterpart in the liberation movement ... started to crumble. Instead of revolution, negotiation; instead of uncompromising transformation, compromising concession; instead of a violent struggle for the seizure of power, negotiation over the distribution of power; instead of sweeping aside the old order and all who had implemented it, dismantling the old order jointly with its old architects; instead of radical exclusion of the old to the benefit of the new, inclusion of both old and new in a newly created social framework (1993a:11).

The dominant discourse came to orbit around postulated common interests and destinies – rather than difference, contradiction and antagonism – as the fundamental dynamics at work in society. Commonalities (whether authentic or invented) are emphasized and amplified in service of a hegemonic project which, for the first time in South Africa's history, seeks to organize society on the basis of inclusion.

The settlement and the launch of the transition depended on an activated awareness of 'common interests' between the old order and the popular movement – on an acknowledgment that friend and foe have to pass through a gateway of concessions and compromises in order to avert disaster for their respective agendas. This principle of inclusion became the central ideological tenet of the new South Africa. Not only were all South Africans deemed equal in one nation-state, but the reconstruction and development of society would become presented as a common endeavour, hence the intense pressure on the popular sector to 'exercise restraint' in its demands and pursuit of change. The transition proceeded on the basis of mechanisms and structures that attempt to 'reconcile' – even *transform* – conflicting interests into inclusive policies, projects and programmes.

Essentially, this amounted to an attempt to forge a new basis for social consent – an essential ingredient of any sustainable bid to restructure South African society, whether along unequal or more egalitarian lines. The impulse of some leftists to detect in the very principles of inclusion, assimilation and conciliation the seeds of a betrayal and sell-out was wrong.[38] In themselves these principles did not scuttle attempts to marshall a popular transformation project. What mattered were the terms on which inclusion and assimilation occurred – specifically, which social classes' interests would become privileged in the resultant hegemonic project. In the South Africa of 1994, the class content of that project was still undefined. However, as we shall see, several telling clues had emerged.

Evident soon after the 1994 election was a conviction that – in a capitalist country in the post-1989 world – the appeasement of domestic and, crucially, international capital had become unavoidable. Nelson Mandela soon assured investors that 'not a single reference to things like nationalisation' remained in ANC economic policies and that these had been cleansed of anything 'that will connect us with any Marxist ideology'.[39]

Months later Mandela lambasted striking workers in the auto and service sectors for causing instability and putting their interests above those of their compatriots. The auto strike was abruptly called off when the trade and industry minister, with cunning timing, announced the pruning of protective tariffs in that sector. These and other developments (like the property rights clause, the earlier signing of an IMF Letter of Intent, and increasingly strident commitments to macro-economic 'stability') prompted the SACP's Jeremy Cronin to acknowledge that 'real inroads have been made by capital into the ANC ... their arguments are more attractive and more persuasive to a wide range of ANC leadership than the counter-arguments that are less confident, less coherent'.[40]

Not only the counter-arguments were at fault. The ANC negotiated the settlement without a vivid programme geared at dismantling the structural foundations of the 'Two Nation' society.[41] Indeed it was in recognition of this lacuna that trade unionists devised the Reconstruction and Development Programme (RDP), which became touted as the hub of a strategic programme and was adopted by the ANC shortly before the 1994 election. However, the transformative thrust of the RDP was soon dispersed as the ANC sheared its potentially conflictual elements and refashioned it along ostensibly consensual lines.[42]

What the ANC did bring into office was its adeptness at nurturing and consolidating hegemony, which, in the post-1994 context, would be extended to include a much wider range of class forces. As Cronin observed:

> It might be historically equipped to tackle that project, but the problem is whether it is now equipped to be the central vehicle to take forward this transformation project, to deepen the democratic revolution or achieve social-economic transformation.[43]

Once it became the programme of government, the RDP did not represent a coherent strategic programme for popular transformation. Indeed, though for different reasons, it is questionable whether even the vaunted Base

Document did.[44] Neither would the state be re-oriented around a definable social base. The ANC has been *assimilated* into a web of institutional relations, systems and practices tailored to service the interests of (in the first instance) white privilege and (in the final instance) the capitalist class. Compared with its predecessor, the relative autonomy of the democratic state has perhaps *diminished,* furthering curtailing the ANC's ability to redistribute opportunity, infrastructural resources, access to productive activity and institutional power in favour of the popular classes.

The settlement and the 1994 elections in some respects created and in others *punctuated* marked shifts in South African society. The salient achievement was to resolve the political dimension of South Africa's crisis – an outcome desired by both the democratic opposition and the capitalist class. But an organic solution to the crisis requireed more than revising the political basis for hegemonic consent. It also demanded co-ordinated social and economic restructurings – a new development path.

Left unanswered by the settlement was the fundamental question: Which social and economic interests would be privileged by that path? In Morris' words:

> Will the new society perpetuate the highly divisive social elitism of the past, but on a more non-racial basis? Or will it tend towards a more egalitarian system that strives to muffle inherited frictions by redistributing resources and institutional power? (1993c:8)

Broadly sketched, the answer would launch the country in one of two possible directions. The first would see the gradual dismantlement of the country's 'Two Nation' character through the redistribution of resources, power and security in favour of the 'outsiders'. It is on the basis of such strategies that a new, expansive hegemony could be achieved. The other option would entrench the 'Two Nation' society in which a small, increasingly multi-racial enclave of privilege and a massive, impoverished majority co-exist precariously. Social and economic restructuring would benefit narrow layers of society, whilst the costs of that restructuring would be deflected onto the rest of society. Building and maintaining political hegemony is a prerequisite for the success of such a venture and becomes paramount – and would be expressed mainly in the forms of nation-building initiatives. But the basis of that hegemony would gradually become whittled down to the mobilized support of the main beneficiaries of the new growth path, eventually introducing the need for resort to overt coercion.

The convivial ideology underpinning the settlement did not settle or suspend the intense contest to determine which of those outcomes would materialize. That contest continued but on reshaped terrain, in new ways and on new terms. These factors were manifold: the political breakthroughs of the settlement, the opening of new political and social spaces for activity, the assimilation of the new into the old, the ostensible shift from conflict to conciliation, the restructuring of state-civil society relations, the realignment of affinities along class and other lines (even among customary allies in the democratic movement), weakened ideological cohesion and confidence among the democratic forces, South Africa's weak standing in the global economic system, and more. Together they would radically affect the struggles to determine the course and scale of change.

Understood in this manner, the settlement constituted (and inaugurated) not a rupture but a highly ambivalent (and nonetheless dramatic) series of reconfigurations that also extended far beyond the formal political agreements. In some respects these shifts favoured the popular forces; in others they introduced new, or magnified existing difficulties and challenges.

If negotiations started because, as Govan Mbeki noted, 'this was a war without absolute winners',[45] then they also ended without producing a clear victor. This was so not only because of the compromises that produced the settlement. Most importantly, the settlement reshaped the political and ideological bases and affinities on which would proceed the ongoing struggles to determine the nature of a new development path. In short, 1994 marked a sea-change – but in ways and to degrees that far exceeded conventional assumptions.

Notes

1 Anon (1990:10).
2 See, in particular, Friedman (1993b), Sparks (1994), Mandela (1994).
3 Cassius Mandla, *Sechaba* (November, 1985), cited by Lodge (1989:46).
4 Erwin (1989:47). Having apparently abandoned such prescriptions, Erwin was appointed minister of trade and industry in March 1996.
5 Bottomore (1983:195), paraphrasing Gramsci.
6 See Morris and Padayachee (1989); Morris (1993c).
7 See Chapter 5 of this volume.
8 A *hegemonic project* could be defined as 'societally projected policies aimed at concretely resolving particular conflicting (primarily class) interests by defining a socially acceptable national general interest' (Morris & Padayachee, 1989:67).
9 To the extent that, until 1990, it had no economic policy worthy of the description – see below.
10 Memories remained fresh of the events that followed the marginal opening of political space during the early 1980s. Those fears were amplified by the discovery, in 1990, of the SACP-run Operation Vula – essentially a bid to enable the swift resort to underground activities if the negotiations process were abandoned.
11 Mbeki (1996:119). Note Mbeki's retroactive application of the inclusionary rhetoric that would become elaborated in the ANC's nation-building efforts.
12 ANC NEC (1992:48–53).
13 *Op. cit.*
14 *Ibid.*, p. 50.
15 *Ibid.*, p. 53.
16 Comments made to the 'Prospects and Constraints for Transformation' seminar in Johannesburg, November 1994.

17 Slovo (1992:37). Initially Slovo's 'own individual contribution' to debates in the ANC alliance, this perspective was soon adopted by the ANC leadership. See, for instance, the October 1992 'Strategic Perspectives' document drafted by the ANC Negotiations Commission.

18 Mare (1992:3). See also Mare and Hamilton (1987) and Forsyth and Mare (1992).

19 A comprehensive account of the many factors that propelled Inkatha's transformation remains to be written. Hopefully, it will include an examination of the ANC's treatment of ethnic identity (discussed in Chapter 9 of this volume), and a recognition of Inkatha's historical origins in the racist repression of the Zulu *petit bourgeoisie* early in the century. On the latter score, see Cope (1990).

20 Buthelezi in 1985 – two years before the conflict erupted – approached security force leaders for military assistance. In response, the R3,5-million Operation Marion was launched, following a meeting of the State Security Council. A group of 200 Inkatha members received military training at Hippo Camp in the Caprivi Strip and were sent into action against UDF and COSATU supporters in KwaZulu-Natal, with ongoing support from the police and army. These events formed the basis of the trial of 13 top security officials in 1996.

21 See the Human Rights' Commission's 1991 booklet *A New Total Strategy* for a good example of this tendency. For an alternative perspective, see Hindson and Morris (1992:43–59).

22 The violence has been extensively researched and analysed. For examples, see Africa Watch (1991); Human Rights Commission (1991); Everatt (1992); Morris and Hindson (1992). For an overview of the debates, see Marais (1992a).

23 Emerging from the TRC's hearings since April 1996.

24 Its alliance with the IFP ended after the suspension of negotiations.

25 The first Codesa session saw the absurd spectacle of minuscule political parties (dubbed 'one-phone-and-a-fax' parties by observers) accorded nominally equal negotiating weight to the major parties.

26 *The Star*, 15 September 1992, cited by Bond *et al.* (1996:37).

27 Nzimande (1992:17). The quote was drawn from Vilas (1989).

28 The Constitutional Court in September 1996 refused to uphold the final Constitution agreed to four months earlier because it violated some of those principles. Altered accordingly, the Constitution came into effect in December 1996.

29 See 'Schedule 4: Constitutional Principles' of the 1993 *Interim Constitution*, pp. 244–9.

30 Ironically, this recalled the 'group rights' guarantees initially demanded by the NP.

31 See Bond *et al.* (1996:38).

32 Whether this concession was in fact made remains a point of debate. ANC MP Philip Dexter, for instance, has argued that 'nowhere [in the Interim Constitution] is there any guarantee of jobs'. Instead, 'the continuity of public *service*' was guaranteed. See Dexter (1995a:55–7).

33 See Marais (1994b).

34 Of course, it is also available for the defence and advance of popular agendas – an exaggerated potential, however, as the flirtations of popular movements in industrialized countries with constitutionalism have reminded.

35 For a survey of this debate, see Bowles and White (1993).

36 Interview, 'Don't worry, be happy', *Work in Progress*, No. 95 (Feb/March 1994), p. 17.

37 The PAC collapsed in the contest, garnering a mere 1,3 per cent of the vote – less than the urban and largely white DP's 1,7 per cent and the right-wing Freedom Front's 2,2 per cent.

38 See, for instance, Bond *et al.* (1996).

39 Interview published on May Day, 1994, in the *Sunday Times*.
40 Interview with author, October 1994.
41 The ANC's Albie Sachs (now a Constitutional Court judge) admitted as much in late 1993, saying that the ANC had 'no analytical framework at all' and had been reduced to 'merely improvising'. See 'Preparing Ourselves for Power' (interview with Sachs), *Southern Africa Report*, Vol. 9, No. 2 (November 1993), p. 15.
42 The RDP draft the ANC carried into office was an *outline* for such a programme. Its eventual fate, discussed in Chapter 7 of this volume, would reflect, at least provisionally, the outcome of the struggle to determine the class bias of an ANC-managed hegemonic project.
43 Jeremy Cronin, interview with author, October 1994.
44 See Chapter 7 of this volume.
45 Mbeki (1996:119).

CHAPTER FOUR

The battleground of the economy

South Africa entered the transition with an economy buckled by almost two decades of steadily worsening difficulties which manifested in earnest after the 1973 oil shock.[1] Mainstream economists sought solace in the ephemeral cyclical upswings that occurred sporadically (notably the gold-led improvement of 1979–80 and the fleeting consumption-led upturn of 1983–4). But key indicators betrayed the onset of a structural crisis, which Stephen Gelb (1991:6; 1994:3–4) detected in:

- the feeble GDP growth rate, which descended from its 6 per cent average during the 1960s to 1,8 per cent in the 1980s, eventually plunging into the negative range (–1,1 per cent) in the early 1990s;[2]
- declining rates of gross fixed investment (which plunged as low as –18,6 per cent in 1986, and stayed negative from 1990 to 1993), and high rates of capital flight;
- low rates of private investment which led to under-utilization of manufacturing plant capacity (dropping from 90 per cent in 1981 to 78 per cent in 1993) and declining competitiveness;
- plummeting levels of personal savings which, as a proportion of disposable income, dropped from 11 per cent in 1975 to 3 per cent in 1987;
- very high unemployment, and the economy's inability to create enough new jobs to absorb even a fraction of new entrants into the labour market,[3] a trend exacerbated by under-investment in labour-intensive sectors; and
- chronic balance of payments difficulties.

In broad terms, the crisis reflected the breakdown of the post-war accumulation strategy based on primary product exports and inward industrialization (including import-substitution), based on a violently regimented labour supply. The latter feature fuelled increasingly powerful cycles of resistance that ultimately required the profound restructuring of the social, political and ideological basis of this strategy. It also imposed structural limits on the growth of domestic demand, inhibited productivity and led to a severe shortage of skilled labour.

Export earnings remained largely dependent on raw materials (mainly minerals) and were vulnerable to exchange rate fluctuations and fluctuating commodity prices, particularly the gold price, which began dropping sharply in 1982.[4] South Africa did not evade the trend, evident in other industrializing countries, whereby even short periods of sustained economic growth deepened reliance on imported capital goods, leading to balance of payment problems. As Kaplan has noted, South Africa's capital goods sector performed relatively well until the early 1970s when its expansion slowed profoundly – with 'adverse repercussions on the balance of payments, on the development of skills, and the generation and diffusion of more productive technologies through the wider economy' (1991:176).

In the throes of a balance of payments crisis, the NP government in 1982 sought an IMF standby loan of R1,24 billion.[5] Shortly afterwards, exchange controls were lifted for non-residents, triggering a large outflow of capital, which swelled further during the 1984–7 uprisings. Compounding this were the financial sanctions of the late 1980s which had international creditors refusing to roll-over loans or issue new ones. Fiscal spending soared and the budget deficit increased, as the state sought to meet its external 'defence' and internal 'law and order' needs, and bankrolled its reform initiatives.

Against this backdrop, fixed investment levels crumpled from 26,5 per cent of GDP in 1983 to well below 20 per cent in the late 1980s (eventually dropping to 15,7 per cent in 1993).[6] By 1990, net investment was hovering near the zero mark.[7]

The economy was bedridden. Partially in compliance with IMF's prescriptions, the apartheid state responded by applying severe deflationary measures. It tightened monetary policies, hoisted interest rates to encourage savings (with scant success), froze consumer subsidies and off-loaded the fiscal burden onto the poor by increasing indirect taxation. The overall effect was to lower living standards – one of the key, often overlooked dynamics that fuelled the 1984–7 uprisings.[8] It also introduced the dual exchange rate mechanism in a bid to stem capital outflows.

The adjustments, however, failed to address the structural factors hobbling the economy:

- Low investment rates, linked with the tendency of the private sector to direct its funds abroad.
- The state's failure to reverse the latter trend by encouraging or compelling productive investment by business, which 'has led to an orgy of speculative investment and the shrinking of the manufacturing sector in the past 20 years'.[9]
- A shortage of skilled and a surplus of unskilled, poorly educated and low-productivity labour – the cumulative result of business treating

'black workers as a replaceable factor of production rather than as a human resource'.[10]

■ Poor, conflict-ridden industrial relations.

■ Industrial decay, which was reflected in ageing capital stock, limited capital goods production, and the failure to develop exports by beneficiating raw materials and expanding the scope of the manufacturing sector. This compounded the poor export performance in manufactures, compared to other middle-income countries. Matters improved slightly during the early 1990s, but without reflecting a 'fundamental shift in underlying conditions', according to MERG (1993:212).

■ Low investment in research and development, with most technological development occurring in the armaments and telecommunications industries.

■ A heavy bias against the small and medium-sized business sector.

■ Maldistribution of social infrastructure (such as housing, education facilities, health care and transport) which restricted labour productivity.

■ Rampant poverty, entrenched by a very high unemployment rate, which has stifled productive potential and domestic demand for manufactured goods, the latter having been depressed by deflationary policies.

The effects of these inherited weaknesses worsened during the negotiations period. Between early 1989 and late 1993 the economy sank into its longest-ever recession, registering negative real economic growth until 1993, when a strong upturn in agricultural production (after the acute 1991–2 drought) brought some respite. The mood among economic élites was unreservedly downcast, with Reserve Bank governor Chris Stals warning that the country would plunge into ungovernability by 1996 if the annual growth rate remained at around 1 per cent while the population grew by 2,5 per cent.[11]

Other macroeconomic indicators confirmed the gravity of the situation. Ominously, real fixed investment growth remained negative (improving slightly from –7,4 per cent in 1991 to –3,1 per cent in 1993). Private (non-housing) investment amounted to 10 per cent of GDP, well below the 16 per cent deemed necessary to sustain positive economic growth. Domestic savings stood at 16,5 per cent of GDP in mid-1994, down from the 24 per cent mark (achieved in the 1980s) the Reserve Bank calculated was needed for an annual economic growth rate of 3,5 per cent. Per capita disposable income continued to decline (by –11 per cent in real terms between 1980 and 1993).[12]

The impact of these trends was graphically visible in the performances of each economic sector, with disastrous effects on employment levels. The precise unemployment rate is controversial, though. The Ministry of Finance in the early 1990s pegged it at 19,3 per cent; a SALDRU survey put it at about 30 per cent in 1993, the 1994 October Household Survey found it to be 32,6 per cent, while some analysts believe it is closer to 50 per cent. The ILO, using a 'strict' definition, believes it is below 20 per cent, 'still a very high figure [which] should not be belittled'.[13] More than 400 000 formal sector jobs were lost (excluding agriculture) between 1989 and 1993;[14] almost 8 in every 100 positions became redundant.[15] The trend was long-term: the labour absorption capacity of the economy declined from 97 per cent in the 1960s, to 22 per cent in the 1980s, to 7 per cent between 1985 and 1990.[16]

The manufacturing sector was in the doldrums. Local demand remained sluggish and the sector had failed to penetrate export markets – indeed, between 1960 and 1988, manufactured products' share of total exports slumped from 31 per cent to 12 per cent, while growth in manufacturing output in the same period dropped from 9,9 per cent to –1,2 per cent.[17] One result was massive labour attrition from the early 1980s onwards leading to the loss of 200 000 jobs in the metal and related sectors alone since 1982.[18]

The mining sector, responsible for 65,6 per cent of export earnings in 1991, shed 30 per cent of its workforce between 1987 and 1995, with employment levels tumbling from 752 460 to 512 722. Responding to low commodity prices on the world market, companies shut or scaled down mines they viewed as marginal and unprofitable. Employment levels in the two largest sectors (gold and coal) shrank by 35 per cent and 47 per cent, respectively. The platinum sector showed a 7 per cent increase.[19] Analysts expect mining employment to continue dropping, largely due to the sector's vulnerability to 'international economic fluctuations and competition', the lack of major gold fields discoveries and the fact that 'marginal mines become viable or not by virtue of small changes in the gold price' (ILO, 1996:279).

Agriculture's contribution to GDP dropped steadily, from 9 per cent (1965) to 6 per cent (1988), wreaking an estimated 30 per cent drop in employment over the same period.[20] Since the early 1990s, farmers have sacked thousands more, in anticipation of new legislation aimed at bolstering the rights of rural workers and labour tenants. The sector remained hampered by periodic droughts, low levels of return on investment, low levels of liquidity and a steady build-up of debt.

The negligible welfare provisions for unemployed Africans have resulted in income-earners supporting jobless family members and friends.[21] Rising unemployment and falling nominal wage increases (down from 18,3 per cent in 1989 to 11,1 per cent in 1993) have put increased strain on such cross-subsidization as a makeshift safety net.[22]

Meanwhile, the decline of the formal economy was accompanied by the exponential rise of an underground economy, commonly referred to as crime. A 1996 Nedcor survey claimed that crime cost the country R31,3 billion, ignoring the fact that the bulk of this money continues to circulate within the South African economy in ways that range from basic consumption to real estate and productive investment (shopping complexes in rural towns, transport firms, small- and medium-scale enterprises, retail outlets, etc.). Moreover, this underground economy displays astounding levels of innovation and sophistication,[23] and is able to take advantage of the opportunities opened up by globalization to operate outside increasingly porous and ineffective national laws and regulatory systems, as well as to form intricate cartels, associations and business networks.[24]

One potentially positive factor was the country's relatively low external debt to GDP ratio. In 1990 this stood at 27,3 per cent – 'lower than for any Latin American country in that year, with the exception of Chile, [and] lower than for all ASEAN countries' (ILO, 1996:31). By 1994, it had dropped to 22,9 per cent. The country, therefore, had not yet stepped into a 'debt trap' – leaving the new government some latitude in devising an alternative economic strategy.

Balance of payments problems persisted, as the lifting of sanctions and expectations of an economic upturn precipitated an increase in imports (largely luxury items, and new machinery and technology). Great faith was staked on a sharp rise in foreign capital inflows off-setting these difficulties. That hope stemmed partially from a belief that the disinvestment of the 1980s had been strictly politically motivated. Less uplifting were the reminders from Blumenfeld, among others, that the reasons lay elsewhere. South Africa had become an unprofitable zone for investment, as:

> ... rand-denominated profits had been significantly reduced by the long-running recession, and, via the falling external value of the rand, there had been further serious reductions in attributable foreign currency value of these profits. In short, the fundamental problem of the relationship between political risk and financial rate of return ... had finally reasserted itself with a vengeance'.[25]

In response, South Africa's caretaker government (the Transitional Executive Council, which included the ANC) in late 1993 approached the IMF for a $850 million five-year loan in terms of a special facility for countries suffering balance of payment problems. Surprising many observers, the government signed a controversial letter of intent which, as Padayachee recorded, 'was at pains to point to the dangers of increases in real wages in the private and public sector [and] stressed the need to control inflation, promised monetary targeting, trade and industrial liberalization, and repeatedly espoused the virtues of "market forces" over "regulatory interventions"'.[26] Several economists argued that the IMF would have accepted a less conservative letter of intent, suggesting that, even at this early stage, an ideological predisposition towards neo-liberal orthodoxy had taken hold within the ANC leadership.

Clearly visible in that letter were the parameters of the dominant discourse around 'realistic' options for economic restructuring. The NP government and important sections of big business had since the late 1980s already begun implementing elements of a neo-liberal accumulation strategy. This attempted to restrict the state's involvement in the economy by withdrawing it from the provision of goods and services (through privatization programmes, deregulation and fiscal stringency) and by limiting its role to establishing the broad economic parameters that could optimize the operation of market forces (Gelb, 1991:29–30). The continuation of that strategy, though, was by no means guaranteed.

A flood of economic scenarios and policy frameworks was generated while political negotiations proceeded. Business organizations spearheaded this flurry of interventions, aided by the 'Washington consensus' and the remnants of the high tide of Reaganism and Thatcherism, as they sought to forestall the possible adoption of a new economic strategy that might be predicated on increased controls over capital. These intercessions meshed neatly with a political strategy that could meet the demands for majority rule – but, as Morris foresaw, with minimal concessions to demands for restructuring the economic and social spheres in favour of the black majority:

> The thrust of this strategy would be to establish hegemonic consent by politically appealing to the material interests of those classes of the black population who are to become the greatest beneficiaries of a '50 percent solution'. Those on the other side of the divide would be symbolically accommodated but their material needs would not be systematically catered for (1991:57).

Some redistribution would occur, but 'on a differential basis, and over a relatively long time-scale'.[27]

Within the democratic movement, meanwhile, two exercises (carried out by the Economic Trends Groups and the Macroeconomic Research Group) apparently sought to dislodge this 'Two Nation' mould described by Morris – by reconciling the imperatives of growth and redistribution within a new accumulation strategy. Before detailing the outcome of those contests it is necessary to briefly review the socio-economic havoc the new government would preside over.

The contours of inequality

Socio-economic indices provide a glaring testament to the economic decline and the social costs of South Africa's former growth path. There is no[28] guarantee, however, that a qualitatively different growth path will materialize from the mêlée of class interests and agendas at play since 1994. The danger is that the pursuit of consensualism within an overall context that favours neo-liberal options will produce policies that do not meld into a coherent strategy and, instead, prolong the crisis – a crisis that, in the past two decades, has reinforced and deepened disparities that rank among the worst in the world.

Inequality between rich and poor has increased dramatically since 1975. The World Bank describes South Africa as one of world's most unequal economies, with 51,2 per cent of annual income going to the richest 10 per cent of the population (2 per cent more than in 1975) and less than 3,9 per cent of income earned by the poorest 40 per cent (1,3 per cent less than in 1975).[29] South African's Gini coefficient[30] is 0,68, worse than that of the Bahamas, Brazil or Jamaica (and 33 other developing countries), according to a study on income patterns by the HSRC and University of Natal economists.[31] The poorest half of the population accounts for only 10 per cent of consumption, while for the richest 5 per cent the figure is 40 per cent.[32]

These inequalities correspond largely but *not exclusively* to racial divisions. Among Africans huge disparities have opened. The mean income of the lowest-earning 40 per cent of African households declined by almost 40 per cent between 1975 and 1991, while that of the richest 20 per cent of African households (representing 5,6 million people) soared by 40 per cent, 'making them the most upwardly mobile race group, as black professionals, skilled workers and entrepreneurs benefitted from the erosion of apartheid'.[33] In 1975 less than 10 per cent of the richest 20 per cent of households were African; 16 years later the figure had risen to 26 per cent. Interestingly, the poorest 40 per cent of white households' incomes dropped by 40 per cent, while incomes of almost all Asian and 80 per cent of 'coloured' households rose in same period; the richest 20 per cent whites' incomes remained stable. Much has been made of rising poverty among whites, but the phenomenon has been grossly exaggerated: less than 0,5 per cent of whites (20 000 people) were living in poverty in 1993 – compared to 54 per cent of Africans, 25 per cent of coloureds, and 8 per cent of Asians.[34]

South Africa's class and social structures have been significantly restructured. A much more highly differentiated class structure amongst the black population is evolving, including a formidable black middle class and professional stratum, and a tiny economic élite – leading McGrath and Whiteford to conclude that 'the country's maldistribution is increasingly shifting from being race- to class-based' (1994:50). The ILO has also detected evidence of a drop in inter-racial inequality. In 1980 inter-racial inequality constituted 65 per cent of general earnings inequality; by 1993 this had dropped to 42 per cent (1996:21).

These trends became manifest in the 1980s and stemmed from rising wages earned by skilled workers, declining employment opportunities for unskilled workers, the easing of apartheid proscriptions in the economy and the rise of African entrepreneurs (supported by the corporate sector). Homeland bureaucracies played an important role in the process. They were transformed into burgeoning élites, with ministers and officials often utilising their positions in, or links into homeland government structures to build up lucrative business ventures (in retail, transport, construction, property and agriculture). In the rural areas clusters of African entrepreneurs emerged, a trend that has accelerated dramatically in urban townships. There, sophisticated criminal enterprises also intersect with legitimate business empires. Affirmative action programmes are propelling tens of thousands of young, professional Africans into the corporate sector and into well-paying positions in state structures.

There is, in other words, considerable redistribution of wealth occurring in South Africa – but at the expense of the poorest 40 per cent of the population. The Whiteford and McGrath study warns that:

> ... if this trend continues, it could mean that the new government could be associated with black privilege and the growth of a black elite, although [the trend] started under the previous government.[35]

When these figures are disaggregated further an even more disturbing picture emerges, showing the gender, age, and regional contours of inequality in South Africa.

Absolute poverty is largely a rural phenomenon. Africans living in rural areas constitute 70 per cent of South Africa's poor, with the majority of those households headed by or containing only women.[36] In those areas, only 7 per cent of households have access to flush toilets, 11 per cent to electricity, 5 per cent to garbage collection. Compare this to urban areas, where comparable figures for Africans were 72 per cent, 58 per cent and 80 per cent.[37]

Regional disparities are also striking. According to one survey, per capita income in the richest former province was, in 1989, 50 times higher than in the poorest former homeland.[38] Of the current nine provinces, Eastern Cape and Northern Province have poverty rates higher than 70 per cent, while unemployment rates there and in KwaZulu-Natal are higher than 45 per cent.[39]

Inequality is most fiercely visited upon women, preponderantly African women and especially in rural areas. The most horrifying index of violence is against women, most commonly in the form of battery and sexual abuse. Reported cases of rape and attempted rape soared from 20 458 in 1989 to 36 888 in 1995 (but prosecutions dropped from 10 104 to 8 553 in the same period).[40] Women (of all racial groups) are more likely to be unemployed than men, with almost twice as many African and Asian women unemployed than men. A significant number perform non-wage household and subsistence farm labour, according to the 1993 SALDRU Survey, which found more than 70 per cent of African women aged 16–24 were unemployed. The ILO has found that poverty among African women is linked to the very low wages they earn, prompting it to urge that this group receive 'the highest priority in the development of labour market policy' (ILO, 1996:118). SALDRU also found that Africans aged 16–34 were more than twice as likely to be unemployed as those aged 35 and upwards. The same ratio held, broadly, for coloured and Asian South Africans.

Overcrowding, environmental degradation and poor social infrastructure impels tens of thousands of Africans to flee the former homelands and seek salvation in and around overcrowded townships. In South African's most populous province, Gauteng, surveys have found hostel rooms designed for two people occupied by up to two families, while in formal townships up to 11 people live on each stand (6–7 in three-room houses and 3–4 in a backyard shack).[41] Intensely marginalized squatter communities mushroom on the urban periphery, their residents surviving far below the poverty line on intermittent income drawn from casual labour, informal merchanting (including the circulation of stolen goods), and remittances from working family members and friends. The influx is swelled by retrenched farmworkers. The urbanization rate has risen to 60 per cent, contributing to a housing shortage of at least 1,3 million units. According to the National Housing Forum, 240 000 houses must be built annually merely to keep up with the growth in South African's population.

The crisis extends – in differentiated fashion – into every aspect of black South African's lives. Poor education services combine with the lack of job prospects and social disintegration, resulting in only 11 per cent of Africans graduating from high school (the figure for whites is 70 per cent). Low investment by the apartheid state in the reproduction of African labour has left African communities bereft or badly lacking in basic infrastructure (sewage systems, electricity, piped water, waste removal), support services (hospitals, health clinics) and recreational facilities (sports grounds, libraries, community centres). Since the 1980s, state spending in these areas rose substantially, as socio-economic upliftment schemes were introduced in targeted townships. Still, by 1991, the utility monopoly Eskom estimated that 60–70 per cent of the overall population did not have access to electricity. In all these respects, squatters and hostel dwellers in urban areas, and farm labourers and subsistence farmers in rural areas are hardest hit.[42]

Such statistics, as historian Colin Bundy has reminded, present a world of averages, patterns and contours. They cannot convey the experience of intense poverty and inequality,

> ... its texture: the dull ache of deprivation, the acute tensions generated by violence and insecurity, the intricacies of survival and all its emotions – despair, hope, resentment, apathy, futility and fury.[43]

Those dimensions have become buried even deeper, as expressions of deprivation and trauma are encoded as social deviance, and crime becomes abstracted from its socio-political and socio-economic contexts.

It comes as no surprise that amidst such violently induced deprivation crime has become commonplace,[44] with an absolute increase in crime since 1980. More than 20 000 South Africans were murdered in 1995 (resulting in one of the highest murder rates in the world), while as many attempted murders occurred.[45] Cases of housebreaking, robbery, rape, assault and drug trafficking increased from 1991 onwards, while police claimed that 481 crime syndicates were operating in or from the country in 1996.[46] Most dramatic has been the increase in vehicle hijackings, which more than doubled between 1990 (6 043 cases) and 1995 (12 531).[47] Crime, like poverty, is unevenly spread across the country. When the incidence of serious crimes was measured (per 100 000 people), KwaZulu-Natal, Northern Province and Gauteng appeared hardest hit.[48] Amplified (and often distorted) by media coverage, such figures have spawned a 'crime panic', with polls suggesting most South Africans demand tougher sentencing and the return of the death penalty. Disturbing, too, is the proliferation of weapons in private hands, many of them acquired in an illegal arms trade with roots in the apartheid state's arming of surrogate forces in neighbouring countries during the 1980s. In the midst of all this, private security companies have flourished. There were 3 300 such firms operating in 1996, employing more than 110 000 'security officers'.[49]

Many factors have contributed to this crime trend. Political transitions from authoritarian to democratic systems generally seem to be accompanied by rising crime rates, as 'the bonds holding the society together are loosened in a period of instability'.[50] State apparatuses tasked with maintaining 'law and order' had become thoroughly delegitimized, while the flux of the transition increased the internal dysfunction of these structures for which 'combatting crime [had been] subservient to the policing of apartheid and the maintenance of internal security'.[51] By most reckonings, the standard of policing is poor. A study by US consultants McKinsey in early 1997 found that 70 per cent of staff time was devoted to administration and only 30 per cent to policing.[52] Police corruption, too, remains rampant: Gauteng province alone investigated 8 300 crimes involving police between 1994 and 1996.[53] Incongruously, a moratorium was placed on new hirings in the police service, despite figures suggesting as many as 5 000 police workers were leaving the force annually – due largely to low pay, demoralization and dangerous working conditions.

The anti-crime initiatives forged in townships during the 1970s and 1980s (and generally linked to anti-apartheid structures) all but collapsed during the transition. Some commentators (notably within the SAIRR) have argued also that the 'culture of ungovernability' nurtured during the 1980s helped establish a generalized disdain for authority structures. There is also anecdotal evidence that racial antagonism – which has been suppressed within the consensual rubric of the new South Africa – is occasionally expressed in the form of crime. Indeed, one writer has suggested that 'urban crime has become a replacement for the civil war that never happened'.[54] The signs of social trauma are distressingly evident in many other respects, as well.

Basic elements of social cohesion are lacking, with unhappy implications for efforts to build a nation. The roles of traditionally stabilizing and unifying social institutions like family structures, churches or community bodies have declined or disintegrated, leaving the country's tattered social and moral fabric largely unattended.[55] This is reflected in the frequent resort to violence in conflict situations, low social tolerance, alcoholism and drug abuse.[56] Much of the violent crime is *introverted* and takes the forms of wife battery, rape and molestation within family or friendship circles, fratricide (a large number of murder victims are friends or family members, especially women) and suicides (particularly among whites, where it often includes the entire family).

Affordable and accessible counselling and support services are at a premium, despite the warnings of psychiatric workers that 'as a country, South Africans are exhibiting symptoms which add up to Post-Traumatic Stress Disorder'.[57] British psychiatrist Dr Mark Nathan has warned that:

> ... there is so much mental trauma in this country that as a psychiatrist it is difficult to distinguish classic psychiatric symptoms from a situation where people have simply reached the end of their tether.[58]

Social researchers in the early 1990s 'discovered' a 'lost generation' of youth with little education, agitated political consciousness, poor job prospects, and prone – *en masse*, it seemed – to violence and other 'anti-social' behaviour. Dismissive caricatures of this sort have been rightfully criticized.[59] But the social and political marginalization of large numbers of African youth is confirmed by a growing body of research.[60] In 1995, only one in every 20 youths who finished high school – against all odds – was likely to get formal employment. Youth have been subjected to a culture of systematic neglect, not only by institutions and social processes but within their family structures. Ideologically, African youth have been thoroughly demonized, though the assumption of an allegedly terminal alienation among them is not borne out by research.[61] It is among youth that many observers expect the contradiction between high hopes and lowly realities to flare. Plans to 'reincorporate' these sections of youth into society range from the coercive (draft them into semi-militarized social service and public works projects) to the welfarist (provide better recreational facilities and education opportunities). Happier are the attempts to assemble a national youth development policy that differentiates among youth and goes beyond approaching 'youth merely as potentially productive units in the labour market, or numbers in an education strategy'.

The social desolation is reflected in long catalogues of equally painful statistics. Overcoming such inheritances clearly requires massive efforts to
redistribute resources, security, opportunity and power to the benefit of the
disadvantaged majority. That endeavour is inevitably and deeply entangled
with the need to remedy the country's economic crisis. South Africa,
though, has suffered the misfortune of embarking on such a quest in a historical epoch rocked by seismic shifts in the ideological, political and economic spheres, on a global scale. Few of the verities and possibilities, at
hand only two decades ago, seem to have survived intact or unchallenged.
Any bid to reconstruct the country along more equitable lines has to contend with that context, which deserves some elaboration.

The weight of globalization

That the world has shifted on its foundations is irrefutable. The effects of
collapse of the Soviet bloc have been probed extensively elsewhere. Suffice
to say that the USA has emerged as the single global superpower, commanding massive military force and hegemonic power. Through the global suffu-
sion of its culture, diplomatic and economic pressures, and its subordination of international institutions (notably the IMF, World Bank and UN), it
wields unparalleled influence on a global scale. At the same time, the comparative significance of many developing countries (which stemmed largely
from their geo-political positions within the Cold War context) have all but
vanished. Gone is the partial acknowledgment in previous decades that
countries of the South could choose their own economic systems and that
the imbalances and inequities they suffered required, as Rob Davies has
written, 'some special measures and concessions'. Instead, they are subjected to 'a growing assertiveness and prescriptiveness', with neo-liberal
policies 'held out as universally applicable panaceas and the only road to
growth and development' (1992a:1). Meanwhile, progressive movements
everywhere have been thrown into disarray as their material benefactors
disappeared, their strategic options narrowed and their ideological moorings seemed to dissolve.

The hopes of a 'new world order' of burgeoning prosperity and happiness, however, proved unfounded. For it is equally true that the world
approaches the end of the 20th century in the throes of a profound and
complex crisis – not the least because of 'the apparent failure of all programmes, old and new, for managing or improving the affairs of the human
race' (Hobsbawm, 1996:563).

Occurring with a seemingly relentless momentum and on a disastrous
scale is the dissolution of nation-states, the proliferation of civil wars that
assume the scale of genocide (Bosnia and Rwanda), the rise of extreme
forms of nationalism (sometimes wedded to religious 'fundamentalism'),
the steadily widening gulf of inequality between and within countries, the

economic and geo-political marginalization of whole regions, the ecological havoc wrought in even the most remote parts of the globe, and the renewed spread of poverty-related and other diseases which only a decade ago seemed to have been contained, even conquered.

These developments are intimately linked to profound changes at the economic level. Most obvious is the fact that capitalism is today the dominant world system. This has accelerated and expanded, since the 1970s, the process of so-called globalization which is characterized principally by transnational production, freer passage of commodities, the dominance of finance capital, the increasing authority of supra-national organizations and the rapid development and deployment of new labour-saving or labour-replacing technologies. These developments have been augmented by other trends, mainly the 'shrinking state' and diminished national sovereignty. The latter is commonly associated with the globalized economy but should not be confused with it, for its well-spring lies in a particular ideological response to globalization: neo-liberalism. Indeed, the experiences of east Asian countries show that the reduced state is not an integral element of globalization, but an ideological appendage to it.[62]

Labour-intensive industries now migrate from high-cost rich countries to some low-cost countries on the periphery, with potential hosts luring investments with high growth rates, subsidies, tax breaks, *laissez-faire* export processing zones and by guaranteeing transnational corporations' liberty to repatriate profits. These shifts of production are uneven – of the 42 'low-income' countries, 26 were attracting zero net foreign investment in 1990. Only 22 of the 100 low- and middle-income countries experienced substantial investment, the bulk of them in south-east Asia.[63]

In terms of their relevance in the global economy, whole regions have virtually dropped off the world map, notably sub-Saharan Africa, which remains linked to the world economy primarily through its heavy indebtedness although even its ability to attract loan finance has become limited.[64] There, as Colin Leys has noted, 'most people are facing a future in which not even bare survival is assured ... they are being made into "supernumeraries" of the human race' (1994:34).

Overall, Africa's share of world trade plummeted from 6 per cent in 1980 to 2,6 per cent in 1989,[65] while many countries have suffered substantial disinvestment by foreign companies. Per capita GDP in sub-Saharan Africa fell by an average 0,8 per cent annually in real terms since 1970, although stronger capital flows into some countries since 1995 have spurred hope of an 'African renaissance'.[66] The World Bank claims that half of the 48 sub-Saharan countries' economies grew by at least 5 per cent from 1994 to 1996. However, the performances seem more closely linked to higher commodity prices and good rains than to the adoption of neo-liberal policies. Ghana is often hailed as an African success story, its GDP having soared by

25 per cent between 1980 and 1995 on the back of massive aid flows and a fierce structural adjustment programme. But 'employment actually fell in that period and the greatest contribution to that fall was made by export industries, notably mining'.[67]

New production technologies are causing economies to shed jobs much faster than they can replace them, encouraging the widespread belief that one of the fundamental goals of both socialist and social-democratic projects – full employment – has become a 'pipe dream'.[68] Unemployment is now re-garded as a structural (not a cyclical) feature as manufacturing jobs are lost at alarming rates in many industrialized countries. In the USA, 'from 1979 and 1992, productivity increased by 35% while the workforce shrank by 17%' (Rifkin, 1995b:18). By 1994, only 17 per cent of workers were active in manufacturing, compared to 33 per cent in 1950.[69] Some of these jobs have been transferred into the service sector; by the 1980s, for instance, more Americans were employed in McDonald's than in the steel industry.[70] The introduction of new technologies is removing jobs in the service (especially clerical work in banking and finance) and public sectors (where the trend is accelerated by political commitments to trim public employment). Structural or not, the trend is not restricted to the industrialized countries. Mech-anization in Brazilian automobile factories, for example, has caused massive labour redundancies, despite the comparatively cheap cost of labour.

Equally unrelenting is the pressure for trade liberalization, whereby goods and services (but not labour) are afforded virtually unhindered pas-sage across national borders. Translated into national economic strategies this has produced the fetish of export-led industrialization and growth. The sanguine view holds that the benefits of liberalization accrue to all, narrow-ing the chasm between rich and poor countries (provided they display the requisite competitiveness). This has not happened, as Hobsbawm reminds:

> The real GDP per capita of sub-Saharan Africa declined from 14% of that of the industrialized countries to 8% between 1960 and 1987, that of the 'least-developed' countries (which included both African and non-African coun-tries) from 9% to 5% (1995:424).

Ideologically, free trade has become an almost sacred ingredient of the global economy, despite the controversial effects of the North American Free Trade Agreement (linking the USA, Canada and Mexico). The agree-ment reached in 1994 at the Uruguay Round of GATT established a new world trade order which, according to an OECD and World Bank study, would yield a $213 billion increase in world income. Yet, free trade is hon-oured more in the breach than through observance by successful exporting Asian economies, including Japan.

Since the mid-1980s, as Kevin Watkins has observed, 'the enthusiastic commitment of northern governments to free market principles has been second only to their enthusiasm for protectionist practices' (1994:61). Concessions won by the USA and European countries during the Uruguay Round of GATT allow industrialized countries to protect certain domestic industries against rampant free trade. In some cases relatively high tariff barriers will remain in place until shortly before the deadline of 2005, in others non-tariff barriers (such as 'anti-dumping' duties, 'orderly marking arrangements' and 'voluntary import restraints') have been retained. Noting this trend, former NP finance minister of South Africa, Derek Keys, complained to the annual IMF meeting in 1992 that:

> ... the trade policies of especially the industrial countries continue to be characterised by unjustifiable market distortions, generous subsidies and protectionism ... Yet ... developing countries are expected to show a sustained commitment to sound macroeconomic policies and structural adjustments, while also addressing the problems of poverty, the environment, human resources and democratisation.[71]

Few developing countries have access to, or are politically able to exercise, these privileges (prompting the African group of countries at GATT to admit that 'the impact of the market access arrangements looks quite bleak'[72]), although the south-east Asian experiences suggest that the presumed impotency is not terminal.

The OECD/World Bank study referred to earlier was candid on what awaited developing countries. It calculated that less than one-third of the anticipated $213 billion windfall would go to developing countries (China and a few south-east Asian countries being the main beneficiaries), while sub-Saharan Africa would lose about $1,6 billion in income due to the loss of privileges in the European market.[73] Moreover, the anticipated growth in world trade had slowed demonstrably by 1996, 'when on average the rate of growth of world exports in volume terms fell to only 4%, from the 8,5% achieved in the previous year' (Ghosh, 1997:7).

At face value, these developments seem at odds with the push towards free trade, though only if one ignores the underlying interests, two of which bear mentioning. Firstly, there is the fear that unchecked protectionism would unleash protracted and debilitating trade wars between industrialized countries as they seek to assist corporations in penetrating new sectors and markets abroad, and, conversely, to defend corporations against such penetration. Secondly (and related to that concern), the ability of countries to erect trade barriers to defend industries located on their territories is seen to stifle the growth and expansion of transnational corporations. Bluntly put, the new world trade order is an attempt to resolve growing trade-related tensions and contradictions within the industrialized world in favour of transnational corporations and a few countries (principally the USA), at the (almost incidental) expense of the world's poorer countries. Its global application stems from the need to ease penetration of the markets of OECD countries and, significantly, the newly-industrialized countries of south-east Asia (and similar success stories that might emerge in the decades ahead). It has little to do with any pressing desire to penetrate, *en masse*, low-income sub-Saharan African countries. These command negligible interest and importance in a world where 'all developed countries except the USA sent a smaller share of their exports to the Third World in 1990 than in 1938', and where Western countries (including the USA) 'sent less than one fifth of their exports in 1990'.[74]

It is not surprising that the ideology of neo-liberalism – diminishing the role of the state in society and unleashing the supposedly (self-)corrective powers of unfettered market processes – should have gained currency during a period marked by such changes. Neo-liberalism represents a political/ideological effort to ride the tide of globalization in the best possible interests of the most powerful sets of national economic élites. Its political triumph followed (rather than precipitated) the inability of the left to fashion a viable strategic response to the globalization.

Yet, measured against its stated objectives, neo-liberalism has failed demonstrably – and not only in the former socialist states, where the enforcement of the 'Washington consensus' has wrought cataclysmic results, but also in the UK and USA.[75] It did not halt or even slow the UK's economic regression, which emerged from the Thatcher era with a manufacturing growth rate that ranked 19th out of the 22 OECD countries (NIEP, 1996:17). Between 1979 and 1983 that economy plunged into a deep recession; inflation was lowered but at the cost of a spiralling unemployment rate which rose from 5,4 per cent to 11,8 per cent over the same period,[76] with some three million jobs lost in the manufacturing sector.

In the USA, Washington resorted to Keynesian methods – mainly tax cuts, massive deficit-spending and state subsidies to the arms industry – in response to the 1979-82 recession (Hobsbawm, 1995:412). In both countries the privatization and deregulation crusades did not deliver the promised results. Paul Krugman has noted that, in the UK, 'by 1987, public complaints about British Telecom's performance had become so insistent that the government grudgingly began tightening regulation on its prices and services' (1995:180). Far from 'rationalizing' production, privatization of the electricity networks led to these services producing a 70 per cent excess capacity by 1995.

What neo-liberalism did achieve was a massive redistribution of wealth in favour of the rich. The US trend is instructive: between 1977 and 1989, the incomes of the wealthiest 1 per cent of Americans rocketed by 104 per cent, while that of the poorest 5 per cent dropped by almost 10 per cent, increasing the number poor Americans from 22 million to 32 million.[77]

In reality, neo-liberal programmes not so much 'rolled back' the state than redefined its key priorities. This took the form of redirecting state resources away from the social welfare system towards 'law and order' (the link is obvious) and increased subsidies and support for business, and removing the state's role as 'employer of last resort'.[78] In essence, neo-liberalism represented an attack not on the state *per se* but on the manner and interests in which state resources were allocated in society.

Leaving aside the aggravated inequalities, advocates of neo-liberalism are at a loss to explain its abject failure to produce anything resembling an economic 'miracle'. The first- and second-tier NICs emerged not from neo-liberal policy scripts but, as the World Bank was forced to admit, from 'government interventions [which] appear in some cases to have resulted in higher and more equal growth than otherwise would have occurred'.[79] Of note is Robert Wade's account of Japan's bid to encourage the World Bank to expand its policy directives beyond the narrow perimeters of neo-liberalism on the basis of a thorough study of east Asian economic development. The Bank desisted, leading Wade to conclude that:

> ... the Bank forms part of the external infrastructural power of the US state, even though it by no means bows to every demand of the US government. Whereas the Japanese state uses its strong domestic infrastructural power directly to leverage its external reach – especially in south-east Asia and China – the US state, with much weaker domestic infrastructural power, relies upon its dominance of international organizations like the World Bank and the IMF to keep those organizations pursuing goals that augments its own external reach.[80]

Globalization, therefore, cannot be divorced from the roles of dominant states in augmenting the expansionist and accumulatory projects of national and transnational groupings of capital – an understanding that begs for the reintroduction of the concept of imperialism in leftist efforts to grapple with these phenomena.

The damage done

Far-reaching consequences have been set in motion by these developments. None of the main models for organizing economies seem capable of ensuring both sustained growth and humane living standards. The derailment suffered by proponents of both communist and non-communist variants of socialism is plainly evident. Visions based on the elimination of private enterprise and the rule of the market, and their replacement by state ownership and central planning or by social ownership of production and distribution, have disintegrated. Their antithesis – the *laisser-faire* society ruled by market forces – has proved to be bankrupt. More surprising and worrisome, says Hobsbawm, is 'the disorientation of what might be called the intermediate or mixed programmes and policies which had presided over the most impressive economic miracles of the century' (1995:564–5). In contrast to the other models, these programmes were successful. Though hardly impervious to criticism, they did produce rapid development, stimulated sustained economic growth, improved living standards and dramatically reduced social inequalities.[81] Yet, they have been beaten into retreat – not only by the political/ideological vagaries of the day but by their apparent inability to manage the structural problems that have emerged.

The co-determinist relations nurtured between the state and trade unions were based on largely on the possibility of achieving full employment and the state's capacity to distribute adequate benefits (in the form of monied and social wages) to labour. Both those attractions are under severe attack. The goal of full employment has receded before the conviction that higher levels of unemployment have become a structural feature of the global economy, despite trenchant critiques of this view. Industrialized countries are cutting back on social spending and dismantling their social welfare systems. Trade unions face a dilemma. They can adopt a defensive posture within the old corporatist framework in a bid to limit the damage – an option preferred by the state and business since it tempers renewed instability. Or they can choose the route of attack and assume an overt oppositional role (in concert with other social forces). All the while, however, retrenchments, declining union memberships and attacks by the state and business are likely to sap the strength of the labour movement. The danger in both instances is that the most powerful social force of the past century might be rammed onto the sidelines.

The task of mustering a viable progressive response is complicated further by a generalized retreat from 'old politics'. This is visible in the withdrawal of citizenries from participation in the formal political processes (evident in lower voter turnouts[82]), the unexpected popularity of political contenders whose prime attraction lies in their disavowal of politics and the disaggregation of the left into so-called new social movements guided by identity politics which tend to gravitate not around ideologies and programmes but around 'an amalgam of slogans of emotions'.[83]

The roles and strengths of the nation-state have changed profoundly. In some respects the state has been drastically weakened, delegating its traditional monopoly over certain functions, such as law and order which increasingly is performed by private security firms.[84] In the realms of culture and information, state sovereignty has become radically eroded – as communication satellites beam television and radio programmes into countries, major producers flood world markets with their entertainment and leisure commodities, and computers linked to the Internet disperse and receive vast amounts of data via cyberspace which, by its very definition, transcends the notion of national boundaries. Yet, these phenomena are not pandemic.

States structured around ethnic, religious or nationalist chauvinism (Serbia, Croatia, Chechnya, Iran, etc.) have resisted these trends.

Many states are circumscribed further by the rise of transnational production and liberalized trade systems, and find national prerogatives overridden by supra-national bodies like the IMF and World Bank (in the form of policy dictates attached to loans) or the UN (in the form of UN-mandated military interventions or peacekeeping operations). The very integrity of the nation-state is threatened by the centrifugal pull of ethnic and other minorities seeking 'self-determination'. Where successful, these struggles are often producing entities to which the description nation-state hardly applies – 'a score of empty labels', as one prescient forecast put it, without 'an uncontested territory, nor governments with authority, nor laws, nor tribunals, nor army, nor an ethnically defined population'.[85]

More ominously, state sovereignty is undermined by finance capital which daily traverses the globe on a massive scale in milli-seconds. The phenomenon stems from the over-accumulation of capital which could no longer find enough secure and profitable sites for productive investment. As Sweezy and Magdoff have pointed out, the problem lies with the drying up of profitably opportunities in traditional investment activities. How else to explain, they have asked, why, in the USA, 'in 1948, the capital stock in manufacturing was almost 2,3 times larger than that of finance; by 1988, it was 14 per cent smaller' (1992:7)?

Money, long regarded as subordinate to production, has become an end in itself, despite the obvious fact that production remains the font of capital's expansion. In the liquid form of money, capital now speeds across the globe in search of profit, severely complicating and even upending national economic strategies that are locked into attempts to overcome balance of payments constraints.[86] In David M. Gordon's summary:

> As the rate of return on fixed investment in plant and equipment has declined and as global economic conditions have become increasingly volatile, firms and banks have moved toward paper investments. The new and increasingly efficient international banking system has helped to foster an accelerating circulation of liquid capital, bouncing from one moment of arbitrage to another. Far from stimulating productive investment, however, these financial flows are best understood as a symptom of the diminishing attractiveness and uncertainty about prospects for fixed investment.[87]

Globalization, in this view, 'reflects less the establishment of a stable and new international regime of capital accumulation than an aspect of the decay of the old social structure of accumulation'.[88]

The globalized and highly mobile character of capital seems to be causing relationships between nation-states to be mediated less by competition between national capitals than by the fluidity and mobility of global capital.

In John Holloway's summary, national states now strive to attract and retain within their territories a share of the global surplus value, the presence of which in any one location is increasingly momentary.[89] The pressure to *become* and *remain* attractive to capital increases, producing a mating dance with globalized capital that tends to follow a sequence of routines choreographed by the ideology of neo-liberalism. The state becomes more and more reactive as it tries to attract capital and immobilize it in the form of productive investment, while 'the established links between groups of capitalists and the state come to be seen as a hindrance once it is seen that capital in its money form attaches to no group of people and no particular activity' (Holloway, 1994:41). Again there are several empirical exceptions, notably China and Japan, which suggests that the circle of phenomena associated with globalization is by no means closed. Indeed, Holloway's analysis is open to serious dispute. Susan Strange, among others, has argued that 'there is a symbiosis between the state and transnational corporations from which both benefit ... they are allies as well as competitors and opponents',[90] while Leo Panitch has persuasively critiqued the disavowal of the state's role in the epoch of globalization. In his view,

> ... capitalist globalization is a process which also takes place in, through, and under the aegis of states; it is encoded by them and in important respects even authored by them; and it involves a shift in power relations within states that often means the centralization and concentration of state powers as the necessary condition of and accompaniment to global market discipline.[91]

In fact, as Robin Murray foresaw in a seminal 1971 essay, 'weaker states in a period of internationalization come to suit neither the interests of their own besieged capital nor of the foreign investor'.[92] The state, therefore, has not become impotent nor has capital become disarticulated from it. The reproduction of capital still occurs within the framework of regulations and adjustments introduced and managed by states. This is not to replay the hoary notion that the state is a mere tool of capital but to argue that a tenable understanding of globalization demands emphasis on the relations and struggles among social forces (which 'did not shift to some hyperspace beyond the state') and on the 'nation-state's continuing central role in organizing, sanctioning and legitimizing class domination within capitalism' (Panitch, 1994: 22). It is on the basis of such an analysis that Gordon has concluded that:

> We have not witnessed a movement toward an increasingly 'open' international economy, with productive capital buzzing around the globe, but ... have moved rapidly toward an increasingly 'closed' economy for productive investment, with production and investment decisions increasingly dependent upon a range of institutional policies and activities and a pattern of differentiation and specialization among the LDCs [Least Developed Countries] (1988:63).

In sum, globalization severely complicates but does not preclude efforts by countries like South Africa to implement economic strategies that can serve the interests and improve the well-being of its citizens. Hobsbawm is correct in insisting that:

> … the state, or some other form of public authority representing the public interest, [is] more indispensable than ever if the social and environmental iniquities of the market economy [are] to be countered, or even – as the reform of capitalism in the 1940s [showed] – if the economic system [is] to operate satisfactorily (1995:577).

South Africa in the world system

South Africa's incorporation into the world economy has remained largely unchanged for most of the century, and has rested on three, narrow pillars: as a primary product (mainly gold) exporter, as an importer of capital goods and technology, and as a net recipient of indirect portfolio investment and direct foreign investment by multinational corporations.[93]

Trend swings have occurred in each of these aspects, but they still reflect the essence of the country's incorporation into the world economy. The major and hugely problematic change is that, following the debt crisis of 1985, South Africa became a net exporter of capital.

The similarities with many Latin American countries are striking. Like them, South Africa followed the model of state-led industrialization and import-substitution propagated by Raul Prebish in the 1950s. On both sides of the Atlantic, this yielded impressive levels of industrialization and rates of economic growth. Import-substitution, *per se,* was not a misguided route, as Massachusetts Institute for Technology economist Lance Taylor has pointed out: 'Import-substitution is about the only way anybody's ever figured out to industrialize'.[94] One common problem, though, is the associated maze of regulations, subsidies and tax mechanisms which makes it 'more interesting for firms to play games with the rules than to go out and produce goods',[95] as South Africa has discovered.

But unlike its Latin American counterparts, South Africa did not try to spend its way out of trouble when these growth phases began ebbing. At 22,9 per cent of GDP in 1994, its external debt burden is regarded as small for a developing country – lower than for all Latin American and ASEAN countries (except for Chile and Singapore, respectively).[96] Leaving aside for the moment the political and policy implications of such a move, the country has some scope for increasing its debt load – provided this occurs within the framework and in support of a strategic programme and not haphazardly as the perceived need arises.

In another major departure from the Latin American experiences, South Africa failed to shift its exports to manufactured goods and away from primary products.

This is not to say that the manufacturing sector remained undeveloped. Attempts were made to promote it behind protectionist barriers, enabling it to grow until the late 1960s, after which it 'entered an as yet endless spiral of decline' (MERG, 1993:212). The sector remained heavily dependent on imports, which had to be financed through primary exports. Manufactured products' share of total exports declined steadily from 1970 (31 per cent) to 1988 (12 per cent),[97] only partially because the gold price pushed the exchange rate up, making manufactured exports uncompetitive in global markets.[98] Also hampering the sector's development has been the high cost of locally produced raw materials to domestic downstream manufacturers, as noted by a 1997 Industrial Development Corporation study.[99]

In summary, the economy remains reliant on resource and energy-based products which are of declining importance in world trade and subject to drastic price fluctuations. According to UNCTAD, most African countries rely on one or two primary commodities for 90 per cent of their export earnings; in South Africa's case the figure is about 65 per cent.[100] Meanwhile, its heavy dependence on capital goods imports and foreign technology leaves it extremely vulnerable to global pressures. As result, South Africa is chronically subject to balance of payment difficulties and has never developed an industrialization strategy to promote manufacturing.

Trends in trade

An enduring fallacy is the claim that South Africa was, until very recently, a closed economy. The country has had a relatively extroverted economy, with trade representing about 60 per cent of GDP. Mining is without doubt the most outward-oriented sector (accounting for 62 per cent of exports in 1990, down from 73 per cent in 1980), while the agricultural sector exports grains, wines and deciduous fruits (accounting for 5 per cent of exports in 1990).[101]

This is not to say that it has shared in the more than 30 per cent swell in the volume of world trade that occurred in the 1980s. South Africa has not escaped the fate suffered by the continent generally: increased marginalization in the world economy. South Africa's share of world exports dropped from 1,3 per cent in 1980 to 0,7 per cent in 1989, while Africa's share in the same period fell from 6 per cent to 2,6 per cent.[102]

The particular character of this relative openness must also be recognized. Gold continues to dominate exports (accounting for almost half the total value), followed by non-precious metals. In absolute terms, manufactured exports expanded impressively in the 1960s and 1970s, but the economy's share of global manufacturing exports dropped steadily since 1968, while its share of agricultural exports has also declined.[103] The sectors to perform best in more open markets have been timber and steel. Secondary industry has never been competitive internationally, except in neighbouring countries where South Africa has enjoyed the advantage of lower transport costs, and bilateral and regional trade deals weighted in its favour. Overall, manufacturing's share of exports plummeted from 31 per cent in 1960 to 12 per cent in 1988.

On the import side, capital goods (chiefly machinery, transport equipment and information technologies) have eclipsed manufactured consumer goods. The sourcing of imports has become more concentrated, with its four largest suppliers (USA, UK, Germany, Japan) increasing their share of total imports by 1992.[104]

Although still small overall, trade with Africa has risen by some 40 per cent since 1990 and now comprises about 10 per cent of South Africa's exports, with the trade balance skewed in its favour. One-third is in manufactures, a much higher percentage than for its exports elsewhere in the world. Most of it occurs with neighbouring and West African countries. In 1990, South Africa provided 80–90 per cent of Botswana, Lesotho and Swaziland's imports, 30 per cent of Malawi's, 21 per cent of Zimbabwe's, 15 per cent of Zambia's and 12 per cent of Mozambique's; these figures have swelled since. In turn, South Africa imports mostly unprocessed primary products from the continent, often through barter deals with countries like Nigeria (steel for oil), Mauritius and the former Zaïre. While these deals reduce the strain on foreign currency reserves, they are insulated from the more competitively-driven trade dynamics in the 'open market' and tend not to lead to practices and innovations that can be applied to South Africa's benefit in more conventional trade relations.

Three decades ago, South Africa seemed to be developing into a semi-industrialized country with a relatively diversified export base. At the end of the century, its profile resembles that of most developing countries: as a traditional commodity exporter and importer of capital goods and technologies.

Trends in financial relations

Since its early phases of industrialization, South Africa has received large amounts of portfolio investment (mainly from the UK). During the boom years of the 1960s, it received large inflows of foreign direct investment (mainly from the USA) attracted by low wages, a growing domestic market (mainly due to rising white incomes) and apparent political stability. Much of this capital was invested productively in the manufacturing sector. Syndicated bank loans and bonds raised in the international capital markets contributed the bulk of foreign investment after 1976.

Subsequently, economic decline and political instability combined to wreak havoc on South Africa's international economic relations, and forced the monetary authorities, unilaterally, to declare a debt standstill in August 1985. The country became a net exporter of capital, reversing the positive flows which had prevailed (with minor disruptions) for most of its modern economic history. Massive capital flight occurred in the 1980s – some 40 per cent of transnational firms disinvested[105] and, according to the SA Reserve Bank, the capital outflow in the period 1982–8 amounted to more than $5,5 billion. Many local corporations followed that trend and undertook direct investments abroad, mainly in Europe.

In addition to the net outflows of foreign direct investment and portfolio investment, from 1985 to 1988 the country had no access to long-term debt capital, nor were syndicated bank loans extended or private or public bond issues made. In short, most forms of foreign capital inflows dried up altogether. There was one exception. Although no official development assistance was received in the period 1985–92, there were strong inflows of overseas development aid (ODA) to anti-apartheid and humanitarian organizations.

More positively, Pretoria had repaid and discharged all its loan obligations to the World Bank in 1976. An IMF loan, received in 1982, was repaid by the end of 1987. As a result, the country's ratio of foreign debt to GDP is low by international standards.

Portfolio (equity) capital flows to South Africa increased in the 1990s. The primary causes for this were cyclical: the bottoming out of the recession, the strong coinciding rally in gold markets, and significant progress in political negotiations at the time. Whereas the net outflow of capital from 1985 to 1993 averaged at 2,3 per cent of GDP, net inflows from 1994 to 1996 averaged 2,6 per cent of GDP.[106]

Net purchases of equities by foreigners on the Johannesburg Stock Exchange have increased. But the renewed access to foreign capital has been limited mainly to equity capital and bond issues on the European capital markets – most of which are effectively short-term credits at relatively high costs. This trend in the flow of equity funds to emerging markets is in line with global developments and represents volatile, short-term investments which are swiftly and easily sold off.

Changing the terms of incorporation

While the world fêted South Africa for its successful transition to democracy, other, equally important conundrums remained unresolved. One was how to devise a set of policies that could reconcile the country's insertion into the global division of labour with the commitment to improve the majority's living standards.

New opportunities and new pressures make it possible to alter the manner and terms of South Africa's insertion into the world economy. The new opportunities are patent: the advent of political democracy, a new government, greater international goodwill and the removal of sanctions and trade boycotts.

The 'internationalizing' trend is the paramount pressure, and, politically, is brought to bear mainly by the IMF and World Bank, and to a lesser degree the GATT agreements. Typically, this involves 'liberalizing' trade relations by reducing tariffs and removing non-tariff protective barriers for domestic industry, removing financial controls and guaranteeing the free flow of capital, and remedying other features seen as deterring foreign investment.

That far-reaching adjustments are needed in South Africa's case is no longer in dispute – but that is where the agreement has ended. The platitudes that accompany these debates are often mind-numbing, likening the world economy to 'a picnic', as SACP general secretary Charles Nqakula wryly remarked, where attendance is automatically welcomed if the requisite dress and manners are displayed.[107]

Proposals have ranged from standard neo-liberal packages of free markets, trade and financial liberalization, to supply-side formulas (like those devised by the Industrial Strategy Project), to strategies which envision a creative division of labour between the private sector and the state within the context of a innovative, targeted policies (such as the Macroeconomic Research Group recommendations).

Attracting foreign investment

The argument generally deployed by business and sections of government casually connects 'liberalization' to increased foreign investment and, consequently, economic growth. The emphasis placed by South African business leaders on foreign investment seems disingenuous, however, given the low rate of domestic investment by South African capital. So narrow is the debate, though, that Jeremy Cronin is ridiculed in the business press for suggesting that the best advert for foreign investors is surely when domestic firms make large productive investments locally. On the contrary, 'this is simply not happening, as millions of rands continue to be disinvested, or used speculatively on the stock exchanges and in shopping mall developments'.[108] Private sector (non-housing) fixed investment constituted a scant 10 per cent of GDP in early 1994.[109] At the same time, capital *outflows* persisted in the early 1990s, causing the economy to lose as much as 2 per cent real GDP growth annually.[110] Indeed, while demanding increased liberalization (ostensibly to sweeten investment opportunities in South Africa), the country's major corporations have in the 1990s embarked on a spree of investments *abroad*. Thus, the largest conglomerates have invested substantially in Indonesia, Australia, Zambia, Brazil, Ghana, China, New Zealand, Chile, Venezuela, Ecuador and Vietnam – with trade and industry minister Alec Erwin defending the trend on the basis that the country needs a corporate presence in countries with which it trades.[111]

Nevertheless, the need to attract substantial amounts of foreign investment has become axiomatic. Success, according to Krugman, depends on whether South Africa 'can get any restructuring of property rights behind it; if it can demonstrate that it is more market-oriented than investors now expect; and if it can offer what appears to be a more competitive rand' (in Baker *et al.*, 1993:47).

By mid-1996, substantial adjustments had occurred on these fronts. Property rights are ensconced in the Constitution (without any significant 'restructuring' having taken place), the government's macroeconomic strategy (discussed in detail below) heeds most neo-liberal injunctions, and the rand devalued by more than 30 per cent in six months. The die has been cast, but is the optimism warranted?

The South African debate tends to regard the country as *sui generis* and somehow able to evade the pressures experienced by the rest of Africa – where, overall, foreign direct investment (FDI) grew by a third from 1980 to 1990, but the continent's share of overall global FDI dropped from 6,8 per cent to 2 per cent.[112] Capital outflows, in 1991, equalled 90 per cent of Africa's GDP – more than five times the total investment, 11 times private sector investment, and 120 times foreign investment.[113] 'Not only has the region lost ground to the rest of the world as an investment location,' notes one assessment, 'but within Africa the pattern of flows is heavily skewed in favour of oil-producing nations which account for two thirds of the total [FDI]'.[114] All evidence points to South Africa being locked into these trends. Thus Nigeria attracted 45 per cent of FDI to sub-Saharan Africa from 1990 to 1994, while South Africa experienced a net outflow.

Flows of FDI delineate a much more differentiated 'Third World' than that described in the cheery auguries of orthodoxy. Gordon has shown that 'instead of flowing more and more widely around the globe, capital is on the contrary settling down in a few carefully chosen locations', of four types. The east Asian NICs receive investment mainly for financial services and production for re-export back to the advanced countries. Latin American NICs represent a second category and receive foreign investment aimed almost exclusively at production for large domestic markets. The third comprises oil-exporting countries whose fortunes 'now vacillate with the cob-web cycles of price hikes and oil gluts'. Finally, there are 75–80 developing countries who 'have been shunted off to a side spur, virtually derailed in the drive for access to global resources' (1988:57).

By 1996, foreign investment in South Africa had revived, but along three lines. According to one export promoter, 'investors coming to South Africa want to use us as a springboard to trade in Africa, not necessarily for new investments; they are eyeing the huge tracts of land and stocks of minerals there'.[115] Indeed, South African investors themselves are spearheading this trend, investing in mining, retail networks, tourism, banking, electrification, and agriculture.

The other trend is towards investment in stocks and bonds. The net private capital outflows of 1985–93 were reversing by late 1994, with one estimate putting FDI at $2,5 billion in 1994/95.[116] This climbed to $6,8 billion by mid-1997, according to *Business Map*.[117] But these were 'largely due, however, to investments through the stock exchange', according to the department of trade and industry's Alan Hirsch, who added that FDI 'defined as more than 50 per cent ownership remains relatively small'.[118] Productive investments have targeted the 'traditional middle-class and business market, such as media and infotech investments', hotels and tourism, and the food, appliance and construction industries. But there has been an 'almost total lack of investment in outward-oriented manufacturing'.[119] In Hirsch's summary, 'the problem is that most [FDI] is basically buying market share and going into partnership with South African companies, or buying control of South African resources for export'.[120]

What will it take, then, to encourage foreign investment in export-oriented manufacturing industries? The prognosis looks gloomy, for there 'appears to be little to support the widely held belief that low-cost labour will encourage multinationals to relocate job-intensive operations in parts of Africa,' according to Hawkins. Among the reasons are low labour productivity and the 'relative insignificance of labour costs when compared with material, transport and other costs in many manufacturing operations'.[121]

Simply conforming to the commonly touted requirements – whereby, in former trade unionist Enoch Godongwana's metaphor, the world economy becomes a 'beauty competition' where you stand to win if you can display the 'slimmest legs' and 'skimpiest costume' – is inappropriate. South Africa cannot wish away its geographical location on a continent which barely features in the world economy. Neither can it pretend that neo-liberal adjustments will overcome or even disguise the withering range of structural weaknesses in its economy, and lure foreign investors.

The neo-liberal argument that severe adjustments are needed to attract foreign investment, which spurs growth, thereby triggering a trickle-down improvement in living standards and consumptive patterns, hitches the cart before the horse. International experience shows that foreign investment is more likely to flow to vibrant economies with strong internal demand, and which are integrated into economically dynamic regions.[122] Indeed, the dominant belief that low wages and relatively high skills levels are the key determinants of FDI is not borne out by research. A study of FDI flows to 54 developing countries has showed that those elements ranked lowest among the criteria affecting FDI.[123] Paramount was the size of the domestic market, price/exchange rate stability and political/institutional stability. The reasons are obvious since, as Gordon has argued, 'in many commodities, labour costs are a relatively small proportion of total costs [while] countries with relatively stable price and trade horizons are much more exceptional than those with relatively low labour costs' (1988:58–9).

Moreover, the stress on FDI as a catalyst for growth lets domestic capital off the hook. The two most dynamic performers of recent times in the 'Third World' (South Korea and China) succeeded in mobilizing local capital investment, not by striking supine postures before foreign capital.

Neo-liberal orthodoxy cannot claim credit for any of the east Asian success stories. Meanwhile, its most widely touted success (Chile) offers ample cause for alarm. Along with severely deepened social inequalities, 'whole sectors of industry were wiped out, manufacturing employment fell by half' and growth occurred mainly on the basis of agriculture-based exports.[124] None of the industrialized countries any longer pursues policies of unrestrained 'liberalization' – on the contrary, the OECD countries aggressively maintain protectionist stances (while demanding the inverse from the rest of the world), and are experimenting with neo-Keynesian policies. The world's fastest growing economy, China, has grafted liberalizing elements onto an essentially statist development path (producing a hybrid best described as 'market-Stalinism').

Moreover, there exists no international neo-liberal consensus. Rather, the altered form in which capital circulates globally has produced a need for easier passage in and out of economies, to which different countries are responding dissimilarly – depending on their relative political and economic authority. Adopting neo-liberal policies becomes not a proactive deed but a casual submission to that dynamic, with 'no guarantee', as Krugman admits, 'that [those] conditions will produce large capital inflows'[125] – let alone the broader, advertised benefits.

Becoming competitive

The government strategy for growth centres on invigorating an export-oriented manufacturing sector, an approach that seems in step with the international trend away from trade in primary commodities. The economy's inherited weaknesses, however, make this a daunting task.

The guiding doctrine is one of 'enhanced competitiveness'. This is often glibly distilled into the purported need to get 'prices right', a process that is supposedly propelled by trade liberalization which forces the lowering of input – particularly labour – costs. Hence, the calls from business and ANC leaders for wage restraint. Alongside this is an emphasis on 'improving productivity' which, in business discourse, tends to be reduced to labour productivity, downplaying the importance of capital productivity, social productivity (defined as 'the efficiency with which the population's needs might be satisfied') and managerial productivity.[126]

Both assumptions are problematic. Firstly, as economist Sanjaya Lall has cautioned, 'neither theory nor practice supports the case for completely liberal trade policies'. Indeed, he has found 'no instance of a developing country mastering complex industrial activities ... without protection or subsidization to overcome the costs of learning'.[127] Meanwhile, citing a WIDER study and its own research, the Industrial Strategy Project (ISP) found no evidence of an unambiguous link between export expansion and productivity growth.[128] Summarizing the ISP's findings, Freund noted that:

> South Africa needs more than a trade policy; it needs an overall industrial policy aimed at building research and development capacity, developing industrial exports through targeting strengths, rewarding both job creation and improving productivity, and advancing competition through breaking up conglomerates (although they equivocate on this final point) (1994b:61).

To some extent, this thinking has been incorporated into government thinking. The reformed trade policy is explicitly geared to develop export-orientation, by making a committed move towards trade liberalization, and applying supply-side measures.[129] The latter include efforts to improve productivity and work organization, nurturing small and medium-sized enterprises, helping develop new industries (especially in biotechnology and information technology), encouraging greater investment in research and development, lowering the corporate tax rate (despite the government-appointed Katz Commission's resistance) and providing more tax incentives, and human resource development. However, it does not add up to a strategic policy of the Japanese or South Korean varieties. Measures are predominantly supply-side and bereft of an overt role for the state in targeting and buttressing, for instance, the development of labour-intensive industries or of coaxing and rewarding job creation and productivity advances.

On trade liberalization, the government has leapt out of the starting blocks. Common wisdom has detected in South Africa's tariff system a prime obstacles to competitiveness. The view is both right and wrong. Compared with 32 LDCs (least developed countries), tariff protection is not high, except in the case of final consumer goods. Once the actual utilization of tariffs is considered, South Africa 'appears to be amongst the least protected of all of these 32 countries' (ISP, 1994:98). On the other hand, the inherited system was one of the most complex in the world, and, in Lalls's view '[protected] industries without regard to their competitive potential, [had] no strategy for promoting new infant industries, and [failed] to offset the effects of protection by forcing firms to invest in building export markets'.[130] A strong case could be made for restructuring (as opposed to dismantling) the protective regime.

Who's GATT knocking?

By signing the Uruguay Round of GATT, South Africa committed itself to:
- rationalizing some 12 800 industrial tariffs into no more than 1 000;

■ cutting industrial tariffs by an average of 33 per cent by 1999, with maximum levels for consumer goods set at 30 per cent, for capital goods at
   15 per cent and for raw materials at 5 per cent;
■ cutting agricultural tariffs by an average of 36 per cent over 10 years;
■ scaling down textile tariffs over 12 years to a maximum of 25–45 per
   cent, depending on the product;
■ phasing out local content measures in the automobile industry; and
■ terminating its General Export Incentive Scheme (GEIS) export subsidies
   by 1997.

In August 1994, the department of trade and industry announced deep tariff
reductions in the clothing and textile, and automobile industries that went far
beyond those demanded under GATT.[131] At the time, the cuts did not slot into
a strategic package, aimed at coaxing these industries into new or more competitive directions; it was 'sheer economic Darwinism', as one commentator
put it.[132] Government seemed to recognize the omission, with the minister
responsible declaring weeks later that 'the worst case for this economy is for
us to throw our industries ... to the vagaries of international competition
rapidly and so destroy investment and jobs'.[133] Yet, the government's 1996
macroeconomic strategy described 'the central thrust of trade and industrial
policy' as 'the pursuit of employment creating international competitiveness'.[134] Among the measures employed would be the abolition of import surcharges (already completed), phasing down tariffs by an average one-third
over five years, and phasing out the GEIS by the end of 1997.[135] In the case of
telecommunications, the government was in 1997 aiming to lower tariffs to
zero percent – far below the 20 per cent level required under GATT and the
World Trade Organization (WTO). Worst hit by the tariff cuts has been the
labour-intensive clothing industry (one of the largest industrial employers of
women) and the beleaguered agricultural sector, particularly maize farming.
At the same time, if this leads to lower maize prices for consumers (mainly
the poor) these effects could be mitigated to some extent.

   The GEIS was long trouble ridden and largely benefited conglomerates
'who would have exported anyway',[136] and was plagued by fraudulent
double claims. Moreover, the GEIS was not structured to specifically encourage the export of finished goods. The World Bank, however, is doubtful
whether South African can establish export competitiveness without a
scheme such as the GEIS. Proposals came from labour and other circles to
restructure the GEIS so as to benefit more small and medium-sized, labour-
intensive industries. Government, though, has opted for the harsher option.

Lifting exchange controls

A further liberalizing adjustment demanded is the abolition of foreign
exchange controls. These were introduced in 1961, in a bid to stem capital

outflows after the Sharpeville massacre. Regulations were modified in subsequent years, including strong liberalization in the early 1980s following the gold price boom. The government's debt standstill – and the uprisings – of 1985 triggered massive capital outflows, prompting the reintroduction of the financial rand mechanism and the tightening of controls.

The financial rand, which traded at a lower rate than the commercial rand, was the principal means for moving capital in and out of South Africa, whether in the form of direct or portfolio investments. Capital could only be removed at a discount and was thus encouraged to remain, thereby protecting foreign exchange reserves.

The global trend, however, runs against exchange controls, which are seen as an unnecessary hindrance to the flow of capital and a major factor discouraging foreign investment. As a result, the South African debate is not whether or not to discard these controls, but whether this should be done in one, fell swoop (the 'big bang') or in a phased approach. The debate has been heated, though the government decided against the 'shock-therapy' option, despite overt encouragement from the IMF in late 1994.[137] The financial rand was abolished in 1995 as the first step in the phased removal of exchange controls. According to government policy, 'all remaining exchange controls will be dismantled as soon as circumstances are favourable'.[138]

The irony is that this gradual approach was accompanied by many of the difficulties associated with the 'big bang' approach. In early 1996, the currency began devaluing dramatically. By year-end it had lost more than 30 per cent of its 1995 value against the US dollar. A familiar train of events ensued. Imports costs soared, causing a slow-down in the retooling and upgrading of plants and, more menacingly, a major shortage of foreign exchange. On the positive side, exports have become more price competitive. The devalued rand and mega-projects going into production saw manufactured export volumes rise by 12 per cent in 1996 while its percentage share of overall exports rose from 26 per cent to 29 per cent.[139] In early 1997, however, the rise faltered to 3,4 per cent.[140] But the stunted export capacity of the manufacturing sector prevented it from capitalizing markedly on that boom; the crucial link between an activated new industrial policy and exchange control liberalization was absent. Meanwhile, capital inflows slowed dramatically in 1996 and were down to R3,9 billion from R19,2 billion in 1995, leaving the government tempted to use privatization to boost inflows.[141]

Government announced a range of other relaxations of exchange controls in 1996 and 1997, including allowing foreign investors greater access to domestic credit, enabling finance houses to engage in asset swaps with foreign companies and permitting them to make larger foreign currency transfers, and further relaxing exchange controls on residents, among other 'adjustments'.

The triumph of orthodoxy

By 1996 the government had nailed its colours to the mast of export-oriented growth, eschewing proposals for an inward-looking industrialization strategy geared at servicing domestic needs in the first instance. Even some ANC economists, like Rob Davies, have warned that South Africa seeks to hop aboard the export-led bandwagon at a time when '[a]lmost all semi-peripheral and many peripheral countries are now attempting such a strategy under global conditions that are becoming less and less favourable for all to succeed' (1995:63). Such warnings have gone unheeded.

Admittedly, its attempts to achieve a more favourable and dynamic integration into the world economy have been somewhat ambivalent. In some respects it has adopted a prostrate posture to demands for 'liberalization' – illustrated by its attempts to display the requisite attractiveness to foreign investors, its tariff reduction decisions, and the macroeconomic framework within which this is occurring. On the other hand, there are tentative signs of a more proactive approach of pivoting trade policy on broader industrial policy restructuring – by way, especially, of supply-side measures aimed at bolstering industrial performance. Referring to the experiences of the NICs in south-east Asia, Lall reminds that:

> ... the experience of the most dynamic industrialisers in the developing world suggests that their selective interventions determined the nature and success of their industrial development.[142]

But, as the next chapter shows, government policy does not even pretend to emulate such 'selective interventions'. Whilst not quite 'hands-off', the approach is one of highly restrained facilitation within an overall context governed by the reactions of market forces.

At the same time, the conditions for replicating the policies of the NICs do not seem to exist in South Africa's case. Both South Korea and Taiwan used their geo-strategic significance during the Cold War to great effect, winning preferential access to US markets without having to reciprocate by opening their own markets. Moreover, as Davies has noted, 'they embarked on export-led growth when most industrializing countries were still pursuing import-substitution programmes'.[143] Instead of an authoritarian regime able to suppress labour, South Africa has a democratic government that is committed at the level of rhetoric to consensus-building. It does not have the luxury of a weak capitalist class, nor a homogenous population or an even relatively favourable income distribution (key elements of Taiwan and South Korea's successes). Its rural economy cannot function as an employment and income safeguard. Situated in a sub-region and on a continent that enjoys barely a toe-hold in the world economy, it lacks the luxury of dynamic markets in close proximity. And it starts:

... from a low, narrow and uneven base marked by an inward-looking economic premised on 75 years of import-substitution policies, minimal domestic competition, a continued dependence on our natural resource base, low labour absorption and an insufficient emphasis on human capital formation, falling rates of gross domestic fixed investment and a capital that has aged ...[144]

To be sure, South Africa is not Mauritania or Sri Lanka, but like most developing countries its importance to global capital is negligible. In effect, to apply an unfashionable term, it is being 'delinked', as 'capital adjusts the weaker zones of the world to the requirements of global accumulation'.[145] The gamble taken by South Africa (and many other developing countries) is that by acceding to these adjustments and fine tuning them in some respects, it might attain a niché in the world system. It is not the first country to attempt this; indeed, the ordeals of its forerunners are sobering. The question is whether an alternative route is possible and what it might be.

If the prospects of retaining a robust inward dimension to a development path that, perforce, is also pitched outward are dim in the prevailing global context, hopes seem brighter for an analogous venture on a regional scale. This would entail restructuring South Africa's relations with the southern African region as an integral element of a set of new development strategies. Clearly, the approach cannot be to establish some sort of regional autarchy, for very obvious reasons. Yet, it does offer greater possibility for resisting neo-liberal hegemony in order to pursue paths that prioritize the needs of the country's citizens.

South Africa and the region

Given the pursuit of regional trade blocs and common markets internationally, it is not surprising that there has emerged a virtual consensus on the need for closer economic interaction between the countries of southern Africa.[146] Donor countries, multilateral lending institutions, South African business and the governments of the region have all signalled their support.[147] For the ANC, the objective of closer cooperation seemed clear:

> This will aim at redressing past inequalities which characterised not only North-South relations but some of the South-South links as well. We will do our utmost to avoid the domination of South Africa's economy over the region.[148]

The question, though, is what kinds of interaction are desirable and whether it should extend as far as economic integration. Although several variants of economic integration exist, they all describe a process whereby 'the economies of individual states are merged (in whole or in part) into a single regional entity' (Davies, 1992a). Greater cooperation, on the other hand, stops short of that threshold. It entails states sharing or providing 'to each other resources, technology or expertise, collaborat[ing] in joint projects or act[ing] together in external economic relations'.[149]

Until quite recently, the need for integration was almost axiomatic, with even the World Bank advising that course. The Bank has promoted neo-liberal integration exercises that would be 'consistent with an outward orientated strategy' and entail 'mutual regional liberalization'. The objective would be 'to create conditions which would allow the private sector freely to work, trade and invest across African borders and with relatively low barriers against third parties'.[150] That approach eschews the protection of domestic markets, offers no guarantee that the markets of the North would reciprocate and erodes the potential ability of a regional bloc in the South to resist further liberalization demands from the North (Davies, 1992).

South African business, however, retreated from its earlier enthusiasm for deeper integration, worrying that this would add only to South Africa's own problems. Instead, it propagated a more cautious approach of expanding cooperation more or less in line with the historical patterns that ensured South African hegemony over the region. Similar, though more muted, concerns also penetrated the ANC government's thinking after 1994. As a result, a real prospect exists that the terms of regional integration will be reshaped in ways that entrench South African dominance. With a GDP of US$80 billion, its economy is three times larger than that of the rest of the region. Its transport infrastructure is much more developed, and its financial and productive capacities far outstrip those of other regional economies.

Skewed integration

Southern Africa has been 'integrated' to a substantial degree since colonial times. In historian Dan O'Meara's words:

> [C]ompeting European colonialism fashioned a Southern African region marked by a fairly high degree of what can be called skewed integration – an essentially regional economy in which the central pole of accumulation was the mining and later the agricultural, industrial and service sectors of the South African economy. All other economies in the region, except that of Angola, were locked into this regional economy as suppliers of cheap migrant labour, certain goods and services (water, energy, transport, etc.) to the South African economy, and as markets for its manufacturer and capital.[151]

The gold mining industry was built with migrant labour from the homelands and neighbouring countries; until the 1980s, the industry employed a majority of non-South African workers, mostly from Mozambique and

Lesotho. Remittances sent home by these workers, along with earnings from resource exports, provided the countries with much of the foreign exchange they used to purchase South African manufactured products. Indeed, the manufacturing sector's early growth occurred substantially within this regional context, allowing for the production of goods that were unlikely to penetrate markets elsewhere in the world.

Regional and other markets on the continent remain of great current – and potential – importance to South Africa's manufacturing sector. One study found that, in the 1970s, manufactured exports to Botswana, Lesotho and Swaziland were responsible for some 67 000 jobs in that sector (Davies, 1992b). In 1990, South Africa supplied more than 80 per cent of those countries' imports, while, overall, 32 per cent of its manufactured exports went to African countries other than that trio – mostly steel, food, chemical, and automobile products.[152] Severely distorted trade relationships pertain, with South Africa maintaining a very large trade balance in its favour. According to SADC figures, South Africa's visible exports to the region were more than five times the level of imports during the 1980s.[153] This was not only a mark of superior productive capacities. Theoretically, the Southern African Customs Unions (SACU, joining South Africa, Botswana, Lesotho, Swaziland and Namibia) provides for free trade between member countries. However, South Africa erected sturdy non-tariff barriers to limit manufactured imports from the other members, stymieing the development of manufacturing industries in those countries. In addition, the terms of the Common Monetary Area (CMA, embracing the SACU countries) establish the South African rand as the common trading currency – which implies the surrender of macroeconomic control over their finances to South Africa (Beaudet & Theade, 1994).

The legacies of South Africa's historical domination and of the destabilization strategies of the apartheid regime therefore pose great obstacles to an integration project capable of 'actively promoting economic growth of a type that brings benefits to all members of society'.[154] Immense devastation was wreaked by destabilization. Unicef has estimated that one million people died as a result, while the SADC countries suffered losses of US$60 billion.[155] Mozambique, where South Africa supported the Renamo rebels, is today classified by the World Bank as one of the poorest and most aid-dependent countries in the world. Angola, where South Africa supported and fought alongside Unita, is today racked by crises to the point where, arguably, it is a nation-state in name only. Developmental efforts were either scuttled outright or undermined, as Pretoria sought to exert its political hegemony over countries that had adopted overt anti-apartheid stances. It lessened its use of neighbouring countries' transport services (and, in the case of Mozambique, helped destroy them), and drastically cut back on the number of migrant workers labouring in its mines.

Rob Davies, though, has cautioned against over-politicizing those strategies, emphasizing the economic factors that accompanied the political motives. By the 1980s, South Africa's manufacturing sector had slumped, and was performing very poorly by international standards. In addition, the region (like most of the continent) was being hammered by massive indebtedness, poor terms of trade, desultory economic performances and South African destabilization. In Davies' summary,

> ... goods whose competitiveness was tending to decline were being offered in markets where the foreign exchange needed to buy them was becoming increasingly scarce ... One of the objectives underlying destabilization was clearly to preserve essential elements of the established patterns of regional economic relations intact, while permitting a highly partisan restructuring of others (1992b:79).

Good neighbours?

The challenge is to reshape those relationships in ways that yield mutual benefits. It has become a cliché to assert that the fate of the region as a whole cannot be separated from the fortunes of its individual countries. Certainly, for South Africa, the benefits of closer cooperation are manifest. Increased trade with the region (and the rest of sub-Saharan Africa) could boost South Africa's manufactured exports and help it escape its status as a primary commodity exporter. Energy drawn from the region could augment its efforts to develop the economy. Regional investments that target industrial sectors can boost the income earning potential of other countries, thereby sustaining their status as markets for South African products and services. The latter point is particularly important, since the general level of imports by countries in the region has declined markedly, making it 'in South Africa's own interests to work for a climate of growth and development throughout the region and wider continent'.[156]

More broadly, joint and/or co-ordinated investment projects offer some hope of achieving economies of scale within the region. Combined with stronger political cooperation and co-ordinated trade reform, this could provide the region with greater leverage when bargaining with multilateral institutions like the GATT, WTO, IMF and World Bank.[157] Sharing unevenly spread managerial, professional, scientific, technological and natural resources can remove several of the barriers blocking the revival of more equitable development efforts in the region. The inclusion of social charters in agreements can help expand the rights and conditions of workers, and extend democratic practices across the region.[158] Overall, strategies geared at overcoming existing imbalances and inequities *throughout the region* can help remedy its individual states' frailties *vis-à-vis* the North. Moreover, they are essential if the endemic socio-political insecurities in the

region are to be overcome – insecurities which (in the form of mass migration, refugee movements, political instability and conflicts) inevitably spill
over national boundaries. Thus, the MERG report urged:

> ... positive action to develop new patterns of trade, develop infrastructure
> and influence industrial location, as well as compensatory and corrective
> mechanisms – to ensure that the burden of adjustment to the new integrated
> region does not fall disproportionately on working people and the poor ...
> (1993:279).

This would mean restructuring the existing multilateral institutions in the
region, including the South African-dominated SACU and CMA. Also
affected would be the SADC (which admitted South Africa as a member in
1994) and the eastern and southern African Preferential Trade Area
(PTA).[159]

The problem is that such an approach requires high degrees of reciprocity
from South Africa, which has to be expressed on several fronts, as Davies has
indicated (1992b:14–18). Investment decisions should be guided by other
countries' need 'to promote growth and diversify their productive bases' and
not strictly by short-term profitability. Other countries have to gain greater
access to the South African market, while the regional transport system
needs to be restructured 'to address problems caused by distortion of historic
transport flows'.[160] Crucially, regional – not merely national – solutions have
to be found for the problems of both legal and 'illegal' labour migration. On
the whole, a new regional framework for relationships must enhance democracy in the political, economic and social spheres, along the lines pursued by
trade union and other groupings in the Latin American context.

There has been little evidence of a willingness on South Africa's part to
oblige in many of these respects. There are apparent exceptions, such as the
rehabilitation of the Maputo Corridor, and the Lesotho Highlands Water
Project. But on the whole, the tendency has been to prioritize the interests of
South African business. Thus South Africa slapped 90 per cent tariffs on
Zimbabwean textile imports, while maintaining free access to the
Zimbabwean market. As *Africa Confidential* has observed, the ANC gov-
ernment:

> ... has repeatedly assured its fellow members [in SADC] that it wants to be a
> partner, not a boss. Yet, the facts, economic and military, say otherwise.[161]

Two attitudes are evident in business circles (Davies, 1992a). The first pours
scorn on the importance of the region and sub-Saharan Africa for South
Africa. Instead, the country has to position itself 'as a "first world" player
involved in global markets rather than a "third world" country relegated to
regional markets'.[162] In this view, free trade agreements with the North,
especially the European Union, outweigh any regional initiatives.

The second champions South Africa's alleged role as an 'engine of growth' and recovery in the region. The liberalization of regulatory systems is seen as a prerequisite to 'open up the region to South African exports and capital investment', from which benefits would allegedly trickle down into the targeted countries.[163] Here the demand is for free trade and unencumbered capital movement. The objective is two-fold: to enable greater penetration of the region (and beyond) by South African capital, and 'to reinforce South Africa's image as the "natural gateway" and partner for foreign investors in southern Africa'.[164]

South African trade with the region and the rest of sub-Saharan Africa has swelled markedly since 1990 – rising to $3,8 billion (compared to $0,9 billion in imports).[165] So have its investments which, generally, have not been aimed at industrial development. Most corporations have announced expansion plans in other African countries. South African Breweries (SAB) now runs brewing companies in Botswana, Lesotho, Swaziland, Tanzania and Zambia. 'Our strategy in Africa', according to SAB's chair, 'is to dominate market share'.[166] Retail giants like Shoprite-Checkers and Pick 'n Pay have opened operations in Zambia, Mozambique, Namibia, Botswana, Kenya and Zimbabwe. Financial institutions like Standard Bank now operate in 13 other African countries, prompting the African Development Bank to comment that South African institutions have become 'increasingly important' in the commercial banking and insurance sectors of the region (Esterhuysen, 1994:68). Mining houses have made investments (many of them substantial) in Angola, Ghana, Botswana, the former Zaïre, Zambia, Namibia, Zimbabwe, Burkina Faso and Mali. Leisure companies have set up operations as far afield as West Africa and Egypt, while researchers have noted 'an increasing demand for South African project management in Africa'.[167] In Mozambique, the dismal state of the economy saw the government welcome right-wing Afrikaner farmers' bids to buy up agricultural land, with the blessing of Nelson Mandela. South Africa's emphasis on exports is likely to encourage firms which are unable to penetrate markets further afield to unload products and services on the economies of the region.

A key problem is that the debate on regional cooperation or integration has been restricted largely to government, business and donor circles. Along with regional counterparts, COSATU and NACTU did, in 1991, draw up a Draft Charter of Fundamental Rights of Workers in Southern Africa – but in Davies' view, it 'addressed only a small part of the challenge' (1992b:19).

Meanwhile, South Africa has benefited from a massive 'brain drain' suffered by other African countries as far afoot as West Africa. At least 200 of Zimbabwe's medical doctors emigrated to South Africa in 1991/2, while the country's two universities had to close several departments after losing some 200 lecturers since the early 1980s.[168]

In sum, greater integration and cooperation has been forged but along lines that are not based on the principles of equity, interdependence and mutual benefit which SADC has tried to promote. Instead, the trend has been towards 'hegemonic bilateralism', whereby neighbouring countries seek 'bilateral deals based on a "pragmatic extension" of existing relations' (Davies, 1992b:84). The pattern seems to confirm Patrick Bond's prediction of a:

> ... new wave of SA mining houses plucking non-renewable resources, SA construction firms piggy-backing on aid-funded projects for short term gain and SA manufacturers shipping out products that can't be sold at home, wiping out the SADC industries in the process.[169]

The danger is that restructured regional relationships could bear greater affinity to the abortive Constellation of Southern African States dream of the apartheid regime, than to progressive visions extolled by the ANC and the democratic movement.

Much is made of the SADC's potential role in forging a more equitable process of integration. Yet, the SADC's importance is potential, not existing. Its activities affect a very tiny proportion of the region's economies – only four per cent of the SADC's trade is between member countries, a quarter of that with South Africa. The value of the SADC, in some views,

> ... may be turn out to be mainly as a forum in which South Africa's neighbours can speak frankly to the people who still, as their predecessors did, overshadow the politics and economics of the region.[170]

Such conclusions might be premature, particularly if the SADC Trade Protocol, signed in August 1996, is allowed to mature and define regional economic relations.[171] Aimed at integrating regional markets, the agreement calls for the establishment of a free trade area by the year 2005 – though not in unconditional fashion. Tariff reductions would be introduced in asymmetrical fashion, with South Africa likely to make the speediest and deepest cuts to offset current trade imbalances.[172] Some allowances are to be made also for infant industries, enabling countries to apply for 'extended grace periods' during which tariff and subsidy reductions could be limited (within WTO provisions).

The protocol includes several other, potentially progressive features. An agreement on rules of origin will discourage assembly plants and repackaging operations, while 'local content' will be defined in regional terms and include content originating in any SADC country.

An infrastructural provision is aimed at improving transport and communications, border controls (both external and intra-regional), and harmonizing customs procedures (the latter provision could stem the dumping of illegal textiles and clothing in SADC countries). Meanwhile, existing bilateral agreements (for instance, SACU) will be integrated into the broader multilateral SADC process, and a dispute resolution body will be established. Poorly detailed, though, are provisions aimed at cross-border investment promotion.

Other recent SADC advances have included a Shared River-Basin Protocol which binds countries not to alter the courses of waterways, a Southern African Power Pool (geared at joint research into regional energy sources, production and distribution), and an anticipated Integrated Transport System geared at co-ordinating road, rail and air transport in the region. Also planned is a Finance and Investment Protocol to co-ordinate the banking and finance sectors in southern Africa.

The 1996 Trade Protocol has been registered with the WTO, thereby granting the SADC some leeway in negotiating regional agreements that might inhibit the impact of some WTO strictures. Another fortuitous development has been South Africa's decision not rush into a free trade agreement with the European Union (EU); instead, it has opted for a trade and development accord between *southern* Africa and the EU – though it is unclear whether this represents a principles stance or a negotiating tactic.

Potentially, these initiatives buoy hopes for a regional integration process that could exhibit progressive features. The test, though, will be South Africa's willingness to make good on the need to redress the stark imbalances that characterise relations currently – particularly when such concessions entail short-term 'sacrifices'. Powerful historical and current structural pressures – emanating from within South Africa and internationally – favour a continuation of South African hegemony in the region. Countering them will require more than the (perhaps ambivalent) political will evident in the SADC Trade Protocol.

Notes

1 Grateful thanks to John Sender for his valuable comments on this and the next chapter.
2 SA Reserve Bank figures (June 1995), calculated in 1990 constant prices.
3 During the 1960s, with the economy at its peak, 74 per cent of new entrants into the job market found jobs in the enumerated sectors. By the late 1980s, this had dropped to 12,5 per cent, prompting the NP government to admit that the unemployment crisis was structural (Gelb, 1994:3). Currently, fewer than 7 per cent of new entrants find work in the formal sector. See Dave Lewis in Gelb (1991, 244–66), and ILO (1996) for overviews of the unemployment crisis.
4 In 1993, 63,7 per cent of exports were primary or primary processed products.
5 For more, see Vishnu Padayachee's 'The politics of South Africa's international financial relations, 1970–1990', in Gelb (1991).
6 ABSA Bank, 1994, *Quarterly Economic Monitor* (July).
7 Gelb (1994:2).
8 Anthony Marx was one of few analysts not guilty of this oversight: 'With no cushion for hard times, South Africa's urban poor have been highly vulnerable to

economic shifts reflected most directly in higher prices for corn "mealies" and other food on which they spend much of their income. Their anger over increased hardship has exploded during economic downturns ... the unrest in 1976–1977 and 1984–1987 came in the wake of major recessions' (1992:245).

9   COSATU spokesperson Neil Coleman, writing in *Business Times*, 3 July 1994.

10   *Op. cit.*

11   SAIRR (1992:406–7). Whilst reflecting poorly on Stals' political acumen, the prediction underlined the widespread concern over South Africa's economic malaise.

12   Standard Bank, 1994, *Economic Review* (Third Quarter), Johannesburg.

13   For a survey of the controversy, see ILO (1996:65–71, 101–23).

14   Minister of Finance, Derek Keys's Budget Speech, June 1994, Cape Town.

15   See *SA Reserve Bank Quarterly Bulletin* (March 1994).

16   See *SA Reserve Bank Quarterly Bulletin* (September 1991).

17   For more, see Kahn (1991); Black, A., 'Manufacturing Development and the Economic Crisis: A Reversion to Primary Production?' in Gelb (1991).

18   Former NUMSA general secretary Enoch Godongwana, cited in *Business Day*, 7 April 1997.

19   Mineral Bureau figures, cited in ILO (1996:277).

20   SAIRR (1992:396).

21   According to the 1994 October Household Survey, only 2,4 per cent of unemployed African men and 0,9 per cent of African women received unemployment benefits; see ILO (1996:109).

22   The informal sector functions essentially as a substitute for an absent social welfare system for unemployed Africans and, with few exceptions, provides for subsistence level survival. However, many South Africans depend on unenumerated wage employment. Little is known about the numbers involved or trends in their wages.

23   The car theft and hijacking industry can, by some accounts, 'fill orders' faster than vehicle manufacturers, and as far afield as Zambia, Mozambique, Zimbabwe and Malawi. Its nodes extend from procurement (car thieves), to reassembly operations (so-called 'chop shops'), transport networks, state licensing and customs departments, and the police itself.

24   See Simone, A., 1995, 'Draft Background Paper for All Africa Ministers Meeting on the Future of African Cities', p. 2.

25   Blumenfeld, J., 'The International Dimension' in Schrire, (1992:71).

26   Padayachee (1994a:26). He went on to note the 'striking' similarities between these commitments and the NP government's controversial Normative Economic Model which earlier had earned the wrath of the ANC.

27   Gelb (1991:30).

28   The extent of poverty and inequality has been widely documented. See, for example, RDP (1995); SALDRU (1994); World Bank (1994). For a critique of some of the data and analysis, see ILO (1996:177–222).

29   World Bank (1992). Compare this to Brazil, where the poorest 20 per cent of the population earns 2,5 per cent of the country's income while the richest 20 per cent earns more than 65 per cent (*UN World Development 1992*, pp. 276–7). The pattern is not restricted to the developing world: in the USA, Australia and Switzerland, the richest 20 per cent earns on average eight to ten times the income of the poorest 20 per cent.

30   The Gini coefficient is the most common measure of income inequality. Perfect equality measures 0 and perfect inequality 1.

31   See Mcgrath and Whiteford (1994:47–50).

32   RDP (1995).

33   Whiteford, A. 'The poor get even poorer', *Mail & Guardian*, 18 March 1994.

34 Andrew Whiteford, 'Debunking the poor white myth', *Mail & Guardian*, 20 January 1995, citing the World Bank-funded 1994 *Living Standards and Development Survey*.

35 Whiteford and McGrath (1994).

36 This translated into about 11 million citizens. Africans living in towns made up 15,2 per cent, those living in cities 11 per cent, whilst coloureds, Asians and whites accounted for the remaining 3,8 per cent; *Living Standards and Development Survey*, 1994.

37 ILO (1996:19), citing CASE, 1995, *RDP-relevant selection from the October Household Survey* 1994, CASE mimeo, Johannesburg.

38 Development Bank of South Africa, 1991, *South Africa: An Interregional Profile*, DBSA, Johannesburg, cited in ILO (1996:23).

39 SALDRU Survey, 1993. A broad definition of unemployment was used to calculate these figures.

40 SA Police Service figures, cited in *The Citizen*, 27 May 1996. According to some estimates one in two South African women will be sexually assaulted in their life times.

41 SAIRR (1992:344). Rural housing conditions are even worse.

42 The differentiation in services for 'coloured' and Indian communities is much less extreme.

43 Bundy, C., 'Development and Inequality in Historical Perspective' in Schrire, R. (1992:25).

44 Official police statistics show increases in crime rates. But they reflect *reported* crimes, prompting some observers to question whether the incidence of crimes such as rape, assault and housebreaking may, in fact, have remained relatively constant but have been reported more frequently since 1990. There is, however, general agreement that 'recorded crimes ... substantially under-represent crime rates'; see Shaw (1995).

45 'People don't talk anymore. They kill. And we're starting to see kids acting this way' – Marilyn Donaldson, Trauma Clinic counsellor (author's interview, March 1997, Johannesburg).

46 Most specialize in drug trafficking and vehicle theft, while at least 180 operate internationally; *Financial Mail*, 6 September 1996, pp. 64–5. These figures are also disputed.

47 South African Police Services statistics.

48 Shaw (1995:25–6).

49 SAIRR, *South African Survey 1996/97*, p. 87.

50 Shaw (1995:20).

51 *Op. cit.* p. 11.

52 *SouthScan*, Vol. 12, No. 14 (11 April 1997).

53 *The Star*, 6 January 1997.

54 Mike Nicol, *The Star*, 3 July 1996.

55 The vacuum has been filled by a plethora of charismatic 'churches', and the abidingly strong Zion Christian Church.

56 In addition to its estimated one million alcoholics, South Africa is the world's largest consumer of the banned depressant Mandrax which, typically, is mixed with marijuana and smoked.

57 Marilyn Donaldson, author's interview, March 1997.

58 Quoted in *Sunday Independent*, 21 July 1996.

59 See Marais (1993) and Seekings (1993).

60 For example, JEP and CASE (1993).

61   The 1993 'Growing up tough' national survey of South African youth by CASE and JEP found that 69 per cent of school drop-outs still wanted to study to the level they had originally planned. For a summary, see Marais (1993b).

62   For an instructive summary of the state's role in the growth paths of first- and second-tier NICs in the region, see Ghosh (1997:1–19).

65   Hobsbawm (1994:423).

64   Taken as a whole, sub-Saharan African owes more in debt than it produces. The figure stood at $340 billion in 1996, with annual servicing totalling $24 billion; see 'Africa's recent growth may be sign of better days', *Business Day*, 18 April 1996.

65   *UN World Economic Survey*, 1992.

66   These flows are 'off an extremely modest base, and Africa's share of total capital flow still lags other developing or newly industrialised countries by a long way', as noted by a *Business Day* editorial, 22 April 1997.

67   'Conventional economies fail to deliver on promises', *Business Day*, 22 April 1997.

68   For a critique of this sentiment, see *ILO Global Employment Report*, October 1996.

69   For a critique, see 'How jobless is the future?', *Left Business Observer*, No. 75, 16 December, 1996.

70   Vadney (1987:391).

71   Cited in Kentridge (1993:77).

72   *Op. cit.*, p. 63.

73   *Ibid.*

74   Hobsbawm (1995:572), citing Bairoch, P., 1993, *Economics and World History: Myths and Paradoxes*, Hemel, Hampstead, p. 75.

75   For a sobering summary, see Jeff Faux, 'The "American Model" Exposed', *The Nation*, 27 October 1997.

76   Krugman (1995:174). Unemployment dropped sharply in 1988, only to bounce back past the 10 per cent mark within two years.

77   *Op. cit.*, p. 135; NIEP (1996:17).

78   It is also worth noting that, in the UK, citizens were more heavily taxed after Thatcher's 14-year reign than before.

79   World Bank, *The East Asian Miracle: Economic Growth and Public Policy*, World Bank Policy Research Department, Washington, cited in Davies (1995:62–3).

80   Wade (1996:36).

81   Sweden, a backward economy at the beginning of the century, was perhaps the most striking testament to these programmes.

82   In the USA, for example, the number of blue-collar workers casting votes in presidential elections fell by one-third between 1960 and 1988 (Hobsbawm, 1995:581).

83   Hobsbawm's caustic sentiment (1995:567). The trend has acquired many labels and triggered an avalanche of debates, to which the following texts are a useful introduction: Laclau and Mouffe (1985), Hall and Jacques (1989), Osborne (1991) and McRobbie in Morley and Chen (1996).

84   In South Africa, for example, these companies employ more people than the entire police force.

85   The 1949 prediction of anti-communist Russian Ivan Ilyin, cited by Hobsbawm (1995:567).

86   John Holloway has argued that 'this is not an "internationalization" or "globalization" of the economy ... but a change in the form of the global existence of capital' (1994:41).

87   Gordon (1988:59).

88   *Ibid.*

89   Holloway (1994:33–42).

90 See Strange, S., 1986, 'Supra-nationals and the State' in John A. Hall (ed.), *States in History*, London, cited in Gordon (1988:61).

91 Panitch (1994:14).

92 Murray, R., 1971, 'The Internationalization of Capital and the Nation State', *New Left Review*, No. 67 (May–June), pp. 84–108, cited in Panitch (1994:19).

93 Parts of this section are indebted to comments and material provided by Vishnu Padayachee.

94 'Agents of Inequality', *Dollars and Sense*, November 1991, p. 15.

95 *Ibid.*

96 ILO (1996:32).

97 MERG (1993: 241, table 7.4).

98 These factors by no means exhaust the list of structural handicaps plaguing this sector – for a comprehensive account, see the Industrial Strategy Project's 'Meeting the Global Challenge: A Framework for Industrial Revival in South Africa' in Baker *et al.*, (1993:91–126).

99 'Exports rise as domestic demand cools', *Business Day*, 13 June 1997.

100 Kahn (1992).

101 The five largest export markets in 1992 were the USA, Germany, UK, Japan and Switzerland. Only in the latter instance did the trade balance lie in South Africa's favour.

102 *UN World Economic Survey*, 1992, cited by Paul Krugman, 'Trends in World Trade and Foreign Direct Investment' in Baker *et al.* (1993:24).

103 Freund (1994a:46) has noted that 'South African agricultural capitalism is characterised by a negative international trade balance in most years, heavy debts and low productivity in many spheres'.

104 *Trade Monitor*, August 1993, p. 11.

105 Although, in many cases, they retained an indirect presence through financial and technology agreements.

106 'Indicators point to progress on growth', *Business Day*, 11 June 1997.

107 'As South Africa is welcomed back into the international economic fold and prepares itself for full participation in the global economy ...' is a standard cliché in economic circles – in this case it introduced the Standard Bank's journal, *Economic Review*, May 1994.

108 See Cronin, J., 'Exploding the myths of the neo-liberal agenda', *Business Day*, 9 November 1994.

109 The rise in private sector fixed investment during 1994 (by approximately 13 per cent) was 'mainly limited to a number of major projects, spurred by tax concessions', according to the Reserve Bank, *Quarterly Bulletin*, No. 197 (Sept. 1995), p. 5.

110 Standard Bank chief economist Nico Czypionka, quoted in the *Argus*, 25 June 1994.

111 *Business Map Update*, 10 February 1997.

112 World Bank, *Global Economic Prospects 1996*.

113 According to the International Finance Corporation (the World Bank's private sector investment arm), cited by Hawkins, T., 'Africa left out in the cold', *Financial Times* , 15 June 1996.

114 *Ibid.*

115 Cited by Bond, P., 1992, 'South Africa's comic investment image', *Africa South* (April).

116 *Business Map Quarterly Review* (January 1996).

117 *Business Map South African Investment Report* (May 1997), p. 5.

118   Hirsch, A., 1995, 'Productive Investment Trends in South Africa' (workshop paper).
119   *Ibid.*
120   Cited in *Business Map Quarterly Review* (Jan 1996), p. 12.
121   Hawkins, T. 'Africa left out in the cold', *Financial Times*, 15 June 1996.
122   As even a 1995 Ernst & Young survey noted, 'the primary motivation for entering countries' was 'not low production costs' but the 'potential rate of return and local market demand' – a self-evident point.
123   Schneider and Frei (1985:167–75).
124   See *Trade Monitor*, No. 3 (August 1993), p. 3.
125   Baker *et al.* (1993:47).
126   See the Industrial Strategy Project's (ISP) 'Meeting the Global Challenge: A Framework for Industrial Revival in South Africa' in Baker *et al.* (1993:93–7).
127   'What Will Make South Africa Competitive?' in Baker *et al.* (1993:56).
128   See Baker *et al.* (1993:99).
129   See the Department of Trade and Industry's *Support Measures for the Enhancement of the International Competitiveness of South Africa's Industrial Sector* document, released in 1995. An earlier version prompted one business journalist to ask whether its 'brand of economics' represented 'Keynesian Thatcherism, or the opposite?'; *Business Day*, 14 September 1994.
130   Lall, S. in Baker *et al.* (1993:61–2).
131   The announcement ended a bruising, five-week autoworkers strike within hours. There is a suspicion that the announcement was timed to end the strike, after the labour ministry had refused to intervene in the dispute.
132   The department's 'industrial policy' was only released in late 1995.
133   Former trade and industry minister Trevor Manuel, quoted in *Business Day*, 1 September 1994.
134   Department of Finance (1996:11).
135   *Op. cit.*, pp. 11–12.
136   ISP, 'Meeting the Global Challenge' in Baker *et al.* (1993:98). These conglomerates received 55 per cent of pay-outs in 1992/3.
137   See 'Forex controls "need to with a big bang"', *Sunday Times*, 18 September 1994.
138   Department of Finance (1996:11)..
139   'SA's big export surge', *Mail & Guardian*, 27 March 1997.
140   'Growth forecasts drop as GDP dips', *Business Day*, 3 June 1997.
141   Thus, three-quarters of the record capital inflow in May 1997 was derived from the partial privatization of the telecommunications giant Telkom; see 'Reserves soar as capital soars into SA', *Business Day*, 3 June 1997.
142   Baker *et al.* (1993:69).
143   Davies (1995:63).
144   Former trade and industry minister Trevor Manuel, *Business Day*, 1 September 1994.
145   Samir Amin, interview, Johannesburg, August 1993.
146   Rob Davies has produced among the most lucid and sustained investigations of South Africa's relations with the region. This section draws in particular on his writings.
147   Donor countries' support stems primarily from their desire to be released from aid commitments to economically decrepit countries in the region.
148   Nelson Mandela, quoted in *Southscan*, 29 March 1991.
149   Davies (1992:3).
150   World Bank, 1991, *Intra-Regional Trade in sub-Saharan Africa*, Economics and Finance Division, Washington, cited in Davies (1992:9)

151 O'Meara, D., 1991, 'Regional Economic Integration in Post-Apartheid South Africa – Dream or Reality' in A. van Nieuwkerk and G. van Staden (eds), *Southern Africa at the Crossroads*, Institute of International Affairs, cited by Beaudet and Theade (1994:233).

152 *Ibid.*

153 *SADC Regional Economic Survey*, 1988, Gaborone, cited by Beaudet (1994:236). In 1990, South African imports to SADC totalled R12,4 billion, while its imports amounted to a mere R2,4 billion (Davies *et al.*, 1993:21). Formed originally in a bid to wean neighbouring countries of their dependence on South Africa, the renamed South African Development Community (SADC) in 1994 admitted South Africa as a member.

154 ICFTU/Organizacion Regional Interamericana de Trabajadores, 1991, *Economic Integration, Development and Democracy: An International Conference*, Costa Rica, cited by Davies (1992:17).

155 See, for instance, Hanlon (1986b); and various essays in *South African Review*, No. 4 and No. 5 for overviews of that strategy and its effects.

156 Davies *et al.* (1993:19).

157 The UNDP's 1992 *Human Development Report* warned that unilateral trade reforms would further diminish the already precarious bargaining positions of countries of the South.

158 See MERG (1993:279).

159 For more detailed proposals, see Davies *et al.* (1993:49–59), while Esterhuysen (1994) contains an overview of these institutions.

160 *Op. cit.*, p. 15.

161 'Still the boss', *Africa Confidential*, Vol. 36, No. 17, 25 August 1995.

162 Davies (1992a:80)..

163 *Ibid.*

164 *Op. cit.*, p. 81.

165 Esterhuysen (1994:64). The exports comprise mainly manufactured and processed goods, such as steel and paper products, chemicals, foodstuffs, automobiles and mining equipment. Its imports are mainly agricultural commodities.

166 Quoted in 'A new scramble', *The Economist*, 12 August 1995. In Tanzania, SAB sacked 700 workers when it took over the state-run brewery.

167 *Business Map Quarterly Review*, September 1995.

168 *Op. cit.*, p. 72.

169 'South Africa's Comic Investment Image', *Africa South* (April 1992), quoted by Beaudet and Theade (1994:238).

170 'Still the boss', *Africa Confidential*, Vol. 36, No. 17, 25 August 1995.

171 This section is indebted to notes provided by Dot Keet.

172 South Africa's import:export ratios with other regional economies are hugely skewed, rising as high as 1:7 with Botswana, 1:11 with Zambia, 1:12 with Lesotho.

CHAPTER FIVE

The evolution of ANC economic policy
A short walk to orthodoxy

On May Day, 1994, Nelson Mandela declared in the country's largest news-paper that:

> In our economic policies ... there is not a single reference to things like nationalisation, and this is not accidental. There is not a single slogan that will connect us with any Marxist ideology.[1]

The announcement drew ritual praise from business leaders who, despite ample evidence to the contrary, still worried that ANC economic policy might lurch in a radical direction. In their discomfort they recalled Mandela's assurance four years earlier, upon his release from prison, that:

> ... the nationalization of the mines, banks and monopoly industry is the policy of the ANC and a change or modification of our views in this regard is inconceivable.[2]

Those words had exposed Mandela for the first time to the fickle and fierce dynamics ANC economic policy would become subjected to – within hours JSE traders were, as one observer put it, 'unceremoniously falling out of bed' to launch a selling spree.[3]

As the idiom advises, 'Never say "never"'. More than any other aspect of ANC policy, the party's economic thinking was launched on a roller coaster ride – buffeted by threats, cajoling, ridicule and injunctions from business organizations, banks, Western governments, activists, trade unions, foreign lending institutions, economists and consultants.

The first target for attack was the ANC's alleged penchant for national-ization,[4] which it soon dropped – to the alarm of many supporters. Nationalization was a red herring, though. Its resonance in popular dis-course stemmed less from its literal prescription than from its symbolic power; encoded in that instrument was the overriding commitment to redistribute resources and opportunity in favour of the majority. The retreat from nationalization was read, therefore, as hinting at the likely dilution of that broader avowal.

Mandela's May Day statement reflected the extent to which the terms of the political transition had been projected also into the sphere of economic policy-making. The need to build consensus among key stakeholders – 'to bring everybody along' – reigned supreme, and the ANC assumed the task of trying to harmonize and distil from antagonistic interests economic policies that could win consensual endorsement. This, in a context where the ANC had paid scant attention to economic policy during the 1990–3 negotiations and, when it did, relied on weak advice. As South Africans celebrated the 1994 election results, there was already unambiguous evidence that post-apartheid economic policy would conform to the pronouncement, seven years earlier, by Anglo American Corporation's Clem Sunter:

> Negotiation works. Rhetoric is dropped, reality prevails and in the end the companies concerned go on producing the minerals, goods and services.[5]

By 1996, as we shall see, the ANC government's economic policy had acquired an overt class character, and was unabashedly geared to service, the respective prerogatives of national and international capital and the aspirations of the emerging black bourgeoisie, perhaps above all – at the expense of the impoverished majority's hopes for a less iniquitous social and economic order. It was a momentous shift for a party with a strong working class constituency, that was closely allied with the SACP and COSATU, and replete with avowed socialists in its leadership ranks. But it also betrayed the ideological ambivalence of the organization.

This section tracks the evolution of ANC economic policy which, in sweeping and telling terms, was consummated in the ANC government's macroeconomic plan, the Growth, Employment and Redistribution (GEAR) strategy, released in June 1996.

Smoke and mirrors

When the ANC was unbanned in 1990, it had no economic policy, a peculiar situation for an eight-decade-old liberation organization despite the efforts internationally on the left to train a cadre of ANC exile economists. Its 1988 Constitutional Guidelines had committed it to a mixed economy. But that avowal hung in a policy vacuum, and invoked vague, sweeping passages of the Freedom Charter which pledged that:

> The People shall share in the country's wealth!
> The national wealth of our country, the heritage of all South Africans shall be restored to the people;

The mineral wealth beneath the soil, the banks and monopoly industry shall be transferred to the ownership of the people as a whole;
All other industries and trade shall be controlled to assist the well-being of the people;
All people shall have equal rights to trade where they choose, to manufacture and to enter all trades, crafts and professions.[6]

The ANC's first serious attempt to fill this lacuna came in the form of a 1990 'Discussion Document on Economic Policy', issued by its new Department of Economic Policy (DEP). In its main themes (and several other respects) the document echoed policy work done by COSATU's Economic Trends group which, until then, had been responsible for the most substantial efforts to chart a sustainable, progressive economic strategy. Central to the ANC document was the 'restructuring' of the economy which, as economist Nicoli Nattrass noted, could 'include anything from extensive state intervention to conventional market-driven structural adjustment' (1994c:6). The document envisaged an active role for the state in planning industrial strategy and overcoming racial, gender and geographic inequalities. It stressed the need to restructure the financial sector which, it said, 'does not sufficiently direct savings into productive activity nor into critical areas of infrastructural development' and, instead, encourages 'a scramble for short-term speculative profit'.[7] This would include funnelling foreign investment into targeted areas of the economy. Basic needs would not be met through 'inflationary financing' but by marshalling domestic savings and raising corporate tax rates. Also advised was the unbundling of conglomerates in order to stimulate competition and allow entry by small and medium-sized enterprises into the economy. Calls from business for a low-wage economy in order to achieve 'international competitiveness' were rejected, while a central role would be reserved for organized labour in devising and implementing policy.

The overriding theme was '*growth through redistribution*', a formula 'in which redistribution acts as a spur to growth and in which the fruits of growth are redistributed to satisfy basic needs'.[8] The logic was that growth could be spurred by satisfying 'the basic needs of the majority through a redistribution of income which would increase employment, demand and production' (Kentridge, 1993:6).

Economists like Nicoli Nattrass have contended that the 'growth through redistribution' route was chosen largely 'because it served the political purpose of uniting various constituencies within the ANC' – implying a certain degree of expediency and an awareness that the policy had a short shelf life. One could argue the converse: that it reflected the influence of the left (mainly SACP and COSATU-aligned) within the ANC at the time. Strengthening that leverage was the fact that the ANC's economic debate was still occurring within its own circle (and had not yet been subjected to the imperatives of broader consensus-building), and was being waged largely at the ideological (and not the *technical*) level. That would soon change.

The 'growth through redistribution' approach was severely censured by mainstream economists and in the media. Attacks ranged from consternation about the 'socialist' undertones of the document to a more sophisticated set of objections to its alleged overtones of macroeconomic populism. The latter variant argued that it tended to:

> ... underestimate the negative effects on investment, overestimate the existence of spare capacity, and fail[ed] to predict the continuing high demand for imports and the inflationary impact of large deficits.[9]

The argument held that a state spending spree (geared at redistribution) would overheat the economy, and bog it down in a morass of foreign exchange shortages, currency devaluations, rampant inflation, severe indebtedness and cuts in real wages. Chile (1970–3) and Peru (1985–9) were invoked as typical examples of such folly. In short, the 'growth through redistribution' path was deemed unsustainable, with the Mont Fleur scenario later likening it to the fateful flight of Icarus, warning:

> After a year or two the programme runs into budgetary, monetary and balance of payments constraints. The budget deficit well exceeds 10%. Depreciations, inflation, economic uncertainty and collapse follow. The country experiences an economic crisis of hitherto unknown proportions which results in social collapse and political chaos (Le Roux *et al.*, 1993a:8)

Still, it is worth recalling the thinking behind the 'growth through redistribution' slogan. In a 1991 Development Bank paper it was described as a growth path resting on both export promotion and inward industrialization, geared at significantly expanding domestic demand and social infrastructure. The Keynesian overtones are clear. In Kentridge's summary it argued that:

> ... the poor consume goods made with a higher labour component, in which direct import content is lower, and that spending by the poor not only multiplies the GDP more than that by the rich, but that it does so primarily among the poor. In short, growth from redistribution would boost output and employment more than a similar injection among the rich (1993:8).

Such thinking quickly withered before the criticisms it evoked, although this opposition was never elaborated into anything resembling a coherent intellectual critique. The ANC's May 1992 policy guidelines made no reference to the formula. In workshops activists were discouraged from referring to the slogan. Over the next two years, the party's economic thinking would increasingly bear the imprints of neo-liberal thinking, as the need for macro-economic stability became interpreted as demanding fiscal and monetary stringency and calls for deregulation, liberalization, privatization and export-led growth gained favour among ANC leaders and their economic advisers.

It is difficult to pinpoint the factors that led to the conversion of ANC economic thinking to orthodoxy. But, as Patrick Bond has suggested, the plethora of corporate scenario planning exercises unleashed after 1990 had a telling impact.[10] The first was Nedcor/Old Mutual's *Prospects for a Successful Transition*, launched in late 1990 and completed in 1993.[11] This was followed by the insurance conglomerate Sanlam's *Platform for Investment* scenario and the social-democratic *Mont Fleur Scenarios*. Meanwhile, other documents, like the South African Chamber of Business' (SACOB) *Economic Options for South Africa* document, were wheeled into the fray.

In reflecting on the scenario exercises, it is helpful to distinguish between their form and content. On the latter score, there was some dissonance in their prescriptions – although an overarching set of precepts was common to all of them. Most important was their shared demand that economic policy had to become grounded in relationships of trust, negotiation and consensus-building. Decoded, this implied imposing 'a kind of "coerced harmony"', analogous to the central dynamic applied in the political negotiations.[12] In Bond's view, 'the scenario exercises reflected the desire of the masters and carefully hand-picked participants to come up with a deal – rather than with good analysis'.[13] Undergirding that process was a set of elementary truisms, notably the need for macroeconomic stringency, restraint in efforts at social restructuring, an outward-oriented economy and a facilitating (as opposed to regulating) state. Their common thrust was to demonize as 'macro-economic populism'[14] any attempt to ground future economic policy in the mutually reinforcing dynamic of growth and redistribution.

Also important was the form of the exercises and the activities that accompanied them. Their language was that of melodrama, laden with populist flippancies and cartoon-like metaphors.[15] Lavishly promoted (in the form of books, videos, multi-media presentations, newspaper supplements), their impact was ensured by a bewildering assortment of seminars, conferences, workshops, briefings, international 'fact-finding' trips and high-profile visits by carefully chosen foreign 'experts' – financed by business and foreign development agencies. ANC leaders were fêted with private 'orientation' sessions and confabs at exclusive game resorts. The ideological barrage was incessant, and amplified by the corporate-owned media which gleefully attacked any signs of heterodoxy and dissonance in ANC thinking. By 1993, Sanlam's *Platform for Investment* document could justifiably gloat about the:

... close working relationship between the ANC, the World Bank, the Development Bank of Southern Africa, the Consultative Business Movement, and other organisations which are painstakingly pointing out the longer run costs of many redistributive strategies.[16]

Broadly indicative of the counsel arrayed in those interventions SACOB's *Economic Options for South Africa* document. It insisted that free enterprise was 'the remedy for poverty and ensured economic growth', though it did see a need for some economic reforms. Unsurprisingly, it roundly rejected the 'growth through redistribution' formula. Instead of a new development strategy the country needed to create optimal conditions for free enterprise to flourish. This meant that the task of achieving social and political stability rested with the state, which had to alleviate poverty and homelessness – within policy and other parameters that favoured capital. On that score, the document proved to be prescient. As summarized by Kentridge, it advocated 'the promotion of small business, the reduction of corporate tax, the maintenance and upgrading of the country's infrastructure, and a reordering of government spending priorities to tackle poverty, unemployment and the skills shortage' (1993:18). Similar thinking would later infiltrate the government's RDP White Paper and become displayed in macroeconomic policy.

The sub-text was far from innocent. The welfarist elements admitted to by institutions like SACOB were to function as a 'political accessory' appended to an economic strategy, 'necessary evils rather than the basis for creating a new set of social alliances, a new era for economic growth and the bedrock for social stability in post-apartheid society' (Morris, 1993c:9).

Slightly less orthodox were the Nedcor/Old Mutual scenarios. These focused on the need to achieve competitiveness in manufactured exports and envisaged two stages of recovery. The government would make large investments in social programmes and infrastructure, after which a manufactured export drive would commence, founded on a compact between business, labour and government. Noteworthy was its downplaying of the need for massive foreign investment.

It must be noted that around economic policy in general, but especially around industrial policy, South African capitalists were not (and had never been) of a single mind. Broad agreement existed around the need for a market economy, but different fractions of capital demanded different restructuring interventions that best favoured them.

The plethora of research projects launched by the IMF and World Bank conformed with and elaborated the same overarching perspective. While the IMF issued customarily strident injunctions, the World Bank, soon after the 1990 thaw, opened channels to the ANC and the trade unions and enlisted researchers associated with the democratic movement in its projects. 'This is the only country in the world where we speak to the oppo-sition,' its representative later boasted.[17] The soil of conciliation and con-sensus was being diligently toiled. The Bank's *Reducing Poverty* report became the public component of an intensive process of lobbying and 'trust-building' with the ANC and other popular organizations. It melded detailed analyses of South Africa's economic plight with somewhat restrained neo-liberal directives that were often offset by incorporating aspects of progres-sive thinking. In the Bank's view, growth hinged on private sector-led expansion in labour-intensive sectors of the economy – though it also reserved a subsidizing (through incentives and credit) and facilitating role (through investment in health and education) for the state:

> South Africa's unequal legacy cannot be reversed solely by market reforms because those disenfranchised by apartheid will be unable to obtain the resources necessary to exploit market opportunities.[18]

The Bank's *Reducing Poverty* report criticized the capital-intensive character of industry, the heavy state subsidy support for large-scale capital intensive projects, and claimed that 200 to 400 thousand fewer jobs were created in the 1980s as a result of the African workers' wage increases. However, along with the reminder that growth required 'continuing fiscal discipline' and 'happier industrial relations', the Bank made the rather unusual point that labour should not 'bear the brunt of reduction in real wages'.[19] On the latter score, the Bank diverged from the IMF's pronouncements. The latter's *Key Issues in the South African Economy* document paraded the institution's cus-tomary arguments in forceful fashion. Along with slashing the budget deficit, lowering inflation and maintaining macroeconomic stability, liberalized trade and financial relations were posed as essential precursors to increased exports, foreign investment and access to credit. It warned against 'excessive' government expenditures on education, health, training and complementary infrastructure, while declaring that the 'remedy for structural unemployment is to increase the productivity of labour, to lower the real wage, or some com-bination of the two'. Although fallacious,[20] the argument found many a receptive ear. The National Manpower Commission's chair, Frans Baker, declared for instance that while wage cuts were 'not necessarily' the answer, the ideal approach would be 'to let employers and unions negotiate wages in the face of the cold winds of international competition'.[21] In the business press, some commentators openly advised the speedy implementation of IMF-style structural adjustment:

> The IMF will want measures such as currency liberalisation, reducing gov-ernment spending, cutting subsidies to blue chip companies, privatising state assets and busting the cartels in labour and other markets. Some will com-plain about a loss of sovereignty, but we would have undertaken these

reforms years ago had we not be thwarted by vested interests ... we've been unable to make the reforms that will give us 6% growth. Perhaps the IMF will help.[22]

Drawing heavily on IMF thinking was the apartheid government's Normative Economic Model (NEM, released March 1993). This was an attempt to add some coherence to the bedraggled and erratic economic policies pursued by Pretoria. Having hopped the supply-side bandwagon in the mid-1980s, the government touted privatization, trade liberalization, spending cuts and strict monetary discipline as the way forward. The conversion to free market economics, however, was not unequivocal. The zeal for privatization proved short-lived, as caution set in on tariff cuts and former finance minister Derek Keys advocated a strong government role in facilitating an investment-driven economic recovery (Kentridge, 1993). Government economic policy remained ramshackle, a pastiche of Thatcherite adjustments and statist legacies. The NEM sought to establish a more coherent policy framework.

The NEM bore the hallmark of a January 1992 IMF 'occasional paper' which reversed the 'growth through redistribution' formula, and proceeded by way of elimination to argue for adjustments that were in step with its standard directives to the South.

Paving the way to growth, according to the NEM, would be an ensemble of measures that included tax cuts for companies, increased indirect taxation, wage restraint (and higher productivity), lower inflation, restricted capital outflows, budget deficit cuts, higher spending on research and development and training to raise exports, improvements in the social wage, restricting unions' positions in collective bargaining and corporatist relations between government, labour and business. In sum, a trickle-down model with government providing some support (through welfare and public works projects) to the 'short-term' victims of adjustments.

The ANC and COSATU unreservedly slammed the government model, and the NEM seemingly was ushered onto the sidelines of the debate – although, three years later, the ANC government's macroeconomic strategy would contain several of its elements. Even mainstream business journals concurred, suggesting that 'neither the model's scenario nor that of the IMF have any hope of whatever of being achieved'.[23]

In late 1993, there appeared the ostensibly social-democratic *Mont Fleur* scenario. In retrospect it ranked as an important factor in the march of orthodoxy – less for its content details than for its theme song and the range of progressive (including ANC) economists and union figures it drew into the exercise. The scenario resolutely assailed heterodox strategic options by daubing them in the grim colours of macroeconomic populism. Striking was its dissuasion of redistributive state spending. The intervention was made all the more notable by the fact that it occurred several months before the release of the MERG report, *Making Democracy Work: A Framework for Macro-economic Policy in South Africa* – the outcome of a process which, since 1991, had ostensibly been the main site of ANC economic policy development. As we shall see, MERG died an unceremonious and speedy death – confirmation of the extent to which the ANC had surrendered to the voices of realism.

By late 1993, noted Kentridge, 'the language and tone [of ANC and business policy documents] are so similar that at times they appear interchangeable' (1993:26). The capitulation did not occur unchallenged, however. From 1992 onwards, the ANC's policy resolutions had increasingly hedged progressive state regulation with caveats clearly aimed at mollifying business. This triggered angry reactions within the ANC's grassroots constituencies and COSATU. During the negotiations process, consultation by the ANC with its membership and political allies was patchy and perfunctory, and the relationship between the negotiations and economic policy formulation virtually non-existent. Pressure from ANC and trade union activists had kept on the agenda demands like restructuring the financial sector and progressive taxation – but only until 1992 when they were dropped from ANC resolutions. At the same time, the ANC began mooting the need for property rights guarantees and privatization. Its visions of change came to orbit around a 'developmental state' which would 'lead, coordinate, plan and dynamize a national economic strategy' aimed at job creation and redistributing resources to the poor.[24]

Activists did fight back. At the May 1992 ANC Policy Conference they pushed privatization off the agenda and softened the wording of other placatory pledges. But the gist of the post-1990 retreats were endorsed, thanks partly, as Nattrass has suggested, to the personal presence of ANC leaders Nelson Mandela, Walter Sisulu and Cyril Ramaphosa in the economic policy debates at the conference. The draft policy guidelines emerged substantively intact though semantically adjusted. Thus the word 'privatization' was replaced with an unwieldy phrase designed to mollify dissent.[25] The exception was the re-appearance of the call for greater control of financial institutions.

ANC economic thinking came to reflect, according to ANC economist Viv McMenamin, 'a shift away from policies which may be morally and politically correct, but which will cause strong adverse reaction from powerful local and international interests' (Kentridge, 1993:10). Its draft policy guidelines (released in April 1992) had been stripped of references to higher corporate taxes, made no mention of restructuring or regulating the financial sector and mooted the possibility of privatization in the public sector – portentous changes that betrayed the waning influence of the left in ANC economic policy-making. Increasingly, the labour movement was being portrayed as representing a narrow and relatively 'privileged' constituency. The 'labour aristocracy' argument would later be vigorously pursued by main-stream economists (notably Nicoli Nattrass) and resonated profoundly with the *petit bourgeois* constituency in the ANC (who, themselves, would be threatened by measures such as minimum wages).

The ANC's commitment to an export-oriented growth strategy was also assured, despite warnings from unlikely quarters such as the GATT, that:

> ... export-led growth, while beneficial to the balance of payments, is unlikely to immediately affect levels of unemployment, given the capital intensity of the export sector, unless labour-intensive downstream industries can be developed.[26]

The endorsement of an export-led growth path stemmed not simply from 'cajoling by business', but was promoted also from within the left's ranks – by the COSATU-initiated ISP.[27] Improved manufacturing export perform-ance had been acknowledged on the left as an important factor in address-ing South Africa's endemic current account difficulties and its reliance on revenue from primary commodity exports. This required restructuring industries which had been declining since the 1970s and which produced a range and volume of manufactured exports that were negligible compared with Brazil and Mexico.[28] But a revived manufactured export capacity could not become the central vector of an economic growth strategy which, at least some left economists still argued, had also to focus on restructuring, developing and expanding the *internal* market. Such perspectives were marginalized, however.

Unlike business, the ISP stressed that competitiveness derived not so much from lower input costs (such as cheaper wages) as from product quality and variety, speedy innovation, capital and labour productivity, and 'the endow-ment of widely spread skills' (Joffe *et al.*, 1994b:17). Instead of suppressing wages to lower input costs, it advised enhancing productivity (through skills upgrading, better training and wages, and greater democracy in the work-place), increasing the social wage and allowing producers to 'take advantage of the lower wages in rural areas and disadvantaged areas'.[29] Special empha-sis was placed on high-value products. Rather than subject industry to a process of attrition by randomly removing protection, the ISP proposed 'a trade policy that attempts to sharpen the flow of incentives from the interna-tional market' within an overall industrial strategy.[30] The desired alchemy required a state hand in applying supply-side measures and in providing a range of (dis)incentives that could make the market function better – 'a kind of liberal Keynesianism', as one of the team members joked. Many of the ele-ments of the ISP plan could have augmented an industrial revival strategy geared at servicing popular domestic needs. Instead, they were deployed in a framework that pivoted South Africa's economic revival on an export-led growth strategy. This despite the team's own admission that:

... entry in external markets is increasingly difficult, partly because of the growth of protectionist barriers in key large economies and partly because of heightened competition. At the same time, most of the developing world (including South Africa) is being forced to open domestic markets to imports.[31]

Rearguard actions

COSATU tried to oppose many of the developments surveyed here. Two counter-attacks in particular were devised. The first was a push for a greater institutionalized role in economic and industrial policy-making.

In late 1992, it issued an economic policy document that emphasized job creation and meeting health, education and housing needs. Its broad thrust towards social transformation belied attempts to portray the federation as defending a narrow set of interests. Moreover, arguments that a social contract was needed to advance these objectives were winning ground in COSATU. Since the early 1990s, several affiliates had already put this into practice at industry and company levels – NUM's 1992 profit-sharing deal with mining houses and NUMSA's agreements with employers around restructuring the auto industry were two examples. COSATU's push for the creation of a National Economic Forum (NEF) was in line with this thinking. Such a bargaining body would transfer decision-making on key economic issues from government into a forum where trade unions could wield influence. Key ANC leaders like Trevor Manuel, the party's shadow finance minister, openly disapproved, claiming for example that macroeconomic policy was the preserve of government, not the trade union movement.[32] Still, the NEF was launched in October 1992, amidst confusion about its role and the extent of its powers.[33] COSATU wanted it to function as a negotiating body; business wanted an advisory body. That tension would plague the body in its later incarnation, NEDLAC (National Economic Development and Labour Council), which would officially become described as a '*consultative* structure'.

As important was the development of a Reconstruction Accord, which began in 1991. The aim was to make COSATU's electoral support conditional on the ANC adopting the accord as a government programme once it assumed power. COSATU saw this as a way of maintaining leverage with its ally, although labour analyst Karl von Holdt warned with prescience that 'the working class movement may ... find that its quest for influence is the very thing that holds its captive to ANC policies' (1993:22). The accord would eventually mature into the RDP, which the next chapter investigates in more detail.

A battle lost

By 1994, though, the left had lost the macroeconomic battle. To be fair, the ANC had not entirely subordinated itself to the prerogatives of capital.

Some progressive elements still lay encrusted in its economic proposals, but a strong conservative tilt had emerged in ANC economic policy. It endorsed financial and monetary stringency, saw a restricted role for the state in redistribution and supported the restructuring of trade and industrial policies in line with an export-led strategy. Economic revival would be market-led and geared at achieving sustainable growth by attracting foreign and encouraging domestic investment. Exchange controls would be removed, tariff and non-tariff protection to industries gradually lifted, and supply-side support provided to help stimulate industrial renewal. Social and industrial unrest would be checked through social accords, co-determination agreements and restructured labour relations.

The pat view is that the ANC simply 'saw the light', thanks to the determination of business to 'patiently and systematically educate blacks into the economic realities of the world'.[34] Nattrass believes that as 'the ANC leadership began to worry about ensuring long-term sustainable growth – and hence also its long-term political future' its policies became more 'pro-business', with current finance minister Trevor Manuel 'instrumental in this process' (1994c:20). But such explanations assign to orthodoxy the status of self-evident 'truth' – which is hardly borne out by international experience – and fails to explain why certain options won out over others.

The question, therefore, stands. One view holds that the country does not possess the comparative advantages that allow countries like China or Malaysia to fashion hybrid strategies which incorporate (but are not determined by) neo-liberal adjustments. Saddled with a structurally weak economy, handicapped by balance of payment constraints and a sizeable (but not extravagant) debt burden and situated in an economically stunted region, the state's room for manoeuvre is severely cramped. The argument suffers several weaknesses. Multilateral lending institutions like the IMF and World Bank hold little material leverage over South African economic policy since the country has not taken out major loans from them. Also, their desire for an African 'success story' provides leeway for innovations that might violate many of the injunctions issued to other developing countries as conditions for loans. At approximately $20 billion, South Africa's foreign debt is, as a percentage of GDP, small by international standards. Moreover, a compelling moral and political argument can be mounted for the negotiated repudiation of the share of that debt incurred by the apartheid regime.[35]

Another argument points to South African state's current 'incapacity' to act effectively as the guiding force in reconstruction and development. The intra-state dysfunction allegedly encountered by the RDP is presented as evidence, while sceptics are reminded that, for instance, even the much more sophisticated South Korean state allegedly 'got it wrong' as often as it 'got it right'. Linked is the belief that the ANC's conversion is based strictly on pragmatic concerns. A large section of the left within the ANC draws solace from such analysis – mistakenly, as the 1996 GEAR macroeconomic strategy confirmed.

Equally prevalent is the accusation that the ANC 'sold out'. This, however, presumes an ideological unanimity within the party which did not, and does not, exist. It also assumes that the party entered the 1990s with a relatively coherent and progressive economic view which, of course, was not the case. The answers have to be sought elsewhere.

One factor resided in the shift of the economic debate from the ideological to the technical terrain. This had two important effects. Firstly, the ANC and its left allies were poorly equipped to wage battle on technical grounds, a direct consequence of the democratic movement's historical neglect of the social and economic spheres. Indeed, there was a patent absence of technically rigorous economists at the helm of the ANC's DEP. Thus, business could successfully conduct a vigorous political and ideological struggle at a nominally technical level, deploying massive resources to great effect.[36] This also emboldened conservative figures in the ANC who drew heavily on business thinkers (paraded as being in step with 'global standards') to steer ANC policy along more 'realistic' paths. Secondly, and as a result, policy-making increasingly became dislodged from the social and political objectives proclaimed by the ANC, and increasingly impenetrable to its activists. The quest for policies acceptable to business proceeded as if the process were politically and ideologically neutral, and could then be appended to a set of strategic (and politically palatable) objectives.

By the time MERG produced its report in late 1993, ANC economic thinking was becoming reconciled to orthodoxy. But the left also has to bear a deal of the blame for the eventual capitulation. Paramount was its failure to politically defend MERG and advance its proposals within the ANC. Whatever the perceived shortcomings of MERG's macroeconomic framework, it was the most coherent left-oriented scenario available and appeared at a time when a progressive vision could still be salvaged. Instead it was seen to threaten the emergent consensus being assembled (on the economic front and in the political negotiations) as well as put at risk the career ambitions of DEP figures. It was impolitely set aside.

What happened to MERG?

MERG was set up in 1991 by the ANC to develop a new macroeconomic model for South Africa.[37] It published its main report – *Making Democracy Work* – in late 1993, amid controversy over the strong contingent of foreign economists on the team and, more tellingly, resistance from members of the ANC's DEP, who felt that MERG was usurping their roles. MERG members, meanwhile, complained that their work was 'frustrated by DEP delaying or spoiling tactics'.[38]

The net effect was the dismissal of MERG's recommendations, despite the acknowledgement by economists like Nattrass that they were 'carefully costed and situated in what appears to be a sound macro-economic model'.[39] At the core of the report stood the argument that the economy could best be restructured through the labour market (improved training and higher wages) and through interventions aimed at improving the structure and operation of business. A new economic system would depend on a 'strong private sector interacting with a strong public sector'.[40] If its key proposals were implemented, the MERG model predicted annual growth of 5 per cent in 2004 and the creation of 300 000 new jobs a year. It presented a two-phase growth plan (comprising a 'public-investment-led phase' and a 'sustained growth phase') that tied growth to expanded and efficiently deployed savings and investment (rather than the demand-led path of large increases in state spending advocated under the old 'growth through redistribution' formula). A robust role was reserved for the state, including:

> ... state intervention in output and pricing decisions in the minerals sectors, regulation of the housing and building supplies market, tightening and extending controls on mergers and acquisitions, monitoring the behaviour of participants in oligopolistic markets, and creating supervisory boards (consisting of bank, trade union and other represented interests) for larger companies.[41]

The report saw state investment in social and physical infrastructure (housing, school education, health services, electrification and road development) in the first phase accounting for more than half of growth, and triggering sustained, growth-inducing effects throughout the economy. In addition, it proposed that the state strategically apply a mix of incentives and regulations to restructure and improve industrial performance, and recommended a national minimum wage, pegged at two-thirds the subsistence level for a household of five.

Two elements in particular drew a barrage of invective. MERG argued that the minimum wage would improve productivity 'by reducing absenteeism, illness and labour turnover', and provide the incentive for firms 'to undertake the necessary adjustments to make human resources more productive' (1993:163). Nattrass was among many economists to counter that 'the low-wage sectors will shed labour once the minimum wage is introduced' (1994b:5), an argument that was reinforced by chiding from business. The other aspect to ignite wrath was the proclaimed need for the state to 'provide leadership and co-ordination for widely-based economic development' and to 'intervene directly in key areas' (MERG, 1993:281). This included the argument that no coherent macro-policy could be operated without more control or oversight of the Reserve Bank.

The plan represented the most sophisticated popular economic strategy ever devised in South Africa. Yet it was allowed to die an ignominious death soon after the report's release. *Making Democracy Work* was savaged in the media and by mainstream economists, responses which some ANC leaders reportedly shared.[42] To be sure, some of its key proposals would be exhumed in COSATU's *Social Equity and Job Creation* document two years later, itself a reactive intervention prompted by the neo-liberal arrogance of the South Africa Foundation's *Growth for All* plan. But by then it was too late.

One the whole, the perspectives gathered in the MERG report fell victim to a dominant discourse and a balance of forces that had tilted ineluctably rightward. So much so, that President Nelson Mandela could, at the 1994 COSATU congress, invoke the examples of low-wage Asian economies and tell delegates that 'unless we sacrifice, [unless] we have that determination to tighten our belts ... it is going to be difficult to get our economy to grow'.[43]

At this stage already, some economists were detecting signals that triggered alarm bells:

> Serious and honest analysis of South Africa's history, its stage of development and of current local and global conditions suggests that a strategy of development based on an essentially neoliberal, free-market ideology, or the magic formula of privatisation, liberalisation and convertibility spells disaster ... The government has chosen to understand the possibilities for local and national development on the basis of a narrow and (arguably) ephemeral interpretation of the nature of global interdependence (Adelzadeh & Padayachee, 1995:11).

Two years later, the ANC government's GEAR strategy would apply more nails to the coffin.

All GEARed up

South Africa's surplus of acronyms was augmented in June 1996, when the government rushed out its macroeconomic strategy. Finance minister Trevor Manuel immediately declared the Growth, Employment and Redistribution (GEAR) plan 'non-negotiable' in its broad outline, although the government was willing to negotiate 'the details with our social partners'.[44] GEAR was preceded by no consultation within the ANC; even top ANC figures were not acquainted with its details before the public release, as President Mandela eventually admitted to COSATU's 1997 national congress.[45]

The rush partially explained the document's palpable lack of rigour, a point confirmed a year later by the astonishing remark by deputy director-general of finance, Andre Roux, that more research was required into the link between economic growth and job creation.[46] But the rush did not explain the specific set of choices expressed in GEAR.

Drawn up by a coterie of mainstream economists,[47] and apparently based on a Reserve Bank model similar to that used for the apartheid government's NEM proposals a few years earlier, GEAR's prescriptions lit the faces of business leaders but shocked many within the ANC alliance. Critics immediately dubbed the plan neo-liberal. There has been much handwringing over the applicability of that adjective, much of it unnecessary and disingenuous. A 1996 government document (*Gear, the RDP and the Role of the State*), sent out to provincial leaders, pointedly admitted that 'in isolation certain measures in Gear are similar to many neoliberal packages'.[48] The document's claim that this was 'because there is an objective character about certain economic relations' is nonsensical, for reasons already stated. A year later, deputy president Thabo Mbeki would still contend that 'anyone who is rational can't come to any conclusion other than our (economic) policies'.[49]

Like motherhood and apple pie, GEAR's stated objective defied criticism. It would achieve, claimed the government, growth with job creation *and* redistribution, superficially reconciling it to the RDP. But rather than determine how the RDP could be achieved *without* unleashing unmanageable fiscal laxity and monetary instability, GEAR predicated the RDP on fiscal and monetary stringency, as deputy president Thabo Mbeki made clear:

> This policy is the central compass which will guide all other sectoral growth and development programmes of the government aimed at achieving the objectives of the RDP.[50]

In fact, the document contained only four references to the RDP – all flippant, except for an annexe which described how the budget deficit target could be met by trimming the RDP Fund.

Although the comparison was seldom drawn explicitly, the superficial correspondence between GEAR and the apartheid government's NEM perhaps explained the angry responses in activist circles. According to the National Institute for Economic Policy (NIEP), GEAR 'represents a recourse to the policy goals and instruments of the past apartheid regime' – a harsh but plausible judgment.[51]

GEAR promised to increase annual growth by an average of 4,2 per cent, create 1,35 million new jobs by the year 2000, boost exports by an average 8,4 per cent per annum through an array of supply-side measures, and drastically improve social infrastructure.

The rancour that greeted GEAR stemmed from the methods chosen to achieve these targets. The plan hinged fundamentally on an implausibly massive increase in private sector investment. This would be elicited by:

- slashing state spending to drive the budget deficit down to 3 per cent of GDP by the year 2000;
- keeping inflation in single digits;

- reducing corporate taxes and providing tax holidays for certain investments;
- gradually phasing out completely exchange control regulations;
- encouraging wage restraint by organized workers;
- creating a more 'flexible' labour market, possibly by deregulating certain categories of unskilled work and exempting small businesses from aspects of the new labour regime; and
- speeded-up privatization.

Unsurprisingly, the corporate sector hailed GEAR as 'investor friendly' and praised the manner in which it 'responds to many of the concerns expressed by business'.[52] Most observers concurred with that view. Business journalist Jenny Cargill noted that 'the government has met most of [business'] macro-economic demands' and went on to remark that 'it is certainly difficult to identify social equity as an explicit feature of the strategy'.[53] Little wonder that Mbeki could later bait critics at a media briefing, by inviting them to 'call me a Thatcherite' – which one journalist declared 'an apt comment on the overall direction of GEAR'.[54]

Surprising many activists, the SACP reacted with disarming ambivalence. Its verdict that the strategy resisted 'free market dogmatism' and 'envisage[d] a key economic role for the public sector, including in productive investment', betrayed a highly superficial reading of the document, hardly surprising given the absence of well-trained analysts in the party's top echelons.[55] (A year later, the SACP hardened its stance, calling for the scrapping of GEAR and its replacement by a 'coherent industrial policy'.)[56]

It was left to COSATU to strike the discordant notes. The federation expressed 'serious reservations' over GEAR's 'conservative fiscal policies', and warned that 'if you try to get the lowest paid people to pay for growth, there will be problems'.[57] COSATU also protested that the plan's prescriptions 'do not take into account the state of development in the economy and the need for massive spending on infrastructure and development'.[58] Strangely, however, COSATU did not release a detailed response to GEAR – despite having commissioned such a study from NIEP.[59]

Two key tests have to be applied to GEAR. Most fundamentally, in the unlikely event of the strategy meetings its targets, would this increase social equity? Secondly, given the political and economic context, and the matrix of postulated causes and effects on which GEAR rested, could the strategy meet those targets? The next section explores these questions.

Boosting growth

GEAR's growth projections (from 3,5 per cent in 1996 to 6,1 per cent in 2000) hinged on increases in private investment and net non-gold exports, as well as substantial (delayed) state expenditure in social infrastructure.

The strategy unloaded the duty of economic salvation squarely onto the shoulders of the private sector – not only as the source of private investment but through partnerships in the public sector (created by a programme of privatization). Those partnerships would enable the state to meet its infrastructural and other obligations while, simultaneously, trimming state expenditure. The government justified its privatization programme in several ways – as a way to 'facilitate economic growth', 'fund the RDP', 'create wider ownership in the South African economy', 'mobilize private sector capital', 'reduce state debt', 'enhance competitiveness of state enterprises', 'promote fair competition', and 'finance growth and [other] requirements for competition'.[60] Semantics aside, many of the professed aims could quite comfortably have been inserted into the NP government's justifications for its privatization drive during the 1980s.

GEAR's crux, though, lay in an anticipated, massive increase in private investment. The document's calculations showed import expenses (over the five-year GEAR period) depressing the fiscus by –0,2 per cent, while state spending was scheduled to add a fiscal stimulus of only 0,5 per cent. It follows that achieving the projected 4,2 per cent average annual growth would require a huge fiscal stimulus of 3,9 per cent (or 93 per cent of the total stimulus) from private investment. Thus, as NIEP warned, 'the projected growth rate is almost completely dependent upon the rapid success of government policy in stimulating private investment' (1996:6).

What specific measures were proposed to ensure that business met this duty? The answer was 'none'. Presented instead were a set of adjustments which, according to the orthodox view, would create an optimal climate for private investment. Most important was a reduced fiscal deficit and low inflation rate.[61]

By buying into the argument that a fiscal deficit of 1996 proportions[62] 'crowds out' private investment, GEAR posed state spending as an impediment to economic growth. Summarized, the 'crowding out' argument holds that when the state borrows to finance a deficit it competes for funds with the private sector. This is said to reduce investor confidence, drive up interest rates and slow growth.[63] Consequently, GEAR aimed to reduce the fiscal deficit (to an average 3,7 per cent), which would lead to lower real interest rates (average 4,4 per cent), boost investor confidence and trigger a dramatic rise in private investment (average 11,7 per cent).

The entire sequence rested on rickety assumptions. Most obvious was the danger that a deteriorating external current account (which the document correctly saw as an enduring difficulty) would lead the Reserve Bank to intermittently intervene sooner rather than later by further hoisting interest rates, thereby interrupting the purported chain reaction (NIEP, 1996:7). With the 'independence'[64] of the Reserve Bank entrenched in the Constitution and the institution screened from parliamentary scrutiny, the government has no authority to persuade the Bank to desist from such responses.

The need to slash the deficit has become an article of faith for supporters of orthodoxy, who see a fiscal deficit in the region of 5–6 per cent of GDP as anathema to a sustainable growth strategy. Yet, even the World Bank does not offer unambiguous succour for this view. In a momentary *lapsus cerebri* in 1993, the Bank allowed for instances where a fiscal deficit of even 12 per cent might be acceptable, as long it were integral to a growth pattern.[65]

This is not to argue that the size of the fiscal deficit is irrelevant, which it is not (incurring a large debt burden to finance the deficit and a high inflation rate are two, possible and important consequences). It is merely to acknowledge that considerable controversy exists about the presumed need to cut state expenditure to a *particular* level irrespective of the stage of the business cycle, whether this does act in fact as a trigger for private investment, and whether it does not become counter-productive (by depressing levels of demand). The Keynesian approach stresses the latter danger, since 'it is the ability to sell what is produced that guides investment decisions'.[66] Two Development Bank economists have calculated that 'a 1% reduction in the deficit before borrowing ... will reduce the average growth rate by about 1.5% for each year' and concluded that 'while fiscal discipline is attractive, it is expensive in terms of forgone output and lost jobs'.[67]

Rather than see investment as a direct function of investor confidence, for instance, a more empirically valid approach would view it as 'primarily determined by *profitability* of investment and the complementarity between investment by the state and the private sector'.[68] Active state involvement is deemed essential to develop conditions for profitability. NIEP has reminded that, internationally, greater attention was being paid to:

> ... the role that public productive expenditures on infrastructure (such as investment on roads, transportation and housing) and social services (such as education, health care and welfare) play in promoting not only a country's economic well-being and growth, but also in encouraging private investment (1996:8).

In that approach public expenditure 'crowds in' private investment by helping create a structural bedrock for sustainable growth. This would appear particularly apt for an economy that requires structural changes to achieve comparative advantage in the world economy, *and* where the government is committed to overcoming or at least lessening social inequalities.

In contrast, GEAR viewed such public spending as part of the problem and only envisaged significant increases in public capital expenditure very late in the day – towards the year 2000 when it could be 'afforded'. Yet it was bereft of measures that could increase the likelihood of large-scale, *sustained* productive investment by the private sector. Its central pillar, as

Cargill noted, 'rests on a leap of faith', although she and GEAR's advocates took heart in Nedcor figures which claimed that new investment projects at any one time [in 1995] amounted to between R100 and R140-billion. What the figures did not disclose was that the preponderance of this investment was in capital-intensive plant upgrading and a handful of existing and highly subsidized gargantuan projects. By late 1995, the growth in manufactured exports (commonly seen as an index of the success of this approach) was slowing, 'primarily because that sector had reached optimal capacity' without the hoped-for 'investment in new plant and machinery'.[69] It revived again in 1996, thanks to the devaluation of the currency, and by early 1996 was growing at a modest 1,5 per cent. Accompanying this, however, was a steady loss in employment in the sector.[70]

Neither did GEAR explain satisfactorily why the 1996 deficit was incompatible with a growth strategy, or why the target had to be precisely 3 per cent (and not 2 per cent or 4 per cent). Beyond the 'crowding out' argument, a deficit is typically seen as constraining growth because (i) it diverts government funds towards interest payments and away from social spending, (ii) if it is financed through foreign loans it increases the external debt burden (leading to balance of payments difficulties), and (iii) it leads to inflation (ILO, 1996). In 1996, the government paid R34,4 billion ($7,5 billion) interest on its debt. Debt levels of 1996 would push that figure to R63 billion ($13,8 billion) in 2000 – hardly alarming for a country whose public sector debt stood at a respectable 56 per cent of GDP (compared to an average 72 per cent for OECD countries) and whose external debt was decidedly low.[71] The latter point is vital, since a deficit at 1996 levels would not significantly destabilize the balance of payments situation. Servicing loans taken to finance the deficit do diminish the funds available for social spending. But GEAR's remedy (driving the deficit down to an apparently arbitrary figure by cutting public sector spending) would have the same effect – by draining the pool of government funding. One supposed 'evil' has been replaced with another, incontestable evil. Thus GEAR's logic pivoted on a 'leap of faith' that a reduced deficit would spur private investment to dramatic levels. Indeed, the 1997/8 budget was geared at achieving a 4 per cent budget deficit by effecting cleverly disguised public spending cuts. The ensuing, postulated growth (coupled with more effective tax collection) would then swell state coffers, enabling a massive increase in real government investment growth during GEAR's final two years (7,5 per cent in 1999, 16,7 per cent in 2000). What if this tenuous chain reaction did not occur? Would public sector spending remain at the diminished 1996–8 levels?

GEAR did not entertain such incredulity. Neither did it acknowledge other trends that contradicted the sequence of effects the strategy relies on. The ILO has pointed out that, unless they are massively inflated in a bid to kickstart growth, budget deficits 'tend to be counter-cyclical': they *fall* with rapid growth, and *rise* when the growth rate falls (ILO, 1996:32–3). The ILO concluded that:

> ... if deficit reduction were desired, the most effective way to achieve it would be through faster economic growth. However, deficit reduction as an *ex ante* policy constraint results in slower growth and greater difficulty in reducing the deficit.[72]

Such reasoning, however, has been shouldered aside in the South African debate which has tarred any resistance to deficit reduction with the brush of macroeconomic populism, blurring the rather obvious distinction between fiscal control and fiscal austerity.

Even if the presumed need to reduce the deficit were inviolable, methods other than slashing state spending were available – including more effective tax collection, more progressive tax rates for the top 20 per cent of income earners, the use of differential rates of value added tax (VAT) on luxury consumption, or a capital gains tax. GEAR recoiled from such options and instead offered an array of tax breaks to business.[73]

What about the inflationary impact of deficit spending? As the ILO has pointed out, there is no inevitable correlation between inflation and fiscal deficits. Inflationary pressure may be caused by an increase in the money supply. Thus, if the deficit were financed through money creation,[74] higher inflation might result. But, unlike most developing countries, South Africa has a developed private sector market for government bonds which allows it to sidestep the inflationary effect by financing the deficit 'in a manner that does not increase the money supply in excess of the rate of output growth' (ILO, 1996:34).

The current monetarist obsession for managing relatively minute shifts in the inflation rate borders on the pathological. In academic Ha-Joon Chang's view, it is 'misinformed' and serves the interests of the financial sector to the detriment of industry.[75] South Africa's inflation rate has not been high; in the period 1981–91 it averaged at 14 per cent, after which it dropped below 10 per cent. Yet GEAR explicitly made reducing the inflation rate one of the main objectives of monetary policy, without demonstrating how this would impact on other factors.[76] The cross-country evidence on the relationship between inflation and growth certainly does not support the view that the relationships is negative.[77] The fixation added another fly to the ointment – by demanding that the Reserve Bank apply contractual, *growth-inhibiting* measures whenever the inflation rate seems poised to step out of line.

A broader point on macroeconomic stability must be borne in mind. In dominant discourse, the monetarist view has become crudely contrasted with 'macroeconomic populism' (unbridled deficit-led social spending), as if these are the only alternatives. There are other options, as economist Vishnu Padayachee has argued. Macroeconomic balances can be assessed,

maintained or restored over chosen periods (for instance, a ten-year reconstruction cycle). This allows for the positive results of particular policies to
work their way into improved growth rates, rather than doggedly enforcing
the often arbitrarily chosen macroeconomic targets throughout the cycle.
Whether or not the economy is growing has to affect the decisions. Within a
sustained growth environment certain macroeconomic (im)balances can
temporarily be stretched beyond the strictures of stringency if key social and
economic indicators (such as employment figures, spending power, savings
rates) are positive. In the words of the SACP's Charles Nqakula:

> We may, or may not, have to reduce inflation or government spending. We
> may, or may not, have to meet the GATT requirements. Whether we do or
> not, must depend on whether these measures will help us meet in a *sustain-
> able way* the social needs of our people.[78]

In the South African debate, however, such perspectives have become
heretical.

Creating jobs

The experience of 'jobless growth' from 1994 to 1996 brought home the
realization that economic growth does not necessarily ease unemployment.[79] GEAR therefore presented specific job creation targets. It predicted
1,35 million new jobs by 2000,[80] of which 833 000 would be created
through GEAR adjustments – 308 000 through higher economic growth,
325 000 through 'changes in the flexibility of labour markets', and 200 000
through 'government-induced employment' (mainly infrastructural development and public works programmes).

Politically, this was GEAR's Achilles' heel, for the prickly notion of
labour market flexibility was central to this aspect of the plan. In finance
minister Trevor Manuel's words:

> As South Africa proceeds with trade liberalization and adapts to international
> competition, downward pressures will be placed on unskilled wages. If this is
> not accommodated by the labour market, then unemployment will rise.[81]

Manuel went on to remark that 'it is likely that wage bargaining in
unionised sectors has contributed somewhat to the slowdown of employment'[82] – a sentiment that harmonized neatly with the SA Foundation's
demand for a two-tier labour market (segmenting better-paid, organized
workers and low-wage unskilled entrants into the job market). Having seen
most of its macroeconomic demands heeded in GEAR, business, understandably, has pushed hard to extract further concessions in the sphere of
labour.

The assumptions imbedded in GEAR's call for 'regulated flexibility'
demand scrutiny. Job creation stood at the centre of GEAR's efforts to

alleviate poverty. Its premise, however, was that employment levels are determined largely by the real wage rate. Thus the trend of jobless growth could be reversed by introducing (among other adjustments) wage restraint and flexibility, and selective deregulation of the labour market. This thinking is questionable on several grounds. Firstly, according to the ILO, South Africa already has an extremely flexible labour market where 'even large-scale firms resort to "informal" forms of employment, through sub-contracting, out-sourcing [and] use of casual labour'.[83] The ILO found that 82 per cent of firms use temporary labour and 45 per cent contract labour. Moreover, '[m]any workers have little employment protection, retrenchments are fairly easy and widespread, [and] notice periods are short or non-existent'.[84] Secondly, the economy is already characterized by considerable wage flexibility, with wages in certain industries fluctuating dramatically. The ILO has found that in sectors 'such as metal goods, footwear, paper products, furniture and plastics, average black wages relative to subsistence actually fell' between 1984 and 1992.[85] Thirdly, the truism that rising black wages have encouraged capital-intensive production, thereby depressing private sector employment,[86] has been soundly debunked, leading the ILO to conclude 'that the available studies have not demonstrated either that real wages have been rigid or that they have had a strong negative effect on employment'.[87] Fourthly, while employment creation is one way of reducing poverty and social inequality, it does *not necessarily* have this effect if employment creation occurs mostly in low-wage jobs.[88]

Yet GEAR saw regulated flexibility in the labour market as a key element of its job creation strategy. This could entail, for instance, exempting categories of workers from aspects of labour regulation, reducing real wage increases in the private sector to 0,7 per cent per annum, opting for sector-based standards rather than introducing a national minimum wage and extending industry-wide agreements to non-parties only if job losses are avoided. Some of the anticipated adjustments would violate existing labour laws, but Manuel stressed that 'laws could be changed, if necessary'.[89] Again, comparative studies reveal a more complex picture. In the east and south-east Asian economies, as Ghosh has noted, 'a number of mechanisms which span policies across sectors have been used, rather than labour market policies alone' (1997:18).[90] These include strong public investment in housing, education, transport and agriculture, as well as price controls on basic goods (especially food) which have the effect of subsidizing elements of the wage basket.

To cement its measures, GEAR (and the Labour Market Commission) called for a 'social accord' that would traverse issues such as investment, service delivery and equity. In the short-term, however, the emphasis would be on cobbling together a deal in which labour would accept wage restraint in exchange for a commitment from business to exercise price restraint.

The political strains this might induce were patent, particularly in relations between the ANC and COSATU. Two further aspects warrant careful consideration. Firstly, NIEP drew attention to the impact of the gradual lifting of exchange controls on attempts to hold business to its side of the bargain in a social accord (1996:22). Labour and government would find themselves hostages to increasingly strident demands from business for further adjustments, with capital threatening to exercise its veto by taking flight. Secondly, the labour movement cannot ignore the tensions such an accord will cause within unions between leadership and rank-and-file membership. As Boris Kagarlitsky has noted, 'in periods of expansion, the skilled and educated strata can see more concrete benefit in allying with modernizing elites', but those affinities tend not to survive the end of those periods (1995:246). Moreover, they are highly tentative in periods of mild and uneven growth. The depressed wages and prolonged income inequality envisaged by GEAR are likely to spark renewed labour struggles by workers, leaving union leaderships in an unenviable position.

Finally, GEAR recognized the need to improve labour productivity, but focused on training as the remedy, at the risk of downplaying the ensemble of other factors that cause low productivity – low capital and managerial productivity, low wages and the apartheid wage gap (which sees managers earn as much as fifteen times the wages of unskilled workers), poor management, and the under-utilization of production capacity.

Trade, taxes and financial controls

GEAR's other main features require brief mention. The strategy correctly assumed a continued drop in the share of foreign revenue provided by gold exports. Thus it aimed to boost manufactured exports and trigger a staggering 23 per cent increase in the export:GDP ratio within four years. NIEP regards this target as 'unrealistic and unattainable', particularly because 'the government has not developed a carefully formulated and precisely targeted industrial strategy geared to those sub-sectors that have potential for export growth' (1996:14). The allegation seems harsh, since industrial strategy is supposed to rank among the more advanced policy areas of the ANC government. Yet, GEAR provided no detailed linkage between its macroeconomic adjustments and industrial policy. Furthermore, growth in export:GDP ratios registered by other countries prompt scepticism about GEAR's 23 per cent target – between 1970 and 1994 the average figure for OECD countries was 6 per cent, for Brazil 5 per cent and South Korea 4 per cent. The scepticism is amplified when one considers that neither GEAR nor current industrial policy provides for an active state role in targeting sectors, and that the time lag in achieving comparative advantage through human resources development makes *rapid* export growth unlikely.

On exchange controls, GEAR wisely resisted the 'big bang' approach but called for the gradual, complete removal of those controls. Foreign investors are to gain easier access to domestic credit, with wholly foreign-owned firms able to borrow up to 100 per cent of shareholder equity. Inexplicably, though, exchange controls were to be eased for local residents as well, allowing institutional investors (insurance companies, pensions funds and units trust) to obtain foreign assets of up to 10 per cent of their total assets. The concession amounted to government-sanctioned capital flight – this, in a strategy that rested squarely on encouraging massive domestic investment. The promised, ongoing relaxation of exchange controls for residents has momentous implications. South African finance capital dearly wishes to escape the constraints of the domestic sphere and gain freer access to global financial circuits. If the desire is satisfied (and GEAR indicated it would be), the investment patterns of domestic capital will become even more capricious.

The abandonment of financial controls effectively renders a strategy like GEAR hostage to the vagaries of finance capital. By allowing the uncontrolled penetration of domestic financial markets by foreign capital and encouraging the migration of local capital, patterns of investment are swept out of the ambit of government policy. Again, the south-east and east Asian experiences roundly contradict the efficacy of financial liberalization. In almost all cases, 'the financial systems of these countries have been tightly controlled and have operated in ways very different from the free regime' (Ghosh, 1997:17).

GEAR's restructuring of taxes was manifestly non-progressive.[91] In 1996, 37 per cent of tax revenue was derived from indirect taxation (VAT, which as currently structured discriminates against low-income earners) and so-called 'sin taxes' (levies on tobacco and alcohol which have a similar, discriminatory effect), with the likelihood of increases. Several options existed to achieve greater progressiveness, including a capital gains tax (the absence of which enables companies to lower their effective tax rates by converting income into capital gains), a tax on luxury consumption and a tax on unproductive land (NIEP, 1996:9). Reportedly, a tax on capital equipment was mooted, but rejected.[92] Instead, personal and corporate taxes were to be reduced if growth occurs, and tax holidays would be offered for selected investments. Overall revenue was slated to increase by way of more effective tax collection.[93]

Can GEAR reduce social inequality?

There is no disputing that economic growth is essential.[94] Yet, it is no panacea – as the 1960s remind. Then, with growth rates averaging between 5 per cent and 7 per cent, white per capita income rose by 43 per cent, while for Africans the increase was a mere 13 per cent. The lessons are twofold. Firstly, as the

ILO has reminded, wealth generation does not necessarily reduce poverty. Secondly, poverty and inequality are not synonymous. The richest country on earth, the USA, exhibits disturbing levels of inequality, while one of the poorest, Cuba, justifiably earned kudos for lessening inequality.

In the final analysis, one question remains paramount: Would GEAR reduce inequality? The strategy offered little comfort on this score. It provided no targets for reducing inequality and viewed job creation as the main avenue for income redistribution – a path the ILO admits 'is a way of reducing inequalities', although 'one would be a little sceptical that it would do so quickly or substantially' (1996:18). That scepticism is likely to be compounded by the fact that restricting wage increases for organized workers and allowing payment of sub-poverty level wages to certain sections of the labour force counted among GEAR's prerequisites for meeting its employment targets. Moreover, the Reserve Bank model (upon which GEAR is based) reportedly did not provide information on income distribution or sectoral employment effects, nor did it bring the potential effects of lower government expenditure to bear on income distribution (NIEP, 1996:23).

Once scrutinized, GEAR seemed to hover between different worlds. Rhetorically, attempts were made to align it with the socially progressive objectives of the RDP. But the central pillars of the strategy were fashioned in accordance with standard neo-liberal principles – deficit reduction, keeping inflation in single digits, trade liberalization, privatization, tax cuts and holidays, phasing out exchange controls, etc. This was alarming for several reasons. There exists no example internationally where neo-liberal adjustments of the sort championed by GEAR have produced a socially progressive outcome. Despite its overall objective of attaining 'growth with job creation and redistribution', GEAR set no redistributive targets and demurred on the linkage between growth and income redistribution. Moreover, it failed to integrate its main elements: for instance, the impact of restructuring government spending on employment and redistribution was sidestepped, while the relationship between the plan and industrial policy was left undeveloped. GEAR offered no direct causal link, as ANC MP Rob Davies noted, 'between the measures proposed' and the achievement of its 'growth and employment targets' (1997:2):

> These results depend on assumptions that lie beyond the macro-economic policy measures proposed, viz that the new policies generate 'confidence' among domestic and foreign private investors, who respond by significantly increasing investment ... Whether investors really do respond to policy packages of this nature in this way, rather than to a record of growth and profitability, is clearly much more debatable.

GEAR was plagued also by glaring internal contradictions. Social infrastructure was to be expanded, while public sector spending would be drastically cut. Job creation was presented as a signal objective while deficit reduction would require the shedding of hundreds of thousands of public sector jobs. As part of the measures meant to encourage foreign investment, exchange controls would, incongruously, also be relaxed for residents, while rapid growth would be pursued through policies (such as monetary stringency) which typically constrict growth.

The early indicators were dismal. According to the Reserve Bank, the GDP growth rate dropped to −0,8 per cent in the first quarter of 1997, down from 3,3 per cent in the last quarter of 1996. The announcement startled economists, prompting some to warn of an impending recession while others adjusted their growth predictions to about 2 per cent for 1997.[95] GEAR had predicted a 2,9 per cent growth rate for 1997. Figures released by Central Statistical Services showed employment fell by 1,3 per cent in 1996 (a net loss of 71 000 jobs), whereas GEAR had predicted 126 000 new jobs. By mid-1997, business leaders eager to assuage growing doubts within the ANC about GEAR could point only to 'tentative signs that foreign direct investment is starting to grow' while admitting 'the fragile nature of these inflows', the 'bulk of which has been in the form of portfolio investment'.[96] Yet, GEAR's failure to deliver on its targets has not weakened but galvanize business' demands for an even more relentless embrace of neo-liberalism. The plan, SACOB urged,

> ... must not become the victim of cynicism and fatigue because of perceived procrastination ... We must prove the skeptics wrong. SA will not get another chance like it.[97]

In 1991, economist Stephen Gelb (later one of the architects of GEAR) warned against:

> ... an accumulation strategy which focuses on restructuring and regenerating the manufacturing sector in particular, by using 'neo-liberal' (market-based) policies to alter cost structures and restore profitability and to expand markets for manufacturers, above all through exports ... [a strategy that] would, in sum, reinforce and extend the dualistic structure of South African society.[98]

Yet that formulation captures the strategic direction adopted by the ANC government which, at the same time, claims commitment to a vision that states 'we cannot rebuild our society at the expense of the standard of living of ordinary men and women. We cannot develop at the expense of social justice'.[99]

Notes

1   *Sunday Times,* 1 May 1994.
2   *Sowetan,* 5 March 1990.

3   Labour consultant Duncan Innes, quoted by Kentridge (1993:3).

4   Based on a disputable reading of the Freedom Charter's phrase: 'The mineral wealth beneath the soil, the banks and monopoly industry shall be transferred to the ownership of the people as a whole'.

5   The quote is drawn from Sunter's 1987 book, *The World and South Africa*, cited by Bond (1996b:4).

6   See Karis and Carter (1997:206).

7   ANC Department of Economic Policy, 1990, 'Discussion Document on Economic Policy', p. 12, cited by Nattrass (1994c:7–11).

8   *Op. cit.*, p. 8.

9   Nattrass (1994c:9).

10 See his 'The Making of South Africa's Macro-economic Compromise' in Maganya (1996).

11 For a critique, see Bond (1996b).

12 Bond (1996b:2).

13 *Op. cit.*, p. 3.

14 First popularized, according to some accounts, by economist Terrence Moll who later, in the service of Old Mutual, would author the ultra-conservative *Growth for All* document for the South Africa Foundation.

15 The *Mont Fleur Scenarios*, for example, translated the country's economic options into the flights of ostriches, flamingos, lame ducks and Icarus – illustrated by cartoons.

16 Cited in Bond (1996b:7).

17 Isaac Sam, *Business Day*, 15 August 1994. The Bank went further; leading one of its teams, for instance, was Geoff Lamb, a former SACP member.

18 *Ibid.*

19 *Ibid.*

20 As economist Neva Seidman Makgetla put it, 'At least since Keynes, no serious economist would use it to explain joblessness of the order of half the labour force, as in South Africa' (*Business Day*, 10 August 1994).

21 *Sunday Times*, 17 July 1994.

22 Editorial, *Business Times*, 21 August 1994.

23 *Finance Week*, quoted by Bond (1996b:10).

24 ANC, 'Draft Resolution on Economic Policy' p. 3, quoted by Nattrass (1994c:15).

25 'Privatization' became 'reducing the public sector in certain areas in ways that will enhance efficiency, advance affirmative action and empower the historically disadvantaged while ensuring the protection of both consumers and the rights of employment of workers'; ANC, 1992, Department of Economic Policy, *ANC policy guidelines for a democratic South Africa – as adopted at the National Conference (May 28–31)*, p. 24.

26 As argued in a 1993 study by GATT staff, cited by Bond (1996b:8).

27 Its extensive recommendations do not bear repetition here; see Joffe *et al.* (1994a).

28 See Amin (1993).

29 *Op. cit.*, p. 21. This contradicted unions' demand for a minimum national wage.

30 Former ISP co-director Dave Lewis, quoted in *Business Times*, 10 July 1994.

31 Joffe *et al.* (1994a:91).

32 It is plausible that at the root of Manuel's position lay a bid to bolster his DEP role.

33 The key negotiations on macro-policy in the NEF, according to at least one account, were led by former unionist Alec Erwin, who 'consistently adopted a conciliatory and defensive posture towards government and business'; author's interview, December 1996.

34 The *Financial Mail's* admonishment in 1990, quoted by Kentridge (1993:4).

35   See Rudin (1997).
36   Neither the Mont Fleur, Nedcor or NEM scenarios were of high technical quality.
37   Its tasks went further – training black economists, and supporting COSATU on economic issues. MERG was later replaced by the National Institute for Economic Policy (NIEP).
38   Kentridge (1993:56).
39   Nattrass (1994b:2).
40   MERG (1993:265). The report described the pre-1994 state as 'neither strong nor slim'.
41   As summarized by Nattrass (1994b).
42   For an illuminating debate on the MERG report, see Nattrass *et al.* (1994).
43   *Sunday Times*, 11 September 1994.
44   Neo-liberal policies, according to Gelb, 'involve the state limiting its own economic activity in relation to the provision of goods and services, for example by a process of privatisation. Secondly, state intervention in the activities of other economic agents is limited to defining the broad parameters of market processes – that is, the general cost levels of productive factors (labour and capital especially) and other incentives (such as tax allowances and subsidies)' (1991:29–30).
45   *SouthScan*, Vol. 12, No. 34, 19 September 1997.
46   'Govt pessimistic about job creation', *Business Day*, 13 May 1997.
47   Including Iraj Abedian, Brian Kahn, Stephen Gelb and Andre Roux.
48   Cited in Davies, R., 1997, *Engaging with GEAR* (draft), Cape Town, p. 3.
49   'The Rational Heir', *Financial Mail*, 3 October 1997.
50   Speech to the National Assembly, Cape Town, 14 June 1996.
51   NIEP (1996:2). Based in Johannesburg, NIEP nominally became the institutional successor to MERG.
52   *Business Times*, 16 June 1996.
53   'Growing Pains?', *Democracy in Action* (August 1996), p. 27.
54   *Business Times*, 16 June 1996.
55   SACP statement, reported by SA Press Association, 14 June 1996.
56   SACP media statement, 10 June 1997.
57   *Sunday Times*, 23 June 1996.
58   COSATU media statement, reported by SA Press Association, 14 June 1996.
59   The study was presented to COSATU, which apparently used it to brief top leadership; author's interview, October 1996.
60   See *Discussion Document by the Government of National Unity on the Consultative and Implementation Framework for the Restructuring of State Assets*, Ministry of Public Enterprises, July 1995.
61   The other key variable – political stability – lies somewhat beyond GEAR's grasp.
62   Officially measured at 5,1 per cent of GDP, although finance department officials admitted off-the-record that it stood closer to 5,8 per cent.
63   The argument was forcefully advanced in the SA Foundation's ideologically-charged *Growth for All* economic strategy document, although NIEP claims that there exists 'no empirical evidence to suggest' that this process 'has ever occurred in South Africa' (1996:6).
64   Jeremy Cronin is correct in dismissing this notion of independence: 'They have close personal and historical ties with the corporate, and particularly the financial sector. The "independent" policies of the Reserve Bank closely reflect the strategic interests of this privileged minority'; see his 'Exploding the myths of then neo-liberal agenda', *Business Day*, 9 November 1994.
65   See World Bank (1993:5) – for the Bank, a curious scenario which was quickly abandoned; World Bank (1994:48–52).

66 Bill Gibson and Dirk van Seventer, 'Economics has changed since the days of Robinson Crusoe', *Business Day*, 28 July 1995.
67 *Ibid.*
68 ILO (1996:29).
69 *Business Map Update*, 30 April 1996.
70 Employment levels in manufacturing industries fell by 0,5 per cent in the first three months of 1997; 'Exports rise as domestic demand cools', *Business Day*, 13 June 1997.
71 In 1994, it stood at 23 per cent of GDP, prompting many observers to regard the country as 'under-borrowed'.
72 ILO (1996:33).
73 These included tax holidays and accelerated depreciation for all new investments in manufacturing.
74 For instance, if the government sold bonds to itself via the Reserve Bank.
75 'Bank's monetary policy "misinformed" ', *Business Day*, 13 June 1997.
76 The World Bank, incidentally, is much more circumspect on this front. It has warned that reducing a moderate inflation rate like South Africa's might have significant impact on output and employment costs; see its *Reducing Poverty in South Africa*, p. 164.
77 See Ghosh (1997:9).
78 SACP secretary general, Charles Nqakula, addressing COSATU's Fifth National Congress, Soweto, 9 September 1994.
79 According to the Reserve Bank, only 12 000 new jobs were created in 1995.
80 This represents employment growth of 2,9 per cent, while the labour force will grow by 2,5 per cent – slightly lowering the unemployment rate.
81 *Sunday Times*, 23 June 1996.
82 *Ibid.* The sub-text is familiar and dastardly: organized workers, who have fought courageously to win humane wage levels and working conditions, are deemed a hindrance to social equity, a privileged interest group that defends itself at the expense of the unemployed.
83 ILO (1996:12). This document represents the most extensive study to date on the country's labour market.
84 *Op. cit.*, p. 19.
85 *Op, cit.*, pp. 194–5. The department of labour is currently investigating claims that in the clothing industry 'wages as low as R1,11 an hour, in practice R49,95 a week, are not uncommon'; *Business Report*, 15 October 1996.
86 The World Bank has shown a particular penchant for this empirically unsubstantiated argument (parroted by Manuel); see, for example, Fallon *et al.* (1994).
87 See ILO (1996:188–96).
88 The US experience in the 1980s is sobering. Low-wage jobs grew substantially during the decade, but poverty levels increased dramatically, with 10 per cent of the population experiencing a 16 per cent drop in real earnings (Hobsbawm, 1995:573). In South Africa, many of the poorest rural households fully participate in poorly paid employment which indicates that they are poor because of their low wages (ILO, 1996).
89 See *Business Times*, 16 June 1996.
90 See also Gordon (1988:51).
91 Corporate taxes contribute only 16 per cent of the overall revenue; *Mail & Guardian*, 19 July 1996.
92 The aim would be to encourage investment in labour-intensive enterprises. However, this could backfire and merely discourage productive investments.

93 Interestingly, the 1997/8 budget's attempts to introduce such regressive taxation were rejected by the parliamentary finance committee in May 1997.

94 A point eloquently made by Colin Bundy in his 'Development and Inequality in Historical Perspective' in Schrire (1992:33).

95 'Growth forecasts drop as GDP dips', *Business Day*, 3 June 1997.

96 SACOB director general Raymond Parsons, writing in *Business Day*, 11 June 1997.

97 SACOB director general Raymond Parsons, 'SA must gear itself for winds of change', *Business Day*, 13 January 1997.

98 Gelb (1991:29–30).

99 Expressed in the words of President Nelson Mandela, cited in ILO (1996:1).

CHAPTER SIX

The RDP: a programme for transformation

As South Africa's political negotiations drew to a close in 1993, the RDP emerged as the most concerted attempt yet to devise a set of social, economic and political policies and practices that could transform South Africa into a more just and equal society. Its starting point was an allegedly integrated analysis of South Africa's developmental crisis – of a 'growth path' that had lost its way – and an awareness that a new path would depend on the achievement of social, political and economic goals (Freund, 1994c). More than a development framework, it aimed at completely reordering politics, the economy and society (Rapoo, 1996). In the shape of the RDP Base Document, it revolved around five sub-programmes: Meeting Basic Needs, Developing Human Resources, Building the Economy, Democratizing the State, and Implementing the RDP.

Originating within the popular movement, the RDP passed through wide-ranging consultation and discussion which eventually included corporate business. A programme that began as a potentially formative framework for progressive transformation was reshaped into a document where 'any issue which might suggest a serious conflict with the interests of the rich and powerful has been smoothed over' (Von Holdt, 1993:25). Partly, this occurred because the paradigm of the political transition (inclusion, conciliation, consensus, stability) applied also to the RDP, a non-surprising development. It was promoted as a unifying, national endeavour that allegedly transcended parochial interests; the RDP 'belonged to everybody'. In class society, of course, the notion of common interests serves essentially as an ideological device to generalize and attribute specific class interests to all of society. What surprised many progressives, though, was the extent to which the scope and content of the RDP became circumscribed by conservative government policies which ignored most of its progressive components (Bond, 1996b). By 1995, an earlier comment by Reserve Bank deputy governor Jaap Meijer – that the RDP could transpire to be 'little more than a somewhat grandiose appellation for a not very ambitious collection of departmental expenditures'[1] – had become prophetic.

Worsening matters were the problems encountered in the RDP's implementation. These included departmental hostility towards the 'intrusive' role of the RDP Office, difficulties in drawing in and keeping on board a wide range of actors throughout the processes of project planning and implementation, lack of co-ordination between government departments, the privates sector's reluctance to engage in potentially 'risky' initiatives and the ineffective performances of some state and RDP structures. With exceptions, the programme seemed to advance from one faltering phase to another, as it fell woefully short of most delivery targets. April 1996 the national RDP Office, which had functioned as a co-ordinating unit within the President's Office, was shut down and its functions were transferred to the offices of the deputy president and the finance minister.

Despite protestations from the ANC government, the question could justifiably be asked whether the RDP indeed remained a 'programme' or whether it had been disaggregated into a compendium of poorly co-ordinated, conventional development projects. Within many popular organizations, the latter diagnosis prevailed. Seemingly dashed were the expectations raised initially – of one million new houses, the redistribution of 30 per cent of good farming land, equality in education and health services, strengthened environmental safeguards, and major inroads into the power of big business:

> [A]side from a few upgrading projects and expanded water and electricity hookups (though under highly commercialized conditions), the only major promises that have survived the retooling of the RDP are free primary health care and constitutionally-guaranteed reproductive rights (Bond *et al.*, 1996:3).

That assessment seemed overly pessimistic. RDP monitor Gavin Lewis argued that 'real achievements have been made in the delivery of essential services to millions', tallying 1,3 million new electricity connections, one million new water supply connections, a primary school nutrition scheme, the building of health clinics and more.[2]

More to the point, though, is an analysis of the political-economy of the RDP in order to ascertain whether and in which respects it remains a possible touchstone for a popular transformation project.

Genesis of the RDP

The original impetus for the RDP came from the trade union movement, particularly the National Union of Metalworkers (NUMSA),[3] which envisaged it as a set of socio-economic targets against which the performance of a new (ANC) government would be judged. At first the conceptualization of the RDP was the preserve of COSATU. The process was broadened to include other popular organizations grouped in MDM, around the political leadership of the ANC. After a wide-ranging consultation process, COSATU adopted (at a special 1993 congress) a draft which spelled out the programme's broad objectives.

Serious disagreements had already surfaced at the 1993 COSATU congress. Delegates complained that the draft under discussion had relegated a commitment to meeting basic social needs to the end of the document, that the nationalization of strategic sectors had been omitted and that the emphasis on macroeconomic stability would hinder redistribution. Emerging even within the comradely enclave of allied forces were starkly differing notions of the role of the RDP. As labour analyst Karl von Holdt wrote, 'COSATU has chosen to help the ANC draft a broad programme for transformation that tries to anticipate and accommodate the interests of most forces in our society' (1993:25). Some union activists were more openly dismayed, claiming that in the first four COSATU drafts 'every single clause is already ANC policy ... apparently, COSATU was trying to bind the ANC to its own policy' (Etkind & Harvey, 1993:85). Meanwhile, visiting Canadian trade unionist Sam Gindin had noted with dismay an ANC which 'comfortably blends a drive to consolidate formal development with an extremely non-transformative model of development'.[4]

The ANC participated in subsequent drafts which swelled the document to a 146-page manifesto of change. Shortly before the April 1994 election the RDP Base Document was adopted by the ANC as its principal guideline for overcoming the legacies of apartheid. The stridency of the Base Document was gradually excised or checked, as weaker 'compromise' sections were pushed to the fore at the expense of its more radical injunctions. The RDP metamorphosed from being the programme of the 'democratic forces' to becoming the policy framework for a government of national unity. The result was a programme that was 'less what it is, than what it might become', as Canadian analyst John Saul noted at the time.[5]

A 'Green Paper' discussion document, tilted towards the supply-side biases of a Development Bank of South Africa team tasked with proposing modifications, was prepared in mid-1994 and met with fierce resistance from popular organizations for its departures from the Base Document. An RDP White Paper discussion document was then drafted and released in September 1994, evoking more muted concern. It contained an amalgam of developmental approaches – mixing neo-liberal prescriptions with some residual Keynesian regulation, corporatist processes with a 'people-driven' approach, ostensibly firm commitments to redistribution with stern macroeconomic strictures. As a road map towards transformation the White Paper pretended to lead divergent social forces to their respective promised lands.

As the RDP metamorphosed into a programme that established a 'comfort zone' between conflicting forces and interests, intense contestation erupted over its content. Popular organizations tried to distinguish between the Base Document (taken to reflect, broadly, a popular agenda) and the White Paper (which displayed more clearly the imprints compromise and realpolitik). Capitalist organizations welcomed its 'realistic' aspects while criticizing those popular elements that were retained.

The road to development

The RDP was conceived as an attempt to programme measures aimed at creating 'a people-centred society which measures progress by the extent to which it has succeeded in securing for each citizen liberty, prosperity and happiness'. Less prosaically, it claimed to be 'an integrated, coherent socio-economic policy framework'[6] aimed at redressing the poverty and deprivation of apartheid, developing human resources, building and restructuring the economy, and democratizing the state. As conceived in the White Paper, the programme would integrate growth, development and reconstruction and redistribution into a unified programme.[7] The key to that link would be an infrastructural programme that would provide access to modern and effective services like electricity, water, telecommunications, transport, health, education and training.[8]

Initially, the RDP Base Document had pledged, among other things, to:

- create 2,5 million new jobs in 10 years;
- build one million low-cost homes by the year 2000;
- provide electricity to 2,5 million homes by the year 2000, doubling the number of households with such access from the then 36 per cent;
- provide running water and sewage systems to one million households;
- redistribute 30 per cent of agricultural land to small-scale black farmers within five years;
- shift the health system from curative services towards primary health care,[9] with free medical services for children under six years and pregnant women at state facilities – by 1998, all South Africans were to receive their basic nutritional intake, thanks to school-feeding and other schemes;
- provide 10 years of compulsory, free education as well as revise the curriculum, reduce class sizes and institute adult basic education and training programmes;
- extend infrastructure through a public works programme; and
- restructure state institutions to reflect the racial, class and gender composition of SA society.

These targets were criticized in business circles as a 'wish list', while other observers warned that clearer priorities and more realistic time-frames had to be set. Evident in the Base Document, though, was an attempt to establish a mutually reinforcing dynamic between basic needs provision and economic growth – the 'growth and redistribution' formula which had been all but discarded by the ANC by late 1993.

Drafted on the basis of submissions received from 'different offices of government, parastatal agencies, multiparty forums, development institutions, organisations of civil society, business organisations and individuals',[10] the White Paper reflected government policy and established 'a policy-making methodology and outline[d] government implementation strategies within the framework provided by the Base Document'.[11] The latter claim was moot. Several qualitative changes distinguished the two documents. Some of the Base Document's targets survived in the RDP White Paper, while others were replaced by more general goals. Most importantly, the core principles of the RDP Base Document were altered.[12] In place of the earlier focus on redistribution and meeting basic needs was a stern emphasis on factors deemed to inhibit growth and investment. Indeed, the broad parameters and some of the specific assumptions of the GEAR strategy were already evident in the White Paper. The economy was seen as suffering from 'government dissaving and a comparatively high proportion of our gross domestic product (GDP) absorbed in government consumption expenditure', while 'a review of exchange controls along with fiscal discipline' was declared necessary 'to facilitate growth'.[13]

The Base Document's starting point was essentially Keynesian. It represented an attempt to establish a mutually reinforcing dynamic between basic needs provision and economic growth – the 'growth *and* redistribution' formula which already had been all but discarded by the ANC by mid-1993. The key catalyst would be an active state, unequivocally biased towards the interests of the disadvantaged majority. The targets it set were ambitious but patently justified in a society regarded by the World Bank as one of the most unequal on earth. Evident throughout were injunctions and proposals that animated the transformative visions of the left – non-market mechanisms for the provision of basic goods and services, decommodifying and democratizing access to certain economic resources, and more. Noble as its objectives (and the consultative process that yielded them) were, the Base Document hardly represented a development *programme*. Its various elements were left unintegrated, leaving unexpressed, for example, the impact of land reform on rural economic strategy or the effect of a national minimum wage on sectoral investment and employment trends. Neither did it achieve even a nominal integration of macroeconomic policy with industrial policy, state restructuring endeavours and its developmental injunctions. Business' smirking description of the document as a 'wish-list' was not altogether inaccurate. These shortcomings, however, would remain glossed over by the left as it tried to fight a rearguard action to force the government to return to 'the people's programme'.

Who pays the piper?

According to the White Paper, the programme would be funded mainly through the 'better use of existing resources' – meaning rationalizing and reallocating the state budget according to RDP priorities and, in so doing, 'unlocking' private sector funding. But the budget would not be increased by raising taxes (acceding to a key demand of business). A special RDP fund was created to fund Presidential Lead Projects which would kickstart the RDP and become models to be followed by line ministries. The fund was intended to 'assist the Government in directing expenditure away from consumption and towards capital investment'.[14] All this would occur within the confines of fiscal and monetary discipline. As deputy president Thabo Mbeki told Parliament in July 1994:

> The government is committed not to increase the tax burden, which could impact on revenue and was also committed to reducing the budget deficit. The government's capability to deliver on the RDP depends on the economic growth rate.[15]

The general approach was to define social objectives and then devise measures to meet them in macroeconomically sound ways. However, the approach was not as neutral as it appeared. As demonstrated, an assembly of economic (and other) policy decisions would severely narrow the options for meeting the RDP targets. Several of those decisions were already presaged in the RDP White Paper. In his preamble to that document,[16] President Mandela described a restrained programme in which the government was, among other things, committed to:

- 'the gradual reduction in the fiscal deficit',
- ensuring 'that recurrent government expenditure does not increase in real terms',
- 'reduc[ing] government dissaving over time',
- changing 'the ratio of government spending towards increased capital expenditure', and
- financing 'the RDP primarily through restructuring the national, provincial and local government budgets to shift spending, programmes and activities to meet RDP priorities'.[17]

The final phrase was key since it predicated the programme on the national budget, the scale of which would be determined by the application of 'fiscal discipline' and the refusal to increase taxation.[18] The upshot was that a tightly controlled macroeconomic balance took precedence over redistribution, despite the rhetoric of the preamble which described growth and development as 'mutually reinforcing'. Envisaged was a scenario in which 'addressing inequalities will expand markets at home, open markets abroad and create opportunities to promote representative ownership of the economy' – with the resultant revival of the economy raising 'state revenues by expanding the tax base, rather than by permanently raising tax rates'.[19] Essentially, adjustments aimed at establishing 'an environment in which winners flourish'[20] were to catalyse economic growth, expand the tax base, eventually swell the budget and increase government funds available for RDP projects.

Of note, too, was the formulation that the 'empowerment of institutions of civil society is a fundamental aim of the Government's approach to *building national consensus'*.[21] In other words, the RDP was seen as subject to (but also instrumental in) bolstering and extending the inclusive terms of the political transition into the socio-economic realms. In theory a division of labour would be organized, allowing the 'national government to set overall priorities and goals' but relying on 'provincial and local governments to interpret those priorities in the context of local conditions' and on 'communities to determine the actual form and content of the development'.[22] A complex network structures and processes were devised to bring about the RDP, including requirements for detailed business plans for development projects and a 'zero-budgeting' system whereby line ministries had to draw up annual budgets *ab initio* to avoid inefficient expenditure. RDP structures were set up in the nine provinces, though to uneven effect (Rapoo, 1996), while attempts were made to set up local development forums as part of the 'people-driven' approach. The role of NGOs, whilst acknowledged, was unclear. Some government figures seemed willing to see NGOs subjected to a process of Darwinist attrition (at the hand of market forces), with the survivors working within the ambit of a state co-ordinated RDP.[23] Several options (including licensing NGOs) were mooted, but met with strong resistance.

The RDP as a 'terrain of struggle'

By late 1994, the RDP had achieved sacrosanct status, a remarkable development since Nelson Mandela, according to some reports, had shown scant interest in the programme a year earlier.

As a government programme, the RDP seemed to accommodate the divergent interests of contesting social and economic forces. As indicated, the prime function of the transition was the establishment of a new historical bloc under whose tutelage a new growth path could be devised and pursued. For the popular forces, that growth path had to be based on a substantial redistribution of resources, opportunity and power. The Base Document did not encompass such a venture – but it did include several benchmarks some of which survived in the White Paper, albeit in haphazard and isolated manner. Moreover, they were undermined severely by shifts of emphasis within the document itself and by decisions taken elsewhere in the system.

Generally, South African business was charmed by the thrust of the White Paper. Conservative commentator Kevin Davie, for example, remarked that, 'all signs now are that our policy makers see that the objectives of the RDP are wholly compatible with the three words [privatisation, liberalisation and convertibility] which so interest the money men'.[24] Yet, concerns remained about the 'repeated reference to the entrenchment of trade union and labour rights' and the 'centrality of the role of the state'.[25]

Views from business

As outlined earlier, a range of (overlapping) stances cohabit within the main business groupings. At one extreme is the view that the role of the state should be restricted as far as possible. Applied to the RDP, this meant that the parameters of the programme had to be determined by policies singularly aimed at maximizing economic growth. Thus corporate tax hikes were opposed, fiscal and monetary austerity demanded, greater 'flexibility' sought in the labour system, property rights demanded and international competitiveness made a priority.

Redistribution would be played off against growth, with the RDP's socio-economic objectives subordinated to the enveloping and more pressing need to achieve robust economic growth. Eventually, the benefits of the ensuing growth cycle would trickle down to the poor. The state would bear the central responsibility for the RDP, within the confines of overarching, growth-inducing requirements. Importantly, the maintenance of law and order was seen as a key element of the RDP. In this view, business, in other words, wanted to 'get on with its business' which might also include exploiting opportunities provided by RDP projects.

Overlapping with that neo-liberal view was a more 'centrist' perspective. Still privileged was the need for economic growth, but it was shadowed by the recognition that growth would falter without adjustments that favoured capital accumulation in two respects. Firstly, dysfunctional features in the social and economic spheres (low social wage, productivity, education and skill-levels, consumption and unstable labour relations) had to be addressed. Secondly, the RDP process enabled profitable forays into new or expanding sectors and markets. The approach was crypto-Keynesian. Rather than spectate, business would position itself in partnerships or as leading agents in RDP projects, on the precondition that the key financial risks were taken by the state. The state's role would be to facilitate, regulate and guarantee – not challenging the market but rather assuming its 'hegemonic role in the ordering of society' (Bond, 1994b). This would occur against a background of macroeconomic adjustments similar to those demanded in the neo-liberal vision.

The approach harmonized richly with the ANC government's remoulding of the RDP, as trade and industry minister Alec Erwin well understood:

The programme to meet basic needs will in fact open new opportunities for the private sector to take up a wide range of economic activities, and for market forces to come into play in areas where they never operated.[26]

SACOB's Raymond Parsons announced with relish that the 'pre-election RDP belonged to the ANC, but the private sector now also owned it and wanted it to succeed'.[27] Meanwhile, it was reported that researchers at the JSE were 'racing to bring out market reports outlining which listed companies will benefit from the implementation of the Reconstruction and Development Programme'.[28]

Ideologically, the centrist approach was buttressed by the extension of the conciliatory principles of the political settlement into the socio-economic spheres. The RDP became seen as a partnership of 'everyone … every organisation, every opinion-making group that can contribute', as Jay Naidoo put it, 'that's the protection this government needs to ensure that if anything goes wrong, it will be our collective responsibility'.[29] In the housing sector, especially, this wrought sad results. In 1994, a national accord was struck with private sector investors and developers for a large, low-cost housing programme. Government sweetened the deal by underwriting business's involvement in the scheme with funds it would provide. Yet, as an editorial in the *African Communist* noted a year later, '[t]he greatest strike in our country at present is not the nurses' or the municipal workers' strikes, but the investment strike by the banks and building societies'.[30]

Views from the left

Contesting these approaches was an embryonic 'left-wing' vision of the RDP which deserves some exposition.[31] The fact that the RDP emerged from the left of the 'popular movement' was no longer obvious by mid-1994. Promoted as a national endeavour around which conflicting interests could converge, the RDP had been pruned of most of its earlier, radical outgrowths. In response, the left began to try and reclaim 'ownership' of the RDP. This perspective was strongly influenced by debates about how a radical programme of change could be achieved within a negotiated transition and, specifically, within the integuments of capitalism.

The South African left's visions of societal change had long centred on formulaic models that hinged on Leninist notions of rupture and the seizure of state power.[32] Gaining ground in the 1990s was the notion that an ensemble of revolutionary or *structural reforms* could build socialism within a capitalist system, with those innovations eventually achieving a critical mass that would tilt society into a socialist transition.[33] Drawing especially on an essay by Andre Gorz[34] and on the Russian Marxist Boris Kagarlitsky's book *The Dialectic of Change,* Canadian social scientist John Saul attempted to draw a distinction between structural reform and reformism.[35]

He proposed two essential criteria for the former. Structural reform must:

> ... be allowed self-consciously to implicate other 'necessary' reforms that flow from it as part of an emerging project of structural transformation [and] must root itself in popular initiatives in such a way as to leave a residue of empowerment – in terms of enlightenment/class consciousness, in terms of organizational capacity – for the vast mass of the population, who thus strengthen themselves for further struggles, further victories (1993:91).

A spirited debate ensued, spanning numerous journal articles and essays.[36] Some critics questioned whether, as Ralph Miliband later put it, 'an altogether different social order can be achieved by a smooth accumulation of reforms, so that one day we will wake up and find that we have been living in a socialist society without being aware of it'.[37] Supporters approached the future on a train of metaphors. But Saul's intervention resonated strongly in left thinking. NUMSA's Enoch Godongwana, for example, advocated 'a turn from exchange-values to use-values in our conceptualisation of why we are restructuring the economy and society',[38] and urged the building of 'certain alternatives within the capitalist framework that will tend to undermine the capitalist logic'.[39] The ANC's Pallo Jordan argued for 'establishing a number of strategic bridgeheads which enable you to empower the working class and the oppressed, and from these bridgeheads you begin to subordinate the capitalist classes to the interests of society in general'.[40]

Unnerved by a perceived retreat from the earlier RDP drafts, the SACP issued a call to 'defend the RDP from the Left'. Jeremy Cronin saw the RDP as a cornerstone for the reconstitution of the popular movement around concrete popular campaigns that would be grounded in the radical pronouncements of the programme.[41] According to the SACP's Langa Zita, this included '[transferring] certain areas of economic activity away from the mediation of the market to society',[42] a process that would concentrate on decommodifying certain economic resources and services (such as housing, education, health and other basic services), and on establishing producer and consumer co-operatives.

The tendency was to subject the RDP document to a meticulous reading, treating it as a sealed text which determined decisions and policies generated elsewhere in the system.[43] Patrick Bond (who participated in the drafting of some of the RDP's sections) detected in the Base Document what he termed 'substantially socialist reforms' and hailed its 'explicitly non-capitalist logic', declaring that 'the discourse over whether society is willing to fund ... essential goods and services has been won'.[44] Fuelling this triumphalism was a variety of proposed innovations such as a Housing Bank, changing the directors of major mutual insurance companies, a commitment to reproductive rights, anti-trust legislation ('and other challenges to the commanding heights of capitalism, racism and patriarchy'), an alleged refusal to take out foreign loans to fund 'RDP programmes that do not directly contribute to raising foreign exchange', and 'the commitment to a strong but slim state which will continually empower civil society' (Bond, 1994b).

Left in such wistful form, this approach seemed to be animated more by expectancy than strategic clarity, though the SACP's Langa Zita did attempt to cast a left vision of the RDP in clearer focus.[45] At root, it meant finding ways to advance 'a political economy of the working class' around the RDP. Zita argued that the RDP's method – underscoring the role of civil society in development – compensated for the weaknesses in content and the constraining effects of policy decisions taken outside the RDP. SACP, union, civic, health, student and church activists saw the RDP as a potential catalyst for reviving popular organizations around a transformation project which, in most respects, had become secreted in the domain of the state. This meant focusing on the RDP's progressive features which could 'be changed and radicalized as we shift the balance of forces' (Zita, 1995). But it also demanded that the state be restructured along democratic lines and the tendency towards technocratic insularity be checked. Processes had to be introduced and support provided to enable weaker sections of civil society to effectively engage with the state – an essential innovation if the trend towards social accords was not to degenerate into corporatism.[46] Without dismissing their utility out-of-hand, Zita noted that none of the conditions which had laid the basis for successful social contracts in social democracies were present in South Africa. Nevertheless, he allowed for a 'qualified embrace of the concept of a social contract ... as an element of other measures' (Zita, 1995). The trade union movement was assigned the task of representing the interests of the broad working classes, in concert with civic and other CBOs.

In a similar vein, development forums were assigned important roles, in keeping with the ubiquitous trend towards multiparty forums since 1990 – essentially efforts to anoint processes with legitimacy. These forums had to be transparent, their negotiators accountable to their constituencies and they had to be reproduced at regional and local levels. The aim was noble: to bolster civil society's role in reconstruction and development. But the effect was to stymie much of the dynamism and creativity associated with civil society organs by corralling them into new pockets of bureaucracy – where they would often find themselves disempowered by the infinitely greater resources deployed in those forums by state and business structures.

In large part impressionistic and sketchy, these approaches have broadly mapped the left's faltering attempts to utilize the RDP as the touchstone for a transformation project.

Deconstructed development

While the left tried to 'reclaim ownership' of the RDP by amplifying its sur-viving progressive elements, economists Vishnu Padayachee and Azghar Adelzadeh were less sanguine about the trajectory of the White Paper. They concluded that:

> ... those welcoming the White paper will share a belief that policies involving any form or degree of effective state intervention are antithetical to economic growth. Sadly, it appears that there are far too many in this latter category inhabiting the corridors of state power in the new South Africa.[47]

Read superficially, the White Paper seemed riddled with contradictions. It was directed at 'fundamental transformation' and was 'not an add-on pro-gramme'[48] while, at the same time, it was described as a programme of 'renewal' which 'should not be seen as a new set of projects, but rather as a comprehensive redesign and reconstruction of existing activities'.[49] Read closely, it transpired that key elements of the Base Document had either been omitted, replaced or severely circumscribed.[50] Plans to restructure the financial sector were abandoned, the 'independence' of the Reserve Bank was guaranteed[51] and a possible national social security programme was dropped. Pervasive was the stern and overriding caveat that '[a]ll levels of government must pay attention to affordability given our commitment to fiscal discipline and achievable goals',[52] and the instruction that 'attention will be paid to those economic factors inhibiting growth and investment and placing obstacles in the way of private sector expansion'.[53]

The emphasis on fiscal discipline rang throughout – not, as the MERG report had proposed, in a manner that enabled (simultaneous) redistribu-tion but as an inflexible prescription that would predetermine the scope of redistribution. As the GEAR strategy would confirm, the government's fiscal policy was not merely 'disciplined', but 'austere'. The distinction is crucial. Fiscal discipline, as Adelzadeh and Padayachee have reminded, makes it possible to 'utilize both the revenue and expenditure aspects' to 'create employment, develop the infrastructure, provide basic needs, reduce the concentration of wealth and improve income distribution, and finally help achieve sustainable economic growth' (1994:3). Fiscal austerity, the writers noted, removes such flexibility and defines an approach that:

> ... commits the government at the national, provincial and local levels to reduce expenditures, finance the RDP primarily from restructuring the bud-gets, maintain or reduce the level of direct taxes, consolidate business confi-dence, enhance the environment for private sector expansion, and liberalize the economy'.

The White Paper also buckled to pressures for trade financial liberalization. The document stated than an export-oriented trade policy depended 'upon the application of an effective industrial policy'[54] – yet, the government had, in mid-1994, already begun implementing the GATT injunctions in the *absence* of such a policy. Moreover, it conveniently refrained from spelling out the wide-ranging impact of the GATT on a programme like the RDP. As Adelzadeh and Padayachee reminded, the GATT obligations extend beyond tariff reductions and the elimination of quotas to include restrictions 'related to government procurement policies, subsidies, intellectual property rights, investment, trade in services, custom procedures and anti-dumping' (1994:6). Their combined effect would be to erode regulatory domestic laws and government regulation at all levels, promote programmes for privatization and deregulation, and weaken worker rights and unions.[55] Moreover, foreign investors 'would enjoy the same treatment as domestic investors' without any mention of reciprocal performance requirements geared at the achievement of RDP objectives.

The White Paper did contain principles and policy options of value, as Adelzadeh and Padayachee acknowledged. The rhetorical commitment to a 'people-driven' programme survived, as did the stated resolve to end the exploitative labour practices of the past and to support racial and gender equality. Yet,

> … the reconstruction and development programme – as a co-ordinated, integrated core investment programme, linking reconstruction, development, growth and redistribution (along the lines set out in the Base Document Vision) – has been disfigured, leaving an incoherent and fragmented RDP White Paper (1994:11).

It is difficult not to conclude that the fate of the RDP was consonant with government policies which, far from lurching unexpectedly to the right, have shown considerable consistency since 1994. Indeed, the closure of the RDP Office in 1996 seemed quite compatible with this trajectory. Imprinted in the RDP's post-1994 theory and practice was a perspective that predicated reconstruction and development on liberalization, free markets, and the cultivation of business and investor confidence. Development and reconstruction would occur *in terms* of those priorities. The 'basic needs' concept survived as a rhetorical device aimed at massaging possible political tensions within the tripartite alliance. Within such an understanding, a separate institutional structure like the RDP Office became redundant since it merely prolonged the fiction that the programme represented an overarching framework that determined government policies and activities. In fact, the reverse held true. Considerably more truthful than many critics realized was deputy president Thabo Mbeki's explanation that the programme had become so well integrated into the different government departments that a separate 'ministry' was no longer needed.

The RDP in practice

Even in its reconstructed form, the RDP has proved difficult to implement.[56] Serious obstacles were encountered within the state, sections of which proved highly resistant to change. Predictably, the intransigence of incumbent officials caused problems. According to some assessments, these were compounded by the tendency to rely on 'existing government personnel and agencies such as the World Bank and Development Bank of South Africa', agencies with 'a very different ideological perspective to that embodied in the RDP'.[57] As common, though less obvious, have been these officials' difficulties in adapting to new organizational styles and cultures, and servicing new priorities. At the same time, the 'self-organizing' and co-opting capacities of bureaucratic systems has tended to disorient the initiatives of newcomers.[58]

Serious problems occurred at the level of line ministries, many of which balked at the allegedly intrusive role of the RDP Office and 'tended to use the RDP Fund as an additional source of operating funds, leaving their existing programmes untouched and untransformed'.[59] There were also logistical problems related to co-ordination, policy-making, planning and failures to identify or design projects that met RDP criteria (Rapoo, 1996). Millions of rands earmarked for RDP projects were left unspent – the RDP Fund 'rolled over R2-billion in unspent funds from 1995 into the 1996/7 fiscal year' while 'overall government "roll-overs" increased from less than R3,5-billion in the 1993/4 fiscal year to R8-billion in the 1996/7 fiscal year' (Kraak, 1996:39). A range of initiatives were introduced to overcome these problems, including the secondment of special management teams to national and provincial ministries. A further complication, hindering the housing programme in particular, was the failure of key private sector participants to adhere to multi-party agreements.[60]

These problems were amplified at the provincial level. In most provinces 'a widespread lack of skills and capacity in drafting business plans' plagued RDP projects (Rapoo, 1996:15). In some, the involvement of community organizations was negligible (Mpumalanga), while in others (North West) an overall government strategy had not been devised by 1996.[61] In addition, there was a lack of co-ordination between provincial and national governments in strategic planning.[62]

At the local level, the setting up of local development forums was often delayed by wrangling over the criteria for inclusion – much to the dismay of state bureaucrats who preferred to concentrate on the technical aspects of 'delivery', at the expense of community participation. Blame rests also on community and popular organizations which have generally refrained from making real the rhetoric of a 'people-driven' process.[63] Even the 'Community Constituency in Nedlac' was forced to admit that 'on the whole, community influence has declined since the initial formulation of the RDP' (1996:5).

Unexpected difficulties emerged in comparatively simple projects. Efficient, small distributors for the school-feeding scheme, for instance, seemed difficult to find and contracts were awarded to corporate distributors (violating one of the objectives of the scheme).

Despite all this, valuable accomplishments had been registered. Most impressive was the connection of electricity to 1,3 million homes and the official claim of one million new water supply connections (in both cases on strict commercial terms). The housing department claimed (in 1997) that some 192 000 houses were being built, compared to the 40 000 built by late 1996. A primary school feeding scheme to combat malnutrition among children was operating in 12 300 schools,[64] free medical care was (in theory) available to pregnant women and children younger than six year, and 297 new primary health care clinics were built in rural areas.[65] Almost 500 public works programmes were launched, providing temporary employment for 28 000 people,[66] while several hundred municipal upgrading projects were started in townships. The land reform programme (comprising land restitution and redistribution) was less successful because of 'capacity problems, limited budgets and slow bureaucracy',[67] although many NGOs criticized the reliance on market mechanisms to redistribute land. By mid-1997, only two of some 15 000 land claims had been settled.

Yet, the overall performance fell well below expectations. Weeks before the RDP Office was closed, in March 1996, a dejected Jay Naidoo was forced to admit that 'very little has happened in the past two years'.[68]

The utility of the RDP

The RDP no longer expresses the interests promoted by its original architects or by a left eager to tie its colours to a programmatic mast. As researcher Thabo Rapoo has written:

> [T]he RDP has lost its meaning and coherence. It has come to mean anything anyone wants it to mean; with a little ingenuity, anything can be made to fit in with the goals of the RDP (1996:5).

It could be argued that, given the nature of the transition, the RDP could not unambiguously express the core of a progressive programme for change. Yet, the document would become severely undermined by policy decisions that unabashedly favour the interests of the privileged[69] – which suggests that the balance of forces, in a period of supposed triumph, had shifted manifestly against popular organizations. In late 1996, deputy president Thabo Mbeki belatedly sought to reconcile the GEAR macroeconomic strategy with the RDP, to the temporary relief of many SACP and COSATU figures.[70] Far from announcing the resurrection of the RDP, Mbeki's merely confirmed its malleability and, indeed, its eminent compatibility with a development path governed by the prerogatives of capital.

Among the factors that produced these setbacks, several tend to be over-looked. The left mistakenly assumed it had achieved sufficient hegemonic weight within the ANC and the tripartite alliance (the same applies *within* each of the alliance partners). It also disregarded the extent to which the parameters of the RDP in practice would be drawn on the basis of setbacks suffered outside the political negotiations. Most obvious was the abandon-ment, first, of the growth *through* redistribution formula and, later, of the substitute formula, growth *and* redistribution. Instead, the left sought solace in the predictable rhetoric of the ANC government which, for obvi-ous reasons, continued to pay lip service to the transformative elements of the RDP which, in practice, have been superseded. Unsurprisingly, the RDP was subjected also to the terms of the transition which, along with the con-servative economic policies, mitigated against diverting substantial resources towards the poor. Worsening matters has been the disorientation and disorganization of popular organizations which failed to muster the systematic pressure and influence needed to halt those shifts.[71] As Patrick Bond lamented,

> ... progressive forces in civil society have provided only sporadic reminders – whether in the form of policy advocacy, demonstrations, best-practice pilot projects or political interventions – of deviations from the RDP (1996b:42).

By mid-1997, elements within the government had begun an attempt to graft a developmental framework (based on RDP principles) to GEAR – a futile bid since a social development programme cannot be appended to (let alone integrated with) a macroeconomic strategy characterized by privati-zation, deregulation, fiscal austerity, trade liberalization and the predomi-nance of the financial sector over production and commerce. Not only the programme's sweep, but its very character and logic has been overwritten by the regressions that were consummated in the GEAR strategy. Indeed, the actual utility of the RDP as a government programme has changed dra-matically.

As phrased by Mexican sociologist Carlos Vilas, 'neoliberalism considers the growth of poverty to be a pathology, not a consequence of the economic system'. The upshot is a development strategy that 'isolates poverty from the process of capital accumulation and economic development, and reduces the solution to designing specific social policies' (1996:16). The reconstructed RDP is captured smartly in that formulation. As a patchwork of developmental activities, the RDP functions not as a developmental framework but as an aggregation of social policies designed to alleviate poverty without impacting on the complex of economic policies and prac-tices that reproduce poverty and inequality. In essence, it has become a social containment programme which acts as a quasi-welfare cushion, while purportedly self-adjusting market forces run their course.

Related is another, less visible function located in the ideological realm. Inscribed in the RDP is the political-historical continuity between the Freedom Charter and the reality of an ANC government. Its political resonance as a programme of mooted transformation has prevented it from being discarded formally, despite the private derision of some leading ANC figures. Within the context of the national liberation struggle the RDP signifies continuity. Within the transition it signifies unity. In fact, it is against the background of the nation-building project that the RDP's utility becomes manifest. There it functions as an axis around which the principles of inclusion, conciliation and stability can be promoted in tangible form. Within its ambit, disparate interests are seen to become reconciled in a unifying 'national endeavour'. In this discourse, the self-help activities of working class residents and the unbundling exercises of corporations share the same stage as expressions of a postulated 'unity of purpose', of a new patriotism. The question 'Who killed the RDP?' vanishes, and is replaced by the liturgical reminder that 'the RDP died for us all'.

Quo vadis, the RDP?

Popular on the left has been a revivalist approach hinging on the belief that the dragon of GEAR could be slain with the sword of the Base Document. The argument pivots on the notion that GEAR was an aberration and should be subordinated to the 'people's programme'. As demonstrated, GEAR was not a momentary lapse but the outcome of a systematic ideological conversion achieved among powerful sections of the ANC. Moreover, several of its measures (especially the abandonment of financial controls) have severely undermined efforts to reinstate the vision of the Base Document at the centre of a new growth path.

Reversing the current trajectory requires broad-ranging recoveries. But hampering them are crucial shortcomings in leftist visions of the RDP, principally the tendency to overstate the power and sweep of the progressive elements in the programme. Diagnoses of the RDP typically refer to the 'unravelling of the consensus around the RDP' as one of the main problems.[72] On the contrary, after mid-1993 there was no seamless 'consensus', even among the 'national democratic forces'. The subsequent versions themselves reflected the ever-broadening range of interests that were being marshalled around the programme. The RDP became a 'one size fits all' programme – some elements thrilled leftists, others gratified business.

The Base Document remains both relevant and valuable, not as a blueprint but as a complex of development benchmarks that arose from a consultative process and which, in many respects, distilled the ideals that had propelled the struggle against apartheid. Those benchmarks represent the basis for a new development strategy which will have to be integrated with progressive macroeconomic and industrial policies – areas in which the Base

Document fell woefully short. Merely hoisting it to prominence or predominance will not suffice.

Such an enterprise has to occur also on the basis of rigorous analyses of the transition – its terms, the recasting of social alliances, their class nature and the political/ideological reconfigurations in the democratic movement. Several concerns arise, most notably the cursory treatment of the political-organizational aspects of such a project. Typically, references to the ANC, the tripartite alliance and 'national democratic forces' have been distressingly a-historical and decontextualized, with the formations presented as unproblematic entities, largely untouched by the reconfigurations and contradictions unleashed during the transition.[73] Other dilemmas have remained not only unresolved but timidly addressed. 'To speak of alternatives is pointless,' as Boris Kagarlitsky has written, 'so long as there is no force on the political scene that is capable of putting them into practice.'[74] Does the SACP function as the political axis for the project? If so, how does this affect its alliance with the ANC? And what role can COSATU assume in such a recovery?

The boundaries of permissible change have been established. Whilst not inviolable, they are formidable. The most crucial retreats from the Base Document vision have become concretely expressed in government policies and practices. They cannot be reversed along the discreet avenues of intra-alliance persuasion and lobbying. Needed are systematic and more overt intellectual and popular challenges that summon the involvement of a broader range of popular organizations. A 'high road' approach might concentrate on building a critical consensus against the main blockages in the transformation process – principally, economic policies, as well as efforts to stunt or circumvent social contract processes or remould them into élite, corporatist forms, and attacks on the social, economic and political rights that underpinned the Base Document. Running parallel could be a 'low road' along which (temporary) united front-type activities and campaigns are launched, drawing together forces across class, sectoral and geographic divides around specific issues. In education, for instance, efforts aimed at the democratization of the school system and of tertiary institutions, the revision of syllabi, and the realization of education as a right and not a privilege determined by 'affordability' are not only justified but encouraged by the RDP. Similar examples abound in other sectors. The ideological legitimacy the RDP bestows on divergent activities can be exploited, not only to register real gains but also to reanimate flagging organizations. In some cases, the two approaches could overlap, by mobilizing around the specific, tangible effects of broad policy positions (for instance, the impact of rampant tariff reductions on the communities of clothing and textile workers). At the same time, these approaches have to penetrate and build alliances with sections of the state. As we argue below, a schema that strictly counterposes (progressive) civil society to the state is theoretically bankrupt and practically self-defeating.

For reasons stated, the Base Document cannot serve as the core programme for a popular hegemonic project – its potency is largely ideological and political. More realistic would be to use *clearly defined* elements of it as reference points around which such a project could be assembled. Nor can it be regarded as the sole source of such reference points which could serve as the catalysing elements for an organic process of reconfiguring and rebuilding a popular movement for transformation. The alternative is for the popular forces to remain towed along in the wake of a development path that adapts but ultimately reinforces the insider/outsider mould of society. Meeting those challenges, though, requires overcoming a complex of theoretical, strategic, political and organizational dilemmas that confront these forces.

Notes

1 *Business Day,* 2 September 1994.
2 'RDP is on long road to success', *The Star,* 6 May 1997.
3 At first, the approach was somewhat 'syndicalist' and aimed at an accord that would guarantee workers' rights in the post-apartheid era. Later this was expanded (with union strategist, now trade and industry minister, Alec Erwin and former COSATU general secretary Jay Naidoo at the helm) into a broader programme for transformation.
4 Paraphrased in Gindin (1993).
5 Saul (1994:40).
6 *RDP White Paper,* p. 4 (section 1.1.1).
7 Significantly, in the White Paper the word 'redistribution' appeared only twice in this context.
8 For a summary see Shepard (1994:38–41).
9 Annually, South Africa spends 10 times ($183 per capita) on health care what the World Bank calculates is needed to provide basic public health services for all. Most of the expenditure, however, is on expensive curative care (Shepard, 1994).
10 *RDP White Paper,* p. 2 (Preface).
11 *Ibid.*
12 See *RDP White Paper,* pp. 6–7 (section 1.3).
13 *Op. cit,* pp. 9, 26–7. More positive was the 'central proposal ... that we cannot build the South African economy in isolation from its southern African neighbours' (p.10).
14 *RDP White Paper,* p. 16 (section 2.3.1).
15 Speaking during the budget debate.
16 *RDP White Paper,* pp. i–ii.
17 *Op. cit,* p. i.
18 *Op. cit,* p. 28 (section 3.4).
19 *Op. cit,* p. i (Preamble).
20 Trade and industry minister Trevor Manuel, speaking at an awards banquet, *Business Day,* 1 September 1994.
21 *RDP White Paper,* p. 48 (emphasis added).
22 As interpreted by the South African National Civic Organization's (SANCO) Moses Mayekiso; see *Taking the RDP to the Streets,* address to SANCO Southern Transvaal

RDP conference (May, 1994), Johannesburg. The role of the private sector in SANCO's model was unclear.

23 'They will not be forced to close, but have been asked to reconsider whether they remain relevant,' as former unionist Bernie Fanaroff phrased it in the *Business Day*, 24 August 1994.

24 *Business Times*, 9 October 1994.

25 As summarized by the *RDP Monitor*, August, 1994.

26 Erwin (1994:42). A former trade unionist, Erwin was one of the main architects of the original RDP. In fact, the private sector already had a major stake in basic needs markets like housing and communal taxi transport – with 'disastrous results' (Bond, 1994b).

27 *Cape Times*, 27 July 1994.

28 *Mail & Guardian*, 10 June 1994.

29 Former 'RDP minister', Jay Naidoo, quoted in the *Cape Times*, 4 July 1994.

30 *African Communist*, No. 142 (3rd Quarter, 1995), p. 2.

31 See, for instance, Dexter (1994); successive articles by Patrick Bond in *African Communist*, Nos 137, 138, 144; the SACP's 1995 'Strategy and Tactics Document', reprinted in *Links*, No. 6 (January–April, 1996).

32 This legacy is discussed in more detail in Chapter 8 of this volume.

33 See the special feature 'Social democracy or democratic socialism', *SA Labour Bulletin*, Vol. 17, No. 6 (Nov/Dec 1993) pp. 72–99; and John Saul, 1991, 'Between "barbarism" and "structural reform"', *New Left Review*, No. 188 (July–August), republished in Saul (1993). See also Moses Mayekiso, 1993, 'Nationalisation, socialism and the alliance', *SA Labour Bulletin*, Vol. 17, No. 4 (July/August); 'What's left for the Left?' (special edition) *Work in Progress*, No. 89 (June 1993); Karl von Holdt, 1992, 'The Rise of Strategic Unionism', *Southern Africa Report* (November); 'Strategic objectives of the National Liberation Struggle' (discussion paper), *African Communist*, No. 133 (2nd Quarter 1993); 'The present situation and the challenges for the South African left' (SACP discussion paper for the Conference of the Left), July 1993, unpublished.

34 Gorz (1973).

35 *Ibid.*, and 'Thinking the Unthinkable: Globalism, Socialism and Democracy in the South African Transition' in Miliband and Panitch (1994). For a cautioning response from Kagarlitsky, see his 'Letter to South Africa', *Links, No.* 4 (January–March 1995).

36 For volatile examples, see Callinicos, A., 1992, 'Reform and Revolution in South Africa: A Reply to John Saul', *New Left Review*, No. 195; Saul's reply in the same issue; Godongwana (1994b); and Lehulere, O., 1996, 'Social Democracy and Neo-liberalism in South Africa', *Links*, No. 7 (July–October).

37 Miliband (1996:19).

38 Paraphrased by Bond (1994b:19).

39 Cited by Saul (1994a:40).

40 *Ibid.*

41 Interview with author, October 1994. See also his 'Eight Theses' discussion document prepared for a 'Socialist Conference on Reconstruction and Development', October 1994.

42 Cited by Bond (1994c).

43 For a critique of this approach, see (Marais, 1994a).

44 Bond (1994c).

45 Zita (1995).

46 For a fierce critique of the social contract in the South African context, see British Marxist Alex Callinicos's *Between Apartheid and Capitalism* (1992).

47 Adelzadeh and Padayachee (1994:1), which strongly influenced this section.

48 *RDP White Paper,* p. 4 (section 1.1.2).

49 *RDP White Paper,* p. i (Preamble).

50 Many ANC activists came to describe the RDP White Paper as the 'Omo document' –
the reference was to a well-known detergent, packaged in garish containers, which
(its manufacturers claim) 'washes whites whiter'.

51 In order 'to ensure that it is insulated from partisan interference and is accountable to
the broader goals of reconstruction and development' (*RDP White Paper*, p. 33) – an
Orwellian phrase, given the Reserve Bank's structural location in the economy.

52 *RDP White Paper,* p. 6 (section 1.3.2).

53 *Op. cit.,* p. 6 (section 1.3.6).

54 *Ibid.*

55 *Ibid.*

56 For a more detailed survey of the manifold difficulties, see Kraak (1996), Marais
(1997a) and The Community Constituency in NEDLAC (1996). The latter grouping
comprises SANCO, the Women's National Coalition, the South African Federal
Council of the Disabled and the National Rural Development Forum.

57 The Community Constituency in NEDLAC (1996:3).

58 This structural reality is often overlooked in favour of personalizing the causes of
institutional dysfunction. See, for instance, Postman (1992:85), where he describes
bureaucracy as a 'meta-institution that largely serves itself' and vigorously replicates
its culture. Also of note is Manuel De Landa's analysis of the self-organizing principles of complex machines and institutions (1991).

59 *Southscan,* No. 28, 19 July 1996, cited by Kraak (1996:38).

60 For an overview of these and other travails, see Marais (1997a).

61 For an overview of RDP performance in Gauteng, Mpumalanga and North West, see
Rapoo (1996).

62 Naidoo, J., 'Taking the RDP Forward' (report to Parliament, 8 June 1995), Cape
Town.

63 When a new Education Bill was filibustered in Parliament in 1996, for instance, not a
single protest action was mounted by the supposedly robust range of progressive student and education organizations in the country.

64 While commending the programme, the National Progressive Primary Health Care
Network (NPPHCN) suggested the R623 million (US$138 million) project should
have been directed at pre-school children. Operation Hunger slammed the project,
saying 'If we are trying to improve the nutritional status of children, the [project] is a
waste of money'; see *Mail & Guardian,* 15 March 1996.

65 For a critical assessment of progress in the health sector, see Bond *et al.* (1996:6–9).

66 Unfortunately, these programmes were used by some construction companies to
'casualize' their labour forces by sacking full-time employees and hiring contract
workers; see *Mail & Guardian,* 13 September 1996.

67 'RDP is on long road to recovery', *The Star,* 6 May 1997. See also Marais (1997a).

68 *Mail & Guardian,* 15 March 1996, cited by Kraak (1996:39).

69 Inaccurate was the SACP's claim that, in the RDP, 'macro-economic concerns like the
growth rate, the inflation rate, or our international competitiveness are all subordinated to [the] critical objective' of meeting the basic needs of South Africans; see
SACP, 1995, *Strategy and Tactics Document,* Johannesburg, p. 18.

70 In a presentation to the ANC's national executive committee in early November.
Reportedly, COSATU's Sam Shilowa and other union leaders drafted core parts of
Mbeki's paper.

71 Surveyed in more detailed in Chapter 7 of this volume.

72 See, for instance, The Community Constituency in NEDLAC's 1996 critique, *Return to the RDP*.

73 Analysts who probe these questions are routinely fobbed off for not 'understand[ing] how the democratic movement works' (*Mayibuye* editorial, June 1996). Only in late 1996 did the SACP, for instance, devote sustained attention to these matters; see its *Let Us Not Lose Sight of Our Strategic Priorities* (discussion document), October 1996.

74 Kagarlitsky (1996:229).

CHAPTER SEVEN

The popular movement in flux
The state of play

Since the 1970s there revived in South Africa a dynamic range of progressive organs within civil society, grouped broadly under the rubric of the
anti-apartheid struggle and referred to here as the 'popular movement'.[1]
The sweep encompassed labour, women's, civic, student, youth, human
rights, church, legal, health, education, media, community advice, legal,
housing, land and other groups. Many of them functioned as 'institutional',
organized bases of resistance and provided much of the oppositional impetus that led to the negotiated transition. Indeed, their seeming pervasive-
ness, maturity and sophistication gave rise to grandiose expectations.

In some respects the reputation was deserved. Until the early 1990s, the
trade union federation COSATU ranked among the fastest-growing union
federations in the world and it remains by far the strongest on the continent.
Though of uneven strength, civic associations are active across the land. A
huge array of professional, community and service organizations remains
active. A fledgling women's movement has mustered national lobbying campaigns (notably on women's reproductive rights) and more. Land and housing organizations have remained active in education, training, lobbying and
policy work. Compared to most other developing countries, the accumulated achievements, experience, skills, infrastructure and resources within
progressive civil society organs seem formidable.

Assuming this state of affairs as a constant given would be foolish. Indeed,
some unionists have disputed the strength and vibrancy of the 'popular
movement', arguing that 'outside of the unions (and churches) and excluding business, civil society is fragile' and that 'many organizations really exist
only in embryonic form' (Bird & Schreiner, 1992:31). One might retort that,
'embryonic' or not, those structures at least exist. Other analysts have tempered the praises sung to autonomous, community-based organizations
(CBOs) by reminding that they were principally 'mobilisation organisations,

and to convert them into development-oriented instruments' would prove difficult (Narsoo, 1991:27). Still others have counted heads and discovered that less than 5 000 of the 54 000 non-governmental organizations (NGOs) in South Africa are involved in anything resembling development work.[2]

The point, though, is not to conduct a roll-call but to assess whether the popular components of civil society can live up to the expectations heaped upon them. This calls for two enquiries. Are the roles assigned grounded in a coherent and viable theoretical framework? This requires a survey of the debates around the state and civil society in South Africa. And, practically, which are the key challenges to be met if these organizations are to achieve the levels of efficacy demanded of them?

The 'discovery' of civil society

In South Africa the infatuation with civil society grew intense after two, coinciding developments: the collapse of Eastern Europe's statist models, and the prospect of a negotiated transition from apartheid to democracy.

Like the Bandung generation of anti-colonial movements, the anti-apartheid struggle viewed the state as the tangible embodiment of concentrated power which, in turn, was seen as 'a quantifiable substance that has to be seized'.[3] Strategies were therefore aimed at the seizure of the state in order to work its levers to the benefit of the masses. The implied conflation of the state with 'the people' and the 'public good' (once it rested in the 'right' hands) is obvious.[4] Also implicit was the notion that power could be centralized within certain institutions and exercised from above.

Yet, the struggles waged inside South Africa during the 1980s also revealed an awareness of the diffuse nature of state power, as social movements, professional groups, churches and trade unions waged resistance struggles in civil society.[5] At the forefront were the black trade unions. Reflecting on that decade, Fine has detected in their activities a search for a 'third road' that departed from the neo-classical and neo-Marxist routes, both of which represented top-down models of change in which formations of civil society become subsumed within a centralized project (1992:74–5). In several respects the new trade unions broke with the orthodox approaches and provided 'the practical foundations for the rebirth of "civil society"'.[6] The self-organization of workers implicitly challenged the weight of nationalism in South African political culture, while struggles for reforms in the workplace diverged from the 'all-or-nothing' perspectives of the ANC. Invested in the notion of worker control (emphasizing participatory democracy, accountability of leadership and open debate) was the conviction that power should be exercised from below. Analogous approaches percolated in other popular organizations.

These approaches implied a more sophisticated understanding of the dispersal of power in class society which contrasted with the reifying thinking employed in the ANC and SACP. The discourse there remained virulently Leninist, to which Gramscian understandings were at best *appended* – yielding interpretations of the 'war of position' approach that implied the 'encirclement of a fortress state'.[7] In this manner, the harnessing of autonomous activities of popular organizations into dual power and insurrectionary strategies seemed to present no contradiction. Persistent was the conception of the state as a monolithic bloc in which pure power resided. The strategy was to attack the state from the outside, besieging and weakening it until it could be seized.

The struggles of civil society organs were seen in purely instrumental terms and became incorporated into the external assault against the apartheid state. Indeed, their utility would dissolve once power had been won. The effects were most pronounced in trade unions, some of which attempted to develop political identities and organizational styles distinct from the liberation organizations. In Fine's summary,

> ... a formal ANC-SACP-COSATU alliance was effected; members of the trade union left were recruited into the Communist Party or drawn into its ambit; those who continued to oppose the SACP-ANC were generally isolated (1992:77).

Amid the uprisings of the mid-1980s the autonomous strategies attempted by trade unions became caricatured as 'workerism'. The choice presented was 'either "political" or "non-political" unionism [which] was really no choice at all: it meant the assimilation of unions into the political frame of the national liberation movement' (Fine, 1992:78). Dominant once again was a perspective of frontal assault on the state, expounded in the slogans calling for ungovernability, non-collaboration, people's power and insurrection.

These perspectives were not periodic 'aberrations'. They lay at the very heart of the ANC and SACP's strategic thinking and endured after 1990, when the ANC set about dissembling and incorporating many of the organizations that had driven the protests of the previous decade. Controversially, the UDF was disbanded, while youth and women's organizations were folded into ANC structures which quickly slumped into moribundity. They were set elemental tasks: mobilizing support for the ANC during negotiations, membership recruitment, and fundraising.

That this occurred through a mix of coercion and consent showed how deeply the instrumentalist view had permeated the democratic movement. There existed, according to Jeremy Cronin, a 'B-team mentality' which viewed the internal movement as a substitute for the exiled ANC. As writer Dan Connell pointed out:

> This was notably the case in the women's and youth movements where there had been strong grassroots organisations with their own distinct and diverse

agendas, but which were folded into the ANC and then turned almost overnight into vehicles for mobilizing their constituencies for the political agendas set at the center (1995:33).

A further example of this instrumentalism was the manner in which mass action by popular organizations was 'turned on and off' by the ANC leadership at key junctures during the negotiations phase.[8] This was intimately related to the view that power is best exercised from above by a national liberation movement functioning as the reservoir and guardian of the masses' interests. Typically, the perspective was associated with Stalinist statism, overlooking its affinities with Western social welfare states which displayed a similar distrust of popular initiatives and grassroots democracy, and a comparable veneration of the state. Questioning these assumptions therefore required more than critiques of Stalinist tradition. Conceptions of the state and civil society had to be re-examined.

The jolts of 1989–90 prompted many left intellectuals to take up that challenge.[9] Two shifts quickly occurred. In the SACP, the scepticism about 'bourgeois' democracy ebbed and was replaced by the (sometimes grudging) acceptance that rights and liberties associated with liberal-democracy were (however insufficient) not mere 'window-dressing'. Related was a sudden infatuation with civil society which was endowed with magical properties – becoming, as writer Monty Narsoo remarked,

> ... the panacea for the ills of the failed East European regimes, the decline of the welfare state, the ailing economies of the African continent and for reconstruction in South Africa (1991:21).

A fetish of civil society emerged. Encouraging it also were two related international trends: leftist critiques of the welfare state[10] and the anti-state crusades of neo-conservatism. Though politically irreconcilable, both trends recognized the inadequacy (for their respective political projects) of the cult of state worship.

In South Africa, the definition and role of civil society resided very much in the eyes of its beholders. The concept was made to describe politically independent social movements, or 'a robust, locally-constituted voluntary sector' (Swilling, 1991:22), or everything from 'a little jazz collective [to] a multi-billion rand company' (Narsoo, 1991:25). Some included in it the institutions of capitalism,[11] others conveniently decided that it excluded the market. These divergent definitions produced bewildering anomalies in left discourse, where, as analyst Steve Friedman noted, 'the aim is no longer only to win state power but to limit it' – leading him to ask whether 'yesterday's populists and socialists [are] today's liberals and libertarians?' (1991:5). Although posed with some mirth, the question captured the giddiness that characterized debates around the state and civil society.

A brief history

Several sets of meanings have, over the centuries, adhered to the concept of civil society. It originated in Roman times to distinguish between private property and state or community property, making its modern 'association with the specific property relations of capitalism', as Ellen Meiksins Wood has recalled, 'a variation on an old theme' (1990:61). The concept was revived by French and English liberals in the 17th and 18th centuries, followed by Hegel, who proceeded to conceptualize a dichotomy between state and civil society. For him, the latter represented the arena of fractious and self-interested competition, with a potential for self-destruction. Thus the advancement of the public good rested with the state, a perspective Marx then complicated by demonstrating that the state embodied the particularities and class relations of civil society. Ergo, communism implied the withering away of both the state and civil society.

Departing from a rigid demarcation between state and civil society, Antonio Gramsci later emphasized their interrelatedness and likened the latter to a system of trenches that protects the state. In his famous formulation,

> ... when the state trembled a sturdy structure of civil society was at once revealed. The state was only an outer ditch, behind which stood a powerful system of fortresses and earthworks ... (1971:238)

Unlike Marx, Gramsci saw the state not as force, in the last instance, but redefined it as force plus active consent. Civil society, in this view, is a sphere where a ruling class organizes hegemony – essentially the activated consent of a broad range of social forces, including the subordinate classes. The state is protected by hegemony organized in civil society while the hegemony of the ruling class is buttressed by the state. The domination by a ruling group therefore cannot be traced to concentrated points in the state. It is diffuse and pervades society. The signal lesson is that civil society is not 'independent' and 'separate', and that the spatial opposition between state and civil society serves to disguise the processes by which class *and other* forms of domination are achieved and maintained.

This most crucial ingredient of domination – cultivating the 'active consent' of subordinate groups – occurs at the superstructural and not the structural level. At the same time, Gramsci did not view civil society as being wholly intertwined with and functional to class domination.[12] Rival ideologies and organizations could acquire *relative autonomy* from the relations of production. Gramsci generated drastically different conceptions about how state power – and class rule – is contested and consolidated. The fetish of the state yielded to an emphasis on civil society – although some readings of Gramsci deemed this shift 'opportunistic', 'a merely tactical position, in which civil society is a necessary site of a contest for the state'.[13]

The pluralist view is quite distinct and regards civil society as a counter-vailing sphere where multiple interests and relations intersect and freedom is realized. While avoiding the disingenuous anti-statism of neo-conserva-tives,[14] the view sees civil society as the zone of freedom and voluntary action. Emancipation requires 'the autonomy of civil society, its expansion and enrichment, its liberation from the state, and its protection by formal democracy' (Wood, 1990:74). Superficially stirring, the conception suffers a severe flaw. It requires that capital be seen as merely one among a multiplic-ity of forces and interests active in civil society, thereby concealing capital-ism's overarching coercive power. Capitalism 'disappears into a conceptual night where all cats are grey' (Wood, 1990:66), while civil society's main dysfunctions are attributed to intrusions by the state. A variant of this con-ception is to be found in the post-Marxism of Ernesto Laclau, where class struggle forms 'only one of the subject positions of social agents, since the workers themselves participate in many others'.[15]

In the eyes of the beholder

Circulating in the democratic movement are various hybrids of these approaches. The statist traditions of the ANC and SACP have encouraged a wariness of state power, expressed in several forms. In one, an autonomous and vibrant civil society is seen as a prerequisite to *deepen* liberal democ-racy (within the framework of laws, rights and liberties conferred by the state) and to systematically carve out toeholds for socialism. This is to occur through grassroots voluntary associations that 'influence and even deter-mine the structure of power and the allocation of material resources'.[16] The boundaries of civil society are tightly defined to exclude capitalist institu-tions (its 'essence ... is a robust locally-constituted voluntary sector'[17]). Its role becomes especially important when the post-apartheid state's capacity to deliver on promises of reconstruction and development falters.

Another adds a thin leftist gloss to the pluralist outlook and views the com-promised state with deep distrust. Not only have its new administrators not shed their statist compulsions but by assuming the task of managing the revival of capital accumulation in a volatile political and social context, they might be tempted to resort to authoritarian measures to achieve the requisite stability. Consequently, the left is urged to defend not only the 'space' provided by liberal democracy but also the historical project the ANC-dominated state is said to be betraying. The state has to be quarantined, and its reach restricted while civil society becomes an external terrain for a permanent left opposition. This approach reverts to the state/civil society schism, ignoring the fact that 'civil society does not exist independently of the state, it is situated in rules and transactions which connect state and society' (Beckman, 1993:29).

Conversely, elements in the ANC still eye civil society with grave suspi-cion. Those structures that ascribe to the Congress tradition are encouraged to forego their claims to autonomy and rather operate within the folds of the ANC. The dissolution of the UDF sprang from this thinking, as did the disdain shown towards ANC members who opted to stand as independent or civic candidates in the 1995 local government elections. Civil society is valued as one of several instruments for achieving state power, after which it becomes an (unavoidable) irritant or, worse, a sphere of anti-state harassment and reaction. The tradition of state worship (and the notion that power resides in and can be exercised from specific spatial or institutional points) lives on.

More common is a view that combines the pluralist and Gramscian conceptions. An autonomous and diverse civil society is extolled, on one hand, as a corrective counterweight to the state,[18] and, on the other, as the site where hegemony is built and maintained. ANC discourse seldom disentangles these two meanings, though within the SACP the emphasis has come to rest more clearly on civil society's role in hegemonic struggle. It argues that the legitimacy and mass-base of the ANC make the tripartite alliance the natural vehicle for that hegemonic project which has to involve also a struggle 'for the heart and soul of the ANC'.[19] Basically Poulantzian, the approach rejects the choice 'between a struggle "within" the state apparatuses ... and a struggle located at a certain physical distance from these apparatuses'[20], arguing instead for an articulation of those engagements.

Finally, one encounters (particularly among development NGOs) a ritual clamour for a vibrant and independent civil society that is freed from the weight of the state and of political parties. The posture tends to be poorly theorized, dogmatic and ignorant of the danger that 'strengthening the independence of civil society does not necessarily mean greater equity or freedom'.[21] Its anti-statism and disdain for party politics disregards the pre-eminence and sweep of capitalist institutions in civil society, and the ways by which 'many of the coercive functions that once belonged to the state [have been] relocated in the "private" sphere, in private property, class exploitation, and market imperatives' (Wood, 1990:73). Indeed, the approach is closely linked to neo-liberal discourse and practice.[22]

The South African debates continue to orbit around such contradictory and confusing conceptions of the state and civil society – yet they cut to the heart of the dilemmas facing the popular movement. Many of the assumptions and affinities inherited from the anti-apartheid struggle have translated poorly into the new context. Disaffection with statist routes of transformation has coupled with the perception of the state as being 'withered away' by globalization, yielding hugely amplified assessments of the scale and role of civil society. The trend is visible worldwide, most profoundly in the industrialized countries where, in new social movement theory, popular organs and initiatives have acquired an almost messianic status. 'State-centred marxist theory' is deemed obsolete, because it 'can no longer offer either a practicable path to freedom or a desirable one'.[23] Yet the new, substitute paths remain vague and appear equally impracticable, because 'the new conception of civil society is intentionally formless',[24] and because it rests on the erroneous notion that the state has shrunk into small fortresslike spaces in the field of society. The complex relationship between the state and civil society is still rendered in archaic terms of externality and opposition, leading to a neglect of the ways by which conditions for the exercise of power are established and reproduced.

Civil society in the new era

Having laid the groundwork for South Africa's fledgling democracy, the popular movement has been struggling to find its footing in the transition. Buffeted by changes, neither its mass-based organizations nor the array of NGOs that function in their support have evaded the dilemmas thrown up by internal dysfunctions, funding crises, political incoherence and overall strategic disorientation. Recuperation has been complicated by the constantly shifting contexts in which these organizations function. While not in crisis, they are in flux and prone to a pervasive mood of disengagement and disorientation – termed 'post-liberation depression' by some. Among the many causes one can discern the disorganizing and demoralizing effects of the intense violence and trauma experienced in African townships, a well-nurtured belief that the onus of introducing and directing change now rests with the post-apartheid state, the alienating effect of discreet and remote negotiations processes, misgivings about the abilities of existing organizations to service people's needs and confusion about those organs' role in post-apartheid society.[25]

Symptomatic of these difficulties is the question whether one can justifiably speak of a popular movement that orbits around a broadly distinct culture and set of goals. Until 1990, it was possible (though already controversial) to singularize the assortment of organizations gathered under the mantle of a struggle for national liberation. The struggle functioned as an ideological and political 'glue' that drew in and bonded popular organizations into uneven (and contested) unity. Broadly, two currents of organizations merged in that process – what Narsoo (1991) has termed 'organisations of survival' and 'organisations of resistance'. The former included professional bodies (teachers, health practitioners, legal workers), *stokvels* (informal saving schemes), burial groups, black business associations, cultural groups, sports clubs and some trade unions. Prominent among the latter were student and youth groups, women's organizations, land and squatter groups, civic associations, and independent media projects. Straddling the two categories were human rights groups, advice offices and some church organizations. As internal resistance swelled during the 1980s those distinctions became highly porous, as organizations chose or were coerced into adopting more overt political postures. This process was both organic (pro-pelled by rank-and-file demands) and externally imposed (through the demonization of efforts to work within spaces demarcated by the apartheid state).[26] In short, organizations 'were being squeezed by a state seeking legiti-macy and liberation movements seeking hegemony in civil society' (Narsoo, 1991:27). By the mid-1980s, the homogenizing sweep of the resistance cur-rent was extensive as politicized and often militant organizations came to dominate civil life in many black townships.

Two important factors contributed to this situation. The ANC became adept at a key aspect of any hegemonic project: it managed to deploy an array of ideological precepts and symbols, and asserted their pertinence to the lived realities of millions of South Africans. The Freedom Charter was resurrected and popularized as the programme for change; the liberation struggle was personified in the form of Nelson Mandela; the colours, flags, songs and slogans of the ANC became ubiquitous features of resistance activities. The idea of 'the people' was 'turned into a formalism whose sin-gular consciousness was homogenised by the movement which spoke in its name', while a 'plurality of opinions' was 'negated by the singular notion of public opinion', as Fine has written (1992:80). The armed struggle, too, functioned impressively in this process. Although armed attacks multiplied in the 1980s,[27] their efficacy lay not at the level of military strategy but as cathartic, galvanizing signifiers of resistance and in their symbolic refutal of the apartheid system's alleged invincibility. Overall, the ideological field through which millions of citizens experienced reality was dramatically altered. In short, the ANC had, by the late 1980s, succeeded in extending its hegemony within the broad popular movement.[28]

The other factor was material. Foreign NGOs and funders provided mas-sive amounts of financial support to internal popular organizations. This meant that many initiatives that would have remained informal and ephemeral could establish a sustained and 'organized' presence. At the same time, groups that might have preferred a more 'apolitical' role recognized that choosing sides also carried material implications.

The national liberation struggle therefore acted as an ideological epoxy that bonded a miscellany of organizations. The collapse of the apartheid system, and the winning of political power by the ANC, however, diluted that adhesive effect – leading to accentuated divisions and tensions within and between the constituents of the popular movement. As argued below, many of these tensions were not new but had been submerged in the dis-course of anti-apartheid struggles. Indeed, the descriptive power of the term 'popular movement' has become questionable. Generally, it has referred to a combination of political and community-based organizations and NGOs (mostly professional, service-oriented groups). Defined nar-rowly as those organizations whose objectives fit broadly within the rubric of the national liberation project (i.e. liberty, democratization, reconstruction and development) the popular movement encloses about 5 000 organizations. But even that definition poses problems. Does it, for example, include black business organizations which historically supported the broad aims of the liberation struggle but which currently promote élite black capitalist aspirations or function as building blocks of a 'patriotic bourgeoisie', depending on one's analytical vantage point? The answer to such questions is being postponed by the elevation of the RDP into a national, consensual venture – which mirrors the inclusive sweep of the Freedom Charter, extending it to embrace both (former) friend and foe. Translated into a nation-building and national development endeavour, the national liberation project survives as the prime ideological bonding agent. Its adhesive power, though, is weak.

Despite this disorienting context, the popular movement is by no means dead in the water. Membership of its most powerful component – trade unions – more than doubled between 1985 and 1995. Almost half of all unionized workers belong to unions affiliated to COSATU which had 1,4 million members in 1995.[29] It and, to a much lesser extent, the National Council of Trade Unions (NACTU), remain formidable forces on the shopfloor and, potentially, in the theatres of economic policy-making. Civic associations are still ubiquitous, though of sharply differing strength and character from one township to the next. There exists the rudiments of a women's movement (though weakened by the failures of the ANC Women's League) which has won gains in the legislative arena and continues to challenge gender oppression within popular organizations.[30] The land movement comprises both organized structures and more ephemeral organs which arise, often spontaneously, in response to local crises. High schools, universities and colleges boast students' councils, although their vanguardist postures tend to alienate them from many students. While South Africa's religious institutions are disparate and often socially reactionary, some retain the potential of becoming vital social actors (as demonstrated during the 1980s).[31] Despite funding crises and the departure of skilled personnel, a strong and diverse range of NGOs remain active.

Many of these organizations have tried to engage creatively with government departments (notably in the labour, land, health and education sectors) and in the constitution-making process.[32] At the local level others have instituted innovative housing schemes for squatter communities or compelled the democratization of universities and colleges. These kinds of achievements suggest a healthy popular sector. Yet, in most cases, they were made *despite* an array of inhibiting factors that beset these organizations. The next section surveys some of those factors, most of which apply also to the main liberation organization, the ANC.

Shocks of the new

Three months after the 1994 election, the ANC's organizational apparatus was 'in tatters', according to President Mandela. It had been hollowed out by the exodus of leaders into government, state and corporate structures. Compounding matters were poor administrative systems, inadequate intra-organizational communication, confusion about its powers and roles vis-à-vis colleagues in government, financial troubles and the increasing difficulty in answering the question 'What's our mission now?'.

As the ANC approached the 1999 elections, activists reported that many party branches, denuded of active memberships, existed in name only.[33] An official report on the ten ANC regions in the Free State province, for example, lamented 'a lack of collective leadership, of political direction, of contact with branches and a lack of resources'.[34]

Many of the same ideological and material processes that brought this about were being experienced by other popular organizations and the NGO service sector. Some trends can be discerned.[35]

Identity crises

Popular organizations are beset by a crisis of role and identity. With the ANC in government, their former oppositional character has been declared an anachronism and they have been urged to move 'from resistance to reconstruction'. This implies abandoning mobilizing and overt political activities in favour of 'delivering' development, a process that requires reorienting organizational objectives towards project development and implementation, and participation in policy-making. It demands new skills, organizational systems, forms of interaction with constituencies and the state, even a new ethos. It also calls into question the sheer relevance of some organizations when the state is seen to be better equipped to perform their tasks.

But for some, the 'from resistance to reconstruction' slogan glosses over many complexities. Lechesa Tsenoli, former South African National Civic Organization (SANCO) president, has judged the slogan 'undynamic and undialectical' since it presumes that South Africa in 1994 passed through a magic portal beyond which the contradictions that had fuelled resistance dissolved into a common, national endeavour. He argued that ostensibly discordant actions (like 'land invasions') remained an integral, reinforcing element of reconstruction:

> We recognize the problems that can arise from such 'invasions', but there is no doubt that they could be one of the most efficient mechanisms for land release'.[36]

Such actions highlight a central conundrum: the relationship between the state and civil society within the context of a national reconstruction effort.

Officially, the government insists that popular organizations should function not as mere agents of state-defined and state-led development initiatives but as autonomous participants in a grand reconstruction effort. Emphasized is the need to build 'dynamic partnerships' between the state and civil society, a formula that confirms rather than resolves the dilemma. Schooled in launching external, frontal assaults on the state, these organizations now have to engage with and within a state which, in formal terms, is controlled by a political ally. What are the appropriate divisions of labour in such a relationship and where lie the boundaries of dissent? The initial answers have been either irresolute or depressing. Some government departments (like housing) prefer delivery-oriented NGOs and CBOs which can slot into state programmes.[37] Those structures emphasizing social development over swift delivery have found themselves bypassed by bureaucrats keener on 'product-driven' relationships with the private sector. Other departments (education and health, for instance) have sought less prescriptive relationships with NGOs and CBOs. As for dissent, the government has proved less than indulgent when it has involved outright criticism.[38]

With the partial exception of the trade union movement, few organizations can draw on historical traditions to meet these novel challenges. This central weakness can be traced back to two core features of the resistance struggles. Efforts to exploit spaces and weaknesses in the state were denounced as collaborationist and rejected in favour of outright conflict. Hardly any experiences of engagements with and within state apparatuses were allowed to accumulate. And change 'was conceptualized as starting with a seizure of state power and from there the transformation of society would flow in a very centralized manner', in former trade unionist Enoch Godongwana's words.[39] Conceptually, civil society had been virtually collapsed into the post-apartheid state. 'The irony,' SACP deputy secretary-general Jeremy Cronin has admitted, 'is that we fought for decades to arrive at a point where we seem unable to devise a clear strategy to move forward'.[40]

The rise of technicism

The post-1990 plethora of negotiating forums and the huge demand for policy proposals and action research pushed to the fore those organizations capable of rendering 'technical' services (training, research, policy development, advisory support, etc.), and increased the influence of urbane technical specialists. By drawing on such expertise, many popular organizations were able to influence new policies. But it also introduced new difficulties. One was the marginalization (wittingly or not) of the constituencies those processes were supposed to serve.[41] A 'tyranny of expertise' took hold, in Tsenoli's view:

Ideally, it should be a relationship where the 'expert' develops options for us and we then decide on an informed basis which is the most appropriate option. But often the relationship does not work that way. The issue is power – who ends up controlling the agenda?[42]

In some cases, the rarefied nature of these processes has been overcome.[43] In many others, they have aggravated tensions within constituencies, heightened distrust of organizations' leadership, and inadvertently helped scuttle ostensibly viable projects. Trade unions and civic associations have been especially susceptible to these dynamics.

Another variant of this problem occurs when (mainly urban) development NGOs second or provide staff to remote CBOs in a bid to launch or improve faltering projects. The pressure to make a project operational (to 'deliver') often overrides the more arduous process of transferring skills to the CBO. A typical complaint has been that the support ends up stymieing rather than enhancing grassroots capacities. More general is the danger that complex social dynamics become submerged and overlooked when tasks are framed in purely technical terms. Former trade unionist (now ANC MP) Preggs Govender has detected this tendency in the RDP where:

> ... lots of numbers are thrown around, yet social relations are talked about in the abstract as broad statements. They end up being in the top of the document – as in 'this is why were are doing this' – but exactly what we are going to do is rendered in a totally technicist manner.[44]

The irony, as progressive movements in other societies have discovered, is that a propensity for strictly technical solutions both depoliticizes and repoliticizes the problem at hand. Once decoded into 'purely rational' terms, the problem is shielded against the grasp of insurgent or antisystemic politics (which, perforce, is geared at excavating and challenging the underlying power dynamics). Far from being politically 'neutral', the resultant decisions, by overlooking those dynamics reinforce and legitimize them. This was glaringly evident in the GEAR macroeconomic plan, a strategy drawn up by a purportedly ideologically neutral team of economists and politically propelled by technocrats within the ANC government. COSATU, in its 1996 *A Draft Programme for the Alliance*, regarded GEAR as one of several examples where policy and implementation by government ministries occurred in technocratic and atomized fashion, while the SACP's Cronin and Blade Nzimande later correctly related the trend to 'statist exaggerations'.[45]

Urban concentration, rural isolation

The largest and best-resourced popular organizations tend to be concentrated in and around urban zones, where most resources and skills are concentrated. However representative civics might be in those areas where they are well organized (generally the 'established sections of townships rather than shack settlements'[46]), in huge swathes of society such structures are non-existent, disorganized or unrepresentative. Because those communities are generally poorly positioned to access funding and other support, the discrepancy is endemic, particularly when the overall funding pool shrinks. The resilience and determination that distinguishes many of the structures that do emerge in these areas is undermined by their lack of material and institutional resources. In addition, media, information and consultation circuits and networks operate largely within the urban realm, adding to the isolation of rural constituencies.[47] As a result geographic divides – overlapping with the 'pre-modern' and 'modern' divide – are reinforced.

The cheque is in the mail

The vitality, resilience and 'enterprising' flair displayed by popular organizations drew billions of rands in overseas funding. The role of this money in building, bolstering – and distorting – South Africa's vaunted popular movement cannot be underestimated.[48] During the 1990s, much of that funding has been directed away from South Africa or into bilateral funding arrangements with the government. As the flood of funding for civil society has dried up, three trends could be observed:

- NGOs began following a supply-side logic, tailoring their activities to access diminishing pools of funds that donors were earmarking for particular areas and types of work.[49] The practice has become widespread, with donors like USAID pushing it to new extremes by inviting *tenders* from NGOs for earmarked funds. As a result, donors have acquired much greater influence over what work is performed in which sectors, while organizations' dependency on outside funding undermines their abilities to independently design programmes and to respond to (unforeseen or, for funders, unattractive) emerging needs. The representativeness of organizations is also compromised, since 'people are not having to account to the local residents but to donors'.[50] The blame must be shared, however, since some organizations (like civics) could avoid this with member fees and other forms of fundraising.
- A process of attrition began abruptly after 1990, with projects and organizations collapsing in sectors that were struck from donors' lists of priorities. Media, culture, community advice service and some education projects have been hardest hit.[51] These projects often served as resource, training, information and infrastructural anchor points for other popular organizations. The impact of their demise extends far beyond the projects themselves.
- Development NGOs in particular have turned towards cost-recovery methods to make up for funding shortfalls. The rule of the market is

being introduced into areas which hitherto were able to socialize access to services and resources – effectively reproducing the marginalizing dynamics many NGOs profess to be combatting. Cost-recovery operations tend to structurally favour better organized and more sophisticated groups, since accessing those services presupposes some integration into existing circuits of funding and expertise. In addition, the cycle of dependency is extended, since organizations that contract NGOs often themselves have to fundraise from donors.

Most of these trends are prevalent worldwide and reveal the actual function of most NGOs in societies experiencing neo-liberal adjustments. In Samir Amin's judgment,

> ... far from constituting the basic structure of a powerful civil society, these reorganized NGOs accompany the management of society by the dominant forces of capital (1997:10).

Under the canopy of economic policies like GEAR, NGOs' roles tend to harmonize with standard neo-liberal logic as they toil in the wake of development and welfare responsibilities shirked by the state. Their function becomes one of (at once) legitimizing and cushioning the effects of that economic strategy on the most destitute sections of society.[52]

Migrations

Popular organizations (and service organizations linked to them) suffered a massive exodus of experienced and skilled personnel after the April 1994 election. Benefiting from this drain were government departments and state institutions, as well as companies implementing affirmative action programmes. In rare cases, individuals have made principled decisions not to accept the enticing offers of lavish salary packages and benefits. COSATU elected to send 20 top union officials into government while affiliates like NUMSA (which discouraged mass departures) lost almost 40 regional and local leaders. The ANC's infrastructure has been hard-hit with top figures leaving for the corporate sector (former secretary general Cyril Ramaphosa now heads the business consortium New Africa Investments Limited). A wealth of experience and institutional histories departed with these individuals, leaving in their wake diminished capacities for the kinds of innovations required in the transition.

These departures have become an ongoing trend as people enter a spiral of upward mobility and migrate from job to job. The result is a high turnover of staff which causes chronic delays and instability in organizations' work schedules. A minor benefit is that many veterans of the popular sector now work in state structures, which might make it easier to forge links between the two sectors. But the revolving door phenomenon is also

aggravating existing weaknesses in popular organizations. Many development NGOs, for instance, 'are good at devising innovative projects but lack
the capacity to ensure their wider implementation – they lack lobbying and
advocacy skills and the financial skills to cost projects on a wider scale'.[53]
As a result, innovation is stunted and localized.

Complications of difference and identity[54]

Less tangible but more pervasive and enduring is the legacy of homogeniza-
tion. A constantly admired feature of the anti-apartheid era was the success
of the ANC (and the UDF) at enveloping different classes, ethnicities, generations and ideologies. Distinct identities were submerged and swept along
by the currents of resistance. In their place, levelling categories were applied
– 'the people', 'the oppressed', 'the community' – which blanketed the multifold identities through which people live their realities. The tactical utility
of this response was obvious. But it carried hidden costs which did not go
entirely unnoticed in the democratic movement. In a famous 1984 exchange
of letters in the ANC's *Sechaba* magazine, the editor warned that:

> [o]ur strive for unity should not blind us from seeing the differences which if
> ignored can cause problems for that unity we are striving to achieve.[55]

Despite such sporadic declamations, the popular sector was left, in Cronin's
view, 'unable to discern and deal with the different interests and identities
within communities and constituencies'.[56] Those differences have erupted to
the surface as the dissolution of the apartheid system removed one of the
central unifying factors in the popular movement. By enforcing difference
and division, that system, paradoxically, had bolstered a homogenizing
reaction. Ideologically, the democratic movement countered the system of
racial exclusion by defining itself in inverse terms, stressing inclusiveness
and playing down difference. At the grand level, this yielded the ambitious
concept of non-racialism, based on the conviction that race is not immanent
but socially constructed and therefore subject to contestation.[57] In practice,
however, this concept failed to dissolve racial boundaries and retained 'a
reactive nature, synonymous with non-discrimination, and indistinguish-
able from the dominant one of multi-racialism'.[58] Inscribed in the non-racial
project were the very categories that it sought to transcend, which led to
serious contradictions in the discourse of the democratic movement.
Rhetorically, racial difference was eschewed; yet, social realities encouraged
organizing on the basis of race. Racial difference was at once denied and
reinforced. These contradictions haunt the movement – tangibly, for
instance, in the Western Cape where the majority of coloured voters have
sided with the NP while African voters *en masse* are allied to the ANC.
Racial tensions between coloureds and Africans have long been explicit in
everyday life in that province. Yet, the ANC failed to recognize the

profound clashes of identity and interests that underlay those tensions, preferring to regard them as the product of a 'false consciousness' engendered by apartheid ideology. As antidotes it opted, for example, to engineer the election of a former coloured priest to head the party in the province, ignoring the multifold layers on which Africans' and coloureds' self-perceptions rested. Six months after the election defeat, the problem had still not been analytically probed; at the ANC's September 1994 provincial congress, the matter was merely alluded to, despite the fact that the organization itself had become openly riven by racial divisions.[59]

The popular tradition was not equipped to process the reality of overlapping, heterogenous identities. Allegiance to the ANC, for instance, entailed the adoption of a singularized world view and (political/social) identity, purged of paradoxical or contradictory interests and identities. It was into this blindspot that Mangosuthu Buthelezi, leader of the IFP, inserted a political programme with which he succeeded in mobilizing a potent social and political movement around Zulu chauvinism and (re)invented tradition.

Other layers of difference (notably class and gender) were played down in less ambiguous ways in a liberation struggle forged around the central theme of nationalism. Working class politics was subordinated to the imperative of national liberation, a historical process Fine (in Fine & Davis, 1990) has documented in detail. This was facilitated by the SACP's Colonialism of a Special Type (CST) theory, which became official policy in 1962, although its main tenets had been constructed already in the 1940s. The CST thesis argued that South Africa 'combines the characteristics of both an imperialist state and a colony within a single, indivisible geographical, political and economic reality'. According to historian Colin Bundy's critique, it:

... purports to rest on class relations of capitalist exploitation [but] in fact it treats such relations as residual. That is to say, the conceptualization of class relations, which is present in the theory, is accorded little or no role in the analysis of relations of dominance and exploitation, which are, instead, conceived as occurring between 'racial', 'ethnic' and 'national' categories (1989).

At its centre was the conviction that 'no acute or antagonistic class divisions exist among Africans' – a view which, as some SACP leaders admitted, yielded a strategy whereby 'the class struggle subordinates itself to and is for some time obscured by the national question'.[60] That approach was inscribed in the 'two-stage theory' of revolution, which distinguished between a 'national-democratic' phase (theorized as a specifically South African variant of anti-colonial struggle) and a 'socialist' phase (in which class struggle would move centre-stage).[61] Acceptance of this approach was, however, never unanimous and was fiercely disputed in the 1980s,[62] when it fuelled occasionally violent conflict between so-called 'workerists' and 'populists'[63] – labels which, to an extent, disguised a broader conjunctural struggle in which the exiled ANC sought to assert its dominance over an increasingly vibrant and independent internal movement.

This denial of class differences among Africans (which, by the 1980s, had become empirically untenable) and the subordination of class struggle within the national liberation project today haunts the 'popular movement' – sometimes in curious and cynical ways. The segmented labour system mooted by the ANC government in 1996[64] offers an example. It fits into a discourse that prolongs the view of class struggle as a potentially disruptive dynamic in the broader liberation project. The overall *political* aim of such a system is to dislodge the organized working class from the broader popular movement and to corral it into a strictly economic unionism. Roughly sketched, this entails assigning to an allegedly privileged layer of the oppressed majority 'special interests', which are counterposed to those of other popular sectors and addressed through corporatist methods and structures (most patently a 'social accord' between labour, business and government). Whereas class differences were earlier denied, they now become explicitly acknowledged. The objective, though, remains the same: to domesticate or subdue class struggle by subordinating trade unions to the imperatives of the national liberation project (administered in foreshortened form by the ANC government). Strategic continuity is maintained.

The monolithic notion of 'the oppressed' and 'the community' drew some of its currency from the fact that until the 1970s class differentiation within African communities had been substantially inhibited by the apartheid system. As discussed earlier, the state reforms led to a profound process of class decompression, which accelerated markedly since the 1980s. Civic associations in particular were caught off-guard by this development which generated sometimes virulent tensions between different class layers in African townships. Often cited is the example of rent boycotts organized by civics which claimed to represent 'the community' in toto: while tenants in formal houses stopped paying rent, they often continued to collect rent money from sub-tenants living in the backyard shacks and garages. Thus, a protest to defend the interests of a presumed 'community' in some cases favoured its more privileged sections.[65] Other examples abound: of conflicts between hostel dwellers, shack dwellers and residents in formal housing, as well as between South African residents and immigrants from neighbouring countries.[66] It must be stressed that the existence of multiple interests and identities does not dissolve or atomize a community (as post-modernists would have it), but that those differences are mediated through complex dynamics which, too often, have been overlooked.

Unsurprisingly, the representativeness of popular organizations like civics has been called into question, prompting some commentators to dismiss them as 'unelected gangs that call themselves "the community"',[67] a stance closely related to the neo-conservative desire to rule community organizations out of the equation by dealing directly with residents as 'consumers' of services.

The blunting of difference had its roots not only in the unifying discourse of the resistance struggle but also in the reality of apartheid-engineered townships, where civics 'had to in practice embody the entirety of local civil life' (Simone, 1994:2). Still, civic leaders like Moses Mayekiso have admitted that the assumption of an undifferentiated community is spurious:

> Civics cannot claim to represent an entire community ... a process must be established so that other popular organizations can play a role alongside the civics.[68]

Such formulations, however, beg crucial questions. What structures qualify as 'other popular organizations'? Do civics remain 'first among equals' and, if so, on what basis do they stake that claim? If they do not represent the entire community, whom do they represent (a point further complicated by the arrival of democratically elected local government structures)? The conventional response has been to assign civics a bridge-building role whereby they 'try and reconcile conflicting interests around a particular issue'.[69] In this conception, civics mediate 'relations between a heterogeneous network of established groups within a community and larger structures of power and authority' (Simone, 1994:2). But this emphasis on formal civil society tends to obscure the informal, associational, almost subterranean networks that cohere many informal settlements and townships. These include sub- and illegal networks as well as highly informal (but well-observed) 'rules of conduct' that mediate between conflicting interests in a community – much of it invisible to the conventional gazes of development NGOs and state officials.[70]

The repressive weight and ideological principles of apartheid both enabled and made attractive responses that denied difference, emphasized unity, and enforced homogeneity. Some of the handicaps that now hobble popular organizations stemmed directly from that approach. Nowhere has the streamlining and regimenting effect of African nationalism been felt more acutely than among women, a matter that deserves more elaborate attention.

Gender and the democratic movement

The experience of organized women in the democratic movement has been an ambiguous and often unhappy one. Certainly, a long path was travelled between the affiliation of the Bantu Woman's League to the ANC in 1913 (denied voting rights, its main task was to organize catering and entertainment for ANC meetings), and the establishment of the ANC Women's League (ANCWL, 1943) and the Federation of South African Women (FSAW, 1954).

Formally, at least, women had won equal status in the ANC, while FSAW could declare boldly that 'freedom cannot be won for any one section or for the people as a whole as long as we women are in bondage'.[71] The anti-pass law protests mounted by women (and organized principally by FSAW) in the late 1950s rightfully earned a prime place in resistance lore.[72] But the 1958 decision to call off that campaign also revealed the contradictory dynamics between women's organizations and the male-controlled ANC leadership. Controversies persist to this day over where the blame for that decision should rest. Walker (1982) has pointed to the bashful manner in which ANC leaders reacted throughout to political protests organized by women. Budlender *et al.* (1992) and Fine (1990) have stressed that neither the ANCWL or FSAW were *feminist* organizations, and that their self-perceived role was to organize women 'in the liberation struggle of all the oppressed in South Africa, with the emphasis on class and colour oppression'.[73] The overall supremacy of the national liberation struggle – and the authority of its leadership – was not questioned, leading Fine to suggest that:

> [t]he Women's Federation withdrew from its mass civil disobedience campaign in 1958 for the same reasons that SACTU withdrew from its week-long stay-away that same year: because the united front strategy pursued by Congress was to restrain such forms of worker militancy and because leaders in the Federation just as in SACTU recognised the ultimate authority of Congress (1991:181).

In subsequent decades, women would regularly spearhead resistance activities – from the 1959 Cato Manor protests to the land and squatter struggles of the 1980s in the Western Cape. Thanks to the work of organizations like the Federation of Transvaal Women (FEDTRAW) and the United Women's Congress (UWCO), and woman leaders in the exiled ANC, a greater awareness of women's issues had taken root when the liberation organizations were unbanned in 1990. Semantically, this was evident in the ANC's professed commitment to build a 'democratic, non-racial and *non-sexist* South Africa'. Yet, the phrase also betrayed the ongoing subordinate and appendage-like status of women's issues within the national liberation project. The August 1990 relaunch of the ANCWL rekindled many feminists' worst fears, with one delegate reflecting that:

> [i]t was difficult to say what made it a women's rally. There were men speakers encouraging women, some men performers entertaining the crowd, lots of ANC fashion clothes, drum majorettes, and women doing their usual thing – cooking ...[74]

Women's organizations were collapsed into the ANCWL, whose immediate task was to recruit members into the ANC, after which women could be recruited into the League.[75] In feminist and union activist Pat Horn's view, the struggle against gender oppression still 'only feature[d] as an addendum or an afterthought in our liberation struggle, to the extent that it feature[d] at all' (1991:87). As in the 1950s, however, many women activists assisted in this subordination. At a 1991 women's conference in Durban, organizers were berated by women delegates for not having sought the prior approval of political organizations – a response that confirmed that 'the loyalties of activist feminists to our political organizations are still by and large much stronger than our commitment to unite with all women to challenge the patriarchal domination we all feel so keenly'.[76]

Not only was the organized unity of women still refracted through nationalist politics, but it was also fraught by class and racial divisions which had been blunted by the unifying imperative of the liberation struggle. The prospect of building a national women's movement seemed as remote as ever. Undeterred, women activists formed the Women's National Coalition (WNC) in 1992 to draw up a Women's Charter and ensure that women's rights would be entrenched in the new Constitution. The WNC drew in 79 women's organizations and 13 regional coalitions. There, too, the divisions manifested although they were somewhat tempered by the legalistic focus of the WNC and by the need to impact on a negotiations process that was careening along. In negotiations chambers women delegates occasionally defied their parties and fought against measures that compromised women's rights.[77] Several pieces of discriminatory legislation were altered or struck from the statute books, and agreement was won for setting up a Gender Commission as a statutory body. The new Constitution now guarantees women equality before the law and provides for affirmative action, while a 'right to life' clause was skilfully worded to enable the later passing of legislation legalizing abortion on demand.[78]

For the majority of women, though, the practical impact of those and similar gains will remain limited and largely dormant – unless accompanied by other, more dramatic changes. ANC politician Preggs Govender has argued that giving tangible effect to the often vague demands of women in a particular sector requires a much greater role for women in 'strategic and intellectual policymaking', as well as organizing women in new ways.[79] At root, this means that more women should occupy the middle and top echelons of state structures and popular organizations, and a women's movement needs to be built (the reinforcing dynamic between the twin tasks being patent).

On both fronts, there has been little cause for celebration. Thanks mainly to the ANC's decision to include a quota of women on its party lists, women fill 101 of the 400 seats in the National Assembly.[80] But only four of the 23 cabinet ministers are women, two of them assigned portfolios in line with standard gender stereotypes (health and welfare). Women are markedly under-represented on all but four of the 25 select parliamentary committees. In 1990, less than 20 per cent of the 17 300 people active in legal occupations were women, while women held less than 15 per cent of the 5 600 senior ranking posts in the police force.[81] Generally, according to the drafters of the *Beijing Conference Report*, women 'remain invisible at most levels in public structures' (1995:52). In the popular sector, the situation is more distressing: about 8 per cent of national and regional officials in COSATU affiliates are women, while the figure for SANCO is believed to be even lower (ILO, 1996:153). The skewed representation is registered, for example, in the abject failure of the RDP, economic policies and national budgets to gauge the specific impact of measures on women. Gender earns only a rhetorical presence – thus 'job creation' plans are devised on the assumption that women and men would benefit equally.[82]

The view taken by activists like Govender has been that women 'have to take a deep breath, go into the existing power structure and transform it'.[83] Implicit is the belief that the historical subsumption of women's struggles under the national liberation project paradoxically offered women easier access to circuits of state power during the transition.[84] Similar arguments have peppered the histories of many other women's movements in the Third World. Unfortunately, as Hassim has reminded, they evaporate in the light of experience:

> As structures are established and process becomes increasingly rigidified, these spaces disappear and the marginalisation of women again becomes entrenched (1991:67).

While women in positions of power might lever new opportunities, their potential remains arrested without popular organizing. Yet, there is no agreement on what form this should take. Should energies go towards building a *national* movement, rather than consolidating existing strengths at regional or sectoral levels? Should women be organized in overtly political organizations, rather than by 'trying to incorporate those zones (like churches and *stokvels*) where they are already organized but politically passive'?[85] No less important are the types of issues such a movement takes up. Arguably, the very category 'women's issues' risks perpetuating women's marginal status by feeding the notion that women's needs can be distilled from the various spheres of society and addressed independently, while leaving intact the structural underpinnings of oppression.

Complicating matters further have been the sobering lessons drawn from the WNC experience. The insulating effect of bureaucratizing such an endeavour became apparent. Even ANC activists disagreed whether a movement should be built from the grassroots level or from the centre (by kickstarting it with high-profile events and campaigns). And the assumption of cohesion among progressive women proved wrong; racial, ethnic, class, cultural, geographic and religious tensions fissured the assumed unity and common-mindedness.[86] Imbedded in the latter realization is the question of where the axis of a movement should be located – and, indeed, of what a women's movement is. Govender has argued that it should emerge from local campaigns and activities with black working class women at their core: 'At its inception it cannot be something for all women, although ultimately that is what you aim to achieve'.[87] Supporters of this view take heart from the localized activities of groups like the Rural Women's Movement and Natal Organization of Women. But, as Hassim's research into the Inkatha Women's Brigade has cautioned,

> ... a women's movement per se does not guarantee that women's position in society is being fundamentally challenged or indeed that there will be any impact on existing political organisations or parties, trade unions or policy makers (1991:73).

Women's organizations, even when aggregated into a movement, can engage in activities that do not question power relations in wider society or their social base. The assumption of progressiveness (because they centre on a particularly disadvantaged sector of women) seems misplaced. Some activists believe the rudiments of a movement already exist. Lacking are the ideological and political visions that can cohere them into a movement, visions a minority of activists argue should rest on the shared and overtly feminist understanding that all political issues have a gender dimension.[88] A *feminist* movement that shifts the emphasis from women to gender would, it is argued, avoid the pitfalls of obfuscating difference and, instead, oblige 'women to confront contradictions in their own self-definition'.[89] Thus, unity around the right to abortion could be achieved precisely by acknowledging that 'access to health care and child care is more limited for working class and black women'.[90]

To some extent, the truism that women have endured the 'triple oppression' of apartheid, capitalism and patriarchy has not aided the emergence of organized feminist politics in South Africa. The metaphor of layered, cumulative oppression obscured the problematic ways in which race, class and gender intertwine in women's lives. It also validated the practice whereby:

> ... even in those moments in which women confronted the male domain directly, they did not articulate their campaigns either in terms of a struggle between men and women, or an exclusively female struggle against an oppressive system (Hassim, 1991:69).

As a result, the history of black South African women has, perforce, been engulfed in the history of the national liberation struggle. Blaming the confining effect of the national liberation project for the dilemmas that bedevil the emergence of a cohesive and strategically focused women's movement

might seem unfair. But its suffocating effect on the honest expression of difference – and the autonomous pursuit of overlapping agendas – meant that
the conundrums that confound such a movement were shielded from
earnest attention and remedy. They were allowed to incubate for decades,
only to emerge in impetuous forms during a phase of historic opportunity.
The repression of the apartheid era discouraged many women from organizing politically. But it was also popular organizations' long-standing dele-
gitimizing of women's concerns as 'soft political concerns' that fuelled political alienation and forced hundreds of thousands of women to withdraw
into secluded zones of organized activity (Hassim, 1991:70-71). As a result,
the social landscape is replete with apolitical women's structures like church
cooperatives and self-help groups which are 'detached from feminist visions
which could make connections between such groups and wider politics'.[91]

The ghosts of the past haunt efforts to develop a women's movement
built around a feminist politics. Steered into the slipstream of nationalism,
and waged in profoundly different political and material conditions, South
African women's struggles were fought in isolation from the upsurge of
feminism in the industrialized world. Whether bearing the label or not,
feminism was scoffed as an irritant in the lubricated workings of the
national liberation struggle. So much so that in the 1990s, in perhaps its
most opportune time in the country, it is peppered with the calumny of
being élitist, anti-African and purely 'intellectual'.

Trade unions – *the* movement?

The considerable faith vested in the ability of the trade union movement
(specifically COSATU) to lead a popular transformation project and its
organized strength and strategic importance demand that it be scrutinized
more closely.

How many times has the liberation movement worked together with the
workers, and at the moment of victory betrayed the workers? There are
many examples of that in the world. It is only if the workers strengthen their
organisation before and after liberation [applause] ... if you relax your vigi-
lance, you will find that your sacrifices have been in vain. You must support
the African National Congress only so far as it delivers the goods, if the ANC
does not deliver the goods, you must do to it what you have done to the
apartheid regime [prolonged applause, shouts of 'Buwa! Buwa!']. – Nelson
Mandela speaking off-the-cuff at the September 1993 COSATU Special
Congress.[92]

The legalization of black trade unions and the large shift of unskilled
African labour to skilled and semi-skilled labour led to the emergence of the
largest labour movement in Africa. Between 1985 and 1993 union membership more than doubled and by 1995 between 2,6 million and 3,1 million

workers belonged to unions.[93] Almost 40 per cent of the total workforce is unionized, one of the highest rates in the South.

These unions vary in degrees of militancy, strategic prowess, organizational character, democratic depth and political bent. But those joined in the two main federations (COSATU and NACTU) constitute the most formidable organized popular force in South Africa. The largest, COSATU (with 1,4 million members), has retained the achievement of socialism as its long-term goal and adopted a broad social and political role.

The modern labour movement arose during periods of intense repression, which later combined with attempts by the state and capital to subject black labour to a more sophisticated containment and adjustment programme. As unionist Bobby Marie has recalled, unions' main objectives were 'to recruit membership, establish basic trade union rights and improve wages and working conditions at plant or factory level' (1992:21). They did this in assiduous and militant fashion – vigorously recruiting and organizing members, and launching successive strike waves. By the mid-1990s, many of the basic rights sought had been won at the factory level.

The coming of age of the modern black trade union movement can be divided into three phases (Barrett, 1993). After the 1973 strikes, organizing was concentrated in the manufacturing sector and 'unions eschewed mass mobilization and high profile campaigns in order to build a disciplined power base' (Friedman, 1987:33). Following the Wiehahn reforms massive unions like NUM were formed, militant actions grew, especially on the mines, the giant federation COSATU was established, and controversies raged over the role of the labour movement in broader political and social struggles. From the late 1980s onwards, a new regime of labour relations was instituted, and public sector organizing commenced and boomed.

COSATU is by far the strongest federation. Almost half of all union members belong to its affiliates and their power is rivalled only in the public service, printing, construction and chemical sectors.[94] COSATU's greatest feats have been of two types: its role in the struggles which helped stalemate the apartheid state and its affiliates' successes which, since the mid-1980s, led to sharp rises in workers' wages, improved conditions of employment and the introduction of the 'rule of law' into the workplace (Baskin, 1991). One can add an array of other achievements: COSATU's birth and consolidation under emergency rule, its defence within the popular movement of the need for critical debate, freedom of expression and democratic organization, its attempts to nurture a tradition of participatory democracy, blocking the repressive 1988 amendments to the Labour Relations Act, initiating and developing the RDP, and more. More recently, it campaigned successfully for the establishment of the tripartite National Economic Development and Labour Council (NEDLAC) which promised to extend the movement's influence to fiscal, industrial and development policy. It fought for, and won, a progressive new Labour Relations Act, and participated in dozen of negotiating forums (ranging from drought relief to electricity policy and industrial restructuring).

On the debit side, though, some telling failures also occurred. Leaving aside tactical errors (such as the abortive July 1986 stay-away and the muddled attempts to mobilize against privatization a decade later), two major failures stand out. Efforts to organize farmworkers via the Farm and Allied Workers' Union (FAWU) have proved largely unsuccessful and its bid to organize the unemployed has been ineffective.

The ground shifts

Unions were not only agents but also subjects of change. Along with their victories arose several weaknesses and destabilizing factors which have frustrated the movement in the 1990s. Some were related to structural changes in the economy, others specifically to the transition.

The first variety included declining membership in the manufacturing sector (which was hit hard by the recession of the early 1990s), although in the declining mining industry unionization levels rose during the same period and reached 65 per cent in 1995. More positive has been the soaring membership in the public sector following the recognition of public service unions. By 1995, there were 18 unions active in this sector, which is beset by job insecurity, poor pay and high income differentials. The 1995 nurses' strike confirmed the impetuosity of this sector, although the government's regime of fiscal stringency will lead to downsizing and out-sourcing, and likely roll back those gains.

Also taking hold are multiple changes in production systems, as the manufacturing sector tries to gain new footholds in international markets on the basis of enhanced competitiveness and productivity. Accompanied by the standard demand for wage restraint, these include switching production towards smaller volumes of skilled labour inputs, greater reliance on casual labour and flexible specialization, and experimentation with 'participatory' modes of work organization like quality circles. Despite the progressive regulatory system envisaged in the new Labour Relations Act, the labour system has become more pliant, due to the shift towards more flexible forms of employment like sub-contracting, out-sourcing and casual labour. These trends pose major challenges. As the ILO has noted, 'workers in those statuses are rarely easily drawn to enter or remain a body of collective action, especially if that appears to represent the interest of "insiders", those in regular wage or salaried employment' (1996:155). By 1996, COSATU had not decided whether to take on the arduous task of organizing these workers.

Ironically, other weaknesses stem from the movement's successes. Ballooning memberships in the 1980s, the winning of many basic rights at the factory level and participation in negotiating forums increased the responsibilities of national offices. In most cases, they have coped with great difficulty. Many have been leery of introducing efficient organizational and staff management systems, leading to poor co-ordination, communication and discipline.[95]

Another casualty has been the vaunted principle of 'worker control',[96] which demands regular consultation, report-backs and mandated leadership. Many of these practices were trampled underfoot in the scramble to participate in negotiating structures. In one case, an agreement by union negotiators to radical tariff cuts in the auto industry early in 1994 somehow escaped the usual report-back and communication procedures – catching even union leaders by surprise. Considerable resources and time are devoted to policy – and decision-making at the national and industry levels. Increased bureaucratization, the highly technical nature of those engagements, along with poor information flow and communication, have generated alienation and distrust at the rank-and-file level. Shop stewards have complained that they are 'tired of feeling like transmission belts for decisions taken elsewhere'.[97] Arguably, 'worker control' was better suited to an era of small unions battling around tangible and relatively elemental plant-level issues. At least one unionist has publicly declared the tradition 'cumbersome if not impractical'.[98] Others have argued that its ailing status is not terminal and has been caused by the violation of mandates, infrequent and inadequate efforts to inform workers and canvass opinions on key matters. New, professional and effective management and communication systems are needed if worker control is to be revived (Marie, 1996; Godongwana, 1994a and 1994b).

By their own admission, COSATU unions are also not providing members with adequate service and support. Part of the problem lies with poorly trained shop stewards whose plight is worsened by their weak links with union offices. Once elected, most embark on their work having received (at best) one, rudimentary training course, leaving them feeling 'still blank as shop stewards'.[99] A 1995 ILO survey in the Gauteng industrial heartland discovered that 29 per cent of shop stewards had not met a union official in the previous year, 28 per cent had received no training from their unions, while the bulk of those who had went on one- or two-day courses.[100]

All unions have suffered high rates of staff turnover. Experienced shop stewards in particular are being drawn into supervisory and even managerial positions as part of companies' affirmative action programmes.[101] Unions cannot compete with the lucrative salary packages on offer. Other officials and leaders have taken up posts in government and state structures, a move initially endorsed by COSATU who released 23 top unionists to contest the 1994 elections on an ANC ticket. The latter decision (essentially a consummation of the alliance) seemed patently ill-considered and betrayed a 'bankruptcy of strategic planning', according to former NUMSA general secretary Enoch Godongwana.[102] In 1994 alone, some eighty senior officials left COSATU and its affiliates. NUMSA, once regarded as well-organized, was left with a head office, in the words of one observer, 'denuded of leadership'.[103] After the October 1995 local government elections, NUM alone lost 101 members and officials to the new councils.

Finally, there is the ubiquitous reliance on expert advisors as unions sought to participate in 'every negotiating forum under the sun' (Collins: 1994) – ranging from drought relief to electricity policies and economic restructuring. This has stretched resources, removed key union leaders from their organizations and led to sometimes unmandated agreements. This dependency has increased as some unions entered into corporate ventures aimed at building 'black economic empowerment'.

Most of these trends are recognized by COSATU which, in 1996, set up a Commission on the Future of the Unions to investigate the practical and strategic challenges confronting them.[104] Many are shared by other popular organizations. The overall effect is to temper the often lofty expectations these organizations are saddled with. Yet, despite the doomsaying of many analysts, COSATU remains the most powerful, organized social force in the country.

The politics of unionism

The labour movement's situation, however, is further complicated and compromised by a battery of strategic and contextual factors particular to it. Several political traditions cohabit in the movement, most importantly within COSATU itself. Three historical traditions have been detected. In the first, the devoted alliance between SACTU and the ANC during the 1950s led to the crushing of SACTU by the apartheid regime and its retreat into exile by 1964. In the 1970s, the view that 'workers' struggle in the factories and townships was indivisible' resurfaced strongly in general workers' unions (Fine & Webster, 1989:256). This 'national democratic' or 'populist' tradition was grounded in the SACP's CST which privileged a multi-class national liberation struggle over class struggle. By the mid-1980s several 'populist' unions were engaging the state in concert with the UDF. But another tradition had also gathered strength in the 1970s – that of 'shopfloor' unions which were leery of direct involvement in broader political issues and concentrated on building democratic shopfloor structures, accountability and worker control. Some went as far as proposing a mass-based workers' party as an alternative to the SACP. A third current pursued the BC tradition, at first de-emphasizing class but later redefining it in racial terms. Supporters sought to combat the white intellectual leadership of the labour movement and nurture black (understood to include Africans, coloureds and Indians) self-esteem, independence and capacity. The tradition settled loosely within NACTU.

The sectarianism that marked COSATU's creation stemmed from the fact that it encompassed the first two traditions. At the level of debate, the tensions were never resolved. Instead the impossibility of separating the workplace from the upheaval in the townships saw workers embark on joint actions with community organizations. The resultant compromise (that COSATU would participate in the political struggle 'on terms favourable to the working class') postponed but did not settle the debate. At the height of the uprisings, COSATU shifted deeper into 'populist' mode when it pledged to fight the national democratic revolution under the leadership of the ANC. The move revived fierce debates around questions of union independence from political organizations, the defence of working class politics, ensuring accountability of unions and their leaders to members and more – questions that would beset the federation a decade later. Between 1987 and 1989, internal political unity was shored up through a more strategic compromise that linked the priority of ending apartheid to the need to struggle for socio-economic justice after liberation. When the state banned the main popular organizations in 1988, COSATU stepped into the breech and assumed an even more direct political role, which later became institutionalized in the tripartite alliance between itself, the ANC and SACP.

Those two traditions, however, still swirl through COSATU in irresolute fashion. At its 1993 congress, NUMSA stunned its allies when it passed a resolution demanding that the alliance should end 'in its current form' once the ANC ascended to government.[105] Von Holdt has predicted that, if push came to shove, some of COSATU's strongest affiliates would support the dissolution of the alliance.[106]

An accompanying feature has been the emergence of sharpened differentiation within the working class since the 1970s. Historically divided along racial lines, the South African working class has long been a conceptual postulate, never a coherent social force. Increased stratification since the 1970s means that the black (and particularly African) working class can no longer be neatly bracketed as a single category. Potential and existing stress lines run between the employed and unemployed; rural and urban-based industrial workers; organized and unorganized workers; full-time and part-time or contract workers; semi- and fully-skilled workers and unskilled counterparts. Most obviously, organized workers in the formal sector comprise a small portion of the total labour force. Yet, a large share of those with jobs are unorganized in low-productivity, low-paying, highly insecure service employment – like domestic workers, farmworkers, cleaning and security workers, and small retail outlet workers. The implications of these phenomena tend to be over-dramatized in pronouncements that overlook the many common problems that still affect workers. But they do caution against assuming the existence of neatly congruent interests.

Stratification has also increased within industries. Research in the metal industry has suggested that the African workforce in particular 'is becoming more differentiated with respect to occupation and income', a trend which, the author, Warren Crankshaw, claimed, 'has implications for the solidarity of the African working class movement'.[107] One consequence detected by Crankshaw was a rising awareness of specific and differentiated interests. Thus 94 per cent of African workers and staff supported the right to strike; but, unlike their blue collar colleagues (who favoured 'mass-based and militant unionism' to defend collective interests), staff members' main concerns were individual promotion and advancement. This points not to a wholesale dissolution of African worker solidarity, but to the increasingly specific identification of interests.

These apparent trends have prompted controversial but challenging prognoses. Former NUMSA organizer Geoff Schreiner has dismissed as 'unrealistic' the view that COSATU should lead the societal transformation process. As reasons, he cited the federations' 'questionable' capacity to perform such a role and its unavoidable entry into a compromising social contract (1994:43-4). Instead, it will have to 'prioritise and champion the cause of the most privileged sections of the working class – those who have stable, formal sector employment, relatively high wages and those who dominate the leader echelons of the movement'.[108] The causes, according to Schreiner, lay in affiliate unions' diminished organizational capacities, dwindling personnel resources, the rise of flexible specialization in production, and the likelihood that if members' needs are not serviced other unions 'will fill the gap. Unions, wrote Schreiner, would have 'to prioritise the realisation of shop floor bread-and-butter demands'.[109] The alleged thrust is towards 'enclave unionism', where unions' roles become confined to the defence of increasingly parochial interests.

Such analyses have been made to harmonize sweetly with the war cries of business and some ANC leaders,[110] who seek to hive off organized workers as a 'labour aristocracy' whose gains allegedly come at the expense of the unemployed. As Fine and Webster (1989) noted, 'attempts to limit the role of trade unions in post-colonial Africa have often been justified on the grounds that trade unions represent only a tiny fraction of the labour force'. Nevertheless, the fact that a trend is put to cynical use does not erase the trend itself, which has two possible implications. The first concerns the subjective disposition of workers and their willingness to support the demands of colleagues in other wage and skills categories. Labour researcher Dot Keet believes that stratification has not induced parochialism and docility; instead it 'is amongst skilled and better educated workers that many of the most effective – and militant – worker leaders are to be found' (1992:30). The second involves unions' responses to the trend. Do they choose to deploy their strained resources primarily in defence of organized workers, and retreat from acting as the champion of all workers, with and without jobs? Do they confound the hopes of business, and make more vigorous efforts to organize the growing numbers of casual, part-time, contract and marginalized workers? Do they still try to revive practical alliances with other popular organizations around specific issues, of the sorts that emerged during the 1980s? These questions have congealed into COSATU's paramount political challenge – bluntly, to develop 'a new vision of who we are and what we are fighting for' (Von Holdt, 1996:38). The answer is of immeasurable importance to the fate of the popular movement and its visions of transformation.

The catch phrase 'strategic unionism' emerged in the early 1990s to describe COSATU's bid to adapt to the new era, and offered a provisional response to those questions. As defined by Von Holdt, this involved a programme of radical reform:

> ... of the state, of the workplace, of economic decision-making and of civil society ... driven by a broad-based coalition of interest groups, at the centre of which is the labour movement (1992:33).

Three basic prerequisites were posed for this labour-driven process of social change. Broader unity was needed in the labour movement itself (between different federations and categories of workers, and across racial lines). Popular organizations had to be united around a common programme of reforms (the RDP Base Document would emerge as a benchmark for those reforms). And a 'durable alliance' was needed with the ANC.[111] In themselves, though, these elements imposed major challenges. The labour movement remained riven by inherited divisions, popular organizations had become weakened and lacked a coherent vision or role, and a committed alliance with the ANC begged crucial, unresolved questions. In addition, the fact that 'even highly sophisticated national trade union centres have been forced into largely reactive and responsive roles' led observers like Schreiner to counsel against union attempts to lead the process of industrial restructuring, let alone transformation (1994:44). Instead, their sights should be set lower – at securing 'an important range concessions for its members'.

Those factors, along with the disorienting impact of the transition, have cast doubt on the prospects of such a venture – nevertheless, COSATU believed that it should be undertaken. The federation's role in NEDLAC and a host of other fora stemmed directly from that strategic choice. The engagements were motivated by lofty goals which, in hindsight, were tinged with naïvety. For instance,

> ... the flow of investment will be influenced through industry-wide restructuring policies, negotiated with trade unions. New technology and work organisation would be matters of compulsory negotiation at factory level.[112]

Still, the overall shift was profound, and conformed to the paradigms of the political transition. Economic and developmental changes were to be devised and introduced not through conflict and exclusion, but negotiation and inclusion that yielded mutual benefits. The view drew favour among government, business and labour (typically the pillars of a social contract), who recognized that a reconstruction process would founder unless it was politically feasible. Both NEDLAC and the new Labour Relations Act (LRA) were designed to institutionalize this shift from adversarial to more co-operative relations between labour, business and government.[113] Basically, the social contract would function as the economic correlate of the negotiated political settlement. While NEDLAC 'institutionalizes tripartism', the new LRA encourages centralized bargaining at industry level, the setting up of workplace forums and, ostensibly, seems aimed at shoring up union strength – a prerequisite for a codeterminist arrangement (Baskin, 1996b). At the same time, it promotes 'regulated flexibility' in the labour market, albeit along 'union-friendly' lines. The fate of such endeavours is unclear, however, because they presume internal organizational strengths unions lack and because GEAR and the 1996 Labour Market Commission report clearly tilt towards harsher deregulation.

Inside or outside?

The move towards codetermination unleashed a torrent of polemics, as activists explored the political-strategic implications of the envisaged social contract.[114] While Trotskyist groups rejected it out of hand, alliance activists' concerns centred on the divergent expectations of the main players. As the SACP's Langa Zita reminded, capital saw it mainly as a vehicle for steady economic growth and international competitiveness.[115] A modicum of social development would be tagged on as an inevitable 'cost' for enlisting labour's support for the economic adjustments it deemed necessary. The key trade-off would involve business agreeing to some industrial restructuring, government improving the 'social wage', while labour would reciprocate by ensuring industrial peace and exercising wage restraint. A social contract, in Godongwana's view, was 'not intended to make any fundamental transformation of society but to reform capitalism' (1992:23). Yet, the engagement could not be shirked:

> What do we tell the 9000 workers in the tyre manufacturing industry when tariffs are removed and their jobs are at stake? Do we tell them to wait for a socialist revolution?[116]

Even in COSATU unanimity is absent. While SACTWU officially favours codetermination as a means of preventing government and business from acting unilaterally, unions like SAMWU reject it. Glaring ironies are at work, as Baskin noted:

With NEDLAC and the workplace forums envisaged by the new LRA, South Africa has one of the most institutionalized forms of concertation in the world. Ironically, this has emerged without explicit union commitment to codetermination, incomes accords and the social-democratic politics which normally accompany such developments (1996b:14).

Neither is there unanimous support among business and mainstream economists, some of whom argue that negotiated economic policies would prevent the 'strong medicine' of adjustments from being administered.[117]

The biggest peril is that a tripartite social contract could degenerate into a corporatist mode, whereby 'the strongest voices divide the spoils, while the most marginalized and hence the most needy sectors are excluded'.[118] Such a form of élite-pacting would revise and entrench the insider/outsider divide (Bird & Schreiner, 1992) and would, eventually, have to be shored up through authoritarian means. That danger looms large. Tripartite social contracts have tended to work only in industrialized countries with high employment, where organizations of both capital and labour are cohesive, highly representative and organizationally efficient. South Africa hardly fits that bill. In addition, the increasing vertical tensions within COSATU and its affiliates have made it more difficult to ensure that agreements struck in structures like NEDLAC are accepted by negotiators' constituencies. Capital, too, is deeply divided by a 'divergence of interests and views' that 'has been almost comparable to that between black and white workers' (ILO, 1996:159). Business South Africa (BSA) was formed precisely to bridge these divides and brought together 18 major capitalist organizations. However, the National African Federated Chambers of Commerce (NAFCOC) soon withdrew, leaving BSA at risk of been seen as a 'white and big business organisation only'.[119] According to the ILO, 'there are serious questions about BSA's representativeness, and there is doubt about its capacity to support all sectors equally, and about the losing sectors breaking ranks with others' (1996:167).

The future of tripartite social contracts and, more broadly, strategic unionism, hangs in the balance. The situation is aggravated by a third, conjunctural feature that shadows the labour movement's efforts to shape the direction of South Africa's transformation. This relates mainly to the government's conservative economic strategy which has generated contradictory demands on labour – greater stability, productivity and flexibility. Greater productivity and competitiveness, for instance, is made to pivot on organized workers' support for training schemes, changes in production and shift systems and pay deals linked to work performance, as well as greater flexibility in the labour market at large. On the other hand, workers' demands for better wages and working conditions are deemed to undermine investor confidence. Moreover, the forum tasked with securing a resolution, NEDLAC, has seen its authority undermined by all three players – not the least the labour department whose director general, Sipho Pitanya, in

August 1997 launched a sustained attack against the institution. Key to a tripartite framework is the ability of union leadership to win members over (and hold them) to sometimes controversial compromises. COSATU affiliates' poor organizational and communication systems, their neglect of many locals and the growing distance between them and national offices casts serious doubt on the federation's ability to hold up its end of a tripartite schema. Not surprisingly, unions have grown more reticent towards tripartism. NUMSA has argued that its initial misgivings have been validated by the deflection of pivotal decision-making away from NEDLAC, leaving it to deliberate 'detail without discussing the broader picture within which we should locate that detail'.[120]

The restriction of NEDLAC's role harks back to the purely advisory status originally conceived for one of its forerunners, the National Economic Forum. This regressive shift is linked to a broader attempt to steer tripartite structures away from formative policy-making and towards facilitating the implementation of policies decided elsewhere in the system. GEAR's proposed social accord exemplifies this approach. From organized business' point of view, there is little reason why it should subject its fundamental prerogatives to laborious negotiations at NEDLAC if direct engagements with government (followed or preceded by largely theatrical tripartite confabs like 'job summits') seem a surer route to gratification. Likewise, the backroom confabs with COSATU around GEAR and the privatization programme suggest that government, too, prefers the bilateral route.[121] And COSATU itself has occasionally chosen direct engagements with government rather than submitting key concerns to the NEDLAC process.

Debating social contracts in terms of their 'reformist' or 'revolutionary' potential becomes academic in such a context. The central dilemma is much more crass: is the labour movement willing to become an active party to a neo-liberal economic strategy in exchange for concessions that effectively corral it into defending the interests of a section of the working class? The choice made will help determine whether the movement abdicates or salvages its professed role as the linchpin of the struggle to break the insider/outsider mould of society. The quandary, in fact, links to the historical discourse between the labour movement and liberation organizations. In the past labour (and class) struggles were regarded as instruments in the national liberation project. In the post-apartheid era, this has been translated into an analogous domesticating exercise geared at serving a postulated common endeavour of economic growth and social reconstruction. But this time around subservience implies support for a project that is demonstrably structured in favour of the capitalist class.

Troubling as the dilemma is, it should not compel a rejection of tripartite institutions which, after all, never were instruments insulated from class struggle. Their terms can be challenged and broadened to subject policy-making to popular contestation, the forms of which would extend widely (lobbying, worker action, street protests, media campaigns, etc.). Two ingredients are essential. The labour movement must develop the capacity to participate effectively in fora like NEDLAC and, for business, ongoing participation in them should be made the only viable way forward. The burden therefore rests equally on government to forego discreet bilateral deals, abandon its cowed stance towards business and restore tripartite processes at the centre of macro policy-making. However, as Nzimande and Cronin pointed out, by 1997 the ANC government was retreating from even the pretence of being a 'neutral' adjudicator of conflicts between business and labour:

> The so-called golden triangle turns out to be worse than an illusion about class neutrality. No expectations, no pressures are placed on 'capital'.[122]

Given such developments, the hopes (harboured by the SACP and some COSATU figures) of reviving the ANC's purported working class bias seem highly fanciful. Not only has the ANC's class bias always been equivocal but the post-1994 predominance of aspirant *bourgeois* and entrenched *petit-bourgeois* layers in the organization's ranks has become palpably expressed in policies, conduct and rhetoric. In that context it seems daunting enough to force the ANC government to regulate 'even-handedly' the relationship between labour and business.

The failure to invigorate authoritative tripartite processes could spur the labour movement down two routes. It could take up the cudgel for a mix of workers' and broader, popular demands by leading protest campaigns against specific policies. Its already diminished resources will render such engagements sporadic and fitful, and make it difficult to sustain campaigns towards happy conclusions. Almost certainly, such a course will be met by repression. Given unions' poor record in the 1990s of building broad ideological support for strikes, these crackdowns might even be encouraged by much of the public, including the new economic élites:

> It is time to make a choice: have an airy-fairy liberal democracy with a fairly mediocre growth rate or lay it out on the unions at the risk of being labelled a 'union basher', and become another growth-led Taiwan ... my friendly advice to the government is: do the right thing ... and only have sentimental rather than economic regrets.[123]

Moreover, it will further strain the movement's ability to serve its immediate constituency of organized workers, leading to depleted memberships and contributing to a long-term decline.

Alternatively, the movement can reconcile itself to a compromised role in an essentially corporatist framework and concentrate on advancing the interests of its members. This will fulfil a key objective of the ruling class and elements in the ANC: confining the movement to 'economistic unionism' centred on narrow, parochial interests. A type of corporatist chauvinism is consolidated and the labour movement becomes detached from broader popular struggles. Powerful forces are jostling it in that direction. In confronting this dilemma, COSATU in particular finds itself once again having to reconcile the different political traditions that fissured it in the mid-1980s. As Fine and Webster warned in 1989, those differences were never resolved. Rather they were 'buried in the face of the state onslaught of 1987 and 1988' (1989:272). COSATU's prominent location in broad popular movement is by no means guaranteed.

Success at broadening the scope of structures like NEDLAC will not, however, guarantee unions a definitive role in macro-level decision-making. As the ILO has observed, their participation in tripartite forums has been marked by sometimes feeble contributions to public policy discussions, and marred by:

> ... the lack of resources to make meaningful contributions, absenteeism from key meetings, and the resultant tendency for unions to become reactive to initiatives taken by employers or government, rather than policy formulators (1996:157).

Hanging in the balance, then, are not only the strategic routes COSATU chooses in pursuit of radical reforms, but their sweep and content. In the early 1990s, former COSATU general secretary Jay Naidoo declared adamantly that:

> [w]e need to block government policies that are going to entrench things and make it impossible for a democratic government to meet the needs of the people and address the inequalities of apartheid.[124]

Adjusted to post-1994 South Africa, that entreaty seems apposite still, as many factory-level unionists will confirm. Making good on such words, though, requires grappling also with two highly combustible political questions. Should COSATU remain in the tripartite alliance – and if so, on what conditions? Sentiment and tradition serve as inadequate guides on such weighty matters. Ultimately, the answers must rest on COSATU's organizational capacities and (potential) allies in the popular sector, on an interrogation of class dynamics in the alliance and on a clearer analysis of the state and civil society in the transition. The Commission on the Future of the Unions (set up by COSATU in 1996) might help devise an exit from the impasse.[125] The dilemmas, however, extend throughout the popular movement, and, pivotally, affect also the ANC as a party and the SACP – matters we now turn to.

Notes

1   This term is used here largely for convenience and certainly with reservations, since it implies activated organizational linkages, certain levels of political and ideological common-mindedness, and broad strategic confluence. Whether these factors exist is a moot point explored in the next two chapters.

2   NGO worker Zane Dangor, quoted in *The Star*, 22 October 1996.

3   Poulantzas (1978:254); see also Fine (1992) and Mercer (1980).

4   The Freedom Charter's demand that the wealth 'be transferred to the ownership of the people', for example, became interpreted as a commitment to nationalization – a leap that was 'only possible if "the people" are synonymous with the state', as Mark Swilling observed (1991:20).

5   Friedman has argued that 'exclusion from the franchise and the banning of national movements forced [them] to seek a power base in civil society' (1991:8).

6   Fine (1992:75).

7   Poulantzas (1978:258), who argued that Gramsci intended the term 'war of position' in precisely this manner.

8   A variation on the 'encirclement' approach. See also Cronin (1992).

9   Astonishingly, the best-known critique to emerge from the exiled left still contained no reference to the ferment of Western Marxist debates around the state and civil society; see Slovo (1990).

10 Notably John Keane's *Democracy and Civil Society* and *Civil Society and the State*, both 1988, Verso, London.

11 A view which found persuasive support in Ellen Meiksins Wood's 1990 essay 'The Used and Abuses of Civil Society'.

12 On these scores, Gramsci's departure from Marx was dramatic; see Pellicani (1981:33–4).

13 Friedman (1991:8). The allegation stems from a plausible reading of Gramsci, shared among others by Poulantzas (1978) and Keane (1988a and 1988b). Whatever the academic vote, it overlooks the continuing need, *after* the achievement of state power, to reproduce domination through hegemonic struggle.

14 Who, in Keane's view, argue for 'restricting the scope of the state and increasing its power'; cited in Friedman (1991:7). The emphasis, in fact, is not on 'rolling back the state', but on redeploying its resources in favour of capital; see Chapter 5 of this volume.

15 Laclau (1990:163).

16 Swilling (1991:22). This approach is especially prevalent in SANCO; see, for instance, Commission on Development Finance, 1994, *Making People-driven Development Work*, SANCO, Johannesburg.

17 *Ibid.*

18 Broadly indicative is, for example, Albie Sachs' contention that 'the organs of civil society are the principal guarantors that good government will exist', cited in Fine (1992:72).

19 Interview with author, October 1994, Johannesburg.

20 Poulantzas (1978:259).

21 Narsoo (1991:26). See also Kagarlitsky's warning that 'such new ideas are only the mirror image of old illusions' because '[a]uthoritarian structures often grow out of mass spontaneous movements' (1995:242).

22 See Amin (1997:10–12).

23 Mooers, C. and Sears, A., 'The 'New Social Movements' and the Withering Away of State Theory' in Carroll (1992:63).

24 *Ibid.*

25   See *Development Update*, No. 1 (July 1997), NGO Coalition, Johannesburg for an attempt to engage with some of those factors.

26   Most obviously those organizations that sought alliances with political bodies working within the tricameral parliamentary system and homeland structures. By resisting incorporation into a broad resistance front, the Inkatha movement became the salient target of this demonization process.

27   Up from about 23 in 1977 to 228 in 1986, according to political analyst Tom Lodge's count (in Lodge & Nasson, 1991:178). See also Lodge's 'The African National Congress after the Kabwe Conference' in Moss & Obery (1987)

28   Yet, the ANC's visions of post-apartheid society were marked by decidedly non-hegemonic approaches that centred on notions of victory, power, subjugation and isolation (Morris, 1991:46).

29   ILO (1996:149–50). NACTU accounts for 11 per cent of unionized workers, while the third largest federation, the Federation of South African Labour (FEDSAL) claims 8 per cent.

30   Sadly, to limited effect. It is estimated, for example, that only 8 per cent of national and regional officials in COSATU-affiliated trade unions are women (ILO, 1996:153).

31   Signalling a revival have been some church leaders' public calls in 1997 for a repudiation of the apartheid debt and their support for a national campaign against poverty and inequality.

32   *Ad hoc* alliances of organizations won the inclusion of an enhanced set of social and economic rights in the final constitution, as well as clauses protecting women's reproductive rights and citizens' rights to choose their sexual orientation.

33   The Dobsonville branch in Soweto, for example, saw its membership drop from 4 500 in 1993 to 27 in mid-1997! Parallel to this has been the emergence of vibrant ANC (and SACP) branches in some rural areas.

34   'Deep divisions in directionless Free State ANC branches', *The Star*, 17 February 1997.

35   The annual 'Development Updates' published by the international funding NGO INTERFUND are a helpful index to these trends.

36   Interview with author, December 1994. Tsenoli later became a member of parliament. 'Land invasions' describe the often spontaneous decisions by residents to occupy and build shelters on vacant land. In some cases, these actions are organized by shacklords who rent or sell plots to squatters.

37   See Anon (1997).

38   Even Archbishop Desmond Tutu has been rebuked by Nelson Mandela for questioning the lavish salaries and perks earned by MPs, while the SACP's Jeremy Cronin has several times been censured for criticizing government policies like GEAR.

39   Interview with author, October 1994. At the time, Godongwana was general secretary of NUMSA.

40   Interview with author.

41   SANCO's *Making people-driven development* work report was highly critical of this trend which, it alleged, has made many NGOs 'rarely accountable to communities'.

42   Interview with author.

43   The Marconi Beam housing scheme in Cape Town is a happy example of how a politically sensitive and highly technical venture could succeed precisely because it was not allowed to recede into obtuse and alienating processes; see the *Reconstruct* supplement, *Mail & Guardian*, 22 November 1996.

44   Interview with author.

45   Nzimande, B. and Cronin, J., 1997, *We need transformation not a balancing act* (discussion document draft), Johannesburg, p. 3. The paper was a withering critique

of an earlier ANC discussion document *The State and Social Transformation* which it slammed for promoting a 'slide into a technocratic, "class-neutral" approach to politics ... partly based on [the ANC paper's] inability to think clearly about class realities in the new South Africa'.

46   Shubane and Madiba (1992:13).

47   Of course, there are exceptions like land and farmworker NGOs and CBOs.

48   For a trenchant critique of this phenomenon, see Chapter 12 of *Making People-driven Development Work* (Hanlon, 1994).

49   During the 1980s donor monitoring of project spending and work was extremely lax, providing huge latitude which in some cases was abused. After 1990, however, the patron-client relationship applied in the rest of the Third World was reintroduced, its conservatism reinforced in part by the rise of the logical framework analysis (LFA) fad.

50   Author's interview with Lechesa Tsenoli.

51   With the exception of the *SA Labour Bulletin*, all the independent publications loosely allied with the popular sector have shut down.

52   For a survey of GEAR's impact on development NGOs, see Marais (1997a and 1997b).

53   Author's interview with a programme officer of a foreign funder.

54   The premise of this section is not that the assertion of overarching commonalities has to yield before the surge of post-modern identity politics with its parochial pockets of 'communities' bonded by specific, narrowly-defined identities. On the contrary. As Hobsbawm has observed, 'never was the word "community" used more indiscriminately and emptily than in the decades when communities in the sociological sense become hard to find in real life' (1996:40).

55   *Sechaba,* June 1984. The editor was quoting from an earlier *Sechaba* review of Richard Rive's *Writing Black,* in response to a heated debate over the labelling of coloureds as 'so-called coloureds'.

56   Interview with author.

57   See Balibar and Wallerstein (1991).

58   Rupert Taylor, 'Taking Non-racialism Seriously', conference paper, 1993, Johannesburg; see also Marais (1993a).

59   Sandile Dikeni's 'How the West Was Lost', *Die Suid-Afrikaan* (November 1994), Cape Town, remains one of the most lucid analyses of this phenomenon, which continues to confound the ANC.

60   Bundy (1989), citing the SACP's Michael Harmel.

61   With the two stages conceptually and strategically separated by the winning of state power.

62   Also within the SACP, where some members wanted the national liberation movement 'to bring economic (or class) issues before the people' (Bundy, 1989).

63   The 'workerist' label was applied by elements of the ANC to activists who promoted the centrality of the labour movement and its struggles in a 'worker-led revolution'. In response, the tendency to play down the alleged class character of the struggle was dubbed 'populist'.

64   As part of the GEAR macroeconomic plan.

65   Described in more detail by Shubane and Madiba (1992:12–19), who noted that 'by suggesting that black township residents share a common experience despite their differences, they have taken apartheid's definition of the group as their rationale'.

66   In 1995 this led to a nocturnal pogrom against Mozambican residents in Johannesburg's Alexandra township. Media reports suggest the victimization has since become endemic.

67   Ray Hartley, *Sunday Times,* 26 May 1996.

68   Speech to SANCO RDP conference in May 1994, Johannesburg. A former SANCO president, Mayekiso in 1996 gave up his seat in parliament to head SANCO's investment arm.
69   Interview with author.
70   Interestingly, Simone has also noted the 'capability of these syndicates to "invisibly" cut across party, racial and class lines' (1994:15).
71   From the 'Report of the First National Conference of Women,' quoted by Walker (1982:153).
72   In the first six months of 1957, some 50 000 women took part in 38 demonstrations across the country.
73   Budlender et al. (1992:119–22).
74   Anneke, W., 1990, 'Launch of the ANC Women's League', Agenda, No. 8, quoted by Hassim (1991:67).
75   Hassim (1991:67). The decision had been taken at a May 1990 ANC meeting in Lusaka.
76   Horn (1991:86).
77   An attempt to exempt customary law from the Bill of Rights' equality clause was, for instance, successfully staved off by such unity.
78   For a list of other gains, see the Beijing Conference Report (1995:14–18).
79   Interview with author.
80   The quota demand was initially blocked 'as divisive' at the 1991 ANC national conference. It was later successfully revived.
81   See the Beijing Conference Report, pp. 47–8.
82   For a summary of other misassumptions, see Schreiner (1993:25–7), and Budlender (1997).
83   Quoted in Gevisser (1994:5).
84   The analogy with COSATU's decision to send top leaders into government is striking.
85   Author's interview with ANC MP Preggs Govender.
86   Author's interviews with Preggs Govender and Nozizwe Madlala.
87   Interview with author.
88   Such a course has many opponents, however, not the least among some black women's activists who view feminism as a middle-class import from Europe with little application in South Africa.
89   Hassim (1991:78–9).
90   Ibid.
91   Ibid.
92   Speech reprinted as 'Will the ANC sell-out workers?', African Communist, No. 134 (3rd Quarter, 1993), pp. 7–8.
93   The lower figure is derived from the 1994 October Household Survey, the higher one from the Department of Labour statistics. See ILO (1996:150) and Baskin (1996b:10–12).
94   In 1995, NACTU had 360 000 members and FEDSAL 250 000; see ILO (1996:150) and Baskin (1996b:9).
95   See Marie (1992) for a frank account of these problems. Many of them have persisted, as confirmed by Von Holdt (1996:41). For a brief survey of organizational practices in COSATU and its affiliates, see Baskin (1992:455–60).
96   For a summary of the origins of this principle, see Collins (1994:33–42).
97   See Shopsteward, September 1994. COSATU set up the magazine to improve communication with factory level workers and officials.
98   Marie (1992:23).
99   The lament of a TGWU shop steward, cited in Keet (1992:34).

100 ILO (1996:159). The survey was not restricted to shop stewards of COSATU affiliates.

101 Unions' loss has not necessarily been management's gain, because 'once unionists joined management, they often lost their credibility and were not given sufficient support in their new positions, [leading] to a high failure rate'; see *Business Day*, 6 July 1994.

102 Godongwana went on to muse that 'the best we can hope is that these comrades, driven by sheer instinct, will somehow still push a labour agenda from their vantage points' (1994a:23).

103 Tactically, the move was patently foolish. Unions held no practical leverage over the seconded officials, as NUM's Kgalema Motlanthe admitted when former NUM leader Marcel Golding left parliament to head an investment holding company: 'Golding is accountable to the ANC, not the unions. It was his decision to leave. We cannot stand in the way' – *Sunday Times*, 12 January 1997.

104 See Von Holdt (1996:36–42), as well as COSATU general secretary Sam Shilowa's *Towards Developing a Long-term Strategy for COSATU: A discussion paper*, 1994, Johannesburg. Collins noted at the time that it repeated observations made by COSATU office bearers as far back as 1987, adding 'that the fact that they have to be repeated points to the urgency for solutions to be found to the problems' (1994:39).

105 The SACP's Jeremy Cronin later implied in a newspaper article that NUMSA delegates had unwittingly become victims of a National Intelligence Service plot to sow disunity in union ranks – a 'dirty argument that avoided inspecting the merits and motivations of the NUMSA resolution', according to Godongwana (1994:22).

106 These could include NUMSA, SARHWU, NEHAWU, SADTU, SAMWU and SACTWU, while TGWU, NUM, CWIU, FAWU and CAWU would probably defend the alliance (Von Holdt, 1996:37).

107 Crankshaw (1993). Unskilled labourers, for instance, accounted for 36 per cent of the workforce in the metal sector in 1965 but only 8 per cent in 1989, whilst machine operators increased from 35 per cent to 50 per cent of the total workforce.

108 Schreiner (1994:48).

109 Schreiner (1994:44).

110 Dishonestly, it must be pointed out. Schreiner went on to suggest how organizations which attempt to represent different interests of the working classes could support one another through cross-sectoral collaboration (1994:48).

111 Von Holdt (1996:33–4).

112 From the introduction to the economic policy paper adopted by SACTWU at its July 1993 congress.

113 The localized correlates of NEDLAC are the efforts to instill co-determination at the enterprise level. Among the most significant are the workplace forums envisaged in the 1996 Labour Relations Bill. Worker participation in management decision-making has been a long-standing union demand but many unionists have recoiled from this concept, arguing that management has grown adept at using worker participation to introduce new production systems that enable it to bypass unions (ILO, 1996:158).

114 The most lucid texts to emerge from this debate remain those of John Saul (1991, 1992, 1994b). Of note, too, is Boris Kagarlitsky's rejoinder 'Letter to South Africa' (1995a).

115 Interview with author.

116 NUMSA's Enoch Godongwana, cited by Zita (1994).

117 See Kentridge (1993:40–3) for a summary of these views.

118 *Op. cit.*, p. 43.

119 Andrew Levy and Associates, 1995, *Annual Report on Labour Relations in South Africa 1994–95*, Cape Town, p. 38, cited in ILO (1996:166).

120 Former NUMSA general-secretary Enoch Godongwana, cited in *Shopsteward*, Vol. 4, No. 4 (August–September 1995).

121 Informal interviews with union and SACP officials suggest that COSATU's initial, muted response to GEAR stemmed from government's pledge that it would discuss COSATU's problems in *bilateral* meetings.

122 Nzimande & Cronin (1997:6). The authors used a 1996 ANC strategy paper *The State and Social Transformation* as the pretext to air their critique of this tendency in the ANC government.

123 Business consultant Phinda Mzwakhe Madi, 'To be a tiger', *Finance Week* (1 September, 1994). Three years later, the by-then black-owned Johannesburg Consolidated Investments was announcing plans to sack 4 000 mineworkers.

124 Cited in Von Holdt (1992:14).

125 See 'The September Scenarios', *SA Labour Bulletin*, Vol. 20, No. 6 (December), pp. 57–62.

CHAPTER EIGHT

The popular movement in flux
Ways forward

Beyond the conjunctural dilemmas and difficulties outlined in the previous chapter, the revival of a popular project is complicated by enduring theoretical and paradigmatic complications[1] which revolve around conceptions of the transitional state, of civil society and the relationships between them. Adapting a Gramscian schema to the South African situation opens possible routes for advance. But it implies conceptualizing the state and civil society in ways that stand somewhat at an angle to the theorizations that accompanied and defined the anti-apartheid struggle.

Rethinking the state and civil society

The state is incorrectly regarded as the site of concentrated power, to be seized and managed in accordance with the agenda of its new administrators. Neither is it merely a set of institutions through which a dominant class imposes and defends its prerogatives over the subordinate classes. Instead of such precarious domination via coercion and material force, political power implies the *ideological* conquest of society. The political dominion of a ruling class is grounded most fundamentally in the nurturing of the active consent of broad sections of society – the winning of hegemony. Except for extraordinary circumstances, the exercise of force and coercion is secondary.

The struggle between two classes, therefore, is necessarily the struggle between two hegemonies, the basis of which is ideology which (whatever the specific content) has to enable a class 'to escape the confines of its own corporate interests and to enlarge its political action to the point where it can understand and advance the aspirations of the subordinate classes' (Pellicani, 1981:30). In Gramsci's formulation, hegemony is achieved when this ideology is spread throughout the whole social surface, determining not only the unity of economic and political ends but intellectual and moral unity – by locating questions of intense concern not on the corporate level but on a 'universal' level.[2]

Hegemony presupposes that an aspirant ruling class develops and popularizes a coherent world view, an encompassing moral, social and strategic perspective that is antithetical to that of the dominant order. Importantly, the latter cannot be reduced to mere 'legitimation, false consciousness, or manipulation of the mass of the population' (Bottomore, 1983:202). This ideological map has to enable that class to co-ordinate its own class interests with those of subordinate groups in order to obtain their active consent. As phrased by Bottomore,

> ... the material basis of hegemony is constituted through reforms or compromises in which the leadership of a class is maintained but in which other classes have certain demands met.[3]

Naturally, this cannot affect essentials and, in the last instance, the fundamental interests of that class have to prevail. But the perspective has to be equipped with an elasticity that allows subordinate classes to align themselves with the hegemonic project. This is a crucial point. The ideological basis upon which consent is built is not monolithic, neither can it be strictly reduced to the interests of a particular class. Rather, it has to be:

> ... constructed at the intersection of ... multiple subject positions which, though *overdetermined* by class struggle, cannot be said to be directly determined by it or reducible to its effects (Mercer, 1980:126).

Hegemonic struggle entails dispersing and popularizing a coherent set of values, beliefs and ideals (expressed as ideas and actions), and building intellectual and moral unity among the social groups that constitute society. This struggle is waged on the terrain of civil society.

A variety of definitions of civil society are employed in the South African debate, many of them rigidly and expediently counterposed to the state. In contrast, Gramscian theorists have proposed that civil society be understood in *conjunctural* terms, as comprising:

> ... the thick web of interpersonal relationships and [representing] the social surface over which is extended the cultural hegemony of the ruling elites (Pellicani, 1981:33).

This allows for an understanding that locates civil society in rules, transactions and struggles which connect the state and society (Beckman, 1993). It also avoids the pitfall of spatially separating the state from civil society, recognizing instead their interconnectedness. The distinction, in a Gramscian view, is *methodological,* not intrinsic. This allows for the state to be understood as a 'strategic field'[4] that is 'constituted, condensed [and] materialized through a complex ... interplay of economic, political and ideological forces' (Mercer, 1980:119–20). Implicit is a recognition that contradictions of the state do not stem merely from conflicting interests within the ruling class, but are created also by tensions between it and the dominated classes.[5] This allowed Gramsci to arrive at the concept of the 'integral state', as:

> ... the entire complex of practical and theoretical activities with which the ruling class not only justifies and maintains its dominance, but manages to win the active consent of those over whom it rules (1971:244).

Phrased differently, the integral state represents the 'hegemonic moment' that articulates 'diverse elements into relative unity' (Mercer, 1980:121). Formed upon this ensemble of often discordant interests is a historical bloc[6] which represents the objective basis of hegemony and which takes the form of a system of social alliances that are held together by a common ideology and culture. But it is more than a loosely structured set of social classes. As Pellicani has indicated, it is also 'a cultural, economic, political and moral phenomenon' – which means that the hegemony of a ruling class:

> ... lasts as long as it is able to ensure the cohesion of the system of alliances on which its rule is exercised, and [enlarged] to include the other classes, thus satisfying in one way or another their moral and material interests (1981:32).

Finally, any class that seeks 'to advance its candidacy for the ethical-political leadership of society must organize itself into a political party'[7] – a crucial point often disregarded by the fans of social movement theory. The alternative is an aleatory and rudderless process which, while possibly embracing dynamic activities, is determined in the final instance by happenstance.

The rise of post-Marxism and post-modernism in the 1980s spawned an often unquestioning celebration of social movements, with supporters reminding that political parties anchored in the organized working class had failed to register lasting victories. Recommending social movements was their:

> ... flexibility, inclusiveness and decentralized structure that facilitates entry into political action from the various sites of social action in a way that trade unions and electoral parties cannot.[8]

These are valuable attributes. But the fetish of social movements ignores two debilitating trends. Firstly, they tend to become insulated around tight, parochial self-definitions which undermine the broader political and strategic coherence required for a popular hegemonic project.[9] Moreover, as Boris Kagarlitsky has noted, 'authoritarian structures often grow out of mass spontaneous movements' (1995:242). He argues that a 'democratically organized party' has to constitute 'the core of a mass movement', since it can provide political responsibility, accountability of leadership and help stabilize the movement. Party and movement have to collaborate, but from positions of independence. A crucial condition is that:

> ... movements must not be run by the party along bolshevik lines, but neither should the party be subordinate to the movement.[10]

Hegemony and its taskmasters

Gramscian thinking was evident in the practical activities and in some of the intellectual work that accompanied the internal democratic movement of the 1980s. Popular activities (which could be construed as the rudiments of a hegemonic contest) were waged by youth, women and civic groups, and by unions. But, as Fine (1992) noted, these currents became diverted from the mid-1980s onwards back into the more orthodox perspectives held by the exiled ANC and SACP. Activities which constituted hegemonic struggle were incorporated into the statist strategic ambit of the national liberation movement and enlisted in frontal assaults on the 'fortress' of the apartheid state. The post-1994 experience, however, has promoted a more explicit engagement with Gramscian conceptions in some key popular organizations, including the SACP.[11]

Routinely, the 'national democratic forces' have been regarded as the core of a bloc that would advance the interests of the disadvantaged classes. That bloc would be 'centred around the ANC – which straddles government, parliament and the ANC as a broad liberation movement' and 'includes the tripartite alliance – but extends well beyond into a range of MDM formations'.[12] The task, essentially, would be the pursuit of a 'national democratic revolution', the content of which was broadly captured in the RDP Base Document. However, the discourse of 'reconstruction and development' has also been enlisted as the broad ideological frame for another hegemonic project geared at servicing the prerogatives of the more privileged sectors of society.

As argued, a ruling bloc based on the political exclusion of the majority and revolving around beleaguered minority political parties had become an indisputable liability by the mid-1980s. The rise of a militant working class movement politically allied with the excluded political opposition and the spread of other popular organizations drove home that realization. The ruling bloc had to be revised or 'modernized', with the negotiations serving as the gateway for that bid to transform South African into a more conventional capitalist society.[13] Salient were two risky adjustments. For obvious reasons, the ANC had to constitute the political axis of the bloc – but on terms that inhibited its radical impulses and rendered it amenable to servicing key prerogatives of capital. Essentially, this has provoked what Cronin calls a 'struggle for the heart and soul of the ANC'.[14] Secondly, the organized black working class had to be disciplined and weaned from its role as standard-bearer for a popular transformation project. Structural changes in the social composition of the working class (mainly its increased stratification) have abetted this process which is to be propelled by increasing the flexibility and segmentation of the labour market.

Both the ANC and the labour movement are therefore subject to intense contestation. Given their ideologically indeterminate (or, at least, *disparate*) character, the national democratic forces 'are liable to coalesce around two distinct versions of the national democratic project' (SACP, 1996:1) – better formulated as two hegemonic projects, each of which seeks to win the active consent of similar social forces. The one represents a modulation of the ruling bloc's 'modernizing' drive, the other a popular transformation project. Under the motto of 'realism', the first revolves around core themes of normalization, globalization, social unity, law and order, and the economic empowerment of blacks. It is aimed at extending the pre-1994 set of alliances to include the middle and upper strata of the labour movement and the ANC, the black *petit bourgeoisie* (including the ranks of NGOs), the new, emergent (black) capitalist fractions, and new entrants into the executive and administrative layers of the state. Disconcerting is the fact that many of these groupings, as the SACP has noted, 'have constituted the core cadre base of our movement'.[15] Several government policies (notably GEAR) are highly functional to this project. The sale of public assets (wholly or partially) has an 'affirmative action' component that increases the black élite's stake in the economy.[16] Meanwhile, improved social infrastructure becomes accessible to an expanded (but still tiny) group of 'insiders' that includes sections of the working class.[17] As indicated, the working class is viewed ambivalently – as both ally and foe – which requires a strategic compromise along the lines described in the previous chapter.

All this occurs in the context of nation-building, a necessary project aimed at equipping society with an inclusive and unified self-perception by addressing the widespread desire for social peace, conciliation and unity, and satisfying the need for a sort of psycho-social equilibrium. In essence, the concept of nationhood is non-class. Yet, the consciousness that moulds it 'is influenced by the hegemonic class in a particular society' (Alexander, 1993:16). Left unbuttressed by political-economic adjustments that demonstrably favour the disadvantaged majority, the project implies the legitimation of social inequalities. The challenge, then, is to invest it with a content that reflects popular interests and answers the question 'What kind of nation do we wish to build?'. In contrast, the current project is propelled by the axiom that the sheer forging of nationhood ranks foremost, irrespective of its political-economic character.

The basis of a ruling class hegemonic project is being constituted under the very feet of the 'national democratic forces'. South African capital has been assiduously engineering the rise of a black economic élite. A key intervention was the nurturing of the black-owned New Africa Investments Ltd (NAIL), which was set on its feet with the assistance of the insurance giant Sanlam[18] – in a move reminiscent of white, English capital's cultivation during the 1960s and 1970s of Afrikaner corporations as 'junior partners' in economic dominance. The attitude of NAIL executive Nthato Motlana is instructive: 'We want to go into the future hand in hand with white partners'.[19] As many as 200 'black economic empowerment' ventures have arisen subsequently, though many have been derided as mere window-dressing benefitting a tiny black élite and the incumbent white capitalist class.[20]

It is tempting to draw similarities with the bloc established after 1948. Class tensions were blunted by the nationalist (and racist) themes around which hegemony was built, by extending wide-ranging benefits to narrow (white) layers of the working class and by enabling workers to achieve some mobility into entrepreneurial and professional activities. Finally, from capital's point of view, the political project pursued by the NP met but in some respects also exceeded the bounds of necessity – creating an undertow of mild political tensions within the bloc.

Some of these features are evident, in analogous though nascent form, in the 1990s. The most apparent difference, of course, is the multiracial character of the emergent new bloc. Less obvious is the fact that the first decades of the apartheid project were marked by strong growth in economies across the world and in South Africa, which allowed for the distribution of privilege to be sustained and expanded until the 1970s. That context no longer prevails. The world economy has not recovered from the 1973 crisis, and has undergone profound changes that further marginalize developing countries of South Africa's ilk. The economy, meanwhile, remains in the throes of a structural crisis. This suggests that the days of wine and roses will prove shortlived for those layers of black South Africa that are inducted into a new ruling bloc. As a result, the loyalties of the 'new insiders' might prove to be impetuous and the cohesion of the bloc frail. Politically, a new bloc built around such a multiracial class project will rest on a highly precarious bedrock; ultimately, its continued dominance will require resort to authoritarian measures and the gradual dismantlement of South Africa's liberal democracy.

Naturally, within the popular movement (particularly the SACP) another project is envisaged, 'in which the social weight, interests and concerns of the working class as a whole, and the broader rural and urban poor, are hegemonic' (SACP, 1996:4). This is conceptualized as the logical extension of the national liberation struggle which was regarded as 'an emerging hegemonic project' by Cronin. But that struggle centred on unity and common interests derived (at the most fundamental level) from the racial identification of social groupings, and was cast in the form of African nationalism.[21] As one SACP member has asked, 'Can we build a working class hegemony around the fact that people are oppressed as "Africans" or "blacks"?'.[22] African nationalism resonates potently in the post-apartheid era. Yet, it also disguises the conflicting interests that cohabit under its ideological mantle and the aggressive pursuit of those interests. The corporate ambitions of a black economic élite are realized within, and justified by, nationalist discourse. The muffled and marginalized ambitions of unemployed black youth are couched in similar terms. Traditional chiefs invoke nationalist themes to justify their authority – but so can rural women whose demeaned status stems partly from those systems. African nationalism, in the current epoch, therefore buries rather than excavates the systemic sources of inequality and oppression.

Grounded in the firmament of African nationalism is the ANC which (as the 'party of the people') is perforce regarded as the political centre of two contesting hegemonic projects. The ANC, therefore, is both the subject and object of hegemonic struggle which generates a major dilemma. If one follows the Gramscian injunction that any class with hegemonic aspirations has to organize itself into a political party, the question arises whether the ANC is the most appropriate vehicle for a popular, working class hegemonic project. If not, which political forces assumes that mantle?

What's our mission now?

The prime strategic challenge after 1994 has been to regroup a popular movement around a common set of objectives. The RDP seemed to fit the bill but, for reasons already stated, its utility *as a programme* has dramatically changed. The semantics of reconstruction, development and nation-building[23] have become eminently malleable. The popular forces cannot reverse this state of affairs by proclaiming, for example, that the RDP 'is our programme'. Reconstruction and development has to be invested with new, *particular* meanings invested with potentially broad-ranging appeal that privileges the interests of the popular classes. Inevitably, this requires that the class and other contradictions that snake through the democratic forces are not muted but rendered more explicit.

The danger is that, instead, a Bernsteinian 'the-movement-is-everything' approach holds sway on the basis of questionable claims of the ANC's historical working class bias. A strategic perspective is fashioned as loosely and inclusively as possible in order to preserve unity at all costs. The commitment to reconstruction and development remains sacrosanct but is couched within a nationalist discourse that continues to muffle the distinct interests that are privileged or thwarted by resultant activities.

Left in such enveloping terms, a popular project of transformation is likely to remain locked into the homogenizing force field of nationalism. The alternative, in the views of some SACP and COSATU thinkers, is a programme that expresses a 'working class political-economy'. But the

formulation begs important questions. Axiomatically, the role of the organized working class is seen as central, and for valid reasons. Yet, leftists
have to recognize that 'the world of labour is itself heterogenous'.[24] At the
most obvious level, there is the stratification between better qualified,
employed and organized workers, and their poorly skilled, un- or under-
employed counterparts – a reality opponents of labour eagerly exploit, as
COSATU has discovered. While the strategic importance of organized
workers is undeniable, a social bloc led by that force has to genuinely
address and incorporate the interests of the bloc's other participants. In the
abstract, this counsel seems simplistic. In the South African context, it
announces a perplexing task. Specific (and sometimes contending) interests
were for long muffled by the homogenizing weight of the anti-apartheid
struggle. Since the mid-1980s, they have resurfaced with a vengeance. The
result has been disorientation within social and political formations, and
the often traumatic eruptions of internecine conflict. This heterogeneity is
an integral feature – and potential advantage – of a hegemonic project of the
sort envisaged by sections of the South African left. The challenge is to
harness it as a positive feature of a radical project anchored around a political party of the organized working class. Sadly, the traditions of the SACP
and ANC have equipped them poorly for this task.

Related is another prickly matter. The post-1970s anti-apartheid struggles occurred largely in urban and peri-urban areas, and pivoted on
demands derived from visions of modernization. Indeed, the battle lines of
the bloody conflict between Inkatha and the Charterist forces corresponded
to the contradictions between modernist and traditional value systems,
between rural, urban and peri-urban zones, and between proletarianized
and 'peasant' communities. The apartheid state's exploitation of those tensions (and the Inkatha leadership's cynical willingness to become fellow-
travellers of that state) did not warrant the conclusion that the social base of
Inkatha was pro-apartheid or irredeemably reactionary. As a movement,
Inkatha occupied a vacuum. It was built among those layers that had been
ignored by other political forces, layers where the modernizing thrust of
Charterist politics (spearheaded by workers' and student organizations) did
not resonate crisply.[25] KwaZulu-Natal was the only region where a strong,
organized political movement was built on this basis. In contrast, predominantly rural regions like the Eastern Cape and Northern Province have
remained ANC strongholds – largely because of conscious attempts to
reconcile the fault lines between the modern and the traditional.[26] Nevertheless, after 1994 those tensions have resurfaced, most clearly around the
feared 'encroachment' of democratic local government structures on the
authority systems of traditional chiefs. An elementary though often
overlooked point emerges: a hegemonic project that prioritizes the interests
of the working class runs the risk of neglecting or alienating those layers

which doubtless include the poorest and most disadvantaged South Africans.[27] If, within such a project, compromises can be considered with the *petit bourgeoisie* or even, temporarily, with fractions of capital, then surely more earnest efforts are needed to incorporate those 'pre-modern' layers in rural areas into a new set of social alliances?

This does not supplant the central *political* role of organized, skilled workers, but reminds that a popular hegemonic project cannot be constructed on a narrow base of interests. In Kagarlitsky's words,

> ... the main goal of the changes becomes surmounting the gap between the modern and the traditional sectors, between advanced and backward enterprises, between the capital cities and the hinterland (1995a:246).

These types of challenges are being acknowledged among sections of the left. Practically incorporating them into a strategic project, however, remains a 'work in progress'.

It must be emphasized that the ANC government's post-1994 accomplishments have not been bereft of substantive, progressive features. Most striking was the forging of a political system that rests on a progressive constitution and bill of rights, new labour legislation which, in many respects, deserves the envy of workers in industrialized countries, and attempts to transform education. Projects that bring potable water to tens of thousands of rural residents, provide free health care to young children and pregnant women, and feed primary school children are deservedly celebrated.

Their transformative thrust, though, is questionable – for they are submerged in broader strategic shifts that bow to the imperatives of the most powerful sections of capital. In a sense, the government has struck out on paradoxical policy tracks. Within the context of GEAR these apparent contradictions will become reconciled along lines familiar to Latin American victims of structural adjustment: the grafting of World Bank-type social programmes onto neo-liberal economic policies. The outcome is not transformation but social containment. Attempts to rhetorically situate the South African government's policies within a transformative paradigm need to be judged in this context.

How can a new strategic perspective be developed? Some elements appeared in the SACP's 1995 'Strategies and Tactics' document or reside in the RDP Base Document. Others are emerging fitfully in specific sectors (land, housing, gender, health, labour, education) – often in organic and, to remote observers, unspectacular forms. Some of the building blocks for redefining a popular hegemonic project exist, others will continue to emerge as ordinary South Africans resist the sacrosanctity of privilege – an 'organic process' that acquires its form through the activities and campaigns waged by what Neville Alexander has called 'intersecting vanguard or interest groups'.[28]

Practical regroupings

Typically, the ANC is seen as the most appropriate political anchor-point for this process of regrouping and redefinition. In the view of the tripartite alliance it is the:

> ... ANC-led political centre [that is] capable precisely of co-ordinating and driving a political, social and economic transformation programme through a wide network of forums and institutions.[29]

But the ideologically disparate character of the ANC, and the disaggregation of interests occurring within it, raise questions about its suitability for such a role. The customary injunction has been to win the ANC over to a more radical perspective by struggling to revive its putative working class bias, a well-worn precept of the SACP, as shown by Toussaint's stirring words in 1988:

> Working class leadership of the national movement is possible. It is desirable. It is the only safeguard that today's broad front can tread an uninterrupted passage, in unity, to the socialist-building of tomorrow (1985).[30]

Given the fluidity of the ANC (and, within it, the increasing prominence and power of interests anathema to those of the popular classes) a new strategic perspective will be stillborn if its content is determined by the ANC's inclination to adopt or resist it. Von Holdt's prescient warning deserves to be writ large: 'The working class movement may ... find that its quest for influence is the very thing that holds it captive to ANC policies' (1993:22). There is a pressing need to recast the terms of the tripartite alliance.

The need, therefore, is not simply to calculate a formula that can revive the 'national democratic forces'. It is to *reconfigure* a popular movement on the basis of an explicitly transformative perspective. Does this imply an oppositional front? The question betrays, once again, the misconception of a spatially separated state and civil society. In truth, the state and civil society are interconnected, each defining the other through a complex of relations and constantly shifting engagements. Depending on the situation, elements of the one transmute into the other. A popular movement, therefore, is positioned neither outside nor inside the state or civil society. In the course of its activities it traverses the two strategic fields.

Yet, a popular hegemonic project requires a political axis. Recommending the SACP for this role are several attributes: its potentially strategic influence within the ANC (as a party and government, at all levels), the wide-scale presence of its cadres in institutions of the state and civil society which allows for the penetration of seemingly impervious sectors and structures, its historical avowal of radical transformation (despite the ambiguous and problematic routes plotted toward that goal), and its enunciation of class-based struggle. Mitigating against its candidacy is the poor level of political education in its ranks, the timidity of its strategic perspective and the suffocating weight and questionable pertinence of its theoretical bedrock (CST, which remains steeled against rigorous critique). What does this mean for the tripartite alliance?[31] The enquiry invites this proposition: If the alliance cannot be functional to, and survive, the resuscitation of a popular transformation project then its *raison d'être* surely would have expired. The alliance, after all, was never viewed as an eternal fact. Apposite still is Bird and Schreiner's proposal that 'a new alliance or set of alliances – with working class organisations in civil society – get at least the same priority' as the alliance with the ANC (1992:32), a move that carries portentous political implications. The stakes, though, are too high to avoid thoroughly investigating the probable impact of continuing the alliance in its current form.

The tripartite alliance has experienced increased strain as the contradictions have become more pronounced between COSATU's working class (and nominally socialist) priorities and the policies of the ANC government. Considerable apprehension has surfaced also between the SACP and ANC.[32] These tensions were inscribed into a democratic transition that saddled the ANC with the task of managing (and policing) a historic class compromise tilted against the interests of the majority. Muffling them, however, was the strategic view (derived from the SACP's two-stage theory) that the achievement and deepening of the 'national democratic revolution' was not only paramount but eminently congruous with a popular transformation project. The transition reveals a paradox which few foresaw: that a historic breakthrough can be achieved on the basis of accommodations, and set in motion reconfigurations, which actually arrest the transformation project in a severely stunted form.

The most attractive route out of this impasse would be to recast the terms of the tripartite alliance, in general, and the SACP-ANC alliance, in particular by allowing the creation of platforms within the ANC (along the lines of Brazil's Workers' Party). This would render the class and other biases in the ANC less opaque and enable the clear expression and pursuit of divergent interests, enabling a more vigorous pursuit of distinct strategic directions. At the most fundamental level, this could allow the disaggregation of interests and agendas which are being forcibly corralled under the canopy of coerced unity – a prerequisite for the gradual reconstitution of a popular hegemonic project. For an organization as ideologically elastic as the ANC this should pose no threat of implosion. Rather it could place the organization on a more genuinely democratic footing.

Blocking that route are conceptions of liberation as a unilinear process of advance, divided by 'phases' and adhering to a predictable and ultimately unstoppable trajectory of progressive change. Setbacks would occur but without fundamentally recasting this long march of history. 'The forces of reaction could,' as Kagarlitsky has sardonically noted, 'retard or even halt this process, but they could not encroach upon the "irreversible" gains of the workers' (1995b:34). Whether employed in revolutionary or reformist projects, strategies based on such mechanistic notions of progress have met with defeat everywhere in the world. Three lessons can be drawn. Firstly, setbacks and gains do not merely halt or accelerate the wheels of advance – they drastically alter the terms and capacities for engagements. By ignoring these underlying reconfigurations, the stern injunction to 'hold the course' becomes self-defeating. Secondly, setbacks and gains often occur simultaneously, as popular organizations have discovered to their dismay. Simply performing a kind of political arithmetic of pros and cons (and adjusting, accordingly, the nuts and bolts of the project) obscures the qualitatively different implications these shifts hold for engagement. Thirdly, and most importantly, the rectilinear approach impels a headlong strategy of 'forward ever, backward never', denying popular organizations the option of performing strategic retreats in certain areas.[33] The world offers ample evidence of the foolhardiness of such convictions.

The choices made will decide whether South Africa will experience the reconstitution of a popular movement that is able to effectively engage in hegemonic struggle. Its effectiveness, though, will be determined not only by its political coherence and sophistication but also by its ability to overcome the myriad organizational difficulties already catalogued. Alternatively, that movement will remain fragmented and in disarray. At worst, once vibrant sections will continue to decline or disappear, leaving in their wake the emergence of depoliticized initiatives that are primarily geared at enabling marginalized sectors and communities to *survive* the vagaries of the hegemonic class. In political-economic terms, they will function as the 'popular' components of the kinds of poverty alleviation and social containment programmes described earlier. At best, various formations will haphazardly attempt to muster counter-hegemonic activities that will lack the cohesiveness and expansive appeal that characterizes a potentially successful hegemonic project, and sporadically invite repression. Such is the historical juncture reached in South Africa that none of these alternatives are unlikely.

Beyond the borders

This chapter has concentrated on the state of the popular movement. Yet the globalizing dynamics described earlier demand that a rebuilt movement broaden its horizons beyond its national boundaries. Traditionally, this has taken the form of 'solidarity', usually dispensed towards other movements engaged in struggles against repressive regimes or towards beleaguered, progressive experiments by victorious movements.

There is no point being sanguine about the recent histories of solidarity between countries and movements of the South. Generally, it has been overshadowed (in scale and sophistication) by North-South solidarity, and (in prominence) by the less than admirable examples of governmental networks such as the Non-Aligned Movement, the Organization of African Unity (OAU) and the ubiquitous UN-sponsored spectacles. Within civil society, co-ordinated activities geared at challenging common transnational dynamics have been rare in Africa. Yet, such internationalizing initiatives have increased in the 1990s – the 1993 anti-GATT protests, the 1994 '50 Years Is Enough' campaign against the Bretton Woods institutions are two examples. While it is tempting to exaggerate the scale and impact of these activities, they remain rudimentary and experimental. But they represent essential antidotes to the globalizing trends that South African popular organizations are struggling to come to terms with.

Many obstacles hinder vigorous South African participation in transnational solidarity that transcends bolstering specific movement movements in specific countries. Long at the receiving end of international solidarity, South African popular organizations have been curiously reluctant to reciprocate – preferring instead to retreat into a hermetism that, at times, has bordered on the xenophobia and suspicion vented by many ordinary citizens against foreign immigrants. Moreover, most of these organizations have been struggling to weather complex new challenges. Yet, the prospects of a rebuilt popular movement seem feeble if it were to adopt an insular, parochial attitude. Its reconfiguration will have to incorporate activated, internationalist perspectives that focus especially on links on the African continent. If cast in forms that obey the perimeters of the nation-state, the movement's efforts will be stunted.[34]

Notes

1 The discursive nature of this section reflects an alarming shortage of published analysis of these matters. The thoughts that follow are exploratory and, hopefully, could help animate more rigorous debates.

2 *Selections from the Prison Notebooks* (Italian Einaudi edition, 1975), cited by Pellicani (1981:40).

3 *Ibid.*

4 The military idioms employed by Gramsci (ramparts, fortresses, wars of position or manoeuvre), unfortunately, have obscured these crucial points.

5 Mercer, *op. cit.,* p. 121.

6 Distinct from a power bloc, which describes only the moment of force and coercion.

7 Pellicani, *op. cit.,* p. 38.

8 Petras, J. and Morley, M., 1990, *US Hegemony Under Siege*, cited by Kagarlitsky (1995:242).

9 In James Petras's words, this leads to 'an "identity" prison isolated from other exploited social groups unless it transcends the immediate points of oppression and confronts the social system in which it is imbedded' (1997:6).

10 Kagarlitsky, *op. cit.,* p. 243.

11 See, for example, its October 1996 strategy document, *Let Us Not Lose Sight of Our Strategic Priorities*.

12 'Strategic Perspectives' adopted by Alliance Executives' Summit, 1 October 1995.
13 This does not imply some Machiavellian blueprint or that the post-1986 develop-
    ments (from initial overtures to the post-settlement transition) adhered to a seamless
    logic. But they were shadowed by this *objective* need.
14 Interview with author.
15 SACP (1996:3), referring to the national liberation movement.
16 Many government tendering processes are designed in similar fashion.
17 SACP (1996:2–3).
18 Founded in 1918, Sanlam functioned as a credit institution for Afrikaners, transform-
    ing their funds into productive capital. In 1937 it developed close ties with the cabal-
    istic *Broederbond*.
19 *The Star*, 18 July 1994.
20 'There are still only a handful of major black players in the SA economy with limited
    economic muscle. Most of their investments are little more than asset swaps from
    existing white ownership to black ownership,' according to *Business Map Update*
    'Black Economic Empowerment: Fact or Fiction' (August 1996).
21 Despite the commitment to non-racialism, which in practice seldom went beyond
    multiracialism. See, for instance, Marais (1993a).
22 Langa Zita, speaking at SACP cadre school, November 1996, Johannesburg.
23 This refers not only to statements and texts, but also to the ensemble of gestures, sym-
    bols and activities that are deployed – from the RDP White Paper, to Mandela wear-
    ing a Springbok rugby team jersey, to corporations selling assets to black consortiums
    to 'advance the RDP'.
24 See Kagarlitsky (1995:245).
25 The unmistakable rural/urban split in support for the ANC and IFP in the 1996 local
    government elections was graphic confirmation of this.
26 The formation of the Congress of Traditional Leaders of South Africa (Contralesa)
    was one such intervention. By late 1997, however, it was beginning to disengage itself
    from the ANC.
27 It is sobering to recall that it was among such excluded sections that Peru's Sendero
    Luminoso built its social base. In Mexico, the ideologically heterogeneous Zapatistas
    similarly occupied social spaces abandoned by the traditional left. See Castaneda
    (1994) and Casanova (1997).
28 See Alexander (1993).
29 'Strategic Perspectives' adopted by Alliance Executives' Summit, 1 October 1995.
    The document makes instructive reading, both for its insistence that the 'national
    democratic forces' unproblematically represent a progressive bloc, and for its can-
    dour about the feeble functioning of most ANC party structures.
30 Interestingly, Toussaint's formulation implicitly questioned the tenuous notion,
    advanced for example by NUM's Kgalema Motlanthe, that 'the ANC had, as early as
    the 1940s a particular bias towards working people', a bias which 'became stronger
    and stronger over the years'.
31 In fact two alliances are in question: the tripartite alliance, and the much more symbi-
    otic alliance between the ANC and the SACP. COSATU's withdrawal from the former
    (which is not unlikely) would produce a curious situation. The SACP (a working class
    party) would remain in alliance with a party which the most powerful working class
    organization deems anathema to its interests.
32 Most bluntly in the form of a wistful but stridently argued discussion paper by deputy
    minister of environmental affairs and tourism, Peter Mokaba, in 1997, calling on the
    SACP to end its symbiotic relationship with the ANC and allow the latter to assume
    its capitalist character.

33 Indeed, it is strange that leftist projects, steeped as they are in militaristic discourse and conceptions, have proved so singularly unwilling to accept Clausewitz's counselling that retreats cannot be equated with defeats.

34 For an expanded version of this argument, see Bond (1996a).

CHAPTER NINE

Into the new

'I can tell you sirs, what I would not have, though I cannot what I would.' – Oliver Cromwell (attributed)

South Africa corroborates James Baldwin's aphorism that 'people are trapped in history, and history is trapped in them'.[1] Inherited by post-apartheid South Africa is an accumulation of historical currents – the structural continuities that bedevil efforts at transformation, the ideological narratives that both propel and retard that project, and the political alliances serving as vehicles into the future. Their utility for a project that dismantles the insider/outsider mould of society cannot be assumed. In many respects they complicate the passage into the new.

Irrespective of its character and main beneficiaries, a resolution of the South African dilemma cannot occur without the forging of a new national consensus. That process is integral to the contesting hegemonic works-in-progress, none of which has matured to the point of achieving ascendancy. In broad outline it has taken the form of the ANC-administered bid to forge a South African nation around the principles of an inclusive, non-racial democracy.[2] This nation-building project extends beyond the juridical and geographical spheres, towards a provisional bid for unity (or, at least, a kind of truce) at the cultural, social and political levels.

Correctly, the project is seen as the bedrock for the other component of a resolution to the crisis: a new development path which, progressives hope, will spur social and economic transformation. It is aimed at defending the integrity of a unified nation-state, combating racist and ethnic-exclusionist legacies and trends, and establishing in South Africans' lived realities a sense of unity and common belonging while respecting their diversities. Forging such a national consensus around the principles of inclusiveness and unity requires illuminating or inventing a range of commonalities that can supersede and abate the centrifugal dynamics at play in society.

The project rests on several pillars. Its core foundations reside in the terms and details of the political settlement, the post-apartheid political system and the rights and liberties inscribed in the Constitution which, at the political-juridical level, establish the principle of equality as the central axis of political and social relations. Buttressing them are specific compromises imbedded in the settlement (the 'sunset clause', the protection of minority rights at local government level, guaranteeing the expression of cultural diversity), the nominally federalist character of the political system, acknowledgement of Afrikaners' right to seek self-determination, preservation of traditional leaders' authority, as well as the amnesty provisions (and the concomitant processes of the Truth and Reconciliation Commission, TRC). By and large, the latter elements are geared at accommodating social and political forces deemed capable of destabilizing post-apartheid society.

A further pillar comprises a wide range of symbolic and discursive interventions aimed at established commonalities with which broad layers of South Africans can identify. Central is the political persona of Nelson Mandela, in which is vested the principles of reconciliation, tolerance, moderation, consistency and trust. Augmenting it are unifying symbols (the new national flag, the twin anthems),[3] spectacles (sports events such as the 1995 Rugby World Cup and 1996 African Nations football championship, Mandela's *tête-à-tête* with former foes), campaigns revolving around shared anxieties (the 'war against crime'), and adjustments aimed at bestowing legitimacy on discredited institutions (the police, military and judicial apparatuses). Also enlisted are riskier enterprises, like the TRC (tasked with helping engineer a psycho-social catharsis) and the grand gesture upon which it is predicated: amnesty.[4] Signal, too, are the (faltering) attempts to precede restructuring initiatives with broad consultation, geared at ensuring inclusiveness and preventing potentially destabilizing reactions.

That a concerted effort is needed to defuse the manifold enmities, antagonisms and fissures bequeathed by the past is obvious: 'If South Africans do not succeed in building a nation, they will fall apart into warring faction legitimised in ethnic, racial party-political and perhaps even religious terms,' as Neville Alexander has warned.[5] Understandably, there are dissenting voices. Fearful that such a project could spur an upsurge of African nationalist chauvinism, political philosopher Johan Degenaar has argued that the nurturing of a democratic culture should supersede nation-building. Yet that venture is a prime element of the project which, at least in its current form, seems to respond to Jurgen Habermas' counsel that:

> ... the nation of citizens does not derive its identity from some common ethnic and cultural properties, but rather from the praxis of citizens who actively exercise their civil rights.[6]

The stress-lines of the project are perhaps better sought elsewhere. In some respects elements aimed at defusing hostilities could generate the opposite effect. The concessions to Afrikaner chauvinism and conservative African traditionalist forces paradoxically placate and prolong the lifespan of politicized ethnicity. In the former instance, the gamble is more likely to pay off; in the latter, it is already exacerbating social tensions and undermining the authority and effectiveness of new local government structures.[7]

Also controversial is the extent and manner in which unity requires a confrontation with the past. The officially sanctioned response has been the TRC, which deserves some reflection.

The Commission's origins lie in the final months of political negotiations, in 1993. It emerged as a compromise between the need for justice (expressed by the democratic movement) and the demand for a blanket amnesty (made by the NP and its allies and functionaries). The choice, essentially, was 'to consolidate the peace of a country where human rights are protected today or to seek retroactive justice that could compromise that peace'.[8] Struck during a period of intense political instability, the compromise was understandable, though not inevitable. Its contours neatly matched those of the political settlement itself – defusing the threat of 'counter-revolution' by harnessing opposing social and political forces into agreements that could yield stability and build a new national consensus. Rhetorically, its role is described in psycho-social terms – of 'healing the nation'. Victims have the opportunity to publicly air their experiences of human rights violations; perpetrators of abuses are encouraged to disclose their actions in order to qualify for amnesty. The price of the enterprise is steep: full disclosure exempts the perpetrator from criminal or civil action, thereby suspending the administering of justice.

As one of the major building blocks of nation-building, the TRC's function is to extend into the social sphere the consensual (or, at least, conciliatory) dynamics nurtured in the political sphere. The Commission's title ('truth and reconciliation') reflects the hope that truth-telling can help reconcile the contradictory experiences, memories and perceptions that churn through society, thereby changing the ways in which South Africans relate to each other. It is burdened with the hope that the exposure of truths can reinforce a basis for reconciliation and, ultimately, help forge a unified nation.

Considered in the abstract, this makes good sense. But this reconciliatory venture is hindered by other elements of the broader nation-building project, elements geared at placating white South Africans and appeasing capital by drastically tempering progressive adjustments in the social and economic spheres. As a result, the TRC functions within a broader socio-economic – and ideological – context that demonstrably reinforces existing antagonisms. Sadly, in daily life the gestures of reconciliation still emanate primarily from the oppressed. By and large, white South Africans' responses are an admixture of clumsy prevarication, idle bitterness and nostalgia – made possible by the spatial, material and psychological distance they can maintain between them and the 'other'.[9] Absent is contrition and the questioning (on any significant scale) of moral and social sensibilities, about the past and the present. In white South Africa, reconciliation takes the hybridized form of denial and self-absolution. Its arithmetic has remained exploitative, exacting sacrifices and humility from the oppressed, whilst indulging the arrogance of the privileged – a kind of existential analogy to some of the policies pursued by government.

Blame for this is unfairly laid at the feet of the TRC process itself. Rather it rests with some of the terms of the nation-building project. Individual remembrance is demanded, yet collective amnesia is condoned in the name of reconciliation. The evasion of moral (and legal) culpability is sanctioned, most obviously in the case of corporate South Africa whose complicity in a devastated social landscape is rarely, if ever, noted publicly. On the contrary, corporate interests increasingly are conflated with the 'common' and 'national' interests advanced in the nation-building project. These postures are doggedly encouraged by the mainstream media which fall into states of apoplexy whenever signs are detected that the terms of reconciliation and nation-building might violate the comfort index demanded by the privileged.

Superficially, accommodation reached on such terms might appear to till the grounds of appeasement when, in fact, it rationalizes the inequalities of the past and present, and prolongs the alienation of the most marginalized sectors of society.

It bears repeating that building a unified nation and consolidating a stable new political system are imperatives – both in their own right and in establishing a platform for socio-economic transformation. The fundamental problematic of the nation-building project as currently constituted is that it comprises expansive accommodations which, in many respects, entail the perpetuation of values, institutions, systems and practices of 'the past'. Not only do they obstruct socio-economic transformation, but they inhibit the scope of the very 'national democratic revolution' they are deemed to facilitate. As the chapters on the RDP and economic policy have indicated, the reluctance to more forthrightly restructure the circuits whereby wealth and privilege are distributed constitutes an unheralded but prime element of the nation-building project. The tactical arrangements aimed at eliciting allegiance – or, at least, acquiescence – to a new political system have become conflated with a generalized endorsement and reinforcement of the political-economy that defines society currently. In that sense, the nation-building project rests on, and advances, a historic compromise with the fundamental forces and dynamics that determine South Africa's 'Two Nation' character, segmenting it between increasingly deracialized insiders and predominantly black outsiders.

Predictably, this occasions allegations from the left of a 'sell-out', a trite reaction that obscures the dynamics at play. To be sure, there is ample evidence of the absorption of the dominant ideology into the top echelons of the democratic movement. The regurgitation of corporate South Africa's precepts – and their translation into policy – has become commonplace. It is no longer novel to hear ANC figures decry as a woeful 'culture of entitlement' calls for socio-economic transformation along lines that transgress some of the rules of the market. The extravagant perks inherited by new state and parastatal officials have been left intact.[10] The disdain shown towards workers' attempts to further their class interests via strikes sits uneasily beside the tax concessions extended to corporations. Previous chapters have surveyed the many other examples.

This dislocation between rhetoric and reality has become palpable, and has triggered restiveness even within the ANC. Instructive are the cutting criticisms made by the ANCYL in late 1996.[11] Among the difficulties plaguing the ANC, it noted that 'following our resounding victory in the elections, it was inevitable that the organisation and various cadres became much more open to undue influence' and lamented that 'the material benefits which derived for individuals from our position as a majority party, meant a rise in political careerism' (1996:1).

The document also highlighted an array of organizational weaknesses, among them:

> ... a weak deployment strategy, resulting in an overemphasis on governance ... the lack of a cadre policy aimed at new members as well as building political cohesiveness amongst cadres deployed at different levels ... a weak political centre, leading to a failure to integrate the two main strategic tasks (governance and mobilizing our people) ... power struggles and a tendency of some leaders and members seeing themselves as above the organisation ...[12]

In an intervention that self-consciously harked back to the ANCYL's dramatic assertiveness five decades ago, the document then proposed that five pillars define the ANC's strategic objective:

> Socio-economic transformation (with emphasis on affordable services in the areas of health and welfare, housing and education); Economic growth and development that benefits the country as a whole, and seek to uplift the general standards of living of the poorest sections of our society; Transforming the institutions of the state and government; Building a strong and vibrant civil society with the structures of the ANC and the [Tripartite] Alliance leading progressive forces and ensure the continued mobilisation of our people for transformation and reconstruction; Mobilising international support for our national goals as a country (both political and economic).[13]

Coursing throughout the document is a euphemized version of the 'sell-out' allegation, fuelled by a concern that the ANC's principles and strategic objective were in danger of being abdicated.[14] Underlying this is the assumption that the history of the democratic movement's struggle (and the discourses and theoretical underpinnings that have defined that struggle) are beyond reproach. The factors identified by the Youth League are all rooted in the post-1990 era.

Such approaches are inadequate and a-historical. The success of a liberation struggle tends to insulate from scrutiny the strategic frameworks, principles and decisions that steered the struggle towards victory. That these were, in some respects, problematic even in their historical contexts might be regarded as a quibbling matter – for, imperfect or not, they charted a comparatively victorious course. Yet, some of the conundrums and handicaps of the post-apartheid era have their origins in past decisions taken or shirked. Some of those decisions became invaluable ingredients in the eventual, though partial, success of 1994; others were of more dubious utility.

Prime in the former category would be the post-1949 radicalization of the ANC under the ideological mantle of African nationalism. This enabled the establishment of an encompassing unity which, to varying degrees, transcended or muffled class, gender, racial and ethnic divisions. It also provided the basis for the ANC's eventual achievement of hegemony among the anti-apartheid opposition. But it carried important costs: the subordination and active discouragement of class struggle through a reductionism that ascribed the reality of exploitation not only to a system of racial oppression but to the state form managing it, and the wholesale flattening of disparate interests and identities within the construct of 'the people'. Severely complicating efforts to transform post-apartheid South Africa are the very contradictions – principally, class and gender – that were submerged under the rubric of the national liberation struggle.

Related has been the SACP's CST thesis and the attendant division of its struggle for socialism into two stages: a national democratic revolution and a socialist revolution. This provided the theoretical basis for the symbiotic alliance between the SACP and ANC, an alliance which contributed considerably to the victory of 1994. There is no denying that the events of 1989 were a major factor in the SACP's subsequent disorientation which, since 1996, has shown signs of abetting. At the broadest level it swept from under the feet of the SACP, and other socialist and communist organizations worldwide, many of the precepts and tenets that had guided their thinking. But the disorientation lay imprinted also in CST, a thesis which, as the late Harold Wolpe noted, 'purports to rest on class relations of capitalist exploitation, [but] in fact treats such relations as residual', according them 'little or no role in the analysis of relations of dominance and exploitation, which are, instead, conceived of as occurring between "racial", "ethnic", and "national" categories'.[15] Later, Wolpe would question 'the contention within the internal colonialism thesis that racial domination serves to bind the classes within each group to a common struggle';[16] if nothing else, the transition has confirmed the folly of such assumptions. Class exploitation and national oppression are entangled in South Africa. The theoretical challenge facing the SACP (and the popular sector in general) is, as Bundy has written, 'to determine when and how they overlap and complement each other, and when and how they are analytically different' (1993:19).

As noted, there have been signs of a theoretical renewal, basically by appending Gramscian analysis to the CST thesis.[17] Also, the SACP has acknowledged that the two stages of revolution are not separated 'by a Chinese Wall' and, instead, form a continuum – hence its current slogan 'Build Socialism Now'.[18] But a searching debate is needed on whether and to what extent CST today serves as an adequate theoretical framework for the struggles advanced by the SACP. Its overriding analytical frame remains that of race, an important but, in itself, insufficient basis for analysing the dynamics of exploitation, as the transition has made clear. This suggestion is not intended, as Nyawuza charged in 1985, 'to change the orientation and language of our movement and all that we stand for'.[19] On the contrary. There is little cause for complacency about the short-term prospects of a popular hegemonic project. If the party's theoretical framework continues to escape scrutiny, it could find itself unable to emerge from its arrested development and its resultant failure to help define a clear strategy for the left.[20]

The gauntlet has been thrown down to the SACP and COSATU. In anguished tones, the SACP's Blade Nzimande and Jeremy Cronin in early 1997 noted 'a radical and curious shift' from earlier ANC positions. Critiquing the ANC's 1996 *The State and Social Transformation* strategy document, they lamented its 'slide into a technocratic, "class-neutral" approach to politics', accusing it of 'abandon[ing] transformation of existing power realities, and confin[ing] our democratic state to a regulatory role, overseeing "labour" and "capital", helping to co-operate'.[21] Correctly, they asked:

> Can we advance, deepen and defend the national democratic revolution without connecting, in practice, class and national struggles? Do the April 1994 elections simply draw a veil over past capitalist accumulation, and its present consequences? Or should we now, in the 'interest of social stability', just keep quiet about such matters?

The question was rhetorical, obviously. Yet, in attempting to rise to that challenge, the SACP (like the ANC) has to contend with considerable internal contradictions. Coursing through it are three, broad currents. Weaned on a diet of blunted political theory, is a rump of largely unreconstructed 'traditionalists' who appear, in equal measure, angered and dumbfounded by the post-1994 drift of the ANC. Ascendant is a loose grouping of neo-Marxists who are alert to the bankruptcy of orthodoxy and are pursuing a strategic and organizational revival. But arrayed within the party also are powerful 'realists' (exemplified by trade and industry minister Alec Erwin) who argue that global realities preclude an overtly popular path towards transformation, at least for the time being. Like the ebb and flow of the tides, it is not easy to discern where one ends and the other begins.

Complicating matters is a lack of unanimity over the utility of continuing the alliance with the ANC in its current form. Provisionally, the consensus is to redefine the party 'in the context of an ANC-led alliance'. But as the SACP's 1996 strategy document admitted, 'there is a debate in our party about the wisdom of this'. That debate encompasses four scenarios, some of which overlap almost imperceptively.

The first is the Split Scenario. It implies that the ANC has resigned itself to the limited panorama of change that seems imprinted in the transition, leaving the national democratic revolution arrested in a phase that consolidates formal democracy and a political-economy that is geared mainly at servicing the aspirations of an emerging black élite, the black *petit bourgeoisie,* and the demands of the incumbent privileged classes. But an explicit parting of ways seems unlikely. Because the currents spilling through the party blur into one another, dissolving the alliance will also generate splits inside the party. Faced with the choice of pursuing careers and political goals inside the ANC or wandering into the wilderness with a detached SACP, many prominent members will opt for the former route. Moreover, the party's uneven political education leaves it unable to swiftly prepare members for such a radical break with history and tradition.

The real debate is between three other scenarios. Favoured on the left of the SACP is a continuing bid to struggle for the 'heart and soul' of the ANC. The aim is to ensure that the thrust of ANC policies clearly favours the 'interests and concerns of the working class as a whole, and the broader rural and urban poor' (SACP, 1996:15). In short, it presumes that the ANC's class and social bias is not immanent and fixed, but remains (in that hoary cliché) a 'terrain of struggle'. Hence, the ANC can be weaned from a role in which it basically serves as the political manager of a new ruling bloc that shores up privilege. In Cronin's words, 'we're not just looking for a gap in the market so we can hoist the red flag – we're hoping the ANC plays a more effective role as a liberation organisation'.[22] This scenario demands that the SACP more openly challenges government policies and practices that contradict its vision of transformation, develops alternative policies, engages more forthrightly in popular actions, as well as revitalizes and democratizes ANC and alliance structures.

Flanking it is another, comparatively a-historical and revivalist approach – a Watchdog Scenario which presumes that the ANC's purported working class bias is constant and remains intact. The challenge is to ensure that the commitments imprinted in that bias (and expressed in the RDP, for instance) are heeded and resolutely advanced by the ANC. This would demand acceptance of the broad parameters of government policies which, however, have to be held in line with RDP objectives. For example, while recoiling from the neo-liberal, 'trickle-down' character of the GEAR strategy, supporters of such an approach contend that abandoning GEAR would unleash disastrous and punitive reactions from the market. Instead, the SACP is urged to 'engage Gear and try to give it its most favourable RDP spin' – by ensuring, for example, that progressive budget reform accompanies its budget deficit slashing efforts, or that tariff cuts yield demonstrable benefits to poor households.[23] Achieving this also requires democratizing policy- and decision-making to prevent those processes from becoming hived off further into 'narrow technocratic circles'. The difference between these two scenarios is subtle, allowing party figures to commute between them, depending on the issues at hand.

Starkly different is the current reality, that of a Hostage Scenario in which the SACP is strapped into the envelope of government 'pragmatism'. Its influence and authority in policy- and decision-making have been severely cramped and its attempts to dispute dominant perspectives smothered in a context where dissent has been discouraged. Thus, the SACP found itself sternly rebuked for criticizing GEAR in late 1996, a tripartite alliance meeting was not informed of the decision to shut down the RDP national office days later and GEAR became government policy without prior discussion in the alliance (or ANC) structures. In this scenario, debate tends to be encouraged in fits and starts, minor concessions are sometimes proffered, but the boundaries of dissent have been staked out and are decisively patrolled.

The function of this route is to task the SACP with 'policing' the left, tempering unhappiness about government policies and, essentially, acting as a bulwark against any bid to mount overt, leftist challenges against government conduct and policies. It adds up to coerced political stability. The prize for supporters of this scenario (and top ANC figures count among them) is the gradual dissolution of the SACP as an independent political force possibly allied with COSATU in more forthright pursuit of a popular agenda – and, with it, the disintegration of a potential left-wing challenge evolving within and around the party. But this would generate increasingly inchoate and reckless reactions to unpopular policies in the broader body politic. The danger is that it creates a Frankenstein's monster, as disaffected layers peel off (from the SACP and ANC) and retreat into unruly apathy or seek refuge in the soapbox populism exemplified by figures like expelled ANC leader Bantu Holomisa. The outcome is not a 'disciplined' or 'responsible' left flank but a decimated one. The effect is to midwife not a coherent opposition that can enliven a pluralist democracy but a fitful accretion of defiance and disruption which would invite, at best, disdain and, at worst, repression. The upshot would be less, not more stability.

Whether the SACP can unknot the bonds of this Hostage Scenario is unclear. Coursing through ANC ranks are burgeoning anti-communist sentiments which, increasingly, are allied to an aversion towards dissent and heterodoxy, an antipathy mustered and justified under the mantle of 'stability' and 'unity'.

The ANC itself is at a crossroads – not one which will occasion its disaggregation as mainstream pundits tirelessly predict, but one that will force it to more explicitly acknowledge and respond to the *overlapping* interests and tendencies that cohabit within it. The signal event will be Nelson Mandela's retirement. South Africa's providence was that Mandela created a temporary recess in which a sense of unity or nationhood could sink a few tenuous roots. Mandela's historic feat was not only to have helped steer South Africa away from the brink of catastrophe but to have carved out a breathing space where pulses could settle, enmities subdue and affinities become recast.

That interval of reconciliation and precarious stability has commonly been confused with a transition that still has to run its course. It befalls Mandela's successor – deputy president Thabo Mbeki – to oversee what remains a struggle to determine which alliance of social forces will shape the new South Africa.

The grand authority and mythical stature attained by Mandela enabled him to 'float above politics' (in the manner of Charles De Gaulle), unencumbered by the realpolitik of his party and the attendant need to shore up personal power bases. Mandela's success lay in his ability to *traverse* many of the contradictions at play in South African society and the ANC – the 'modern' and the 'traditional', black and white, privilege and deprivation – a feat made possible by personal attributes and by the assiduously constructed mythos that surrounds him. That luxury will not be available to his successor, who will have to wield authority in more conventional ways – by building and fortifying a core base, and constantly cultivating and buttressing support among particular interest groups. With Mandela's departure, South Africa passes from the era of the statesman to the era of the politician, from a dependency on the personal charisma of a leader to reliance on public institutions and democratized political culture. With it comes more intrigue, conflict, uncertainty and, possibly, instability. But it also promises to render more transparent and clearly delineated the tensions that course through society and the ANC.

Submerging contesting interests within the meta-discourse of non-racial unity and reconciliation will become considerably more difficult. More likely is the deployment of increasingly ambiguous variants of African nationalism as stabilizing and disciplinary devices to draw the boundaries of permissible dissent – by distinguishing 'legitimate' interests, activities and criticism from 'deviant' or 'destabilizing' ones.[24] The shift is already evident in the fashionable rhetoric about the need to build a black 'patriotic bourgeoisie' and the casting of criticism in racial terms.[25] Indeed, speeches by Thabo Mbeki during 1997 indicated that the language of African nationalism, perhaps stripped to an 'Africanist' format, would become vigorously invoked to serve as a unifying canopy. For, in Mbeki's view,

> ... running like a structural fault through [post-apartheid South Africa] and weaving it together into a frightening bundle of imbalance and inequality is the question of race colour.[26]

That racism functions as a key dynamic of exploitation is clear; that is represents *the* fundamental fault-line separating privilege from deprivation in post-apartheid South Africa is questionable, as 4 000 mineworkers facing retrenchment at a mine of the black-owned Johannesburg Consolidated Investments discovered in May, 1997. Such a discourse serves as a screen obscuring the other dynamics that lie at the root of inequality in society and which animate dissent and resistance. In such formulations contradictions of class, gender and geography are made to disappear into a twilight zone of race and colour.

However, this discursive shift is unlikely to halt the disaggregation of interests in the ANC, which, after all, are symptomatic of broader social dynamics. No longer stirred into a soup of presumed common mindedness, they can be expressed and pursued in more forthright fashion. Within the ANC such a process could give rise to – or be propelled by prior – calls for platforms within the party, similar to those established in Brazil's Workers' Party, reinvigorating its languishing structures and putting the organization on a more genuinely democratic footing. The effects would spill into the broader movement.

Confounding a popular project, meanwhile, are the multifold conceptual, strategic, organizational and financial difficulties that plague its constituent organizations. In the case of COSATU, these are compounded by other towering dilemmas: the pressures aimed at dislodging it from the broader movement and pushing it towards economic unionism, the corresponding need to (re)define the terms of its participation in tripartite forums such as NEDLAC, and the questions surrounding its continued alliance with the ANC. Overshadowing these complications is the unconcealed arrogance and power of capital, the dominant discourse of liberalization, deregulation, privatization and the like, the prescriptive weight of WTO, World Bank and IMF strictures, the destabilizing encroachments of global capital and the marginalized economic and geo-political status of South Africa.

We are living in a trying age, when, as Colin Bundy has noted wryly,

... revolutionary optimism looks like a cruel joke. We have no prospect of a quick victory or even a clear model of what that victory will look like ... The left is left defending the aims of 150 years of struggle, acknowledging the reality of defeat and evaluating the reasons for it, regrouping and preparing for the second wave of revolutionary struggle. It is an agenda of years and decades.[27]

The process of rebuilding cannot occur by way of blueprint. But neither would it be provident to hitch one's hopes expectantly to some organic alchemy. The obstacles obstructing progress are no longer opaque, as the candid assessments in COSATU's September Commission report demonstrated in late 1997. They demand concerted and pointed remedies – and the courage to interrogate the truisms of old.

At the same time, the social and political transmutations generated by the transition are spawning new forms of organizations that will accompany and even spur this process of renewal, particularly at grassroots level. Perplexing as they might seem at first, their novelty should not invite dismissal, neither should the fact that they tend not to slot neatly into the political, ideological and sectoral categories inherited from the past. South Africans are beginning to coalesce and organize at local level around distinct sets of interests that, historically, were subsumed under the mantle of the anti-apartheid struggle. The ideological weight of that struggle will continue to dissipate and give rise to organized expressions of interests that break with the catch-all categories of the past. The proliferation of local women's initiatives is one, pertinent example of this growing trend. Also, ostensibly 'opportunist' initiatives (land invasions and electricity pirating are good examples) not only represent profound social (and economic) dynamics but are unfairly dismissed out-of-hand as strictly disruptive phenomena. Such organizations and activities are neither intrinsically 'progressive' nor 'reactionary'. Rather, they reflect powerful changes that are occurring both within grassroots layers of society, and between them and other sites of power. Most obviously, these call into question the legitimacy, representativeness and utility of some traditional structures, notably civics. They also represent a shift that sees publics assuming and acting upon more specific social identities, in contrast to the enveloping, homogenizing categories that served the anti-apartheid struggle. Thus, the emptiness of notions such as 'the landless' or 'the rural poor' is vividly evident in the emergence of organizations that seek to represent, for instance, women labour tenants, or in the struggles unleashed within communities that have returned to land dispossessed under apartheid.

A further trend relates to the different levels at which political power is contested and exercised. By 1997, signs were emerging that the statist fixations of the past were being slowly eroded by the exigencies of reality.

The process appeared to be propelled by several, intertwined factors: the modest developmental imprints of the state at the 'community level', the conservative macroeconomic context within which the reconstruction and development enterprise proceeds, and the technocratic and rarefied processes adopted by national and provincial governments. Increasingly, the social and political gaze of citizens is directed both at the central and the more localized levels – hence, the surge of self-help initiatives, new grass-roots formations and the plethora of sub- and illegal activities. Politically, the trend was evident also in the ANC members' defiance of national injunctions to elect hand-picked provincial ANC chairs,[28] while analysts like Mark Swilling have forecast significant shifts at the local and provincial levels towards populist and leftist candidates:

> The emergence of provincial leadership of this sort is an international trend that many governments which have adopted neoliberal economic policies are struggling with. They have found strong leftward shifts at the provincial and local government level.[29]

For the popular forces the upshot is a state of flux and of multifold realignments that will extend well into the next millennium. The challenges that await resolution – the redistribution of wealth, opportunity and resources – will test the firmness of the democratic bedrock laid since 1994 and the authenticity of the new South Africa. They cut to the heart of the liberation struggle and expose afresh the fault lines that fissure the society.

Novel as these challenges are, the popular forces have weathered worse, as those who recall the 'dark decade' of the 1960s will attest. The traditions they draw on are not simply those of valiant struggle against seemingly insurmountable odds but the capacity for invention and creativity, as the 1970s and 1980s demonstrate. In an epoch marked by despondency and cynicism, they remain animated by the impulse to struggle for what *might be* against *what is* ... attributes which can pierce the barriers to change arrayed before them.

Notes

1 *Notes of a Native Son*, 1955.
2 Thanks to Dot Keet for sharing her notes on some of these matters.
3 Grafting together verses from *Nkosi Sikelel' iAfrika* and the Afrikaner-nationalist *Die Stem*.
4 For a survey of the early debates surrounding amnesty, see Marais and Narsoo (1992) and Marais (1993b).
5 Neville Alexander, cited in Rhoodie and Liebenberg (1994:31).
6 See Habermas (1992).
7 As suggested by Contralesa's consideration of forming a new political party to defend the rights of traditional chiefs. See *SouthScan*, Vol. 12, No. 22 (13 June 1997).
8 As phrased in the Uruguayan context by former president Julio Maria Sanguinetti in 1986, cited in Marais and Narsoo (1992:9).

9 Imbedded in whites' anxieties about South Africa's 'crime wave' is a related, racist subtext: a sense of siege and insecurity effected by criminals who, almost by defini- tion in this discourse, are black. In this sense, the 'crime wave' serves as an informal validation of whites' fears of post-liberation retribution.

10 Indeed, South Africa's absurdly large luxury car industry is subsidized in large part by lavish vehicle allowances issued to employees by the corporate sector and the state.

11 ANCY(1996).

12 *Ibid.*, p. 2.

13 *Ibid.*, p. 3.

14 Hence, the repeated references to the ANC's 1994 *Strategy and Tactics* document, and its definition of the party's 'strategic objective as the transformation of our coun- try into a united, democratic, non-racial, non-sexist and prosperous society'.

15 Wolpe. H., 1975, 'The Theory of Internal Colonialism: The South African Case' in Oxaal, I. *et al.*, *Beyond the Sociology of Development*, London, cited by Bundy (1989:9–10).

16 Wolpe (1988:32).

17 See SACP (1996).

18 Making explicit Joe Slovo's 'rather obvious proposition, namely, that it is implied in the very concept of stages that they can never by considered in isolation'; see his *The South African Working Class and the National Democratic Revolution* (1988).

19 See Nyawuza (1985).

20 Parts of Slovo's *The South African Working Class and the National Democratic Revolution* offered the pretence of re-assessment, but proceeded by way of self- validating arguments to demonstrate the inviolability of CST while heaping invective on left critics (bracketed throughout by inverted commas). Thus, he could approve of 'the recent spread of an understanding of the link between *national domination* and *class exploitation* among organised sectors of the working class', while attributing this 'primarily to the heightened experiences of the struggle *against race domination*' (emphasis in text).

21 Nazimande and Cronin (1997).

22 Author's interview, April 1997.

23 Davies (1997:4–5).

24 Less obvious is the extent to which the 'war against crime' aids new distinctions between the legitimate and the illegitimate. The demonization of criminals and the elevation of law and order to a national priority provides a potential bedrock for the criminalization of land invasions, strikes and other protests actions.

25 Examples abound, such as the ANC's reaction to reports linking top ANC Women's League officials to privatized deportation camp, Lindela, near Johannesburg: ANC press statements slammed critics for opposing 'black economic empowerment'. In May 1997, the ANC accused critical black journalists of merely trying to curry favour with their white superiors.

26 Speech to Parliament, 10 June 1997; see 'White people resisting change in SA – Mbeki', *Business Day,* 11 June 1997.

27 Bundy (1993:17).

28 Northern Province delegates in late 1996 voted George Mashamba in as chair, despite a personal plea from Mandela to back the incumbent. In September 1997, Gauteng delegates chose Mathole Motshekga over the ANC national leadership's preferred candidate, Rev. Frank Chikane.

29 'Who needs the provinces?', *Mail and Guardian*, 12 September 1997.

Bibliography

Adelzadeh, A. & Padayachee, P., 1995, 'The RDP White Paper: Reconstruction of a Development Vision?', *Transformation* (February), Durban

Africa Watch, 1991, *The Killings in South Africa*, Human Rights Watch, New York

Alexander, N., 1993, 'Nation-building: An Interview', *Work in Progress*, No. 93 (November), Johannesburg

Amin, S., 1997, 'For a Progressive and Democratic New World Order' (seminar paper), Cairo

Amin, S., 1996, 'Regionalisation in the Third World', Third World Forum document, Dakar

Amin, S., 1993, 'SA in the Global Economic System', *Work in Progress*, No. 87 (March), Johannesburg

Amin, S., 1992, 'The Perils of Utopia', *Work in Progress*, No. 86 (December), Johannesburg

Amin, S., 1985, *Delinking*, Monthly Review Press, New York

Amin, S., Arrighi, G., Frank, A. G. & Wallerstein, I., 1990, *Transforming the Revolution: Social Movements and the World-system*, Monthly Review Press, New York

ANC (African National Congress), 1994, *Reconstruction and Development Programme: A Policy Framework* (base document), Umanyo, Johannesburg

ANC NEC (African National Congress, National Executive Committee), 1992, 'Negotiations: A Strategic Perspective', *African Communist*, No. 131 (4th Quarter), Johannesburg

ANC/SACP/COSATU, 1995, 'The Need for an Effective ANC-led Political Centre', endorsed Tripartite Alliance strategic perspectives paper published in *African Communist*, No. 142 (3rd Quarter), Johannesburg

ANCYL (African National Congress Youth League), 1996, 'Organisational and Leadership Issues in the ANC: A Perspective of the ANC Youth League' (discussion document), Johannesburg

Anon, 1997, 'Compromising Positions', *Development Update*, Vol. 1, No. 1 (June), Johannesburg

Anon, 1994, 'The RDP White Paper: Special Feature', *RDP Monitor*, (1)2 (August/September), Johannesburg

Anon, 1990, 'Prospects for a Negotiated Settlement', *African Communist*, No. 122 (3rd Quarter), Johannesburg

Baker, P., Boraine, A. & Krafchik, W. (eds), 1993, *South Africa and the World Economy in the 1990s*, David Philip, Cape Town

Balibar, E. & Wallerstein, I., 1991, *Race, Nation, Class: Ambiguous Identities*, Verso Books, London

Barrel, H., 1991, 'The Turn to the Masses: the African National Congress's Strategic Review of 1978–79', *Journal of Southern African Studies*, Vol. 18, No. 1 (March), York

Barrel, H., 1990, *MK, the ANC's Armed Struggle*, Penguin Books, Johannesburg

Barrett, J., 1993, 'New Strategies to Organise Difficult Sectors', *SA Labour Bulletin*, Vol. 17, No. 6 (November/December), Johannesburg

Baskin, J. (ed.), 1996a, *Against the Current: Labour and Economic Policy in South Africa*, Ravan Press, Johannesburg

Baskin, J., 1996b, 'Unions at the Crossroads', *SA Labour Bulletin*, Vol. 20, No. 1 (February), Johannesburg

Baskin, J., 1995, 'South Africa's New LRA', *SA Labour Bulletin*, Vol. 19, No. 5 (November), Johannesburg

Baskin, J., 1991, *Striking Back: A History of Cosatu*, Ravan Press, Johannesburg

Beaudet, P., 1991, 'Civics: A New Social Movement?' (mimeo), CIDMAA, Montreal

Beaudet, P. & Marais, H. (eds), 1995, *Popular Movements and the Struggle for Transformation in South Africa*, Alternatives, Montreal

Beaudet, P. & Theade, N. (eds), 1994, *Southern Africa after Apartheid?*, McMillan, London

Bethlehem, L. & Makgetla, N., 1994, 'Wages and Productivity in South African Manufacturing', *SA Labour Bulletin*, Vol. 18, No. 4 (September), Johannesburg

Beckman, B., 1993, 'The Liberation of Civil Society: Neoliberal Ideology and Political Theory', *Review of African Political Economy*, No. 58, Sheffield

Bienefield, M., 1994, 'The New World Order: Echoes of a New Imperialism', *Third World Quarterly*, Vol. 15, No. 1, Oxfordshire

Bird, A. & Schreiner, G., 1992, 'Cosatu at the Crossroads: Towards Tripartite Corporatism or Democratic Socialism', *SA Labour Bulletin*, Vol. 16, No. 6 (July/August), Johannesburg

Blackburn, R. (ed.), 1991, *After the Fall: The Failure of Communism and the Future of Socialism*, Verso Books, London

Bobbio, N., 1979, 'Gramsci and the Conception of Civil Society' in C. Mouffe (ed.), *Gramsci and Marxist Theory*, Routledge, London

Bond, P. et al., 1996a, 'The State of Neo-liberalism in South Africa: Economic, Social and Health Transformation in Question', *International Journal of Health Services*, Vol. 26, No. 4

Bond, P., 1996b, 'An International Perspective on the "People-driven" Character of the RDP', *African Communist*, No. 144 (2nd Quarter), Johannesburg

Bond, P., 1996c, 'The Making of South Africa's Macro-economic Compromise' in E. Maganya (ed.), *Development Strategies in South Africa*, IFAA, Johannesburg

Bond, P., 1994a, 'Reconstruction and Development during Structural Crisis', *African Communist*, No. 138 (3rd Quarter), Johannesburg

Bond, P., 1994b, 'The RDP, Site of Socialist Struggle', *African Communist*, No. 137 (2nd Quarter), Johannesburg

Bond, P., 1994c, 'Election in South Africa', *International Viewpoint* (May)

Bond, P., 1991a, 'Theory of Economy', Pambile pamphlet series, Johannesburg.

Bond, P., 1991b, *Commanding Heights and Community Control: New Economics for a New South Africa*, Ravan Press, Johannesburg

Bottomore, T., 1983, *A Dictionary of Marxist Thought*, Harvard University Press, Cambridge

Bowles, P. & White, G., 1993, 'Central Bank Independence: A Political Economy Approach and the Implications for the South' (draft paper)

Brittain, V., 1994, 'Africa, the Lost Continent', *New Statesman & Society* (8 April), London

Budlender, D. 1997, *The Women's Budget*, Idasa, Cape Town

Budlender, D. *et al.*, 1992, 'Women and Resistance in South Africa: Review Article', *Social Dynamics*, Vol. 18, No. 1, Cape Town

Buhlungu, S., 1997, 'Flogging a Dying Horse? Cosatu and the Alliance', *SA Labour Bulletin*, Vol. 21, No. 1 (February), Johannesburg

Bundy, C., 1993, 'Theory of a Special Type', *Work in Progress*, No. 89 (June), Johannesburg

Bundy, C., 1991, 'Marxism in South Africa: Context, Themes and Challenges', *Transformation*, No. 16, Durban

Bundy, C., 1989, 'Around Which Corner? Revolutionary Theory and Contemporary South Africa', *Transformation*, No. 8, Durban

Bundy, C., 1987, 'History, Revolution and South Africa', *Transformation*, No. 4, Durban

Bundy, C., 1979, *The Rise and Fall of the South African Peasantry*, Heinemann, London

Cabesa, Quadro, 1986, 'From Ungovernability to Revolution', *African Communist*, No. 104 (1st Quarter), Johannesburg

Callinicos, A., 1992, *Between Apartheid and Capitalism*, Bookmarks, London

Carroll, W. K., 1992, *Organizing Dissent: Contemporary Social Movements in Theory and Practice*, Garamond Press, Toronto

Casanova, Pablo G., 1997, 'The Theory of the Rain Forest against Neoliberalism and for Humanity', (AAPSO conference paper), Cairo

Casanova, Pablo G., 1996, 'Globalism, Neoliberalism and Democracy', *Social Justice*, Vol. 23, Nos 1–2, San Francisco

Cassim, F., 1988, 'Growth, Crisis and Change in the South African Economy' in J. Suckling & L. White (eds), *After Apartheid: Renewal of the South African Economy*, James Currey, London

Castaneda, Jorge G., 1994, *Utopia Unarmed: The Latin American Left after the Cold War*, Vintage, New York

Cawthra, G., Kraak, G. & O'Sullivan, G., 1994, *War and Resistance*, MacMillan, London

Cole, J., 1987, *Crossroads: The Politics of Reform and Repression 1976–1986*, Ravan Press, Johannesburg

Collins, D., 1994, 'Worker Control', *SA Labour Bulletin*, Vol. 18, No. 3 (July), Johannesburg

Community Consistuency in NEDLAC, 1996, 'Return to the RDP' (discussion document), Johannesburg

Connell, D., 1995, 'What's Left of the South African Left?', *Against the Current*, (September), Detroit

Cope, N., 1990, 'The Zulu Petit Bourgeoisie and Zulu Nationalism in the 1920s', *Journal of Southern African Studies*, Vol. 16, No. 3 (September), York

Crankshaw, O., 1993, 'On the Doorstep of Management', *SA Sociological Review*, Vol. 6 No. 1, Pretoria

Cronin, J., 1995a, 'The RDP Needs Class Struggle', *African Communist*, No. 142 (3rd Quarter), Johannesburg

Cronin, J., 1995b, 'Challenging the Neo-liberal Agenda in South Africa', *Links*, No. 4 (January–March), Broadway

Cronin, J., 1994a, 'Sell-out, or the Culminating Moment? Trying to Make Sense of the Transition', paper presented to University of Witwatersrand History Workshop (July), Johannesburg

Cronin, J., 1994b, 'The Present Situation and the Challenges for the South African left' (discussion document, July), Johannesburg

Cronin, J., 1994c, 'Towards a People-Driven RDP', *African Communist*, No. 138 (3rd Quarter), Johannesburg

Cronin, J. & Naidoo, Jayendra, 1994d, 'Implementing and Co-ordinating the RDP through Government, the Alliance, Democratic Mass and Community-based Formations, and Institutions of Civil Society', unpublished, Johannesburg

Cronin, J., 1992, 'The Boat, the Tap and the Leipzig Way', *African Communist*, No. 130, Johannesburg

Davidson *et al.*, 1977, *Southern Africa: The New Politics of Revolution*, Penguin, Harmondsworth

Davies, R., 1997, 'Engaging with the GEAR' (discussion paper, March), Cape Town

Davies, R., 1995, 'The International Context', *African Communist*, No. 139/140 (1st Quarter), Johannesburg

Davies, R., 1992a, *Integration or Cooperation in a Post-Apartheid South Africa*, Centre for Southern African Studies, Cape Town

Davies, R., 1992b, 'Emerging Southern African Perspectives on Regional Cooperation and Integration After Apartheid', *Transformation*, No. 20, Durban

Davies, R., Keet, D. & Nkuhlu, M., 1993, *Reconstructing Economic Relations with the Southern African Region: Issues and options for a Democratic South Africa*, MERG, Cape Town

Davies, R., O'Meara, D. & Dlamini S., 1985, *The Struggle for South Africa: A Reference Guide to Movements, Organizations and Institutions*, Zed Books, London

De Landa, Manuel, 1991, *War in the Age of Intelligent Machines*, Zone Books, New York

Department of Finance, 1996, *Growth, Employment and Redistribution: A Macroeconomic Strategy*, Department of Finance, Pretoria

Dexter, P., 1996, '75 Years of the South African Communist Party', *SA Labour Bulletin*, Vol. 20, No. 4 (August), Johannesburg

Dexter, P., 1995a, 'The Big Myth – Sunset Clauses and the Public Service', *African Communist*, No. 139/140 (1st Quarter), Johannesburg

Dexter, P., 1995b, 'The RDP: Ensuring Transformation through the State and Popular Transformation', *SA Labour Bulletin*, Vol. 19, No. 4 (September), Johannesburg

Dexter, P., 1994, 'Make the RDP Make the Left', *Work in Progress*, No. 95 (February/March), Johannesburg

Dikeni, S., 1994, 'How the West Was Lost', *Die Suid-Afrikaan* (November), Cape Town

Ellis, S. & Sechaba, T., 1992, *Comrades Against Apartheid: The ANC and the South African Communist Party in Exile*, James Currey & Indiana University Press, London & Bloomington

Erwin, A., 1994, 'The RDP: A View from the Tripartite Alliance', *SA Labour Bulletin*, Vol. 18, No. 1 (January/February), Johannesburg

Erwin, A., 1990, South Africa's Post-apartheid Economy: Planning for Prosperity, *SA Labour Bulletin*, Vol. 14, No. 6, Johannesburg

Erwin, A., 1989, 'Thoughts on a Planned Economy', *Work in Progress*, No. 61 (September–October), Johannesburg

Esterhuysen, P. (ed.), 1994, *South Africa in Subequatorial Africa: Economic Integration*, Africa Institute of South Africa, Pretoria

Etkind, R. & Harvey, S., 1993, 'The Workers' Cease Fire', *SA Labour Bulletin*, Vol. 17, No. 5 (September/October), Johannesburg

Everatt, D., 1992, *Consolidated CASE Reports on the Reef Violence*, Community Agency for Social Enquiry, Johannesburg

Everatt, D., 1991, 'Alliance Politics of a Special Type: the Roots of the ANC/SACP Alliance, 1950–1954', *Journal of Southern African Studies*, Vol. 18, No. 1 (March), York

Fallon, P. *et al.*, 1994, 'South Africa: Economic Performance and Policies', *Informal Discussion Papers on Aspects of the Economy of South Afroca No. 7*, World Bank, Washington

Fine, A. & Webster, E., 1989, 'Transcending Traditions: Trade Unions and Political Unity', *South African Review No. 5*, Ravan Press, Johannesburg

Fine, B., 1995, 'Politics and Economics in ANC Economic Policy: A Polemic?', *African Affairs*

Fine, R., 1992, 'Civil Society Theory and the Politics of Transition in South Africa', *Review of African Political Economy*, No. 55, Sheffield

Fine, R. & Davis, D., 1990, *Beyond Apartheid: Labour and Liberation in South Africa*, Ravan Press, Johannesburg

Fine, R. & Davis, D., 1985, 'Political Strategies and the State: Some Historical Observations', *Journal of Southern African Studies*, Vol. 12, No. 1 (October), York

Forsythe, P. & Mare, G., 1992, 'Natal in the New South Africa' in G. Moss & I. Obery (eds), *South African Review No. 6*, Ravan Press, Johannesburg

Frank, A. G., 1991, 'No Escape from the Laws of World Economics', *Review of African Political Economy*, No. 50, Sheffield

Freund, B., 1994a, 'The Magic Circle', *Indicator SA,* Vol. 11, No. 2 (Autumn), Durban

Freund, B., 1994b, 'South Africa and World Economy', *Transformation*, No. 23, Durban

Freund, B., 1994c, 'The RDP: Half Full?', *Southern Africa Report*, Vol. 9, No. 5 (July), Toronto

Friedman, S., 1993a, *The Elusive Community: The Dynamics of Negotiated Urban Development*, Centre for Policy Studies, Johannesburg

Friedman, S. (ed.), 1993b, *The Long Journey: South Africa's Quest for a Negotiated Settlement*, Ravan Press, Johannesburg.

Friedman, S., 1991, 'An Unlikely Utopia: State and Civil Society in South Africa', *Politikon*, Vol. 19, No. 1 (December), Durban

Friedman, S., 1987, *Building Tomorrow Today: African Workers in Trade Unions 1970–1984*, Ravan Press, Johannesburg

Friedman, S., 1987, 'The Struggle within the Struggle: South African Resistance Strategies', *Transformation*, No. 3, Durban

Gelb, S., 1994, 'Development Prospects for South Africa', paper presented to WIDER workshop on Medium Term Development Strategy, Phase II, Helsinki (15–17 April)

Gelb, S. (ed.), 1991, *South Africa's Economic Crisis*, David Philip & Zed Books, Cape Town & London

Gelb, S., 1990, 'Democratising Economic Growth: Alternative Growth Models for the Future', *Transformation*, No. 12, Durban

Gelb, S., 1987, 'Making Sense of the Crisis', *Transformation*, No. 5, Durban

Gevisser, M., 1994, 'Crossing the Line', *Work in Progress*, Special Supplement , No. 96 (April), Johannesburg

Ghosh, J., 1997, 'India's Structural Adjustment: An Assessment in Comparative Asian context' (seminar paper), Jawaharial Nehru University, New Delhi

Godongwana, E., 1994a, 'Cosatu Approaches a Crossroads', *Southern Africa Report*, Vol. 9, No. 5 (July), Toronto

Godongwana, E., 1994b, 'Industrial Restructuring and the Social Contract', *SA Labour Bulletin*, Vol. 16, No. 4 (March/April), Johannesburg

Godongwana, E., 1992, 'Industrial Restructuring and the Social Contract: Reforming Capitalism or Building Blocks for Socialism?', *SA Labour Bulletin*, Vol. 16, No. 4 (March/April), Johannesburg

Godsell, B., 1994, 'The Reconstruction and Development Programme: A View from Business', *SA Labour Bulletin*, Vol. 18, No. 1 (January/February), Johannesburg

Gordon, David M., 1988, 'The Global Economy: New Edifice or Crumbling Foundations?', *New Left Review*, No. 168 (March–April), London

Gorz, A., 1973, 'Reform and Revolution', *Socialism and Revolution*, Anchor Books, New York

Govender, P. *et al.*, 1994, 'Beijing Conference Report: 1994 Country Report on the Status of South African Women', Cape Town

Government of South Africa, 1994, *RDP White Paper*, Cape Town

Gramsci, A., 1971, *Selections from the Prison Notebooks*, Lawrence & Wishart, London

Habermas, J., 1992, 'Citizenship and National Identity', *Praxis International*, Vol. 12, No. 2

Habermas, J. 1986, *Autonomy and Solidarity*, Verso Books, London

Hall, S. & Jacques, M. (eds), 1989, *New Times: The Changing Face of Politics in the 1990s*, Macmillan, London

Hani, C., 1992, 'Hani Opens Up' (Interview), *Work in Progress*, No. 82 (June), Johannesburg

Hanlon, J., 1994, 'Making People-driven Development Work', report of the Commission on Development Finance for the SA National Civic Organisation, Johannesburg

Hanlon, J., 1986a, *Apartheid's Second Front: South Africa's War against its Neighbours*, Penguin, Middlesex

Hanlon, J., 1986b, *Beggar Your Neighbours*, James Currey, London

Harris, L., 1993a, 'One Step Forward ...', *Work in Progress*, No. 89 (June), Johannesburg

Harris, L., 1993b, 'South Africa's Social and Economic Transformation: From No Middle Way to No Alternative', *Review of African Political Economy*, No. 57, Sheffield

Harris, L., 1990, 'The Economic Strategies and Policies of the African National Congress', *McGregor's Economic Alternatives*, Juta, Cape Town

Hart, G., 1994, 'The New Economic Policy and Redistribution in Malaysia: A Model for Post-apartheid South Africa?', *Transformation*, No. 23, Durban

Hassim, S., 1991, 'Gender, Social Location and Feminist Politics in South Africa', *Transformation*, No. 15, Durban

Hindson, D., 1991, 'The Restructuring of Labour Markets in South Africa: 1970s and 1980s' in S. Gelb (ed.), 1991, *South Africa's Economic Crisis*, David Philip & Zed Books, Cape Town & London

Hindson, D. & Morris, M., 1992, 'Political Violence: Reform and Reconstruction', *Review of African Political Economy*, No. 53, Sheffield

Hobsbawm, E., 1996, 'Identity Politics and the Left', *New Left Review*, No. 217 (May/June), London

Hobsbawm, E., 1995, *Age of Extremes: The Short Twentieth Century*, Abacus, London

Holloway, J., 1994, 'Global Capital and the National State', *Capital and Class*, No. 52, London

Horn, P., 1991, 'Conference on Women and Gender in Southern Africa: Another View of the Dynamics', *Transformation*, No. 15, Durban

Human Rights Commission, 1991, *The New Total Strategy*, Human Rights Commission, Johannesburg

ILO, 1996, *Restructuring the Labour Market: The South African Challenge* (ILO Country Review), Geneva

Industrial Strategy Project, 1994, 'Industrial Strategy for South Africa: The Recommendations of the ISP', *SA Labour Bulletin*, Vol. 18, No. 4 (January–February), Johannesburg

JEP & CASE, 1993, 'Putting Youth on the National Agenda: Seven Reports (conference document), CASE & JEP, Johannesburg

Joffe, A., Kaplan D., Kaplinsky, R. & Lewis, D., 1994a, 'Meeting the Global Challenge: A Framework for Industrial Revival in South Africa' in *South Africa and the World Economy in the 1990s*, Cape Town, David Philip

Joffe, A., Kaplan D., Kaplinsky, R. & Lewis, D., 1994b, 'An Industrial Strategy for a Post-apartheid South Africa', *Institute for Development Studies Bulletin*, Vol. 25, No. 1, IDS, Sussex

Jordan, P., 1992a, 'Strategic Debate in the ANC: A Response to Joe Slovo', *African Communist*, No. 131 (4th Quarter), Johannesburg

Jordan, P., 1992b, 'Has Socialism Failed? The South African Debate', *Southern Africa Report* (January), Toronto

Kagarlitsky, B., 1995a, *The Mirage of Modernization*, Monthly Review Press, New York

Kagarlitsky, B., 1995b, 'Letter to South Africa', *Links*, No. 4 (January–March), New Course Publications, Newtown (Australia)

Kagarlitsky, B., 1989, *The Dialectics of Change*, Verso Books, London

Kahn, B., 1991, 'Exchange Rate Policy and Industrial Restructuring' in G. Moss & I. Obery (eds), *South African Review No. 6*, Ravan Press, Johannesburg

Kaplan, D., 1991, 'The South African Capital Goods Sector and the Economic Crisis' in S. Gelb (ed.), *South Africa's Economic Crisis*, David Philip & Zed Books, Cape Town & London

Kaplan, D., 1990, 'Recommendations on Post-Apartheid Economic Policy', *Transformation*, No. 12, Durban

Kaplinksy, R., 1994, '"Economic Restructuring in South Africa: The Debate Continues": A Response', *Journal of Southern African Studies*, Vol. 20, No. 4 (December), York

Kaplinsky, R., 1991, 'A Growth Path for a Post-apartheid South Africa', *Transformation*, No. 16, Durban

Karis, T. & Carter, G. M. (eds), 1977, *From Protest to Challenge: A Documentary History of African Politics in South Africa, 1882–1964*, Hoover Press, Stanford

Karis, T. & Gerhardt, G. M. (eds), 1977, *Challenge and Violence 1953–1964*, Vol. 3 of *From Protest to Challenge: A Documentary History of African Politics in South Africa 1882–1964*, Hoover Institution Press, Stanford

Keane, J., 1988a, *Civil Society and the State*, Verso Books, London

Keane, J. 1988b, *Democracy and Civil Society*, Verso Books, London

Keet, D., 1992, 'Shop Stewards and Worker Control', *SA Labour Bulletin*, Vol. 16, No. 5, Johannesburg

Kentridge, M., 1993, *Turning the Tanker: The Economic Debate in South Africa*, Centre for Policy Studies, Johannesburg

Kraak, G., 1996, *Development Update: An Interfund Briefing on the Development and Voluntary Sector in South Africa in 1995/96*, INTERFUND, Johannesburg

Krugman, P., 1995, *Peddling Prosperity: Economic Sense and Nonsense in the Age of Diminished Expectations*, W. W. Norton & Co., New York

Krugman, P., 1992, 'Towards a Counter-Counter Revolution in Development Theory', Proceedings of the World Bank Annual Conference on Development Economics

Kwan, R., 1991, 'Footloose and Country Free', *Dollars and Sense* (March)

Laclau, E., 1990, *New Reflections on the Revolution of our Time*, Verso Books, London

Laclau, E. & Mouffe, C. 1985, *Hegemony and Socialist Strategy: Towards a Radical Democratic Politics*, Verso Books, London

Lambert, R., 1987, 'Trade Unions, Nationalism and the Socialist Project in South Africa', *South African Review No. 4*, Ravan Press, Johannesburg

Le Roux, P. et al., 1993, *The Mont Fleur Scenarios*, University of Western Cape

Legassick, M. & de Clerq, F., 1978, 'The Origins and Nature of the Migrant Labour System in Southern Africa', *Migratory Labour in Southern Africa*, UN Economic Commission for Africa

Lewis, D., 1991, 'The Character and Consequences of Conglomeration in the South African Economy', *Transformation*, No. 16, Durban

Leys, Colin, 1994, 'Confronting the African Tragedy', *New Left Review*, No. 204, London

Lipietz, A., 1989, 'The Debt Problem, European Integration and the New Phase of the World Crisis', *New Left Review*, No. 178 (December), London

Lipietz, A., 1987, *Mirages and Miracles: The Crises of Global Fordism*, Verso Books, London

Lipton, M., 1986, *Capitalism and Apartheid: South Africa 1910–1986*, Aldershot

Lodge, T., 1989, 'People's War or Negotiation? African National Congress Strategies in the 1980s', *South African Review No. 5*, Ravan Press, Johannesburg

Lodge, T. 1987, 'The African National Congress after the Kabwe Conference' in G. Moss & I. Obery (eds), *South African Review No. 4*, Ravan Press, Johannesburg

Lodge, T., 1983, *Black Politics in South Africa since 1945*, Longman, Harlow

Lodge, T. & Bill Nasson, 1991, *All, Here, and Now: Black Politics in South Africa in the 1980s*, David Philip, Cape Town

Macroeconomic Research Group (MERG), 1993, *Making Democracy Work*, Centre for Development Studies & Oxford University Press, Cape Town

Maganya, E. (ed.), 1996, *Development Strategies in South Africa*, IFAA, Johannesburg

Magdoff, H. & Sweezy, P., 1990, 'Investment for What?', *Monthly Review*, Vol. 42, No. 2 (June)

Mandela, N., 1994, *Long Walk to Freedom: The Autobiography of Nelson Mandela*, Macdonald Purnell, Johannesburg

Marais, H., 1997a, *Development Update: An Interfund Briefing on the Development and Voluntary Sector in South Africa in 1996/97*, INTERFUND, Johannesburg

Marais, H., 1997b, 'The RDP: Is there Life after Gear?', *Development Update*, No. 1 (July), NGO Coalition, Johannesburg

Marais, H., 1997c, 'Leaders of the Pack', *Leadership* (August), Cape Town

Marais, H., 1994a, 'Radical as Reality', *African Communist*, No. 138 (3rd Quarter), Johannesburg

Marais, H., 1994b, 'The Skeletons Come out of the Cupboard', *Work in Progress*, No. 91 (August–September), Johannesburg

Marais, H., 1994c, 'Snatching Defeat from the Jaws of Victory', *Work in Progress*, No. 95 (February/March), Johannesburg

Marais, H., 1993a, 'The New South African Identity Crisis', *Work in Progress*, No. 93 (November), Johannesburg

Marais, H., 1993b, 'The New Barbarians (The Criminalization of Youth)', *Work in Progress*, No. 90 (July/August), Johannesburg

Marais, H., 1992a, 'The Sweeping Inferno, *Work in Progress*, No. 83 (July/August), Johannesburg

Marais, H., 1992b, 'What Happened in the ANC Camps?', *Work in Progress*, No. 82 (June), Johannesburg

Marais, H. & Narsoo, M., 1992, 'And Justice for All?', *Work in Progress*, No. 85 (October), Johannesburg

Mare, G., 1992, *Brothers Born of Warrior Blood: Politics and Ethnicity in South Africa*, Ravan Press, Johannesburg

Mare, G. & Hamilton, G., 1987, *An Appetite for Power: Buthelezi's Inkatha and South Africa*, Ravan Press, Johannesburg

Marie, B., 1996, 'Giants, Teddy Bears, Butterflies and Bees: Ideas for Union Organizing', *SA Labour Bulletin*, Vol. 20, No. 1 (February), Johannesburg

Marie, B., 1992, 'Cosatu Faces Crisis', *SA Labour Bulletin*, Vol. 16, No. 5 (May/June), Johannesburg

Marks, S. & Trapido, S., 1991, 'Introduction', *Journal of Southern African Studies*, Vol. 18, No. 1 (March 1991), York

Marx, Anthony W., 1992, *Lessons of Struggle: South African Internal Opposition, 1960–1990*, Oxford University Press, Cape Town

Mayekiso, M., 1994, 'Taking the RDP to the Streets', address to Sanco Southern Transvaal RDP Conference (May), Johannesburg

Mbeki, G., 1996, *Sunset at Midday: latshon' ilang 'emini!*, Nolwazi Educational Publishers, Johannesburg

Mbeki, G., 1992, *The Struggle for Liberation in South Africa: A Short History*, David Philip, Cape Town

Mboweni, T., 1994, 'Formulating Policy for a Democratic South Africa: Some Observations', *Institute for Development Studies Bulletin*, Vol. 25, No. 1, Sussex

McGrath, M. & Whiteford, A., 1994, 'Disparate Circumstances', *Indicator SA,* Vol. 11, No. 3 (Winter), Durban

McRobbie, A., 1996, 'Looking Back at New Times and its Critics' in D. Morley & K. Chen (eds), *Stuart Hall: Critical Dialogues in Cultural Studies*, Routledge, London

Mercer, C., 1980, 'Revolutions, Reforms or Reformulations?', in Alan Hunt (ed.), *Marxism and Democracy*, Lawrence and Wishart, London

Miliband, R., 1996, 'The New World Order and the Left', *Social Justice*, Vol. 23, Nos 1–2 (Spring–Summer), San Francisco

Miliband, R., 1983, *Class Power and State Power: Political Essays*, Verso Books, London

Miliband, R. & Panitch, L. (eds), *The Socialist Register 1994*, Merlin Press, London

Moll, T., 1991, 'Did the Apartheid Economy "Fail"?', *Journal of Southern African Studies*, Vol. 17, No. 2 (December), York

Moll, T., 1990, 'From Booster to Brake? Apartheid and Economic Growth in Comparative Perspective' in N. Nattrass & E. Ardington (eds), *The Political Economy of South Africa*, Oxford University Press, Cape Town

Morley, D. & Chen, K. (eds), 1996, *Critical Dialogues in Cultural Studies*, Routledge, London

Morris, M., 1993a, 'The Legacy of the Past', conference paper presented at the University of Economics, (7–9 December), Prague

Morris, M., 1993b, 'Who's In, Who's Out? Side-stepping the 50% Solution', *Work in Progress*, No. 86, Johannesburg

Morris, M., 1993c, 'Methodological Problems in Tackling Micor and Macro Socio-economic Issues in the Transition to Democracy in South Africa' (conference paper), Slovak Academy of Sciences, Bratislava (May)

Morris, M., 1991, 'State, Capital and Growth: The Political Economy of the National Question' in S. Gelb (ed.), *South Africa's Economic Crisis*, David Philip, Cape Town

Morris, M., 1976, 'The Development of Capitalism in South Africa', *Journal of Development Studies*, Vol. 12, No. 3

Morris, M. & Hindson, D., 1992, 'Political Violence: Reform and Reconstruction', *Review of African Political Economy*, No. 53, Sheffield

Morris, M. & Padayachee, P., 1989, 'Hegemonic Projects, Accumulation Strategies and State Reform Policy in South Africa', *Labour, Capital and Society*, Vol. 22, No. 1

Moss, G. & Obery, I. (eds), 1991, *South Africa Review No. 6,* Ravan Press, Johannesburg

Moss, G. & Obery, I. (eds), 1987, *South Africa Review No. 4,* Ravan Press, Johannesburg

Murphy, M., 1994, 'A Shaky Alliance: Cosatu and the ANC', *Indicator SA*, Vol. 11, No. 3 (Winter), Durban

Mzala, 1990, 'Is South Africa in a Revolutionary Situation?', *Journal of Southern African Studies*, Vol. 16, No. 3 (September), York

Mzala, 1987, 'Towards People's War and Insurrection', *Sechaba* (April)

Mzala, 1981, 'Has the Time Come for Arming the Masses?', *African Communist*, No. 102 (3rd Quarter), Johannesburg

Narsoo, M., 1991, 'Civil Society – A Contested Terrain', *Work in Progress*, No. 76 (February), Johannesburg

Nattrass, J., 1988, *The South African Economy: Its Growth and Change*, Oxford University Press, Cape Town

Nattrass, N., 1994a, 'Economic Restructuring in South Africa: The Debate Continues', *Journal of Southern African Studies*, Vol. 20, No. 4 (December), York

Nattrass, N., 1994b, 'The Limits to Radical Restructuring: A Critique of the MERG Report', *Third World Quarterly*, Oxfordshire

Nattrass, N., 1994c, 'Politics and Economics in ANC Economic Policy', *African Affairs* (July)

Nattrass, N., 1991, 'Controversies about Capitalism and Apartheid in South Africa: An Economic Perspective', *Journal of Southern African Studies*, Vol. 17, No. 4 (December), York

Nattrass, N. & Ardington, E. (eds), 1990, *The Political Economy of South Africa*, Oxford University Press, Cape Town

Niddrie, D., 1990, 'The Duel of Dual Power', *Work in Progress*, No. 67 (June)

NIEP (National Institute for Economic Policy), 1996, *From the RDP to GEAR: The Gradual Embracing of Neo-liberalism in Economic Policy*, NIEP, Johannesburg

NIEP (National Institute for Economic Policy), 1994, *Making the RDP Work: Draft Submission for the RDP White Paper*, NIEP, Johannesburg

Nkuhlu, M., 1993, 'The State and Civil Society in South Africa' (conference paper, August), Cape Town

Nyawuza, 1985, 'New "Marxist" Tendencies and the Battle of Ideas in South Africa', *African Communist*, No. 103 (4th Quarter), Johannesburg

Nzimande, B., 1997, 'The State and the National Question in South Africa's National Democratic Revolution' paper presented at Harold Wolpe Memorial Trust Conference, Cape Town

Nzimande, B., 1992, 'Let us Take the People with us: A reply to Joe Slovo', *African Communist*, No. 131 (4th Quarter), Johannesburg

Nzimande, B. & Cronin, J., 1997, 'We Need Transformation not a Balancing Act – Looking Critically at the ANC Discussion Document' (draft), Johannesburg

O'Meara, D. 1996, *The Apartheid State and the Politics of the National Party (1948–1994)*, Ravan Press, Johannesburg

O'Meara, D., 1983, *Volkskapitalisme: Class, Capital and Ideology in the Development of Afrikaner-nationalism 1934–1948*, Ravan Press, Johannesburg

Osborne, P., 1991, 'Radicalism Without Limit? Discourse, Democracy and the Politics of Identity' in *Socialism and the Limits of Liberalism*, Verso Books, London

Padayachee, V., 1995, 'Debt, Development and Democracy, The IMF and the RDP', *Review of African Political Economy* (forthcoming), Sheffield

Padayachee, V., 1994a, 'Can the RDP Survive the IMF?', *Southern Africa Report*, Vol. 9, No. 5 (July), Toronto

Padayachee, V., 1994b, 'Dealing with the IMF: Dangers and Opportunities', *SA Labour Bulletin*, Vol. 18, No. 1 (January/February), Johannesburg

Panitch, L, 1994, *Globalization and the State*, Universidad Nacional Autonoma de Mexico, Mexico City

Pellicani, L., 1981, *Gramsci: An Alternative Communism?*, Hoover Institution Press, Standford

Petras, J., 1997, 'Intellectuals: A Marxist Critique of Post-marxists' (author's draft paper, February), New York

Phillips M. & Coleman, C., 1989, 'Another Kind of War: Strategies for Transition in the Era of Negotiation', *Transformation*, No. 9, Durban

Pityana, B., Ramphele, M., Mpumlwana, M. & Wilson, L., 1991, *Bounds of Possibility: The Legacy of Steve Biko and Black Consciousness*, David Philip & Zed Books, Cape Town & London

Postman, N., 1993, *Technopoly: The Surrender of Culture to Technology*, Vintage, New York

Poulantzas, N., 1978, *State, Power, Socialism*, Verso Books, London

Poulantzas, N., 1976, *The Crisis of the Dictatorships: Portugal, Greece, Spain*, New Left Books, Manchester

Price, R. M., 1991, *The Apartheid State in Crisis; Political Transformation in South Africa, 1975–90*, Oxford University Press, London

Rapoo, T., 1996, *Making the Means Justify the Ends: The Theory and Practice of the RDP*, Centre for Policy Studies, Johannesburg

RDP, 1995, *Key Indicators of Poverty in South Africa*, Ministry in the Office of the President, Cape Town

Reitz, M., 1995, *Divided on the 'Demon': Immigration Policy since the Election*, Centre for Policy Studies, Johannesburg

Rhoodie, N. & Liebenberg, I. (eds), 1994, *Democratic Nation-Building*, HSRC Publishers, Pretoria

Rifkin, J., 1995a, *The End of Work: The Decline of the Global Labour Force and the Dawn of the Post-market Era*, Putnam, New York

Rifkin, J., 1995b, 'The End of Work?', *New Statesman & Society* (9 June), London

Rudin, J., 1997, *Challenging Apartheid's Foreign Debt*, Alternative Information and Development Centre, Cape Town

SACP, 1996, 'Let Us Not Lose Sight of Our Strategic Priorities', (Secretariat discussion document, October), Johannesburg

SACP, 1994, 'Defending and Deepening a Clear Left Strategic Perspective on the RDP' (discussion document), *African Communist*, No. 138 (3rd Quarter), Johannesburg

SACP, 1962, 'The Road to South African Freedom: Programme of the South African Communist Party', *African Communists Speak*, Nauka Publishing House, Moscow

SALDRU, 1994, *South Africans Rich and Poor: Baseline Household Statistics*, SALDRU, Cape Town

Saul, J., 1994a, '(Half Full) Or Half Empty? Review of the RDP', *Southern Africa Report*, Vol. 9, No. 5 (July), Toronto

Saul, J., 1994b, 'Thinking the Thinkable: Globalism, Socialism and Democracy in the South African Transition' in Ralph Miliband and Leo Panitch (eds), *Socialist Register 1994*, Merlin Press, Toronto

Saul, J., 1993, *Recolonization and Resistance in Southern Africa in the 1990s*, Between the Lines, Toronto

Saul, J., 1992, 'Structural Reform: A Model for Revolutionary Transformation of South Africa?', *Transformation*, No. 20, Durban

Saul, J., 1991, 'South Africa Between Barbarism and Structural Reform', *New Left Review*, No. 188 (July–August), London

Saul, J. & Gelb, S., 1981, *The Crisis in South Africa: Class Defence and Class Revolution*, Monthly Review Press, New York

Schneider, F. & Frei, Bruno, S., 1985, 'Economic and Political Determinants of FDI', *World Development*, Vol. 13, No. 2

Schreiner, G., 1994, 'Restructuring the Labour Movement After Apartheid', *SA Labour Bulletin*, Vol. 18, No. 3 (July), Johannesburg

Schreiner, J., 1993, 'Breaking the Mould', *Work in Progress*, No. 93 (November), Johannesburg

Schrire, R. (ed.), 1992, *Wealth or Poverty? Critical Choices for South Africa*, Oxford University Press, Cape Town

Seekings, J., 1993, *Heroes or Villains?*, Ravan Press, Johannesburg

Seekings, J., 1991, 'Trailing behind the Masses: The United Democratic Front and Township Politics in the Pretoria-Witwatersrand-Vaal Region, 1983–1984', *Journal of Southern African Studies*, Vol. 18, No. 1 (March), York

Segal, L., 1991, 'The Human Face of Violence: Hostel Dwellers Speak', *Journal of Southern African Studies*, Vol. 18, No. 1 (March), York

Sender, J., 1995, 'Economic Restructuring in South Africa: Reactionary Rhetoric Prevails', *Journal of Southern African Studies*, Vol. 20 No. 4 (December), York

Shaw, M., 1995, *Partners in Crime?* Centre for Policy Studies, Johannesburg

Shepard, A., 1994, 'The Task Ahead', *Africa Report* (July/August), New York

Shubane, K. & Madiba, P., 1992, *The Struggle Continues?: Civic Associations in the Transition*, Centre for Policy Studies, Johannesburg

Simkins, C., 1987, *The Prisoners of Tradition and the Politics of Nation Building*, SAIRR, Johannesburg

Simone, A., 1994, 'Local Institutions and the Governance of Community Development in South Africa' (author's draft), Foundation for Contemporary Research, Cape Town

Slovo, J., 1992, 'Negotiations: What Room for Compromises?', *African Communist*, No. 130, Johannesburg

Slovo, J., 1990, 'Has Socialism Failed?', *SA Labour Bulletin*, Vol. 14, No. 6 (February), Johannesburg

South African Government, 1994 (September), *White Paper on Reconstruction and Development: A Strategy for Fundamental Transformation*, Cape Town

Sparks, A., 1994, *Tomorrow Is Another Country: The Inside Story of South Africa's Negotiated Revolution*, Struik, Johannesburg

Stadler, A., 1987, *The Political Economy of Modern South Africa*, David Philip, Cape Town

Stanners, W., 1993, 'Is Low Inflation an Important Condition for High Growth?', *Cambridge Journal of Economics*, No. 17, Cambridge University

Stein, H. (ed.), 1995, *Asian Industrialisation and Africa: Studies in Policy Alternatives to Structural Adjustment*, St. Martin's Press, London

Suttner, R., 1992, 'Ensuring Stable Transition to Democratic Power', *African Communist*, No. 131 (4th Quarter), Johannesburg

Suttner, R. & Cronin, J., 1986, *Thirty Years of the Freedom Charter*, Ravan Press, Johannesburg

Sweezy, P. M. & Magdoff, H., 1992, 'Globalization – To What End?', *Monthly Review*, Vol. 43, No. 9 (February), New York

Swilling, M., 1991, 'The Case for Associational Socialism', *Work in Progress*, No. 76 (February), Johannesburg

Swilling, M. & Phillips, M., 1989a, 'The Emergency State: Its Structure, Power and Limits', *South African Review 5*, Ravan Press, Johannesburg

Swilling, M. & Phillips, M., 1989b, 'State Power in the 1980s: From "Total Strategy" to Counter-Revolutionary Warfare', in *War and Society: The Militarization of South Africa*, David Philip, Cape Town

Toussaint, 1988, 'On Workerism, Socialism and the Communist Party', *African Communist*, No. 114 (3rd Quarter), Johannesburg

Trevor, 1984, 'The Question of an Uprising of the People as a Whole', *African Communist*, No. 97 (2nd Quarter), Johannesburg

Vadney, T. E., 1987, *The World Since 1945*, Pelican, London

Vilas, Carlos M., 1996, 'Neoliberal Social Policy' *NACLA Report on the Americas*, Vol. 29, No. 6 (May/June), NACLA, New York

Vilas, Carlos M., 1993, 'The Hour of Civil Society', *NACLA Report on the Americas*, Vol. 27, No. 2 (September/October), NACLA, New York

Vilas, Carlos M., 1989, 'Revolution and Democracy in Latin America', *Socialist Register 1989*, Merlin Press, London

Virilio, P., 1978, *Popular Defense and Ecological Struggles*, Semiotext(e), New York

Von Holdt, K., 1996, 'David or Goliath?: The Future of the Unions', *SA Labour Bulletin*, Vol. 20, No. 4 (August), Johannesburg

Von Holdt, K., 1993, 'Cosatu Special Congress: The Uncertain New Era', *SA Labour Bulletin*, Vol. 17, No. 5 (September/October), Johannesburg

Von Holdt, K., 1992, 'What is the Future of Labour?', *SA Labour Bulletin*, Vol. 16, No. 8 (November/December), Johannesburg

Wade, R., 1996, 'Japan, the World Bank and the Art of Paradigm Maintenance: The East Asian Miracle in Political Perspective', *New Left Review*, No. 217 (May/June), London

Walker, C., 1982, *Women and Resistance in South Africa*, Onyx, London

Watkins, K., 1994, 'GATT: A Victory for the North', *Review of African Political Economy*, No. 59, Sheffield

Watts, M., 1994, 'Development 11: The Privatization of Everything' (workshop paper), University of California, Berkeley

Wolpe, H., 1988, *Race, Class and the Apartheid State*, James Currey, London

Wolpe, H., 1984, 'Strategic Issues in the Struggle for National Liberation in South Africa', *Socialist Review*, Vol. 8, No. 2

Wolpe, H., 1980, 'Towards an Analysis of the South African State', *International Journal of the Sociology of Law*, No. 8

Wood, Ellen Meiksins, 1995, 'Editorial', *Monthly Review*, (July–August), New York

Wood, Ellen Meiksins, 1990, 'The Uses and Abuses of Civil Society' in Miliband *et al.*, *Socialist Register 1990*, The Merlin Press, London

World Bank, 1994, *Reducing Poverty in South Africa: Options for Equitable and Sustainable Growth*, World Bank, Washington

World Bank (Southern Africa Department), 1993, *South Africa: Paths to Economic Growth*, World Bank, Washington

World Bank, 1992, *World Development Report 1992*, Oxford University Press, Oxford

Zarenda, H., 1994, 'The Inconsistencies and Contradictions of the RDP', address to the Johannesburg Branch of the South African Economics Society, 4 October 1994

Zita, L., 1995, 'The RDP: Towards a Working Class Approach', unpublished
Zita, L., 1994, 'The Limits and Possibilities of Reconstruction', unpublished, Johannesburg
Zita, L., 1993a, 'Unity of the Left', *African Communist*, No. 134 (3rd Quarter), Johannesburg
Zita, L., 1993b, 'Moving Beyond the Social Contract', *African Communist*, No. 133 (2nd Quarter), Johannesburg

Index